Global Garveyism

UNIVERSITY PRESS OF FLORIDA

Florida A&M University, Tallahassee
Florida Atlantic University, Boca Raton
Florida Gulf Coast University, Ft. Myers
Florida International University, Miami
Florida State University, Tallahassee
New College of Florida, Sarasota
University of Central Florida, Orlando
University of Florida, Gainesville
University of North Florida, Jacksonville
University of South Florida, Tampa
University of West Florida, Pensacola

Global Garveyism

Edited by Ronald J. Stephens and Adam Ewing

University Press of Florida

Gainesville / Tallahassee / Tampa / Boca Raton

Pensacola / Orlando / Miami / Jacksonville / Ft. Myers / Sarasota

Frontispiece: Marcus Garvey in 1924. From the Library of Congress
Prints and Photographs Division, Washington, D.C.

First cloth printing, 2019
First paperback printing, 2024

29 28 27 26 25 24   6 5 4 3 2 1

Library of Congress Cataloging-in-Publication Data
Names: Stephens, Ronald Jemal, editor. | Ewing, Adam (Historian), editor.
Title: Global Garveyism / edited by Ronald J. Stephens and Adam Ewing.
Description: Gainesville : University Press of Florida, 2019. | Includes
  bibliographical references and index.
Identifiers: LCCN 2018027407 | ISBN 9780813056210 (cloth) |
  ISBN 9780813080871 (pbk.)
Subjects: LCSH: Black nationalism—Southern States—History—20th century. |
  Garvey, Marcus, 1887–1940—Influence. | Southern States—Race
  relations—History—20th century. | African American political
  activists—Southern States—History—20th century.
Classification: LCC E185.97.G3 G56 2018 | DDC 320.54/60975—dc23
LC record available at https://lccn.loc.gov_2018027407

The University Press of Florida is the scholarly publishing agency for the State
University System of Florida, comprising Florida A&M University, Florida Atlantic
University, Florida Gulf Coast University, Florida International University, Florida
State University, New College of Florida, University of Central Florida, University
of Florida, University of North Florida, University of South Florida, and University
of West Florida.

University Press of Florida
2046 NE Waldo Road
Suite 2100
Gainesville, FL 32609
http://upress.ufl.edu

This volume is dedicated to Amy Jacques Garvey,

the first scholar of global Garveyism, and to

Tony Martin, who originated the idea for this volume.

Contents

Figures

Introduction

Global Garveyism

ADAM EWING AND RONALD J. STEPHENS

Drawing on a rich prehistory of pan-African mobilizations and rhetoric, propelled by the ferment of the Great War, global Garveyism worked its way into the warp and woof of twentieth-century black liberation politics.[1] The Universal Negro Improvement Association and African Communities League (UNIA) established hundreds of branches in the United States and Canada,[2] in the Caribbean,[3] in Central and South America,[4] and in western and southern Africa,[5] organizing dynamic centers of community building and giving local activism a dazzling, and galvanizing, global context. Garveyites carried the news, networks, and self-assured predictions ("Africa for the Africans!") of their movement throughout the diaspora, variously informing, influencing, and cooperating with an eclectic mix of admirers and organizations. By the early 1930s, Garveyism had played a role in shaping everything from trade union politics in the greater Caribbean to Aboriginal politics in Australia; from welfare association politics and independent church building in central-southern Africa to millennial religious revivals throughout Africa, the United States, and the Caribbean.[6] Garveyism's impact was observable in the ways early leaders of the African National Congress and Industrial Commercial Workers' Union in South Africa embraced and translated its methods.[7] It could be glimpsed in the attention and grudging respect granted to the movement by its ideological opponents, whether in the Communist International or the Colonial Office.[8] It was made manifest in the work of Garveyites, former Garveyites, and Garvey acolytes in the several decades following the UNIA's 1920s heyday. Spanning continents and traversing oceans, Garveyites built the largest mass movement in the history of the African diaspora.

Despite the breadth and scope of Garveyism's achievement—and despite the impressive and pioneering work of Garveyism scholars like Amy Jacques Garvey, Robert A. Hill, Tony Martin, Rupert Lewis, Barbara Bair, Emory Tolbert, and others—it has only been in the new century that Garveyism has received serious attention in works published by mainstream academic presses in the United States. In crucial respects, Garveyism's marginalization within mainstream historiographical debates persists. This volume—the first edited collection devoted to Garveyism studies in three decades[9]—showcases original essays by scholars working in Africa, the West Indies, the Hispanic Caribbean, North America, and Australia. Such work has rendered untenable the persistent idea that Garveyism was a brief and misguided phenomenon or that it was a side-show to the normative political trajectories of African American, Caribbean, African, and global history. Rather, the essays appearing in *Global Garveyism* encourage students and scholars to rethink the emergence of modern black politics in a manner that moves Garveyism from the margins of analysis to the center. They suggest the need to revisit global, national, regional, and local histories in light of what Garveyism scholars have uncovered.

. . .

The UNIA was founded in Jamaica in 1914 by Marcus Garvey and Amy Ashwood (later Amy Ashwood Garvey, Marcus Garvey's first wife). Finding his ambitions stifled on the island, Garvey set out on a fund-raising and speaking tour of the United States in 1916, and threw himself into a rising wave of anti-racist, anti-war, and anti-colonial ferment in Harlem—what Hubert Henry Harrison termed the "New Negro" movement. Deploying his prodigious gifts as an orator, publicist, and mass mobilizer, Garvey skillfully shifted the gravity of the New Negro movement away from Harrison's nascent Liberty League and toward his newly restructured UNIA.[10] By 1919, in the eyes of the American intelligence community, Garvey was the most dangerous "Negro radical agitator" in town. Months earlier, the UNIA had launched the Black Star Line Steamship Company, promising to join African-descended people from the United States, the Caribbean, and West Africa in a new triangular exchange intended to foster commerce, cooperation, and racial unity. Later that year, Garvey announced plans to shift the headquarters of the UNIA to Monrovia, Liberia, a central command from which to better pursue the organization's primary aim: the liberation of Africa from foreign domination. In August 1920 the UNIA hosted its first International Convention, drawing thousands of delegates to Harlem to adopt the Declaration of Rights of the Negro Peoples of the World; to select the red, black, and green as a flag to represent Africans at home and abroad; and to elect Garvey "provisional president of Africa." Garvey declared that the scattered sons and daughters of Africa would be united once again, that the race would be reborn and redeemed, and that the UNIA would be the vehicle to bring this about.

Garveyism was born in the cauldron of wartime and postwar radicalism, amid the global insurgencies of colonial populations and peoples of color. Very quickly, however, the moment of instability and opportunity closed; the 1920s was a decade of reaction and repression, of a reinvigorated and reformulated white supremacy. As Garveyites carried their message and their movement across the globe, they were met by a coordinated assault from agents and defenders of the imperial order. The Black Star Line foundered in the face of government intrigue, undercapitalization, and poor business operations. Plans for Liberia were dashed by pressure from the British and the French and by the calculations of the Liberian government. Marcus Garvey was subjected to what the scholar Robert A. Hill has fairly described as a "witch hunt" by the United States intelligence community; failing to secure a sedition charge, the Bureau of Investigations (the precursor to the FBI) built a tenuous mail fraud case, for which Garvey was charged in 1923, banished to federal prison in 1925, and deported in 1927.[11]

As the UNIA entered a period of organizational crisis, Garveyites—in search of practical outcomes—embraced newer strategies for formulating, delivering, and implementing African and black liberation. Amid institutional decline, Garveyism paradoxically retained its vitality as a device for mass politics making. In her pioneering book, *Garvey and Garveyism*, Amy Jacques Garvey (Marcus Garvey's second wife) noted this vitality: the way news of Garveyism was carried from its home base in Harlem to locations around the globe, transported on ships, smuggled by sailors and students, translated into local dialects; the way contacts were maintained from Sydney, Australia, to Honolulu, Hawaii, to Vladivostok, Russia; the way Africans were "indoctrinated in Garveyism in England, France, and the U.S.A., and on their return home, quietly and secretly spread the gospel of Unity and Freedom." Jacques Garvey suggested that nervous colonial states collected voluminous "secret reports" which they held from public eyes. "It would hurt the prestige of colonial powers for the world to know that a lone black man caused them so much concern," she wrote, "that their statesmen had their ears to the ground to hear of his every movement and utterance." The scattered archives of Garveyism, when they became available, would "prove what awakened black minds can achieve in defiance of lashings, imprisonment, and bullets."[12]

This pivot—what Marcus Garvey described as the transition to the UNIA's "second period" of modulated and strategic organizing—is crucial to understanding the enduring legacy of Garveyism. Regrettably, few in the academy were willing to acknowledge *Garvey and Garveyism*, let alone take it seriously, when it was published in 1963.[13] Attention focused instead on E. David Cronon's *Black Moses* (1955), the first historical work on Garvey and the UNIA produced by an academic press. Cronon, who dismissed *Garvey and Garveyism* as a "book of reminiscence," was drawn not to the global organizing work described by Jacques Garvey but to the dramatic rise and fall of Marcus Garvey, to the flashy drama of the UNIA's grand and ill-fated projects, to hopes of liberation dashed and delayed.[14] This framing had the unfortunate consequence of encouraging the impression that Garveyism, for all its bluster, accomplished very little. And indeed, Cronon thought very little of Garvey and his politics. The UNIA's "gaudy uniforms, colorful parades, high-sounding titles, and grandiose dreams," wrote Cronon, captured the imagination of "the unsophisticated and unlettered masses" while repelling the "most thoughtful men." Its appeal to "racial nationalism" revealed the movement's "inherent weakness." In a remarkable sleight of hand, Cronon acknowledged and marveled at Garvey's accomplishment—his leadership of the largest mass movement in the history of the African diaspora—and rendered it somehow meaningless. "Garvey's unparalleled success in capturing the imagination of the masses of Negroes throughout the world," wrote Cronon, "can be explained only by recognizing that he put into words . . . what large numbers of his people were thinking." And yet "little of practical significance" was accomplished. In Cronon's estimation, Garvey's message, which so inspired black people throughout the diaspora, amounted to "an unrealistic escapist program of racial chauvinism." Garvey's ability to catalyze mass support hardly mattered, because the masses, apparently, had their dreams of liberation figured out wrong.[15]

Cronon's chauvinistic dismissal of Garveyites as "unsophisticated and unlettered masses," thankfully, did not survive the test of time. But his perplexing insistence that Garveyism, despite its global mass appeal, need neither be studied as a global mass movement nor taken particularly seriously has become a widely accepted commonplace. For the remainder of the twentieth century, only one other book on Garveyism was published by an academic press in the United States— Judith Stein's *The World of Marcus Garvey* (1986), which nearly matched Cronon's

Adam Ewing and Ronald J. Stephens

work in its skepticism about Garveyism and its lack of attention to Garveyism's global impact.[16] In the new century, Garvey scholars have finally attracted the attention of academic presses. But as the historian Steven Hahn observes, Garvey and the UNIA continue to be briefly summoned in influential histories of the interwar period only to serve as foils, and to be quickly "marginalized, dismissed, or derided."[17] In surveys of American and African American history, Garveyism is deemed worthy of brief mention but hardly worthy of serious analysis. The movement continues to be narrated as a flashy sideshow, an enlivening and quixotic diversion from the *real* story of the black freedom struggle.[18]

This neglect can be partially attributed to the nature and timing of African American history's integration into the white American academy. Bracketed within what Hahn calls a "liberal integrationist framework," and narrowed by the rise of Cold War–era area studies, historical work on the black freedom struggle long emphasized African American connections to—rather than alienations from—the nation-building project of the United States.[19] This uneven acceptance of African American history meant that the types of transnational and diasporic visions that animated the work of black historians like George Washington Williams, W.E.B. Du Bois, Carter G. Woodson, Dorothy Porter Wesley, C.L.R. James, Amy Jacques Garvey, Walter Rodney, Chancellor Williams, and Cedric J. Robinson—the types of framings that allow us to glimpse the contours of Garveyism in its proper, global context—were quieted within the academy. For many decades, to borrow from Michel-Rolph Trouillot, Garveyism was "unthinkable" history.[20] It is no accident that the profession's "discovery" of Garveyism in the new century paralleled the "discovery" of extranational perspectives. The transnational turn, after all, illuminated connections across national and natural borders that black historians, working outside of and on the margins of the academy, had long taken for granted.

This marginalization of Garveyism did not go unchallenged. While the story of the movement was being written out of mainstream historical narratives, its accomplishments were being doggedly and brilliantly traced, cataloged, and preserved by mostly West Indian and African American scholars, and recorded in volumes published by West Indian and independent presses. In 1976, Trinidad-born scholar Tony Martin published his masterpiece, *Race First*, which remains the most complete and most impressively researched work on Garvey's movement to date.[21] And in the 1970s, Robert A. Hill launched his monumental Marcus Garvey and Universal Negro Improvement Association Papers Project, which operated out of UCLA (and more recently Duke University) but

remains powerfully reminiscent of the preservationist efforts of Arturo Schomburg and a host of legendary African-descended archivists who have kept alive
a counter-memory of African diaspora history against persistent pressures of
erasure.[22] The work of these scholars—Jacques Garvey, Martin, Hill, Rupert
Lewis, John Henrik Clarke, Theodore Vincent, Randall Burkett, Emory Tolbert,
E. U. Essien-Udom, Barbara Bair, Arnold Hughes, Ula Y. Taylor, and others—
established the pedagogical framework of global Garveyism that made the
explosion of twenty-first-century scholarship possible. If this volume seeks to
bring attention to the flowering of new work on Garveyism in the past decade,
it also honors the legacy of those who never doubted Garveyism's importance.[23]

. . .

Marcus Garvey and the UNIA arrived at a pivotal moment in global history.
As Michael O. West argues in the chapters that open and close this volume,
Garveyism was both an end and a beginning. It pulled together and catalyzed
the strands of pan-African thought forged during the Age of Revolution and
carried throughout the Atlantic world in the decades that followed.[24] And it
played a crucial role in inaugurating a new struggle against colonial rule and
white domination that would reach its peak—and suffer its ultimate defeat—in
the revolutionary decades of the 1960s and 1970s.

The Great War and its aftermath shattered the illusion of cooperation. At
the outbreak of the conflict, leading black spokesmen from the United States,
the Caribbean, Europe, and Africa encouraged black citizens and subjects to
enlist in the army to "make the world safe for democracy"—to "close ranks," as
W.E.B. Du Bois famously enjoined, in order to secure favorable treatment in the
postwar world.[25] Du Bois's calculation was rooted in the long-standing expectation among leading pan-Africanists that European and European-descended
statesmen would accept, in the end, the challenge of adapting their practices to
more honestly reflect the aspirational rhetoric of the Enlightenment. The Paris
Peace Conference, where the principle of self-determination was explicitly de-
limited to European peoples, and the Covenant of the League of Nations, which
articulated a reformulated mandate for global white supremacy, betrayed this
hopefulness and sparked outrage by anticolonial activists throughout the world.
Many were drawn to the newly constituted Third Communist International,
which loudly declared its commitment to self-determination and liberation
for peoples of color and colonial populations.[26] In the African diaspora, many
more were drawn to Marcus Garvey's vision of a rising tide of color: the inevi-

table resurgence of the world's non-white majority, the rise of a black empire, and the dawning of a new golden age.

Garveyism embodied, at its root, a revolt against the West. To be sure, Marcus Garvey was shaped by the Victorian moralities of the British Empire, and embraced a civilizationist discourse derived from his Western education. He did not set out to overturn Western conceptions of commerce, gender roles, faith, or culture. And yet Garvey understood that the foundation of global order was a racial calculus that granted white peoples resources and power at the expense of peoples of color. His demand of Africa for the Africans, Asia for the Asians, and Europe for the Europeans—in other words, an equitable distribution of the world's land and resources among the world's people—amounted to a revolutionary declaration. Much has been made about Garvey's "philosophy and opinions"—his views on socialism and capitalism, his advocacy of emigrationism, his promotion of racial separatism—but at the core of Garvey's message was a thundering prophecy: Africa will be free. The black race will be free. A new world will be born out of the ashes of global white supremacy. Black people must organize and work and prepare to bring this about.

The UNIA was constituted for the purpose of bringing this prophecy to life. The Great War, Garvey argued, revealed both a declining white civilization and an unprepared, disorganized black race. Now that the conflict had lit the flame of anticolonial agitation, a new war—a war between the races—loomed on the horizon. The medium of the UNIA was thus its message. Building a mass movement was an ideological, theological, and practical imperative.

The success of Garveyism rested on its ability to convey this new message of opportunity and transformation in a way that seemed old and familiar. The rhetoric of the "New Negro" was galvanizing because of this confluence—because, in the words of Lawrence Levine, Garvey "preached it in the right syllables."[27] In the generations before Garvey's rise to prominence, sailors, missionaries, intellectuals, and activists had charted paths across the African diaspora, articulating the outlines of the pan-African vision—racial rebirth, African redemption, and transatlantic cooperation—that would become associated with the UNIA. Garveyites built a mass movement because they were able to translate these old rhythms of community memory and politics in ways that effectively captured the possibilities and constraints of the postwar order. And Garveyism remained a mass politics so long as African diasporic peoples saw it as a usable framework for enacting their own traditions, meeting their needs, and seeking their broader aspirations.

The dissemination of the UNIA relied on what Robert A. Hill has described as a "transmission belt" of British West Indian migration, which facilitated the spread of Garveyism to the urban centers of the United States and Canada, carried it throughout the Caribbean basin, and established outposts for the movement in West and South Africa.[28] As Frances Peace Sullivan argues in chapter 2, the UNIA held a particular and practical attraction for these mobile subjects; the appeal of the organization in "receiving countries" like Cuba, Panama, and Costa Rica was partly the result of the organization's ability to offer a stable "imagined community" for people constantly in transit. From these West Indian enclaves—in Cuba's Oriente Province, in Limón, Costa Rica, in Harlem, in Cape Town, and elsewhere—Garveyism traveled and found new audiences: among rural southerners in the United States; among Afro-Cubans, Haitians, and (although more work is needed) Brazilians; among Africans residing in British, French, Belgian, and Portuguese colonies. The essays in this volume—for all of their geographical reach—only hint at the breadth of Garveyism's spread and reception in communities scattered across the world.

The mapping of transnational phenomena requires more than simply identifying far-flung points of connection. As Emory Tolbert argues in his classic local study of the UNIA in Los Angeles, Garveyism was a product of both global vision and local negotiation. The form the movement took in its hundreds of centers of activity depended on a dynamic process of translation and contestation among Garveyites themselves.[29] As Erik S. McDuffie argues in chapter 3, for example, a distinct "midwestern Garveyism" emerged in centers like Cleveland, Chicago, and Detroit. This "diasporic Midwest," he demonstrates, was an incubator of black internationalist politics, an orientation that bore fruit in the UNIA's later-period organizing in Liberia. In chapter 4, Ronald J. Stephens examines the flowering of Garveyism in Michigan under the leadership of Detroit's executive secretary, Joseph A. Craigen. Focusing on the tumultuous relationship between Garvey and Craigen, who emerged as a leading UNIA official during the period of Garvey's imprisonment and exile from the United States, Stephens uses his case study to delineate the intersecting and at times contradictory demands of global Garveyism and local Garveyism on the ground.

Work on the gendered contours of the UNIA has long suggested the importance of considering Garveyism as a product of both its routes and its roots.[30] If Garvey and his lieutenants embraced a proudly masculinist, and often starkly misogynistic, vision of gender roles that consigned women to a subordinate, "helpmate" status within the movement, Garveyite women found numerous

ways to challenge their subordination in practice. In chapter 5, Nicole Bourbonnais illustrates in her examination of the Harmony Division of the UNIA in
Kingston, Jamaica, how the UNIA's formal articulation of binary and hierarchical gender roles helped frame—but did not determine the outcome of—local
contests among Garveyite women and men to define the parameters of authority, femininity, and politics. The UNIA, Bourbonnais argues, simultaneously
embraced Victorian gender norms and offered a fluid space within which those
norms could be challenged and often creatively transcended. The importance
of this finding goes far beyond Garveyism studies. As Keisha N. Blain points
out in chapter 6, by highlighting discourses at the grassroots and *in production*,
scholars might effectively shift intellectual histories of Garveyism (in particular) and pan-Africanism and black nationalism (more broadly) away from the
singular voices of (primarily) male leaders and embrace a richer, messier dialogue among movement participants, women and men alike.[31] The promise of
this approach can be glimpsed in Robert Trent Vinson's groundbreaking exca-
vation of the South African archives in chapter 7, which reveals the centrality of
African women in the Garveyite Wellington movement, a movement that has
too often been approached by scholars as a mere extension of its colorful (male)
namesake, Wellington Buthelezi.

If the UNIA was a necessary vehicle for the spread of Garveyism across the
world, it was by no means the only container of Garveyite activism. In most
parts of colonial Africa the UNIA was banned, forcing local Garveyites to establish networks and communicate their plans surreptitiously and to organize
by other means. And in both Africa and elsewhere, as Amy Jacques Garvey long
ago noted, the impact of Garveyism easily escaped its bureaucratic and organizational bounds. As Adam Ewing notes in chapter 8, Garveyism was channeled
to productive political ends across sub-Saharan Africa in the form of rumor,
as a device of popular politics making that both fulfilled Garvey's hopes of racial mobilization and pursued those ends in a manner that Garvey could have
hardly imagined. In chapter 9, John Maynard illustrates the generative role of
Garveyism in the rise of Australian Aboriginal political protest in the 1920s.
As elsewhere, the establishment of a short-lived UNIA division in Sydney had
rich, long-term effects. In 1924, the year the Sydney division closed, Fred Maynard, a Garveyite, launched the Australian Aboriginal Progressive Association,
a groundbreaking organization that both addressed itself to Aboriginal politics
and adapted the ideology, symbolism, and rhetoric of global Garveyism.

The essays in this volume suggest that work remains to be done in charting not only Garveyism's spatial dimensions but also its temporal ones. If the centralized, organizational apparatus of the UNIA was greatly diminished by the 1930s, the movement endured—and at times flourished—at the local level. Blain's chapter explores the writing of Garveyite women in the 1940s, the decade after Marcus Garvey's death. And McDuffie looks beyond the UNIA's famous diplomatic entreaties to Liberia in the 1920s to examine the organization's work in the country in the 1960s and 1970s. As the essays by Michael O. West indicate, we can learn much by moving Garveyism from the margins to the center of our multigenerational histories. At the very least, we should acknowledge that Garveyism did not expire with the failure of the Black Star Line or with Marcus Garvey's deportation from the United States. Indeed, the UNIA exists to this day, boasting divisions in the United States, Canada, Jamaica, Costa Rica, Belize, the Virgin Islands, France, Liberia, Sierra Leone, Kenya, Tanzania, and South Africa.[32]

The reach and influence of Garveyism was so broad and so eclectic that scholars are faced not only with the challenge of uncovering its networks but also with problem of delineating its borders. José Andrés Fernández Montes de Oca's chapter on Trinidadian labor politics serves as an important reminder that local organizations like the Trinidad Workingmen's Association might be influenced by the spread of Garveyism and the UNIA but were by no means contained within that orbit. As scholars like Lara Putnam and Frank André Guridy have demonstrated, black internationalism in the interwar years was forged by an unruly and heterogeneous series of migrations, grassroots mobilizations, cultural articulations, religious practices, and political organizations.[33] If Garveyism was the most far-reaching and important thread of black internationalist politics during this era, it hardly captured the rich tapestry of Afro-diasporic thought and practice.

Instead, the success of Garveyism encourages us to think differently about political mobilization and engagement more broadly—to narrate our stories not along the axis of organizational growth and decline, not by following the exploits of exemplary leaders and intellectuals and artists, but rather by pursuing the movement of ideas and associations in space, and by observing how they settle in place, how they are made local, become embedded, are thickened and negotiated. The legacy of global Garveyism becomes fully clear only if we de-emphasize the ability of Marcus Garvey to bend the movement to his will, and only if we acknowledge the limits of the UNIA as a corporate body. It affirms Cedric Robinson's observation that the black radical tradition has not been invented from above but shaped from below—that it emerged organically out of "the revolutionary consciousness of the slaves," out of collective action, out of the historical and cultural formations of black communities.[34] As Garveyism traveled it was transformed by its practitioners, taking root in trade unions, immigrant protection societies, religious bodies, millennial revivals, welfare societies, political organizations, and popular belief and culture. As Robinson would have it, Garveyism did not create the black internationalism of the interwar period but rather found it, gave it a platform, and offered that platform to the masses. This is why Garvey's own fall from grace, and the UNIA's bureaucratic decline, could happen alongside the sustained success of the movement. Garveyism gave voice to a revolutionary demand for the overthrow of global white supremacy in all of its forms. It was a project of reclaiming black power and reaffirming blackness. To follow the history of Garveyism is thus to glimpse something much bigger and much more complex than Garveyism itself: black politics in the making.

. . .

Global Garveyism is the product of a symposium held at Virginia Commonwealth University in Richmond in April 2016. The gathering brought together twenty-one Garveyism scholars for three days of presentations and panel discussions.[35] It was the largest such meeting since 1987, when scholars assembled to celebrate the centenary of Marcus Garvey's birth. The aim of the symposium, and of this current volume, is to catalyze the momentum that has been growing around Garveyism studies in the academy since the beginning of the century. It is an effort, after several decades of neglect in academic circles, to demonstrate Garveyism's centrality in the numerous narratives and historiographies where the movement has been passed over and marginalized.[36]

The acknowledgment of Garveyism's centrality calls us to continue the work of recovery inaugurated by pioneering Garveyism scholars, by Robert A. Hill and the editors of the Garvey Papers, and by more recent historians. The eclectic collection of essays in this volume captures Garveyism studies in an ongoing state of becoming. Evidence of Garveyism's influence remains to be excavated, spread as it is across archives, personal collections, newspapers, and other documents scattered around the world. If this volume reveals the geographical and temporal depth of Garveyism's influence, it is also notably silent on Garveyite activity in Central and South America, in Canada and Europe, and across wide regions of Africa and the United States.[37] Far from representing a final word, this volume (like earlier volumes from Clarke and Lewis) marks an important moment for the field, and demands that more work be done.

Placing Garveyism at the center of our historical narratives does more than call attention to the field: it demands the obliteration of the master narrative. In particular, it shines a powerful light on the erasure of black nationalist perspectives from our stories about and understanding of the black freedom struggle.[38] It reveals the need to rethink the stories we tell about decolonization, about pan-Africanism and nationalism, about the civil rights movement and global Black Power. Michael O. West's sweeping narrative chapters, which open and close the volume, offer a brilliant example of how this might look.[39] For many decades, scholars have been empowered in their belief that the largest mass movement in the history of the African diaspora was little more than a passing, colorful, and quixotic sideshow. As we continue to chart the course of the transnational turn, it would be wise once again to turn the wisdom of the black historical tradition, and to acknowledge and explore what has long existed in plain sight.

Notes

1. For recent books on Garveyism, see Ewing, *Age of Garvey*; Jolly, *"By Our Own Strength"*; Vinson, *Americans Are Coming*; Spady, *Marcus Garvey*; C. B. James, *Garvey*; Bandele, *Black Star*; Rolinson, *Grassroots Garveyism*; Harold, *Rise and Fall*; and Taylor, *Veiled Garvey*.

2. McDuffie, "Chicago, Garveyism"; Marano, "'We All Used to Meet at the Hall'"; Dalrymple, "'Reclaiming the Fallen'"; Harold, "Reconfiguring the Roots and Routes"; McDuffie, "Garveyism in Cleveland"; R. J. Stephens, "The Influence of Marcus Mosiah"; Marano, "'Rising Strongly and Rapidly'"; Roll, "Garveyism"; Jenkins, "Linking Up the Golden Gate"; Issa, "The Universal Negro Improvement Association"; R. J. Stephens, "Garveyism in Idlewild"; Vought, "Racial Stirrings in Colored Town"; Bair, "Garveyism and Contested Political Terrain"; W. James, *Holding Aloft the Banner*; Watkins-Owens, *Blood Relations*.

3. Plummer, "Garveyism in Haiti"; Sullivan, "'Forging Ahead'"; Ewing, "Caribbean Labour Politics"; Guridy, *Forging Diaspora*, chapter 2; Dalrymple, "In the Shadow of Garvey"; Román, "Scandalous Race"; Guridy, "'Enemies of the White Race'"; McLeod, "'Sin dejar de ser cubanos'"; McLeod, "Garveyism in Cuba."

4. Leeds, "Toward the 'Higher Type of Womanhood'"; Burnett, "'Unity Is Strength'"; Kim D. Butler, "Brazil," and Nigel Westmaas and Juanita De Barros, "British Guiana (Guyana)," in R. A. Hill, *Marcus Garvey and Universal Negro Improvement Association Papers* [hereafter *MGP*], 11:clxi–clxxiv; Opie, "Garveyism and Labor Organization"; Macpherson, "Colonial Matriarchs"; Harpelle, "Cross Currents"; Ashdown, *Garveyism in Belize*.

5. McDuffie, "'A New Day Has Dawned'"; Chéry, "Kingdoms of the Earth"; Vinson, "'Sea Kaffirs'"; Sundiata, *Brothers and Strangers*; Bair, "Pan-Africanism as Process"; Pirio, "The Role of Garveyism"; R. A. Hill and Pirio, "'Africa for the Africans'"; Okonkwo, "Garvey Movement in British West Africa"; Olusanya, "Notes on the Lagos Branch."

6. Ewing, *Age of Garvey*; Maynard, "'In the Interests of Our People'"; West, "The Seeds Are Sown"; Edgar, "Garveyism in Africa."

7. Kemp and Vinson, "'Poking Holes in the Sky'"; Vinson, *Americans Are Coming*; Bradford, *Taste of Freedom*.

8. For a good illustration of the Comintern's concern with Garveyism, see Adi, *Pan-Africanism and Communism*. The colonial archives in Africa and the Caribbean and the National Archives in the United States contain voluminous records testifying to surveillance efforts and concerns of European and American governments.

9. Prior to the publication of this volume, the most recent edited collection on Garveyism was R. Lewis and Bryan, *Garvey*.

10. Perry, *Hubert Harrison*.

11. R. A. Hill, "The Case of Marcus Garvey," 58. For a standard account of this story see Grant, *Negro with a Hat*.

12. Jacques Garvey, *Garvey and Garveyism*, 33, 272–74.

13. For an account of the marginalization of *Garvey and Garveyism* by scholars, see Taylor, *Veiled Garvey*, 223–24; and Adler, "'Always Leading Our Men.'"

14. Cronon, "Review of *Garvey and Garveyism*." As far as we are aware, only one other review of *Garvey and Garveyism* was published: G. K. Lewis, "Review of *Garvey and Garveyism*." Lewis, the great Caribbean scholar, is nearly as dismissive as Cronon, deeming the work "a labour of love and an act of dedication," not "a critical book in the academic sense."

15. Cronon, *Black Moses*, 40, 69, 171, 203, 221–24.

16. Stein, *World of Marcus Garvey*.

17. Hahn, *Political Worlds,* 159–60.

18. See, for example, two excellent recent surveys of African American history: Holt, *Children of Fire*, 260; and Tuck, *We Ain't What We Ought to Be*, 163.

19. Hahn, *Political Worlds*, 119.

20. Trouillot, *Silencing the Past*, 70–107. For a longer discussion of Garveyism's marginalization in the American academy and the broader erasure of black nationalist perspectives, see Ewing, "Challenge of Garveyism Studies."

21. T. Martin, *Race First*.

22. Over a period of more than forty years, Hill has remained one of the most prescient voices on the history of Marcus Garvey and his movement. For more recent examples, see his "'Comradeship of the More Advanced Races'" and , "Boundaries of Belonging." Many of Hill's most important writings on the subject will appear in *Dread History: The Essential Writings of Robert A. Hill*, ed. Adam Ewing (Gainesville: University Press of Florida, forthcoming).

23. Smith-Irvin, *Footsoldiers*; R. Lewis, *Marcus Garvey*; R. Lewis and Bryan, *Garvey*; R. Lewis and Warner-Lewis, *Garvey*; T. Martin, *Pan-African Connection*; T. Martin, *Literary Garveyism*; Tolbert, *UNIA and Black Los Angeles*; Burkett, *Garveyism as a Religious Movement*; T. Martin, *Race First*; Clarke, *Marcus Garvey and the Vision of Africa*; Vincent, *Black Power*.

24. The historian George Shepperson draws a distinction between "Pan-Africanism," which he uses to indicate the "clearly recognizable movement" associated with the Pan-African Congresses (1919, 1921, 1923, 1927, 1945, 1974, and 1994), and "pan-Africanism," the eclectic political and religious tradition with roots in the eighteenth-century Age of

Revolution. Unless otherwise indicated by a chapter author, this volume associates Garveyism with the latter formulation of pan-Africanism. See Shepperson, "Pan-Africanism and 'Pan-Africanism,'" 346.

25. Du Bois, "Close Ranks," 111.

26. See Manela, *Wilsonian Moment*.

27. L. W. Levine, "Marcus Garvey," 118.

28. R. A. Hill, "General Introduction," *MGP*, 11:lxii.

29. For further discussion about local Garveyism, see Tolbert, "Outpost Garveyism"; and R. J. Stephens, "Methodological Considerations."

30. Blain, *Set the World on Fire*; McDuffie, "Diasporic Journeys of Louise Little"; Morris, "Becoming Creole, Becoming Black"; Blain, "'We Want to Set the World on Fire'"; N. Duncan, "'If Our Men Hesitate'"; Leeds, "Toward the 'Higher Type of Womanhood'"; N. Duncan, "Princess Laura Kofey"; Dossett, *Bridging Race Divides*, 154–75; Taylor, "'Negro Women'"; Bair, "'Ethiopia Shall Stretch Forth Her Hands'"; Bair, "True Women, Real Men."

31. Groundbreaking work is currently being done in this field. See, for example, Farmer, *Remaking Black Power*; Ransby, *Eslanda*; Gore, *Radicalism at the Crossroads*; and McDuffie, *Sojourning for Freedom*.

32. For division information, the authors corresponded with the UNIA's current international organizer, the Honorable Mwariama Dhoruba Kamau.

33. L. Putnam, *Radical Moves*; Guridy, "Making New Negroes in Cuba."

34. Robinson, *Black Marxism*, 240.

35. In addition to the scholars represented in this volume, the editors would like to thank the following contributors to the Global Garveyism symposium: Brandon R. Byrd, Free Egunfemi, Frank A. Guridy, Stephen G. Hall, Robert A. Hill, Caroline Shenaz Hossein, Jahi Issa, the Honorable Mwariama Dhoruba Kamau, Asia Leeds, Pedro Rivera, Mary Rolinson, Attalah Shabazz, Ula Y. Taylor, and Jonathan Warner. The editors were also honored by the attendance and participation of Nemata Blyden and Emory J. Tolbert.

36. The symposium, and indeed this volume, emerged out of plans by the late Garvey scholar Tony Martin to publish an edited volume on the global contours of Garveyism. It also owes a debt to the efforts of the historian Steven Hahn, who organized a symposium at the University of Pennsylvania in 2009 with the intention of fostering dialogue and connection among an emerging generation of Garveyism scholars.

37. Good work has already been done or is being done in all of these places. See notes 1–6 above.

38. Ewing, "Challenge of Garveyism Studies." As the political scientist Michael Dawson demonstrates, despite the enduring and continuing importance of black nationalist ideology and activism, its historical expressions and manifestations remain "systematically underrepresented" by scholars. See Dawson, *Black Visions*, 30, 133. See also R. Bush, *We Are Not What We Seem*, 2.

39. West and William G. Martin offer another model in "Contours of the Black International: From Toussaint to Tupac," in West, Martin, and Wilkins, *From Toussaint to Tupac*, 1–44. For groundbreaking conceptual models of the black freedom struggle, see Robinson, *Black Marxism*, and Bogues, *Black Heretics, Black Prophets*.

1

Garveyism Root and Branch

From the Age of Revolution to the Onset of Black Power

MICHAEL O. WEST

Seen against the backdrop of the global black liberation struggle over the past two and a half centuries, since the Age of Revolution, the Garvey movement was something of a pan-African commencement, at once an end and a beginning.[1] Although very much a product of its time—the immediate post–World War I era—Garveyism was an end in that it summed up, with such swagger and flourish, much of the preceding pan-Africanist and black internationalist thought and action.[2] At the same time, Garveyism was also a beginning, casting as it did a long shadow on contemporary and subsequent movements against colonialism, neocolonialism, and white supremacy throughout the black world. In short, Garveyism concurrently was a window on the past, present, and future of black struggles and aspirations globally.

Black Power, which emerged in the 1960s and 1970s in diverse parts of the African diaspora and the African continent, well exemplified the sprawling impact of Garveyism over time and space. It is hardly accidental that Black Power, for all its global impact—Black Power was, if anything, even more far-flung spatially than Garveyism—resonated most forcefully in some of the same areas of the black world where Garveyism was most vibrant, or at least most visible—namely, the United States, southern Africa, and the anglophone Caribbean, including the anglophone Caribbean diaspora.[3] Indeed, the two phenomena, Garveyism and Black Power, were often linked organizationally and personally: a number of groups and individuals with direct origins in Garveyism would later reappear as part of the loose political constellation that answered to the name of Black Power.[4] Marcus Garvey, more as metaphor than as man; the

Universal Negro Improvement Association (UNIA), more as inspiration than as institution; and Garveyism, more as method than as movement, served powerfully as backward and forward linkages in the fight for black freedom in the modern world.

Revolution and Revival: Garveyism and the Foundations of Pan-Africanism

Garvey and the UNIA deliberately set out to be both end and beginning, consciously seeking to cohere and inhere previous traditions of black struggle and resistance, especially in the Western Hemisphere. As a historical and political storehouse of pan-Africanism, Garveyism inherited two outstanding traditions. One of these may be termed revolutionary, the other revivalist. Both traditions emerged roughly around the same time, during the Age of Revolution in the late eighteenth and early nineteenth centuries, although they had different foundations.[5]

The revolutionary tradition originated in slave rebellions, of which the Haitian Revolution was the most complete, successful, and glorious. The rise of Garveyism coincided with renewed pan-African interest in Haiti and the Haitian Revolution, with an emphasis on the revolution's iconic male figures, foremost among them Toussaint Louverture. Garvey, a fervent believer in the Great Man approach to history—he saw himself as such a man, potentially if not actually—had long been fascinated with Toussaint, and that fascination reached its apogee in the UNIA. Garvey offered himself as a Toussaint-like figure, and was so accepted in UNIA circles.

As originally formulated, but only as originally formulated, the revivalist tradition stood in contrast to its revolutionary opposite. The revivalist tradition was rooted in the white-initiated Anglo-American Protestant reawakening, or the Evangelical Revival, which emerged in the second half of the eighteenth century and which, like the Haitian Revolution, was an integral part of the Age of Revolution. In Anglo-American lands, especially, the Evangelical Revival was a key factor in facilitating the development of the first important *group* of blacks in the Western world, largely ex-slaves, to become published writers in the language of their oppressors. In turn, this pioneering black intelligentsia would play a seminal role in the rise of abolitionism, which is to say, the political organization of antislavery thought outside of slave communities.

Generally, the founders of the pan-African revivalist tradition, notable among whom were such African-born ex-slaves as Olaudah Equiano and Ottobah Cugoano, steered clear of the politics of revolution. Equiano and Cugoano each published his major work in the years just before the Haitian Revolution, and neither would have been mistaken for a revolutionary in the making. Rather, standing between the Evangelical Revival and the Enlightenment—although generally leaning more to the former than to the latter—Equiano and Cugoano, abolitionist pioneers both, opted for the politics of evolution, that is to say, appealing to the ruling and governing classes and citing scripture (the Bible) and natural law (the Enlightenment) to clinch their argument.[6]

The revivalist tradition may have been founded on pacifism and nonviolent appeal to power, but it did not long remain exclusively so. In practice, if not always in theory, there was no sharp binary between the two modes of struggle—revolutionary and revivalist. Indeed, they were often complementary, and inheritors of the revivalist tradition soon emerged as key custodians of the Haitian revolutionary tradition.

Consider, for example, Prince Hall, noted founder of African American freemasonry, adherents of which (including Garvey) would be well represented in the leadership of black movements in and out of the United States well into the twentieth century.[7] Writing a decade after the British-based Equiano and Cugoano, Hall, who was equally steeped in the revivalist tradition, invoked the sudden and successful slave revolt in the then French colony of Saint-Domingue as the supreme example of the possibility of immediate emancipation, or what other African Americans (following established usage) called the "mutability of human affairs."[8] Hall actually justified the antislavery uprising in Saint-Domingue, which culminated in the Haitian Revolution, in the light of biblical scripture.[9]

Hall was not alone. Consider too David Walker, another outstanding African American scion of the Evangelical Revival. Walker's acclaimed jeremiad urging the enslaved to rebel also extolled the Haitian Revolution. Good evangelical Protestant chauvinist that he was—an impulse he shared with others in the U.S. black struggle, most notably James Theodore Holly and Alexander Crummell[10]—Walker was troubled only by Haiti's putative Catholicism, "that scourge of nations."[11] (He neglected voudou, the religion of most Haitians.) In time, Walker's mantle would be claimed by Henry Highland Garnet, one of the preeminent African American personalities of that era. An ordained Presbyterian preacher, Garnet was even more forthright than Walker in exhorting enslaved African Americans to revolt, evoking as he did so the Haitian revolutionary model and singling out Toussaint Louverture.[12]

Heirs to the Evangelical Revival and free men all, Prince Hall, David Walker, and Henry Highland Garnet were also men of letters seeking to synthesize the revolutionary and revivalist traditions for audiences that included, in the first instance, their enslaved brethren. But it was not just discursively, on paper, that the two traditions in black struggles merged. Theory and practice also joined forces on the field of battle where blood, not just ink, was spilled in the quest for liberty and in the repression of those seeking it. Two such bloodletting episodes occurred in 1831, respectively in the United States and in Garvey's native Jamaica, and then just months apart, when enslaved blacks rose up in arms and struck a blow for self-emancipation, Haitian-style. In both cases, the vanguard of the revolt was decidedly evangelical. The commander of the African American rebellion, Nat Turner (antislavery admirers, such as Frederick Douglass, styled him as "General Turner"), was a visionary Baptist preacher.[13] The leaders of the Christmas Rising, as the Jamaican insurrection was called, after the season in which it took place, were confessing Baptists as well. Not for nothing was the Christmas Rising also called the Baptist War.[14]

Both the Turner Revolt and the Christmas Rising/Baptist War failed in their immediate objective—emancipation. They did, however, succeed in laying down (additional) markers about the determination of the enslaved to break the chains of bondage by all available means, thereby making yet more blood-soaked payments on the great layaway plan that was emancipation. The evangelical-led, aborted servile revolutions of 1831 also may be seen as a kind of rejoinder to a challenge issued at the beginning of the Haitian Revolution. Boukman Dutty, an inaugural leader of the Haitian slave revolt turned revolution, had famously urged his fellow rebels to abandon Christianity and discard the unjust God of the whites. Seen in this light, the Saint-Domingue rebellion was not just a racial, national and class struggle, but also a spiritual battle.[15] As if to respond to the voudou-believing Boukman—and in a dialectical reordering worthy of Georg Hegel, whose Enlightenment-era philosophy owed something to the Haitian Revolution[16]—evangelical rebels like Nat Turner and the Jamaican Baptist warriors converted the unjust God of the whites into the just God of the blacks. By the same sleight of hand, and mind, the "poison book," as one writer has artfully termed the Bible of the enslavers, was rendered into the "good book" of the enslaved.[17] In this way, the revolutionary and revivalist traditions were harmonized, and Boukman and the Baptists metaphorically reconciled, on the earthly battlefield if not in the heavenly hereafter.

The Civil War (1861–65), which made the final payment on the emancipation plan in the United States, was also the last great battlefield reunion of the revolutionary and revivalist traditions in the global antislavery crusade. Here, again, the legacy of the Haitian Revolution took center stage, as the cult of Toussaint as liberator reached its martial apotheosis among African American units in the Union army. For these black soldiers, imbued as they were with an intense combination of zeal, both religious and antislavery—if the two could be separated—the war amounted to a fusion of the revivalist and revolutionary modes of struggle. The key exemplar was Toussaint, who was seen as embodying the capacity of black men to prove their manhood in war, fighting (and dying) for freedom.[18]

Among those seeking to vindicate black manhood on the battlefield of the U.S. Civil War was one Toussaint L'Ouverture Delany, whose father, Martin Robinson Delany, served alongside his son in the Union army.[19] The senior Delany had been the leading black nationalist among African Americans in the decade leading up to the Civil War, at once commended and condemned for his unstinting support of emigration, that is, the idea that the free blacks should leave the United States.[20] When the Civil War came, Delany coolly forsook emigration and joined Frederick Douglass, theretofore his chief political foil and ideological opposite in the African American struggle, in supporting the Union cause, which prophetically both men were sure could only triumph by adopting the emancipation plan.[21] (Douglass's two sons fought in the same military unit, the Fifty-Fourth Massachusetts Regiment, as Delany's son.) Deeply disillusioned by the terroristic and bloody white-supremacist overthrow of Reconstruction, the brief experiment in nonracial (but males-only) democracy that followed the Civil War, Delany once again gave up on the United States and returned to promoting emigration. African Americans in the United States were not the only ones who debated leaving the land in which they and their forebears had been enslaved; so too did people of African descent in other parts of the Americas. In the United States, Delany's was just one of many voices, if one of the more articulate ones, on the emigration question on either side of the Civil War.

"Africa for the Africans": The UNIA, the Occupation of Haiti, and World War I

Garveyism would also become implicated in the emigration question. As befitting its function as a synthesizer of black liberatory strivings, the UNIA adopted emigration as one of its signature issues, building on foundations laid by previous movements and individuals, including Martin Delany. Delany further contributed to the making of the UNIA by archiving, in his best-known work, a mantra that would become indelibly associated with Garveyism. "Africa for the Africans, at home and abroad!" Thus did Garvey, master of propaganda that he was, reduce the UNIA's program to a sound bite, fashioning a rallying cry that became one of its most enduring markers.

As with much else, Garvey's black critics accused him of appropriation, pointing out that the "Africa for the Africans" mantra preceded the formation of the UNIA. Thus Cyril Briggs, a former ally, accused Garvey of stealing the mantra from him.[22] It remained for George Alexander McGuire to answer the critics. Only Almighty God, "none but the Omniscient," rejoined McGuire, a onetime chaplain-general of the UNIA and founder of the Garveyite-inspired African Orthodox Church,[23] "knows who was the first thinker along this line [i.e., who coined the "Africa for the Africans" war cry], but all the world knows that the original doer" was Garvey.[24] McGuire erred on both counts. Garvey, as he implied, was hardly the "original" pan-Africanist, if by that is meant the movement's first major practitioner. Nor would it be left to an all-knowing deity to settle the question of the etymology of "Africa for the Africans" maxim; human research would also be central to the inquiry.

The scientifically inclined Martin Delany—he was a medical doctor who, although "not inclined to be superstitious," thought he could "see the 'finger of God'" in his emigrationist plans—has long been fingered as the original conceiver of "Africa for the Africans" maxim.[25] "*Africa for the African race and black men to rule them*," Delany wrote in 1861, just before abandoning emigration and joining the U.S. Civil War. And, he added for good measure: "By black men I mean, men of African descent who claim an identity with the race."[26] Garvey loyalists, who named him "Provisional President of Africa," would have seen no need for Delany's addition, it being self-evident to them that black men, and in particular one black man, should rule Africa. As it happened, though, Delany was no more the author of the "Africa for the Africans" mantra than was Garvey. The one, like the other, was invoking a catchword for black yearnings worldwide, the antecedents of which remained as elusive as those yearnings themselves.

Happily, Robert Hill, whose decades-long researches have uncovered a series of recondite archives on Garveyism, has now shed new light on the evolution of the "Africa for the Africans" idea. In an arresting PowerPoint presentation opening the conference that formed the basis of this edited collection, Hill showed that the idea had gained currency in abolitionist and black liberation circles in Anglo-Saxon lands well before the publication of Delany's magnum opus in 1852. In Hill's rendition, in its origin "Africa for the Africans" was a riff on another demand, namely, "Ireland for the Irish, and the Irish for Ireland," as first enunciated in 1843 by Daniel O'Connell, the pioneering Irish nationalist who is also known as "The Emancipator." Indeed, the colloquy between Irish and black emancipation would persist down to the time of Garvey, and even into the era of Black Power.[27] Garvey himself was quite fascinated with the Irish cause, as best exemplified in his era by the 1916 Easter Rising.[28]

While perhaps unfamiliar with the origins of the "Africa for the Africans" mantra, Garvey was all too aware of the larger traditions he and the UNIA stood athwart with such majesty and panache. Necessarily, Garvey was also possessed of an acute sense of history, or to be more precise, of historical biography, which became his preferred form of intellectual inquiry as a teenager. In this exercise, which was largely a search for heroes, if not yet for models, Garvey found a favorite: Toussaint Louverture.[29]

By the time Garvey arrived in the United States in 1916—two years earlier, with Amy Ashwood Garvey, he had co-founded the UNIA in Jamaica[30]— Toussaint had become the subject of renewed pan-African interest. The reason was imperialism, about which Toussaint was ambivalent. He refused to take a clear anticolonial stance and declare Saint-Domingue independent of France, leaving that historic task to his successors, led by the wonderfully ferocious former field slave Jean-Jacques Dessalines,[31] after the French had captured Toussaint (along with his wife, Suzanne, and their children) and carted him off to die cruelly in France. Of Dessalines, a noted historian of the Haitian Revolution has offered that "probably no other figure in modern history came from so little and went so far."[32] From Haiti's independence in 1804 to the era of the U.S. Civil War, the American state, beginning with the presidency of the slaveholding white supremacist Thomas Jefferson, shunned the handiwork over which Dessalines had presided and refused to treat with Haiti diplomatically.[33] Then, as if to undo Haiti's independence, historically and symbolically, the United States invaded the country in 1915 and occupied it for two decades.[34]

The U.S. occupation of Haiti was a transformative, and traumatic, event in the country's history. Haiti's writers and artists mounted stiff intellectual and cultural resistance to the occupation, even as segments of the country's peasantry took to the hills to wage guerrilla war against the hated Yankee invaders.[35] Outside of Haiti, the occupation became a major event in the global black renaissance, political and cultural, that followed World War I, a reawakening in which Garveyism stood front and center.

The invasion of Haiti was sandwiched between two signal events associated with World War I: the outbreak of hostilities in 1914 and the U.S. entry into the war in 1917 on the side of the Allied powers, effectively meaning Britain and France, thereby securing victory over Germany. Although the conflict was not of their making, black people the world over became involved in the global and epochal military showdown that was World War I. W.E.B. Du Bois, later to become Garvey's great nemesis, even argued that the war had "African roots." On Du Bois's telling, the deeper determinant of the conflict, if not its proximate cause, was the so-called Scramble for Africa—that is, the brutal and bloody conquest of the continent by the major European powers in the latter part of the nineteenth century.[36]

World War I called forth another kind of scramble, with the chief belligerents turning to the colonies to support the war effort. Britain and France, especially, mobilized vast resources, human and material, from their colonial possessions worldwide, including in Africa and the Caribbean.[37] (As a relative latecomer to the imperialist game, Germany had fewer colonies in fewer parts of the world to exploit, and indeed would lose the colonies it had at the end of the war.) Large numbers of black men were also recruited into the U.S. Army.[38] Everywhere, black civilians fought on the home front to help win the war for production to supply the military front, setting in train vast waves of migrations, within as well as across national and colonial boundaries. In sum, black people worldwide were deeply invested in World War I, even if that investment was not always voluntary.

The war ended in 1918, with much talk about a peace dividend. As partners in the risk, both on the military and civilian sides, black people expected to share in the rewards. In particular, they yearned for relief from colonial and racist oppression and indignity, of which the U.S. invasion of Haiti was but a recent example. But they would be accorded no such relief. If anything, in many cases the black condition actually worsened after the war. From Africa to the Caribbean, from North America to Western Europe, the aspirations of African-descended (and other oppressed) people were rudely and violently denied, both by the repressive arms of the state and by white mobs, sometimes operating in concert with state actors.[39]

The gap between input and outcome, between expectation and reception, could not have been wider. It was a great global white betrayal of black hope, the black laboring and middle classes alike, a political formula that created the greatest pan-African opportunity since the Age of Revolution. The key difference was that, by the era of World War I, the potential circle of global black confraternity had expanded considerably across space. In the Age of Revolution, pan-Africanism, whether as an idea or as a movement, was largely confined to the Americas and Europe, along with certain coastal areas of Africa with significant communities of African-descended migrants from the Americas, such as Sierra Leone and later Liberia.[40] The Scramble for Africa—and this was one of its many unintended consequences—widened and deepened the prospects for the reception of pan-Africanism. Under colonial rule, the African continent more and more came to resemble the African diaspora, with the colonialists reproducing in Africa some of the same systems that had been used to oppress, exploit, and degrade people of African descent in the Americas.[41] In this way, colonialism also created the conditions for the spatial expansion of pan-Africanism, a movement founded not so much on commonality of culture, language, or religion—of which historically there has been little among the descendants of Africa—but on commonality of lived experiences of oppression.

Colonialism did not just create the material conditions for the global expansion of pan-Africanism. Unwittingly, and in further evidence of its internal contradictions, the colonial system also laid the foundations for the emergence of pan-African agents. For their own self-interested reasons—economic, administrative, religious—the colonialists opened up certain limited opportunities for social mobility to small numbers of colonized Africans, mainly through modern schooling with an emphasis on literacy and numeracy, often with a strong religious (Christian) orientation. Graduates of such schools, their aspirations thwarted and denied by racist barriers and white-supremacist practices, soon became frustrated and disillusioned. As they nurtured a budding anticolonial (if not yet nationalist) consciousness, a good many of these individuals turned to the different variants of pan-Africanism that emerged, or reemerged, after World War I.[42]

The Pan-African Revolutionary Tradition, Toussaint Louverture, and Garvey

Bold and brash, Garveyism took pride of place in the new pan-African dispensation that followed World War I. From its headquarters in Harlem, New York, the UNIA emerged as the most dazzling organizational expression of the New Negro, the postwar moniker used to designate the more militant and politically conscious black populace in the United States. An outstanding quality of the

New Negro was a greater interest in world affairs, with an accent on the affairs of the African and wider "colored" world.[43]

Bleeding Haiti, now under the jackboot of the U.S. military, became an important site of contestation for the reconstituted black transnational and transcontinental rendezvous, including Garveyism.[44] Inevitably, parallels—and contrasts—were drawn with that most glorious of moments in the Haitian national experience, namely, the revolution. The resistance within Haiti, and its supporters outside the country, looked to the past for inspiration and examples of heroic, and successful, struggles against the ostensibly superior military power of foreign invaders. Revolutionary heroes, meaning the best-known male military figures of the Haitian Revolution, were metaphorically recalled to active duty. Toussaint Louverture headed the list of such men.

It was not, obviously, a new assignment. Toussaint's name had been on the lips of antislavery freedom fighters everywhere in the Americas for four generations, from the era of the Haitian Revolution to the abolition nearly a century later (in 1888) of slavery in Brazil, the hemisphere's last major slaveholding society.[45] Nor had Toussaint's symbolic value been exhausted with the demise of chattel slavery. He would subsequently be pressed into service, this time as an archetype of the reemergent black international—in short, as an exemplar of the New Negro.[46]

Garvey, too, was offered as an embodiment of the New Negro. In the pages of the *Negro World*, the news outlet which, more than any other arm of the UNIA, validated its claim to universality, Garvey was compared to various revolutionary figures from the past. This list of historical forebears included Oliver Cromwell (English Revolution), George Washington (American Revolution), and Napoleon Bonaparte (French Revolution), all of whom, especially Washington and Napoleon, Toussaint had long been likened to.[47] Garvey himself placed Toussaint, "the greatest Negro to ever come out of the West,"[48] above them all. The Haitian's "brilliancy as a soldier and statesman outshone that of a Cromwell, Napoleon and Washington," Garvey wrote, "hence, he is entitled to the highest place as a hero among men."[49] With characteristic smugness, Garvey also intimated that he was the new Toussaint. Writing in 1919 in the *Negro World*, which had been established the previous year, Garvey gave out: "Yes, the Negroes of the world have found a George Washington, yea more; they have found a Toussaint L'Overture [*sic*], and he will be announced to the world when the time comes."[50] Apparently, no such announcement was ever officially made. But Garvey soon relinquished editorship of the *Negro World*, which persisted in comparing him to the Haitian revolutionary, perhaps unofficially announcing the arrival of the new Toussaint.

Consistent with his biography-centered, Great Man approach to history, Garvey credited Toussaint with single-handedly bringing about Haiti's independence, just as he was inclined to take solo credit for the achievements of the UNIA. Black leaders have come and gone all over the world, Garvey informed an audience in Philadelphia, "and yet we have achieved nothing, except in the Republic of Haiti, where one Negro repelled them and established an independent republic."[51] Of course, Toussaint had done no such thing. Although he assumed personal power over a post-emancipation and autonomous Saint-Domingue, and even promulgated a constitution that made him governor for life (with the right to name his successor), Toussaint steadfastly refused to take the next step and declare independence from France. "The black revolution had passed him by," C.L.R. James, Toussaint's iconic biographer, glumly concluded.[52] Toussaint's apparent inability to imagine a national existence without France, along with his fealty to the "mother" country,[53] would provide a legal pretext for Napoleon's invasion of Saint-Domingue, ostensibly to secure an overseas French territory from external enemies (like Britain and Spain) but actually to reimpose slavery and white supremacy. But although distorting Toussaint's role in the making of independent Haiti, Garvey correctly and succinctly summed up his disposition by the French: "They made a prisoner of him, took him to France, and there he died."[54]

Even as he uttered these words in Philadelphia about Toussaint's end, the thirty-two-year-old Garvey would have been thinking about his own mortality. Actually, his utterances were as much autobiography as historical biography. Just days before the speech, Garvey had survived an assassination attempt, and, against medical advice, checked himself out of a New York hospital to journey to Philadelphia for a previously scheduled speaking engagement. It is revealing that in this, his greatest moment of personal vulnerability since dramatically appearing on the world stage as a black leader, Garvey chose to lash his mast so closely to Toussaint. Now aided by a cane—an outcome of the failed attempt on his life and henceforth a constant companion—Garvey rounded out his address in Philadelphia. "Thank God," he concluded, "as Toussaint L'Ouverture in his time was able to inspire the other men of his country to carry on the work until Haiti was made a free country, so today we have inspired not one, not two, but hundreds of thousands to carry out the work even if they imprison one or kill one."[55] The UNIA leader was copying directly from the playbook of the

Haitian revolutionary. In the most defenseless hour of his public life, the captive Toussaint famously told his French captors that he issued from a tree with deep roots, one that could not be destroyed by chopping off a single branch, no matter how imposing.[56]

As a literary figure, Garvey produced poetry as well as prose, although he was more adept at the latter than the former. Garvey's poetry, like his prose, centered on the liberation and unification of Africa and its descendants scattered all over the world.[57] In his poetry, as in his prose, Garvey summoned Toussaint to bear historical and biographical witness, again in ways that were deeply autobiographical. This is certainly the role assigned Toussaint in Garvey's most notable piece of nonfiction, his long, epic-like poem, "The Tragedy of White Injustice." Garvey penned this poetical protest—it owes a greater debt to protest than to poetry—hard on the heels of his release from a U.S. penitentiary, to which he had been confined for two years on spurious and politically inspired charges of mail fraud. As the title of Garvey's poem proclaimed, his imprisonment was indeed tragic, for he was very much a victim of white injustice. The poem envisioned a world in which black people could at length receive impartial justice, glancing to history for inspiration. Predictably, Garvey's search for a usable past led back to Haiti and Toussaint:

At St. Domingue we struck a clear blow
To show which way the wind may one day go.
Toussaint L'Ouverture was our leader then,
At a time when we were only half men.[58]

It was not the first, or last, time that a sole and solitary Toussaint would be offered as the supreme example of the black liberator and vindicator of black manhood,[59] which to Garvey and many others, both before and after him, amounted to the same thing. Not for nothing was the American occupation often denounced in gendered language, including by Garveyites, as the "rape of Haiti."[60]

Garveyism, Communism, and Black Radicalism: The Struggle over Toussaint Louverture's Legacy

As a masculine archetype of black emancipatory aspirations, Toussaint was hardly the exclusive preserve of Garvey and the UNIA. As had long been the case, rather, Toussaint's legacy was widely embraced within the black liberation struggle, his symbolic value forming a common currency among black freedom fighters (and their supporters) across national and colonial boundaries as well as across political and ideological lines. The fight for black freedom doubled as a battle over the historical bequest of Toussaint Louverture. In this contest, some of Garvey's black opponents—any number of whom were allies turned adversaries—enlisted Toussaint in their battles with him.

A number of these individuals were linked to the Communist International through its national affiliates, including the Communist Party of the United States. Despite the attention lavished on Garvey's quarrel with Du Bois, it remains a truism that Garvey and Garveyism were never more mercilessly and consistently flayed than by black communists worldwide, from the Americas to Europe to Africa.[61] The story of the UNIA is, in part, a story of the struggle—and it was a worldwide contest, waged on multiple continents—between Garveyism and communism for the hearts and minds of people of African descent.

Richard B. Moore was a key actor in the struggle. Possessed of oratorical skills rivaling Garvey's, Moore joined the politics of black liberation as a militant in the Harlem-based African Blood Brotherhood (ABB), which initially offered critical support to the UNIA. The alliance proved to be brief, as Garvey, for reasons to be discussed later, abandoned his more radical position and lurched to the right of the political spectrum. Meanwhile, the ABB went in the opposite direction, effectively dissolving itself and bringing its members into the U.S. Communist Party.[62] Moore was among those who, as a member of the defunct ABB, made the journey from critical support of Garveyism to communism.[63]

Toussaint Louverture was part of the migration. Previously, the ABB had made Toussaint an "illustrious blood brother," and in 1922 it had even planned a convention to coincide with what it described as the anniversary of his death, July 16, although the event never took place.[64] All the same, Moore and his black comrades, who included Cyril Briggs, the founder of the ABB, brought with them into the white-dominated U.S. Communist Party a militant insistence on honoring the black revolutionary tradition, at the helm of which they placed Toussaint.[65] In so doing, they further illustrated Toussaint's appeal across time and space, as well as across the pan-African political divide, and the multiple and conflicting uses to which his legacy could be put.

Garvey had assumed the mantle of Toussaint. Moore, on the contrary, cast Garvey as the anti-Toussaint, an unalloyed admirer of Napoleon Bonaparte, Toussaint's greatest enemy and slow-motion executioner, by "ill-treatment, cold and starvation," in the language of C.L.R. James.[66] According to Moore:

The fact that Napoleon, with a vast and murderous force, had striven to re-enslave the liberated Haitian people did not affect Garvey's adulation of this white supremacist. That Napoleon had caused the peerless leader of the Haitian Revolution, Toussaint L'Ouverture to be seized, imprisoned, and hastened to his death, did not deter Marcus Garvey from continued worship and emulation of this reactionary and deadly enemy of people of African descent.[67]

That Garvey admired Napoleon is well established. Garvey's first wife, Amy Ashwood Garvey, represented him at the point of their courtship as a Napoleon-like figure in search of a helpmeet of commensurate standing. "If as he considered," she wrote of Marcus, "he was a Napoleon, he would need a Josephine," that is, Napoleon's self-assured wife.[68] In turn, Garvey wrote, "Your Napoleon is longing to see you, longing to gaze into your beautiful eyes in fond devotion," and signing off, "Your devoted Napoleon, Marcus."[69] But while noting Garvey's admiration of "men who had fought their way to the top," Amy Ashwood placed Toussaint ahead of Napoleon in the Garveyite firmament, as did Garvey himself.[70] No matter. Such distinctions disappeared in the heat of battle, as evidenced by Moore's attempt to turn Garvey into an unflinching defender of Napoleon's campaign against the Haitians in general and Toussaint in particular.

Everywhere in the world, Garvey drove black communists like Moore to distraction. He had beaten them at their own professed game—mobilizing black workers and toilers—but (in the communist view) toward all the wrong ends. The UNIA proposed a worldwide (universal) united front of all black people, regardless of socioeconomic status, a program centered on "race first." To the communists, black and nonblack, "race first" was little more than an empty slogan, an exercise in "Negro petty-bourgeois nationalism" that was devoid of any vision of revolutionary transformation for the material benefit of the black masses. Rather, the communists argued, the black struggle should be an integral part of the multiracial and multinational struggle for worldwide proletarian or working-class revolution. Garvey, the communists gave out, was a misleader of the black workers. He misunderstood the complexity of race in the modern world and, unforgivably, liquidated the class question. In fine, Garvey was no Toussaint, who had deployed revolutionary means, armed struggle, to end slavery in Haiti.

The communist critique, however, stopped short. It failed to note that Toussaint was also guilty of the same transgression of which Garvey stood accused. In addition to liquidating the national question (refusing to declare independence from France), Toussaint had also liquidated the class question. Far from abolishing the plantation system and redistributing the land to the landless toilers, as the freedpeople or ex-slaves demanded, Toussaint kept the plantations intact, which ultimately proved to be his undoing. The unsung military commander Moise (Moyse), executed by Toussaint for opposing his plantation model of development, and for backing the demand for radical land redistribution—"land to the tillers," in the communist formulation—found no place in the use of Toussaint against Garvey by the communists. Nor in the narrative of their Garveyite foes.

Hubert Harrison also became a foe of Garvey, after having been an ally. As an ally, Harrison staunchly defended the link between Garvey and Toussaint. That is, until Harrison determined that Garvey should not, after all, be linked with Toussaint. A Harlem-based militant like Richard B. Moore and Cyril Briggs—although unlike Moore and Briggs, he never joined the Communist Party—Harrison served variously as editor (without the formal title), associate editor, and contributing editor of the *Negro World*.[71] In these roles he had a direct hand in burnishing Garvey's image, including an article in the *Negro World* placing Garvey in the pantheon of "great Negroes," alongside (among others) Toussaint and Phyllis Wheatley, the African American poet from the era of the American Revolution.[72] But like so many other early supporters, including Moore and Briggs, Harrison eventually parted ways with Garvey.

Possessed of an acid pen not unlike Garvey's, Harrison subsequently published a collection of his articles and essays in book form.[73] Garvey may have survived the assassin's bullet, but he did not escape Harrison's editorial wrath. Readers of Harrison's book learned little about Garvey the great, or his likeness to Toussaint, the UNIA leader having been rudely removed from the list of black icons that appeared in Harrison's original *Negro World* article.[74] Harrison's was one of the first, but scarcely the last, attempts at historical erasure that the irrepressible Garvey would survive.

Harrison may have broken with Garvey, but he never abandoned his unflinching opposition to the occupation of the land of Toussaint Louverture. True to militant masculinist form, Harrison, in an article titled "The Cracker in the Caribbean," denounced "the bloody rape" of Haiti by U.S. marines.[75] He was not alone in his choice of adjective for U.S. racist imperialism. The poet Andy Razaf, a resident of Harlem like Harrison, similarly inquired: "And what of valiant Haiti / Whose liberty has fled / Because of Southern Crackers / What of her murdered dead?"[76] Brimming with indignation, Harrison did not confine his targets to the imperial state. He also lashed out, unjustly and unfairly, at "the silent and shameful acquiescence of 12,000,000 American Negroes too cowardly to lift a voice in effective protest or too ignorant of political affairs to know what is taking place."[77] How, Harrison demanded to know, could "we strike heroic attitudes and talk grandiloquently of Ethiopia stretching forth her hands when we Africans of the dispersion can let the land of L'Overture [*sic*] lie like a fallen flower beneath the feet of swine?"[78] This rhetorical question—posed apparently while Harrison was still formally associated with the UNIA, but perhaps even then an oblique blast at Garvey—identified another exalted plank in Garveyite propaganda, notably, the biblical mantra about Ethiopia stretching out her hands unto God.

Garveyism and the Revivalist Tradition:
The Ethiopian Expectation and the Mosaic Mantle

It had a hallowed place in the Garveyite narrative, the Ethiopian Expectation, as I will call it. If the repeated references to the Haitian Revolution and Toussaint Louverture underlined the UNIA's claim to the legacy of the revolutionary tradition in pan-Africanism, then the group's constant appeal to the Ethiopian Expectation represented its clearest link to the revivalist tradition. Grounded in Psalm 68:31—"Princes shall come out of Egypt; Ethiopia shall soon stretch out her hands unto God"—the Ethiopian Expectation was the most oft-recited biblical passage in the UNIA, an organization that bore, in multiple ways, a striking resemblance to black churches transnationally.[79]

In the revivalist tradition, Ethiopia was generally understood as a synonym for Africa, while Ethiopians referred to people of African descent everywhere.[80] Pan-Africanists of a revivalist hue looked forward to the imminent redemption and regeneration of Africa and Africans, at home and abroad. The UNIA rhetoric about the impending fulfillment of the Ethiopian Expectation—an event that would come as unexpectedly as "a thief in the night," itself a biblical formulation—harked back to the very foundations of the revivalist tradition. It was in the second half of the nineteenth century, however, that the revivalist tradition found its highest and most elaborate literary expressions, nowhere more so than in the writings of Edward Wilmot Blyden,[81] recognized by Garvey as an important intellectual forebear.[82]

To be sure, the Ethiopian Expectation was not the sole biblical passage that became a pan-African refrain. From the outset, the founders of the revivalist tradition also relied on other scriptures, a number of which came from the book of Acts in the New Testament. One of these centered on what I call Divine Impartiality. It declared—in the language of the King James Bible, the accepted pan-African English translation—"that God is no respecter of persons" (Acts 10:34), meaning God is impartial and does not discriminate on the basis of such factors as race, nationality, and (for some) gender. Another scripture popular with pan-Africanists affirmed the doctrine of Racial Monogenesis, that is, the idea that all humans have a single and common origin. Racial Monogenesis was a bulwark against the so-called scientific racism of polygenesis, or the argument that the various "races" of humankind had different origins, based on a hierarchy of superiority and inferiority, with Africans near the bottom.[83] God, the biblically grounded exponents of Racial Monogenesis insisted, "hath made of one blood all nations of men for to dwell on all the face of the earth" (Acts 17:26).

All pan-African revivalists may have affirmed Divine Impartiality, Racial Monogenesis, and, most commonly, the Ethiopian Expectation, but they did not all affirm gender equality. It remained for Christian women, black and otherwise, to search for scriptures to back their demand for equal rights, in church and society alike. There was no shortage of such sacred writs, including in the Old Testament book of Joel, where divine assurance is given that "I will pour out my spirit upon all flesh; and your sons and your daughters shall prophesy" (Joel 2:28). Thus was contested, on the terrain of biblical exegesis, the patriarchal binary between womanhood and prophecy, between women and preaching—a view promoted by many Christian men, including black men subscribing to the revivalist tradition in pan-Africanism.[84]

As a pan-Africanist, Garvey was at least as conversant with the idiom of the revivalist tradition as he was with that of its revolutionary correlate. Accordingly, and significantly, the UNIA was launched on August 1, 1914[85]—eighty years to the day after slavery officially ended in the British empire, most notably in the British Caribbean colonies—under the motto "One God, One Aim, One Destiny." Scholars of Garveyism have been slow to note that this motto transparently was an extrapolation on Saint Paul's militantly monotheistic insistence that there is only "One Lord, one faith, one baptism" (Ephesians 4:5), another scripture much beloved by pan-African revivalists down through the ages, including female ones.[86] Alongside the founding UNIA motto of "One God, One

Aim, One Destiny" appeared the age-old theme song of Racial Monogenesis. In a standard stump speech, Garvey rounded out the portfolio of revivalist biblical mantras with an affirmation of nonracial Divine Impartiality. "God is no respecter of persons," he stated, "whether that person be white, yellow or black."[87]

Yet for all their command of pan-African biblicism, the scripture that Garvey and Garveyites knew best, at least the one they recited the most, was the Ethiopian Expectation. For them, as for pan-African revivalists since the Age of Revolution, Ethiopia was forever stretching out her hands unto God. While the Ethiopian Expectation had always occupied a central place in UNIA propaganda, over time Garvey came to rely on it more and more. The increasing reliance on this, the preeminent biblical trope of the pan-African revivalists, came at the expense of the revolutionary tradition, to which Garvey seemed to become less attentive over time as his political and legal troubles mounted.

These trends are evident in *Philosophy and Opinions of Marcus Garvey*, the first book-length collection of the UNIA leader's speeches and writings. Edited by Garvey's second wife, Amy Jacques Garvey, and published in 1923, *Philosophy and Opinions* was long considered a literary précis of Garvey and the UNIA. As Robert Hill has shown, however, *Philosophy and Opinions* is a much redacted and sanitized text, one designed for a precise political purpose—namely, to present Garvey in a moderate and nonthreatening light during his political and legal battles with the U.S. government.[88] Gone from his wife's edited collection was the radical Garvey, to be replaced with a more cautious figure. The numerous references and allusions to the Ethiopian Expectation in *Philosophy and Opinions*—its very last words are "Princes out of Egypt and Ethiopia shall stretch forth her hands"[89]—offer a jarring contrast to the treatment of the revolutionary tradition as represented by Toussaint Louverture and the Haitian Revolution, which are neglected and essentially written out of the book.

Garvey and his spouse-editor were engaged in a calculated exercise in historical revision. With the American military occupying Haiti and Garvey facing criminal charges in the United States, the pair evidently determined that the inclusion in *Philosophy and Opinions* of material drawing parallels with Toussaint would do nothing to aid Garvey's legal defense. By comparison, the Ethiopian Expectation appeared to be less threatening. For one, it was predicated on the Bible, a text the American political and legal authorities could not very well impeach, as they could the Haitian revolutionary heritage, with the U.S. military occupying Haiti at that very moment. Correspondingly, when placed alongside the Haitian Revolution, the politics of the Ethiopian Expectation looked opaque: it was unclear whether the expected redemption of Africa would be effected through divine intervention or through human agency, such as the UNIA, potentially using revolutionary means, as the radical Garvey occasionally seemed to intimate. The curtailment of the revolutionary tradition in *Philosophy and Opinions*, in relationship to the revivalist inheritance, served Garvey's immediate political and legal imperatives: it seemed to publicly confirm his move to the right. Yet Garvey had not altogether abandoned Toussaint's legacy, as seen in his notable and previously mentioned post-prison poem, "The Tragedy of White Injustice."

If, among the various biblical tropes historically associated with the revivalist tradition, the Ethiopian Expectation took pride of place, then the Mosaic Mantle was a close runner-up. The Mosaic Mantle, like the Ethiopian Expectation, centered on human liberation. As a moniker, the Mosaic Mantle derived from the Exodus story, the celebrated biblical tale of the flight of the Jews from an unpromising condemnation to bondage in Egypt to the promised land of Canaan, a miraculous journey from slavery to freedom starring the patriarch Moses as liberator-in-chief.

Despite a common emancipatory thread, there are important differences between the Ethiopian Expectation and the Mosaic Mantle. One is that the Ethiopian Expectation was unique, even exceptional. Only black people are known to have used the scripture on which it is based in the particular way they did: as a political shorthand, a rallying cry for black liberation. By contrast, the Mosaic Mantle traditionally has been more transracial and transnational, having been used in various parts of the world and at various historical moments by people fighting various forms of oppression.[90] Unlike the Ethiopian Expectation, which is a generic call for liberation, the Mosaic Mantle is an appointment to leadership of a specific liberation struggle, whether that appointment is self-made or made by others, or some combination thereof. In this regard, it should be noted that Christian enslaved Africans in the Americas showed a decided preference for the Mosaic Mantle in relation to the Ethiopian Expectation, which so excited the fancy of many free blacks, especially the intelligentsia.

Personally, Garvey seemed less eager to accept the Mosaic Mantle than he was to invoke the Ethiopian Expectation (or Toussaint's legacy.) In part, the reticence may be attributed to the historic association of the Mosaic Mantle with militant action, the perception of which the more moderate Garvey sought to avoid. Perhaps, also, Garvey was wary of the "Negro Moses" label on account of the mocking tone in which some of his critics delighted in appending it to him. One organ, previously friendly to Garvey, abruptly changed course and repeatedly taunted his as "The Moses that was to have been. The Judas that is."[91]

Such censure did not deter Garvey's admirers, many of whom fondly invested him with Mosaic qualities. Indeed, the investiture was maternal in origin, announced at the point of birth. According to Amy Jacques Garvey, her husband's deeply Christian mother wanted her son's middle name to be Moses, "as she liked Biblical names for her children, and had a hunch that this child would become a leader like Moses of old." Garvey's father, who apparently shared his wife's estimation of their newborn son's leadership potential but whose historical interests were more (European) classical than Christian, countered with the name Aurelius, after the Roman emperor Marcus Aurelius. "Eventually a compromise was reached and the child was baptized as Marcus Mosiah Garvey, although many people called him Mose."[92] Garvey's first wife also thought him possessed of Mosaic charisma. A decade younger than her suitor, the seventeen-year-old Amy Ashwood remembered being initially skeptical about his marriage proposal. But Garvey was not one to be dissuaded. "My doubts and hesitations did not deter the Black Moses," an acquiescent Ashwood reported.[93]

Rev. George Alexander McGuire, too, thought Garvey possessed of the Mosaic Mantle, just as he affirmed the UNIA leader as the "original doer," if not the "first thinker," of the "Africa for the Africans" mantra. In a sermon at the UNIA international convention in 1924, at a time when Garvey was appealing his conviction for mail fraud (the appeal was rejected), McGuire sought to convince the faithful that the leader's setback was really a Moses-like bump on the road to African redemption, as could be expected. His audience, McGuire admitted, did not consist entirely of "friends and sympathizers. Scoffers are here. Doubting Thomases are here. Calamity howlers are here."[94] The biblical Moses faced similar adversity without and opposition within. "As usual, the leader is to be blamed for all vicissitudes even though they be 'Acts of God,'" McGuire bemoaned. "Perishing from thirst, the people assail Moses, becoming violent and threatening his life."[95] As a latter-day Moses, McGuire seemed to imply, Garvey could expect nothing less.

The Mosaic trope would later reemerge as a central organizing principle in the initial wave of modern scholarship on Garvey and the UNIA. E. David Cronon, author in 1955 of the first book-length secondary study of the man and the movement, dubbed Garvey a "Black Moses."[96] In a long letter to Cronon,

Amy Jacques Garvey, who had supplied him research material for his book, commended his efforts, and especially his bibliography, which enabled interested readers "to look up all the references for deeper study" of Garvey. In the end, however, Jacques Garvey's private review of the book was damning.[97] Cronon, she bluntly told another Garvey scholar, John Henrik Clarke, years later, "wrote as a White American, isolating Garveyism and to[a]dying to Colored newspaper and magazine slurs on Garvey."[98] Indeed, Jacques Garvey felt strongly enough about Cronon's text to write a rebuttal, which she eventually published, privately, in book form.[99] Other old-time Garveyites agreed with her assessment and voiced their views soon after Cronon's book appeared. Thus a review in a noted neo-Garveyite journal slammed Cronon as an exponent of the "White Man's Burden," a reference to Rudyard Kipling's (in)famous poem of the same name celebrating European and United States imperialism. Cronon, the anonymous reviewer objected, "started off on the false premise . . . by referring to Garvey as 'The Black Moses' which presupposes that the original Moses was not a black man."[100]

By such reckoning, George Padmore's assessment of Garvey also began from a false premise. In his pan-African vade mecum, published in 1956, the year after Cronon's book, Padmore similarly endowed Garvey with a black version of the Mosaic Mantle. Throughout a distinguished career—he was arguably the greatest solo organizer in the history of pan-Africanism—Padmore displayed a peculiar penchant for getting Garvey wrong, a pattern that extended even to Garvey's name. Repeatedly, Padmore (he was not alone in doing so) wrote of "Marcus Aurelius Garvey"—instead of Marcus Mosiah Garvey—apparently failing to notice that, at least in the naming of his son, Garvey's father did not get his way in an important family decision. Both as a communist and as an anticommunist, Padmore consistently misinterpreted Garvey, first portraying him as a demagogue and tool of white capitalists and imperialists, and then as a well-intentioned but misguided tragicomic figure, "the Negro Moses."[101] Actually, Garvey was just the latest in a long line of reputed Black Moses. Nor was he alone in being portrayed as a black version of a white (or reputedly white) historical figures. His hero and archetype, Toussaint Louverture, has been variously labeled the "Black Jacobin" and the "Black Robespierre" (after the most radical faction in the French Revolution and its most iconic representative); the "Black Consul" and the "Black Napoleon" (after Bonaparte); and the "Black Talleyrand," after the famous diplomat who served a number of French rulers, including Napoleon.[102]

Garvey as John the Baptist: Noble Drew Ali, the *Holy Koran*, and the Moorish Science Temple

Stripped of the Mosaic Mantle, Garvey would reappear in various other guises in several new religious movements that began to take shape in the interwar years. One of those groups was the Moorish Science Temple of America. Led by Noble Drew Ali (formerly Timothy Drew), the formation of the Moorish Science Temple traditionally has been dated to 1913 in Newark, New Jersey.[103] But Edward E. Curtis IV, who has made a career deconstructing "textbook Islam" (what others call "orthodox" Islam) in the study of African American Muslims, has overturned the received wisdom. As a pioneering and seminal form of African American Islam, Curtis has convincingly argued, the Moorish Science Temple was really established in 1925 in Chicago, a city to which Noble Drew Ali had fled, escaping opponents in Newark.[104]

It was in Chicago, an important center of Garveyism,[105] that Drew Ali brought out the religious guidebook of the Moorish Science Temple. Titled the *Holy Koran*, the guidebook was published in 1927, the year Garvey was released from prison in the United States and immediately deported to Jamaica, which may not have been coincidental.[106] Drew Ali, like so many other contemporary religious figures of various theological hues, was fishing in troubled waters, seeking to attract what now seemed to be leaderless U.S.-based Garveyites.[107] Despite its name, Drew Ali's *Holy Koran*, also called *Circle Seven Koran* (after the number 7 set inside a circle on the cover of the original version), at best made only passing allusions to the Koran attributed to the revelations given to Muhammad of Arabia at the dawn of the Islamic era. Displaying far greater knowledge of the (King James) Bible and freemasonry—Drew Ali, like Garvey, was a Mason—the *Holy Koran* presented the genealogy of the "Moors," as Drew Ali called African Americans.

In this melodrama, Drew Ali assigned himself the function of prophet, a notion anathema to "orthodox" Islam, in which Muhammad is the "seal of prophets," which is to say the last one. Apparently believing that that which has been sealed can always be unsealed, Drew Ali paid scant attention to the theological doorkeepers of Islam. He was far more interested in appealing to Garveyites, which his spiritual guidebook did by casting Garvey as his precursor. As John the Baptist heralded the coming of someone greater than himself, notably Christ, so too the *Holy Koran* had Garvey prefiguring the arrival of Drew Ali. "John the Baptist was the forerunner of Jesus in those days, to warn and stir up the nation and prepare them to receive the divine creed which was to be taught by Jesus," the *Holy Koran* announced. "In these modern days," it went on, "there came a forerunner, that was divinely prepared by the great God-Allah and his name is Marcus Garvey, who did taught [*sic*] and warn the nations of the earth to prepare to meet the coming Prophet, who was to bring the true and divine Creed of Islam, and his name is Noble Drew Ali."[108] Garvey, a Methodist turned Catholic, would not have been pleased. (Toussaint was also a Catholic, inviting speculation about a possible motive, presumably one of many, for Garvey's conversion to Catholicism.) For one, Garvey had been upstaged, the *Holy Koran* having relegated him to the rank of Drew Ali's torchbearer. But Garvey may not have wanted any part at all in the Moorish Science Temple theology, disdainful as he was of "religious cranks,"[109] a category in which he may have placed Drew Ali.

Garvey's presumed antipathy aside, Drew Ali's Moorish Science Temple was a foundational pillar in the construction, or reconstruction, of African American Islamic traditions. The Moorish Science Temple, Michael Gomez has noted in a deeply researched and imaginative work, "is necessarily the bridge over which the Muslim legacies" of the slavery era "crossed over into the Muslim communities" that emerged among African Americans in the twentieth century.[110] Of the Muslim communities that came after the Moorish Science Temple, the most important was the Nation of Islam. The leaders of the Nation of Islam, including its chief male organizer, Elijah Muhammad, who officially took command from its apparently nonblack theological originator, Fard Muhammad, denied any connection with the Moorish Science Temple. But scholars have proven them wrong, demonstrating that the Moorish Science Temple was an essential element, organizationally and theologically, in the rise of the Nation of Islam.[111] And like the Moorish Science Temple, the Nation of Islam had deep Garveyite connections, beginning with Elijah Muhammad.

From the standpoint of organizational, if not theological, origins, the Nation of Islam, like the UNIA, was a joint spousal production. If anything, Clara Muhammad (the wife of Elijah Muhammad) may have been even more central to the formation of the Nation of Islam than was Amy Ashwood Garvey to the formation of the UNIA, as the Garvey scholar Ula Yvette Taylor has shown.[112] In turn, the Nation of Islam would become an influential transmitter of Garveyite-inflected ideas to future movements, including largely secular ones like Black Power. If for nothing else, the Nation of Islam would be important for producing Malcolm X, whose parents were both Garveyites and who would become, posthumously, one of the most beloved Black Power icons globally.[113]

Garvey as Apostle: Robert Athlyi Rogers, the *Holy Piby*, and Rastafari in Formation

Rastafari also was a key link in the long and tangled chain that connected Garveyism and Black Power. The theological roots of Rastafari, like those of the Moorish Science Temple and the Nation of Islam, are deep, wide, and varied. But three key texts, building on each other in complex and contradictory ways, are generally agreed to have formed the doctrinal basis of Rastafari. These are *The Holy Piby* by Robert Athlyi Rogers, *The Royal Parchment Scroll of Black Supremacy* by Fitz Balintine Pettersburgh, and *The Promised Key* by Leonard Howell.[114] In conception as well as execution, all three texts and their authors were deeply engaged with one another, with Garvey and Garveyism serving as a common denominator.

Some of the central features in the theological formation of Rastafari first appeared in 1924 in Rogers's *Holy Piby*, also called "the black man's bible." (In like manner, Noble Drew Ali's *Holy Koran* could also have been styled "the black man's Koran.") Given the fact that Rogers was a resident of Newark, New Jersey, at the time his proto-Rastafari text appeared, it may be safely assumed that he was acquainted in some form or fashion with Drew Ali, his contemporary and fellow Newark resident, avant-garde religious personality, and Garvey admirer. Rather like the pan-African revivalists of yore, Rogers's teachings were grounded in the King James Bible and presented the Ethiopians, as he called the descendants of Africa globally, as a peculiar people with a common destiny. Rogers, who immigrated to the United States from the eastern Caribbean island of Anguilla, offered the *Holy Piby* as the guidebook for his Afro Athlican Constructive Church, which he explicitly presented as a religious complement to the UNIA.[115] Rogers at one point even shared a political platform with Garvey.[116]

Garvey appeared early and often in the *Holy Piby*. In this theological framework, Rogers assumed two titles: shepherd and apostle, the former superior in rank to the latter. Next in the lineup came "apostle Marcus Garvey and colleague," namely, Robert Lincoln Poston,[117] a noted Garvey loyalist, UNIA general-secretary, and leader of a UNIA delegation to Liberia who died at sea on the return voyage to the United States.[118] Garvey, however, stood above his colleague Poston in the apostolic alignment. Hailed as "God's foremost apostle,"[119] Garvey was outranked only by Rogers in his function as shepherd, a Moses-like position. Whereas "the holy law of the Israelites was given to Moses," readers of the *Holy Piby* were assured, "God's Holy Law given to the children of Ethiopia was handed to Athlyi [Rogers] by a messenger of the Lord our God."[120] As law-giver (and receiver), Rogers joined his apostolic colleagues, Garvey and Poston, in a sacred mission of African redemption. "The three apostles," the *Holy Piby* asserted, were "anointed and sent forth by the Almighty God to lay the founda-tions of industry, liberty and justice unto the generations of Ethiopia that they prove themselves a power among the nations and in the glory of their God."[121]

Rogers's *Holy Piby*, like Drew Ali's *Holy Koran*, is largely an androcentric document. Both feature outsize male figures, in imagination if not in actual physical stature—Rogers's dimensions are unclear, but Garvey and Drew Ali were both relatively small—charged with executing a divine plan to save black people in the here and now. Yet while hardly a model of gender equality, Rog-ers's text offered women greater prominence and agency than did Drew Ali's. Rogers's wife and daughter appeared in the *Holy Piby* as his co-workers, both addressed as "shepherdmiss," a position transparently subordinate to the shep-herd and, presumably also, the apostles.

The *Holy Piby* further accorded Apostle Garvey a helpmeet, in the person of Henrietta Vinton Davis, an assistant president-general of the UNIA and one of its highest-ranking women.[122] (Davis was a member of the UNIA delegation to Liberia led by Poston.) Significantly, the *Holy Piby* lauded Davis (Garvey called her the UNIA's "Joan of Arc," after the fifteenth-century, self-sacrificing, teenaged French warrior who reputedly gave her king unstinting support in his successful battles against the English) less for her leadership qualities than for her perceived loyalty to Garvey, who was so quick to accuse his co-workers of disloyalty. "Moreover, behold at thy side is the noble woman Henrietta in whom the whole heaven adore because of her greatness of faith and the loyal way in which she fights to save Ethiopia and her generations from everlasting down-fall," the *Holy Piby* instructed Garvey. "Place her at the side of thy colleague, for great is her wisdom, saith the Lord, and send ye also another so that they go and prepare a home for mine anointed."[123]

The *Holy Piby* influentially prepared the way for Rastafari, although it was curiously sparing in references (or even allusions) to the Ethiopian Expectation, a Rastafari touchstone inherited from the revivalist tradition in pan-Africanism. Rogers's guidebook did, however, keep alive the revivalist practice of making Ethiopia synonymous with Africa.

As a proto-Rastafari document, the *Holy Piby* made two important contri-butions. First, it placed Garvey in an apostolic role in relation to African re-demption. Of the new black theological expressions that emerged alongside

Garveyism, the *Holy Piby* was the first to do so, before Drew Ali's *Holy Koran*, which appeared some three years after Rogers's guidebook. And while each text assigned its author a position of preeminence, the *Holy Piby* gave Garvey a more exalted role than did the *Holy Koran*—"God's foremost apostle" in the former as opposed to an untitled John the Baptist–like torchbearer in the latter.

The *Holy Piby*'s second contribution as a Rastafari precursor was that it offered, from a *theological* standpoint, a mundane and materialistic conception of African redemption. In a sharp departure from the pan-African revivalists, Rogers absolutely separated the temporal from the eternal, and then denied the latter's existence. "Hear me O children of Ethiopia," the *Holy Piby* instructed. "There is not a heaven nor a hell but that which ye make of yourselves and for yourselves. . . . The fool slights the things of life and seeketh heaven after death. Verily, verily I say unto you, he shall not find it."[124] Rogers's Afro Athlican Constructive Church was not unique in disavowing the notion of a world to come; so too did the Moorish Science Temple and the Nation of Islam. Among the new Garveyite-engaged theologies, however, the *Holy Piby* was the first guidebook to rule out a heavenly hereafter, a militant Earth-centered doctrine that would reappear in Rastafari.

Garvey as Apostate: F. B. Pettersburgh, the *Royal Parchment*, and Rastafari in Formation

The theological line from Rogers's *Holy Piby* to Rastafari intersected with the work of Rev. Fitz Balintine Pettersburgh. Published in 1926 in his native Jamaica, Pettersburgh's text came with an imposing title: *The Royal Parchment Scroll of Black Supremacy*. Pettersburgh was not the first in the pan-African tradition to speak of black supremacy, by which he apparently meant the rise (again) of African people in the scales of world civilizations. Alexander Crummell (among others) had written along similar lines, essaying on "the destined superiority of the Negro."[125] Lacking Crummell's formal learning and florid prose—perhaps precisely because of such deficiencies—Pettersburgh was also less bound to "orthodox" Christian theology.

A theological innovator on the order of Rogers and Drew Ali, Pettersburgh wrote at a time when the UNIA was in decline and Garvey was in prison. As not just theological innovators but also leaders of religious-oriented movements, all three men—Rogers, Drew Ali, and Pettersburgh—had a common objective in wooing Garveyites apparently adrift, organizationally if not ideologically. Pettersburgh, however, took a different tack. Both Rogers and Drew Ali had, in varying ways and with varying degrees of enthusiasm, positively attached themselves to Garvey. Pettersburgh, on the contrary, hurled sarcasm and mockery at Garvey *and* Rogers. From Pettersburgh's standpoint, his countryman Garvey apparently was guilty by association, that is, the association that Rogers (whose guidebook came out two years before Pettersburgh's) had made between himself and Garvey.

Much like Garvey's UNIA, Rogers's Afro Athlican Constructive Church evinced universal aspirations. Soon after its formation in the United States, the church spread to South Africa, where it was also closely associated with Garveyism.[126] Notably, too, an Afro Athlican congregation was established in Jamaica.[127] In the ensuing competition for potential congregants, many of them presumably of a Garveyite orientation, Jamaican adherents of the Afro Athlican Constructive Church likely would have clashed with Pettersburgh. This, it seems, was one reason—perhaps one of many—for the negative assessment of both Rogers and Garvey in Pettersburgh's *Royal Parchment Scroll of Black Supremacy*, an apparent reaction to the esteemed position accorded Garvey in Rogers's *Holy Piby* and the Afro Athlican Constructive Church in general.

Pettersburgh's guidebook, like those of Rogers and Drew Ali, was offered as a revelatory text for pan-African nation-building. All three authors were firmly grounded in a temporal existence, eschewing the notion of eternal life, even as they couched their messages in religious (largely Christian) idioms. "My dear inhabitants of this world," Pettersburgh wrote at the beginning of his *Royal Parchment*, "we are the foundation stones of the resurrection of the Kingdom of Ethiopia."[128] This was the resurrection of an earthly kingdom, not a heavenly one. "Speak with MORTALS, not Angels," declared King Alpha and Queen Omega, the royal couple of Pettersburgh's Kingdom of Ethiopia.[129] Virtually declaring war on metaphysics, *Royal Parchment* attacked Obeah ("no admittance for Obeah dogs"),[130] astrology ("God Almighty is INSULTED by ASTROLOGERS"), and the Pope of Rome ("The Monarch of Hell's Bottom").[131]

Royal Parchment was not much kinder to Rogers and Garvey. It addressed Rogers variously, and sarcastically, as "professor," "bishop," and, worst of all by Pettersburgh's antipapal lights, "His Holiness Pope Rodgers [*sic*]." Continuing with the battle of the books, *Royal Parchment* deprecated Rogers's *Holy Piby*, dismissing it as the "Athlican's Piby, a good little MESSENGER," and the "Little Piby."[132] As for Garvey, *Royal Parchment* labeled him, again with apparent sarcasm, as "pilot" and "general,"[133] seeming references to the Black Star Line (which the *Holy Piby* appeared, indirectly, to praise)[134] and the Universal African Legion, respectively the UNIA's ill-fated shipping fleet and its paramilitary wing. The UNIA itself fared no better, being described in *Royal Parchment* as "THE EUROPEAN LONG-DISTANCE ITALIAN-JEWISH-ANGLO-TORPEDO."[135] Effectively, Pettersburgh was accusing Garvey of selling out the pan-African faith—in a word, apostasy.

To top it off, *Royal Parchment* discussed both Garvey and Rogers under the heading of "speaking in tongues," a practice associated with the new Pentecostal movement.[136] Once again, Pettersburgh was being disingenuous: the here-and-now doctrine preached by both Rogers and Garvey bore little resemblance to the practice of many Pentecostals, if not to Pentecostal theology.[137] Actually, Garvey, now back in Jamaica and seemingly oblivious to his own professed Catholicism and its attachment to saints, would denounce "religions that howl, religions that create saints, religions that dance to frantic emotion,"[138] seemingly lumping together the tongues-speaking and holy-dancing Pentecostals (who in that period generally called themselves "the saints") and the practitioners of Obeah.

Royal Parchment affirmed as much it denounced, including offering its own unique views on gender. There is even a sense in which Pettersburgh's guidebook may be read as a love story, notably his affection for, and celebration of, his wife, the grandiloquently named Queen Lula May Fitz Balintine Pettersburgh. Theirs was offered not just as "ETHIOPIA'S PERFECT WEDLOCK" but in many ways also as a marriage of equals on a joint quest for black redemption. *Royal Parchment* rejected "white supremacy's" marriage vow pledging faithfulness until death, through wealth or poverty, sickness or health. The alternate "Black Supremacy" vow emphasized parity, with the marriage officer pronouncing: "You are now equal, HEAD and Pillow-Heart and SOUL Life-HOLD COMPANION."[139]

As the second key theological installment on the formation of Rastafari, *Royal Parchment* at once departed from and built on the first installment, Rogers's *Holy Piby*. *Royal Parchment* departed from the *Holy Piby* in dethroning Garvey: Pettersburgh removed the UNIA leader from the spiritual pedestal on which Rogers had placed him. At the same time, *Royal Parchment* reaffirmed, in theological terms, the militantly mundane and materialistic conception of global African redemption advanced in the *Holy Piby*. Each work carried forward the time-honored pan-African revivalist correspondence of Ethiopia and Africa. Both were also deeply indebted to the King James Bible, although Rogers's literary skills and command of the English language are superior to Pettersburgh's. True to its title, *Royal Parchment* also stood out for its unabashed glorification of black royalty, as embodied by Ethiopia's King Alpha and Queen Omega, the beginning and the end, signifying gender complementarity, if not exactly gender equality. With its vigorous antipapal stance, which was entirely consistent with the anti-Catholic démarche of many a pan-African revivalist; its especially harsh denunciation of white supremacy, ideologically and culturally; and its affirmation of an all-wise Ethiopian "dread creator," the *Royal Parchment* all but completed the theological undergirding of Rastafari.

Garvey Gagged: Leonard Percival Howell, the *Promised Key*, and Rastafari Formed

It only remained for Leonard Percival Howell, in the third and final theological installment on the making of Rastafari, to round out the handiwork of Rogers and Pettersburgh. Howell's guidebook, *The Promised Key*, was published around 1935 under the pseudonym of G. G. Maragh, as the British colonial regime in Jamaica inaugurated a decades-long repression of his fledgling movement.[140] *Promised Key* was plagiarism of the rankest sort: large portions (if not the greater part) of it were lifted, more or less verbatim, from Pettersburgh's *Royal Parchment*, with nary a word of acknowledgment. (Much of Drew Ali's *Holy Koran* was similarly cribbed from other sources.)

Howell, however, was not just another run-of-the-mill intellectual appropriator. His *Promised Key*—originally called *Promise Key*, his command of "standard" English being better than Pettersburgh's but not particularly well honed—deployed *Royal Parchment* in novel ways. Howell's use of Pettersburgh's work was strategic and selective, not haphazard and indiscriminate. In this sense, Howell, for all his discursive piracy, qualifies as a theological innovator, comparable to Rogers, Pettersburgh, and Drew Ali.

Like his Rastafari progenitors Rogers and Pettersburgh, Howell's envisioned kingdom was of this world, and this world only. "The white man's doctrine has forced the black man to forsake silver and gold and seek Heaven after death," *Promised Key* protested. But, thanks to the enlightened teachings of the emerging Rastafari, the scales finally had fallen from the eyes of the long miseducated scions of Africa, and the white deceit had been exposed: "We the black man have found out that their doctrine was only a trick, and all their intention was to make themselves strong and to fool the black man."[141] Consistent with

Pettersburgh's *Royal Parchment*, Howell's *Promised Key* disavowed Obeah and astrology ("fortunetellers"), devotees of which were barred from "the Assembly of Black Supremacy."[142] The Catholic Church was similarly condemned. If anything, Howell took an even stronger antipapal stance than did Pettersburgh, describing the pope as "satan the devil."[143]

Howell departed from Pettersburgh on the gender question. For sure, *Promised Key* followed *Royal Parchment* in celebrating King Alpha and Queen Omega. She, however, was very much in the background, as he took center stage. It is in vain that one peruses *Promised Key* for anything approximating the love and affection, to say nothing of the respect and reciprocity, between the royal pair (as embodied by Pettersburgh and his wife, Queen Lula May) in *Royal Parchment*.

Howell's *Promised Key* also did not acknowledge any forebears. Rogers had lauded Garvey. Pettersburgh derided both Rogers and Garvey. Howell ignored all three. The silence on Rogers is understandable, although Howell almost certainly knew of the *Holy Piby*. Howell and Rogers may even have been acquainted, or moved in the same circles, from Howell's sojourn in the United States, including in the greater New York City metropolitan area, where Howell was associated with the UNIA and where Rogers lived (Newark).[144] By the time Howell wrote *Promised Key*, however, he had returned to Jamaica and was spatially removed from Rogers. The exclusion from *Promised Key* of Pettersburgh, whom Howell assuredly would have known, is perfectly logical: plagiarizers often do not cite the authors they plagiarize.

The omission of Garvey from *Promised Key* is rather more perplexing. Howell also would have known Garvey from New York and was certainly in personal contact with him when they both returned to Jamaica. From all accounts, though, Garvey was not favorably disposed to Howell and refused to give him a platform to air his views.[145] All the more perplexing, then, that Howell's *Promised Key* did not return the (dis)favor and, at a minimum, reproduce the barbs against Garvey in *Royal Parchment*, just as Howell reproduced so much else from Pettersburgh's guidebook. It was as if the author of *Promised Key* was splitting the difference between the treatment accorded Garvey by Pettersburgh and Rogers, respectively. At worst, Howell may be said to have gagged Garvey. At best, he declined to apply the doctrine of an eye for an eye, even if he did not exactly turn the other cheek. In this sense, Howell, in his text marking the definitive theological formation of Rastafari, seemed to extend a kind of graciousness to Garvey, albeit through silence. Howell's successors would be more loquacious, and less inhibiting, in offering grace to Garvey, who eventually became an icon of Rastafari, one of its most notable and enduring symbolic figures.[146]

Howell completed the theological foundations of Rastafari begun by Rogers and Pettersburgh in two significant ways. First, *Promised Key* shrank, spatially, the definition of Ethiopia. Rogers had accepted the continental, even global, definition of Ethiopia handed down by the pan-African revivalists, whereby Ethiopia was understood to mean Africa, and Ethiopians meant people of African descent worldwide. For his part, Pettersburgh had spoken of a "Kingdom of Ethiopia," but its geographical dimensions were ambiguous. It was unclear whether this kingdom was a single country, a region, or a continent. With Howell there is no ambiguity: Ethiopia is a country located in northeastern Africa, as the opening sentence of *Promised Key* asserted.[147]

Howell's second outstanding contribution to the full theological construction of Rastafari was his deification of Haile Selassie, the then emperor of Ethiopia, a country also known at that time as Abyssinia. Mostly, *Promised Key* referred to the Ethiopian emperor as Ras Tafari, using Selassie's title (Ras) and his given name (Tafari) before he ascended the throne. Both title and given name eventually would be combined to give Howell's budding movement its signature moniker: Rastafari. Simultaneously, Selassie became the divine-emperor of Rastafari. "His Majesty Ras Tafari is the head over all man [*sic*] for he is the Supreme God," *Promised Key* emphatically asserted.[148] Howell's guidebook promised retribution to those who failed to follow its injunctions, meaning, presumably, black people. (Like the Old Testament, in which it was grounded, *Promised Key* offered a "tribal," or racially specific creed, not a "universal" one.) Mimicking the language of the King James Bible, as the *Holy Piby* and *Royal Parchment* (and also the *Holy Koran*) had done, *Promised Key* concluded: "Woe be unto them that forsaketh H. M. Ras Tafari as being God Almighty, they shall be cast into hell both body and soul."[149] Left unsaid was how such a punishment would be meted out, since Howell did not believe in a literal hell, or heaven.

Rastafari, Pan-African Biblicism, and the Babylonian Captivity

Implicitly, if not explicitly, *Promised Key*, along with its literary progenitors, the *Holy Piby* and *Royal Parchment*, raised the question of emigration, which Garveyism had inherited from previous iterations in pan-Africanism. Over time, Rastafarians would develop a clear-cut position on the emigration question. In so doing, they added mightily to pan-African biblicism, that is, the construction of a biblical basis for pan-Africanism.[150]

Before Rastafari, pan-Africanism biblicism rested on two major pillars, both of them derived from the revival tradition and present in Garveyism. These were the Ethiopian Expectation and the Exodus story, of which the Mosaic Mantle is an integral part. (There were, as we have seen, lesser biblical tropes in pan-Africanism, such as Divine Impartiality and Racial Monogenesis.) Rastafari theology effectively settled the Ethiopian Expectation: Haile Selassie was presented as the fulfillment of the prophecy about Ethiopia's outstretched hands to God, while the Exodus story was folded into the Rastafari demand for a return to the pan-African promised land of Ethiopia.

The Rastafari approach to the Ethiopian Expectation and the Exodus story brought to the fore another biblical trope: the Babylonian Captivity. Under Rastafari tutelage, the Babylonian Captivity became a third major pillar in the architecture of pan-African biblicism, alongside the Ethiopian Expectation and the Exodus story. In the biblical telling, the Babylonian Captivity is post-Exodus: it happened long after the Jews had been freed from bondage in Egypt, arrived in their promised land of Canaan, and established a tradition of national state formation.

In the sixth century BCE, the Jewish kingdom of Judah fell victim to imperialism. The empire of Babylon invaded Judah, crushed the kingdom, and carried off many of its inhabitants into a second slavery. Thus began the notion of the Babylonian Captivity, a captivating tale that would provide fodder for biblically grounded people facing persecution, or feeling persecuted, everywhere. For instance Martin Luther, the German pioneering Protestant reformer, famously penned a disquisition on "the Babylonian Captivity of the church,"[151] a document whose antipapal line concedes nothing to Howell's *Promised Key*. Likewise, exponents of the revivalist tradition in pan-Africanism, which was mainly a Protestant project, held forth on the Babylonian Captivity of the black race.[152]

But while not new to the discourse of a biblically based pan-Africanism, the trope of the Babylonian Captivity never acquired the same iconic standing as the Ethiopian Expectation and the Exodus story/Mosaic Mantle—not, that is, until the rise of Rastafari, whose major contribution was to bring the Babylonian Captivity from the margins to the center of pan-African biblicism. Thus did the demand for Exodus come to include "chanting down Babylon," that universal Rastafari catchall for oppression.[153]

As a biblically based, Old Testament–grounded, and Earth-centered theology, the Rastafari attachment to the Babylonian Captivity is not surprising. The Babylonian Captivity, unlike the Ethiopian Expectation and the Exodus story, is largely free of wonderment. The Ethiopian Expectation, with its temporal imprecision—it was never clear exactly when Ethiopia would stretch out her hand unto God—seemed almost to invite divine intervention, while the Exodus story was an outright miracle, divinely ordered and executed. By contrast, the Babylonian Captivity unequivocally centered human agency, with far less in the way of supernatural entanglement.

The Babylonian Captivity, like the Ethiopian Expectation, was founded on a biblical psalm. There, however, the comparison ends. If the Ethiopian Expectation was a waiting game (albeit one Rastafari claimed ended with the coming of Haile Selassie) reminiscent of a go-slow in an industrial setting, then the Babylonian Captivity was an actual walkout, a strike by the workers, one that seems to bear some resemblance to Du Bois's conception of a "General Strike" by the enslaved during the U.S. Civil War.[154] The story of the older strike is captured in Psalm 137, the key poetical scripture of the Babylonian Captivity:

> By the rivers of Babylon, there we sat down, yea, we wept, when we remembered Zion. We hanged our harps upon the willows in the midst thereof. For there, they that carried us away captive required of us a song; and they that wasted us required of us mirth, saying, Sing us one of the songs of Zion. How shall we sing the Lord's song in a strange land?

This was protest on a grand scale, a rejection not just of economic exploitation and political oppression but also of social degradation and cultural co-optation. Ultimately, the strike signified a repudiation of enslavement and exile. The immediate trigger, however, was a refusal to be made fools of: the strikers would not provide music, their own national music, for the party their oppressors were throwing. The oppressed working people rejected cultural prostitution. Come what may, they would not sing the Lord's song in a strange land for the enjoyment of strange enslavers.

The reggae men and women, those greatest of Rastafari apostles, would throw down a similar gauntlet. They set to music the psalm of the Babylonian Captivity, tweaking it ever so slightly. Instead of refusing to sing the "Lord's song," they disavowed "King Alpha's song," using a Rastafari name for Haile Selassie, as handed down by *Promised Key*.[155] But something had been lost in the translation, the gendering of the story having been reordered. An omission was made in the textual transmission of Rastafari from Pettersburgh to Howell to reggae. Pettersburgh's *Royal Parchment* spoke not just of King Alpha but also of Queen Omega, presenting them as virtual co-monarchs. As in other ways, Howell's *Promised Key* repeated much of what Pettersburgh said about the royal couple, Alpha and Omega. Howell, however, had no companion, no one in his discursive life comparable to Pettersburgh's spouse, Queen Lula May, the embodiment of Queen Omega. The reggae musical reporting, based on the psalm, wrote Queen Omega out entirely, leaving a solitary male figure, King Alpha, whose song would not be sung in exile, and definitely not for the entertainment of the oppressor—or the downpressor, as the Rastafarians prefer to say.[156]

The Ethiopian Crisis of 1935: Rastafari, Garvey, and Haile Selassie

As the omega, if not the alpha, of Rastafari, Howell's *Promised Key* fulfilled multiple functions. It was, in the first instance, an exercise in theological abstraction. But *Promised Key* was more than that; it was also a political manifesto, composed in response to a contemporary crisis. Even as Howell wrote, Ethiopia faced an existential threat: it was an open secret that Italy's fascist dictator, Benito Mussolini, was on the verge of invading Haile Selassie's empire.

For Howell, Mussolini was really a shill for the Pope of Rome, who was seen as the ultimate incarnation of white supremacy in all its forms.[157] The coming military showdown, Howell averred, would be more than just another interstate conflict, or even another act of fascist aggression. It would be, above all, a duel between the Pope of Rome and the Emperor of Ethiopia, and Howell was certain of the outcome. *Promised Key* assured "Inhabitants of the Western Hemisphere," an apparent reference to black people in the Americas, that "the King of Kings [Haile Selassie's] warriors can never be defeated, the Pope of Rome and his agents shall not prevail against the King of Kings host [of] warriors."[158] Howell thus added his voice to the militant and defiant spirit—there was talk of sending black legions to Ethiopia—then gathering over global Africa in response to the fascist threat.[159] "All ye warriors of the King of Kings lift high King Alpha's Royal Banner, from victory to victory King Alpha shall lead his army till every enemy is vanquished," *Promised Key* at once promised and commanded.[160] Howell may have deprecated Christianity, but this call to battle was actually inspired by a Christian hymn, "Stand up for Jesus,"[161] a martial tune wholly consistent with the demands for empire and, perhaps for that reason, an indispensable part of the musical repertoire of English-speaking Protestant missionaries in the colonies.

To the bitter disappointment of scattered Africa and antifascist partisans worldwide, Selassie's army was unable to stand up to Mussolini's war machine.[162] Italy, the fascists now crowed, had been cured of its Adwa complex, that is to say, the psychological effects of the stinging defeat of an Italian army seeking to colonize Ethiopia at the Battle of Adwa in 1896, the single most important setback for European imperialism during the Scramble for Africa.[163] In the rematch of 1935, Mussolini's forces were much better prepared, armed with warplanes, tanks, and mustard gas, weapons the Ethiopians could not match. But even after making allowance for the technological imbalance—the Haitian revolutionaries faced a comparable mismatch against multiple European armies, not just the French—Selassie had proven himself a less-than-inspiring commander in chief. Selassie was no Mao Tse-tung, who at that very moment was leading a people's war against imperialism, capitalism, and landlordism in China and who, significantly, would repeatedly mention the Ethiopian issue in his manual on guerrilla warfare, a text that would later resurface as a Black Power favorite.[164] Selassie further fettered the resistance to the Italian fascist invasion by presiding over an oppressive and reactionary feudal system that kept most Ethiopians in serfdom,[165] a hard reality to which many of his acolytes, Rastafarians among them, turned unseeing eyes.

Garvey was not among the deniers. Downcast at the defeat of the Ethiopians, the thin-skinned leader of the now much diminished UNIA was also nursing a personal grudge against Haile Selassie. In defeat, the Ethiopian emperor sought refuge in London. Garvey, who was now also residing in London, went to the train station to welcome Selassie. It was not to be. The emperor paid Garvey no attention, a snubbing that perhaps called to mind Garvey's own rebuff of Leonard Howell, the Rastafari theologian and founding figure. Previously, Garvey had celebrated, poetically, Ethiopian emperor Menelik's defeat of Italy at the 1896 Battle of Adwa: "Italians, Menelik put to chase / Beating a retreat in uneven haste."[166] In the wake of Selassie's rebuff, Garvey determined that the emperor was a mere epigone, unworthy of Menelik's throne. Accordingly, he mercilessly and bitterly flayed Selassie, accusing him of cowardice and racial treachery, among other transgressions.[167] Garvey's critique was not devoid of merit, but the timing and tone were atrocious. Garvey, always short on grace, could muster none on this occasion, the single most consequential crisis in pan-Africanism in the years between the two world wars, the popular backlash in (and out of) the black world far surpassing the reaction to the invasion and occupation of Haiti by the United States.

The ill-tempered and ill-timed, but not uncharacteristic, response to the Ethiopian crisis helped to confirm Garvey's increasing alienation from the larger pan-African confraternity.[168] The UNIA leader would die, obscurely, in London several years later, during World War II. His had been one of the greatest of meteoric rises in the annals of pan-Africanism, but it was also, arguably, the most precipitous fall. Toussaint Louverture—Garvey's notable model, especially in his most radical phase—had fallen with far greater glory, having been taken captive by the enemy. But, of course, that was not the end of the story; there seems to be no end to the Garveyite story. With Garvey, as with Toussaint, the past was prologue. The one, like the other, would have an afterlife, indeed multiple afterlives. Garvey's legacy would be rekindled, sphinxlike, as if to impersonate his amazing political career.

Garvey and Garveyism: The Black Power Rejoinder

The quarter century or so between Garvey's death and the rise of Black Power marked a low point in the Garveyite narrative, the nadir of Garveyism. During this period, one Black Power bard would bewail, albeit with an element of poetic overstatement, "Garvey was gone . . . / Garvey was forgotten."[169] Garvey and Garveyism would return and be remembered at large, a rebirth in which Black Power would play a determining role. In turn, Black Power found an ally in Rastafari, most especially so in Jamaica, where Garvey, dishonored in his own lifetime by the colonized middle class, eventually would be refashioned and officially transformed into a national hero. Garvey had forsaken Rastafari, shunning Leonard Howell and insulting Haile Selassie. Yet Rastafari generally refused to respond in kind and sup from Garvey's poisoned chalice, including his repudiation of ganja (marijuana), a Rastafari sacrament.[170] Instead, most Rastafarians, although not all of them,[171] held fast to the Garveyite doctrine (or a version thereof) during the nadir, before helping to transmit it to Black Power.

All over the world, numerous organizations, agencies, and individuals stood at the nexus of Garveyism and Black Power. Many were old-time Garveyites. These included the UNIA remnants whom Obi Egbuna, the Nigerian-born pioneer of British Black Power, encountered in London in the 1960s, still "working round the clock" promoting Garvey's message.[172] On the other side of the Atlantic, in Montreal, Canada, Garveyite infrastructure provided a refuge for Black

Power students, many of them from the Caribbean, struggling against racism on campus. One of the few safe public spaces available to the students, it turned out, was Montreal's decades-old UNIA hall.[173]

Sometimes, those transmitting the Garveyite inheritance to Black Power were former Garvey critics who had mellowed over time. Such was the case with Cyril Briggs, chief founder of the African Blood Brotherhood and a leading black member of the U.S. Communist Party. Beginning as a supporter, Briggs soon became one of Garvey's most bitter critics, as we have seen. Yet there was Briggs, at the onset of the Black Power era, writing in the inaugural issue of a Black Power magazine and calling attention to the Garveyite foundations of Black Power in the United States. "Black Nationalism," Briggs offered, using a description applied to both Garveyism and Black Power, "is not new to the American scene." Rather, he continued, Black Nationalism "has long been one of the two main trends in the Black community, even antedating the integration trend. It reached its highest level in this country with the rise of the Garvey Movement which, incidentally, was the greatest Afro-American mass movement in history."[174]

Altogether, Garvey and Garveyism have had a convocational place in the annals of pan-Africanism and black internationalism. From the Age of Revolution to the onset of Black Power, many of the key movements, strains and tendencies in the global quest for black emancipation can in some form or fashion be linked to the UNIA, ideologically or organizationally. At this historical junction, playing the part of traffic director, has stood Garveyism, linking what came before as well as what came after it, connecting the political and the cultural, the sacred and the secular. In the long and still unfinished struggle for black liberation worldwide, Garveyism has occupied the unique position of root and branch. Even now, a century after it first appeared, the Garveyite factor remains unexhausted. It is, truly, a pan-African rock for the ages, Garveyism.

Notes

1. On black struggles in the Age of Revolution, mostly on the western side of the Atlantic, see Frey, *Water from the Rock*; Sweet, *Recreating Africa*; Landers, *Atlantic Creoles*; Knight, *Working the Diaspora*; and Ferrer, *Freedom's Mirror*.

2. The literature on Garveyism is considerable. Not counting edited collections, some of the key book-length studies include Cronon, *Black Moses*; Vincent, *Black Power*; T. Martin, *Race First*; Stein, *World of Marcus Garvey*; Taylor, *Veiled Garvey*; Rolinson, *Grassroots Garveyism*; Harold, *Rise and Fall*; Grant, *Negro with a Hat*; Guridy, *Forging Diaspora*; Vinson, *Americans Are Coming*; and Ewing, *Age of Garvey*. All students of

Garveyism owe a special debt to Robert Hill and his coeditors for their vast documentary project, *The Marcus Garvey and Universal Negro Improvement Association Papers*.

3. The Black Power literature, like the Garvey literature, is growing fast. For a global sampling, see P. E. Joseph, *Waiting 'Til the Midnight Hour*; Swan, *Black Power in Bermuda*; Magaziner, *Law and the Prophets*; Ivaska, *Cultured States*; Slate, *Black Power beyond Borders*; Austin, *Fear of a Black Nation*; Quinn, *Black Power in the Caribbean*; Ford, *Liberated Threads*; and Farmer, *Remaking Black Power*. The anglophone Caribbean diaspora in Central America is charted by, among others, Leeds, "Toward the 'Higher Type of Womanhood.'" For an overview of the reciprocal impact of the anglophone Caribbean diaspora in the greater Caribbean, see L. Putnam, *Radical Moves*.

4. Rather intriguing in this connection is the case of Australia, the Australian Aborigines, and pan-Africanism since the Age of Revolution. See, for example, Pybus, *Epic Journeys of Freedom*; Maynard, "'In the Interests of Our People'"; Maynard, "Marching to a Different Beat"; A. Turner, *On Trial*; and Trometter, "Malcolm X."

5. Michael O. West and William G. Martin, "Haiti, I'm Sorry: The Haitian Revolution and the Forging of the Black International," in West, Martin, and Wilkins, *From Toussaint to Tupac*, 91–97.

6. Equiano, *Interesting Narrative*; Cugoano, *Thoughts and Sentiments*; Bogues, *Black Heretics, Black Prophets*, 25–46.

7. Hinks and Kantrowitz, *All Men Free and Brethren*; Arroyo, *Writing Secrecy*.

8. Moses, *Classical Black Nationalism*, 53–59.

9. Prince Hall, "A Charge Delivered to the African Lodge," in Brooks and Saillant, *"Face Zion Forward,"* 204.

10. Holly, *Vindication*; Moses, *Destiny and Race*. Two of Holly's children, Haitian citizens both, would later emerge as staunch Garveyites.

11. Hinks, *David Walker's Appeal*, 22–23 (quotation on 23).

12. Henry Highland Garnet, "Henry Highland Garnet Calls for Slave Rebellions," in Bracey, Meier, and Rudwick, *Black Nationalism in America*, 67–76.

13. Greenberg, *Nat Turner*.

14. Craton, *Testing the Chains*.

15. C. Joseph, "The Rhetoric of Prayer."

16. Buck-Morss, *Hegel, Haiti, and Universal History*.

17. Callahan, *Talking Book*, 21–48. See also Kidd, *Forging of Races*; and Catron, *Embracing Protestantism*.

18. Clavin, *Toussaint Louverture*; Horne, *Confronting Black Jacobins*; Dillon and Drexler, *Haitian Revolution*; J. A. Dunn, *Dangerous Neighbors*.

19. Clavin, *Toussaint Louverture*, 126.

20. Delany, *Condition, Elevation, Emigration*. This edition (see bibliography) brings together two of Delany's works, the one originally published in 1852 and the other in 1861.

21. R. S. Levine, *Martin Delany*.

22. *Crusader*, October 1921, 9.

23. Terry-Thompson, *History of the African Orthodox Church*.

24. George Alexander McGuire, "What Is That in Thine Hand?" in Burkett, *Black Redemption*, 168–69.

25. Shepperson, "Notes on Negro American Influences," esp. 301.

26. Delany, *Condition, Elevation, Emigration*, 358.

27. Prince, "Do What the Afro-Americans Are Doing."

28. T. Martin, *Race First*, 31; Grant, *Negro with a Hat*, 173, 197–98. For a broader discussion of the subject, see O'Neill and Lloyd, *Black and Green Atlantic*.

29. T. Martin, *Race First*, 82.

30. Amy Ashwood Garvey, "The Birth of the Universal Negro Improvement Association," appendix in T. Martin, *Pan-African Connection*, 219–26. Tony Martin, that surefooted and catholic authority on Garveyism to whom all Garvey scholars are deeply indebted but for whom Garvey seemingly could do no wrong, poured scorn on Amy Ashwood's claim to coauthorship of the UNIA. T. Martin, *Amy Ashwood Garvey*. C.L.R. James was one of the first scholars to acknowledge Amy Ashwood's coauthorship claims. See his *History of Pan-African Revolt*, 98. See also Reddock, "The First Mrs Garvey."

31. C.L.R. James, in a later addition to his magisterial work on Toussaint and the Haitian Revolution, called Dessalines a "barbarian." Perhaps so, but barbarians are made, not born; and Dessalines's reputed barbarism was measured to the existential threat the Haitians faced, the French under Napoleon having literally set out to commit genocide against them. In victory, Dessalines offered a fitting exculpation, hurling his own epithet and assuming sole authorship of the deeply collective project. "I have given the French cannibals blood for blood," he gave out. On the "barbarian" comment, see James, *Black Jacobins*, 393; on the Dessalines quotation, see Geggus, *Haitian Revolutionary Studies*, 27. For the new scholarship on Dessalines, including the idea that he may have been born in Africa, see Girard, "Jean-Jacques Dessalines and the Atlantic System"; and Jenson, "Jean-Jacques Dessalines."

32. Dubois, "Dessalines Toro d'Haiti," 546.

33. Logan, *Diplomatic Relations*; Hunt, *Haiti's Influence*.

34. Plummer, *Haiti and the Great Powers*; Schmidt, *United States Occupation of Haiti*.

35. Shannon, *Jean Price-Mars*.

36. W.E.B. Du Bois, "The African Roots of the War," in D. L. Lewis, *W.E.B. Du Bois: A Reader*, 642–51.

37. Farwell, *Great War in Africa*; Page, *Africa and the First World War*; Strachan, *First World War in Africa*; Paice, *World War I*; Howe, *Race, War and Nationalism*; R. Smith, *Jamaican Volunteers*; S. Das, *Race, Empire and First World War Writing*.

38. Lentz-Smith, *Freedom Struggles*; Mjagkij, *Loyalty in Time of Trial*.

39. Jenkinson, *Black 1919*; Stovall, "Colour Blind France?"; Whitaker, *On the Laps of Gods*; Krugler, *1919*.

40. Geiss, *Pan-African Movement*.

41. Césaire, *Discourse on Colonialism*.

42. See, for example, Kitching, *Class and Economic Change in Kenya*; Zachernuk, *Colonial Subjects*; and West, *Rise of an African Middle Class*.

43. Baldwin and Makalani, *Escape from New York*.

44. On Garveyism in Haiti, see Plummer, "Garveyism in Haiti." Also of interest is Désulmé, "Garvey and Haiti."

45. Clavin, *Toussaint Louverture*; Dillon and Drexler, *Haitian Revolution*; Geggus, *Impact of the Haitian Revolution*; Fischer, *Modernity Disavowed*; Garraway, *Tree of Liberty*; Geggus and Fiering, *World of the Haitian Revolution*.

46. Renda, *Taking Haiti*; Kaisary, *Haitian Revolution;* Figueroa, *Prophetic Visions*; Glick, *Black Radical Tragic*; Dalleo, *American Imperialism's Undead.*

47. Corbould, "At the Feet of Dessalines," 288; Cronon, *Black Moses*, 208.

48. Quoted in M. J. Smith, "'To Place Ourselves in History,'" 186.

49. Marcus Garvey, "African Fundamentalism," in Clarke, *Marcus Garvey*, 156. For all their disagreement, Garvey and Du Bois were united in assessing Toussaint. In an essay on the Haitian, Du Bois approvingly quoted Wendell Phillips, the noted white American abolitionist, as follows: "You think me a fanatic, for you read history, not with your eyes, but with your prejudices. But fifty years hence, when Truth gets a hearing, the Muse of history will put Phocion for the Greek, Brutus for the Roman, Hamden for England, La-Fayette for France; choose Washington as the bright consummate flower of our earliest civilization; and then, dipping her pen in the sunlight, will write in the clear blue, above them all, the name of the soldier, the statesman, the martyr, Toussaint L'Ouverture." See W.E.B. Du Bois, "Toussaint L'Ouverture," in Sundquist, *Oxford W.E.B. Du Bois Reader*, 301.

50. Quoted in Cronon, *Black Moses*, 46.

51. Marcus Garvey, "Address to UNIA Supporters in Philadelphia," in Wintz, *African American Political Thought*, 200.

52. C.L.R. James, *Black Jacobins*, 321.

53. "A good child must show submission and obedience to his mother," Toussaint noted as the French prepared to invade Saint-Domingue. "But should the mother become so denatured as to seek the destruction of her child, the child must obtain vengeance, god willing." Quoted in Girard, "Rebelles with a Cause," 61.

54. Garvey, "Address to UNIA Supporters in Philadelphia," 200.

55. Ibid.

56. Dubois, *Avengers of the New World*, 278.

57. T. Martin, *Poetical Works of Marcus Garvey*. See also T. Martin, *Literary Garveyism.*

58. T. Martin, *Poetical Works of Marcus Garvey*, 8.

59. Writing just over a decade after Garvey, the Negritude bard Aimé Césaire noted in his great epic poem: "a lone man defying the white screams of white death / (Toussaint, Toussaint Louverture) / a lone man who mesmerizes the white sparrow hawk of white death / a man alone in the sterile sea of white sand." Césaire, *Notebook of a Return,* 16.

60. Dalleo, *American Imperialism's Undead*, 101–21. On African American women and the occupation, see B. R. Byrd, "'To Start Something to Help These People.'"

61. See, for example, Padmore, *Life and Struggles*; Solomon, *The Cry Was Unity*; Davidson et al., *South Africa and the Communist International*; Adi, *Pan-Africanism and Communism*; and Weiss, *Framing a Radical African Atlantic.*

62. Solomon, *The Cry Was Unity*, 3–21; W. James, *Holding Aloft the Banner*, 122–84; Makalani, *In the Cause of Freedom*, 45–69.

63. R. B. Moore, *Caribbean Militant in Harlem.*

64. W. James, *Holding Aloft the Banner*, 172. It is established that Toussaint died in April 1803, although there is disagreement over the exact day.

65. Solomon, *The Cry Was Unity*, 98, 184.

66. C.L.R. James, *Black Jacobins*, 363.

67. Richard B. Moore, "The Critics and Opponents of Marcus Garvey," in Clarke, *Marcus Garvey*, 233.

68. Ashwood Garvey, "Birth of the Universal Negro Improvement Association," 220.

69. Quoted in Stein, *World of Marcus Garvey*, 32.

70. Ashwood Garvey, "Birth of the Universal Negro Improvement Association," 221.

71. Perry, *Hubert Harrison*.

72. Perry, *Hubert Harrison Reader*, 180.

73. Harrison, *When Africa Awakes*.

74. Perry, *Hubert Harrison Reader*, 180.

75. Ibid., 236.

76. *Crusader*, October 1921, 20. Razaf's qualified "Southern crackers" was a reference to the fact that the branch of the U.S. military chiefly responsible for the occupation of Haiti, the marines, had a disproportionate number of whites from the South. Or so it was said.

77. Perry, *Hubert Harrison Reader*, 236. On the pan-African reaction to the occupation of Haiti, see Dalleo, *American Imperialism's Undead*; Renda, *Taking Haiti*, 261–300; Kaisary, *Haitian Revolution*, 37–55, 77–106; Polyné, *From Douglass to Duvalier*; A. Putnam, *Insistent Call*, 53–73; B. R. Byrd, "'To Start Something to Help These People'"; Plummer, "Afro-American Response"; Pamphile, "NAACP and the American Occupation"; Lowney, "Haiti and Black Transnationalism"; and M. J. Smith, "Capture Land."

78. Perry, *Hubert Harrison Reader*, 236.

79. Burkett, *Garveyism as a Religious Movement*; Philip Potter, "The Religious Thought of Marcus Garvey," in R. Lewis and Bryan, *Garvey*, 145–63; Bair, "'Ethiopia Shall Stretch Forth Her Hands.'"

80. On the Ethiopian Expectation, see Callahan, *Talking Book*, 138–84; Moses, *Wings of Ethiopia*; and Kay, *Ethiopian Prophecy*.

81. See, most notably, Blyden, *Christianity, Islam and the Negro Race*.

82. Grant, *Negro with a Hat*, 168–69.

83. Eze, *Race and the Enlightenment*; Curran, *Anatomy of Blackness*.

84. Fiorenza, *Searching the Scriptures*; D. S. Williams, *Sisters in the Wilderness*.

85. In choosing that particular day to launch their movement, the UNIA founders were standing in a long tradition, in and out of the British Caribbean, of celebrating August 1. See Kerr-Ritchie, *Rites of August First*; and Kachun, *Festivals of Freedom*.

86. Haynes, *Radical Spiritual Motherhood*, 119.

87. Marcus Garvey, "The Future as I See It," in Jacques Garvey, *Philosophy and Opinions*, 1:73–78 (quotation on 77).

88. Robert A. Hill, "Introduction," in Jacques Garvey, *Philosophy and Opinions*, v–lxxix. See also Theodore Vincent, "Evolution of the Split between the Garvey Movement and the Organized Left in the United States, 1917–1933," in Lewis and Warner-Lewis, *Garvey*.

89. Jacques Garvey, *Philosophy and Opinions*, 2:412.

90. For instance, the Exodus story was part of the biblical arsenal against British colonialism in the American Revolution; the enslaved people in the United States would deploy the same weapon in the antislavery campaign. See J. P. Byrd, *Sacred Scripture, Sacred War*.

91. *Crusader*, November 1921; *Crusader*, December 1921.

92. Amy Jacques Garvey, "The Early Years of Marcus Garvey," in Clarke, *Marcus Garvey*, 29–37 (quotation on 29).

93. Ashwood Garvey, "Birth of the Universal Negro Improvement Association," 223.

94. McGuire, "What Is That in Thine Hand?" 168.

95. Ibid., 167.

96. Cronon, *Black Moses*.

97. Jacques Garvey to Cronon, March 28, 1955, box 29, folder 3, John Henrik Clarke Papers, Schomburg Center for Research in Black Culture, New York Public Library [hereafter Schomburg].

98. Jacques Garvey to Clarke, April 10, 1969, box 29, folder 3, Clarke Papers, Schomburg. Thanks to Adam Ewing for supplying the references for both this note and the previous one.

99. Jacques Garvey, *Garvey and Garveyism*.

100. "Black Moses," *African Opinion* 3, nos. 11–12 (May–June 1955): 14.

101. Padmore, *Life and Struggles*, 125–26; Padmore, *Pan-Africanism or Communism?* 87–104. *Life and Struggles* offered Padmore's views as a communist; *Pan-Africanism or Communism* is the author's anticommunist testament and, alas, the self-produced text that has best come to define his legacy.

102. Girard, "Black Talleyrand."

103. R. B. Turner, *Islam in the African-American Experience*, 71–108; Gomez, *Black Crescent*, 203–75.

104. Edward E. Curtis IV, "Debating the Origins of the Moorish Science Temple: Toward a New Cultural History," in Curtis and Sigler, *New Black Gods*, 70–90. The Chicago origins also find support in Weisenfeld, *New World A-Coming*.

105. McDuffie, "Chicago, Garveyism"; Blain, "'Confraternity among All Dark Races.'"

106. Ali, *Holy Koran*.

107. T. Martin, *Race First*, 77.

108. Ali, *Holy Koran*, 59.

109. T. Martin, *Race First*, 74. Meanwhile, Cyril Briggs, a former Garvey supporter, excoriated the UNIA as "the cult of religious fanaticism." See *Crusader*, August 1921, 26. This assertion appeared in a letter to the editor of the *Crusader*, namely, Briggs himself, who almost certainly wrote it, as was his habit.

110. Gomez, *Black Crescent*, 203.

111. Ibid., 203–75; R. B. Turner, *Islam in the African-American Experience*, 71–108; Essien-Udom, *Black Nationalism*, 33–36; Lincoln, *Black Muslims of America*, 47–52; Clegg, *An Original Man*, 19–20, 69–70.

112. Taylor, *Promise of Patriarchy*, 18–30.

113. On Malcolm and the Garveyite tradition, see Carew, *Ghosts in Our Blood*, 109–33; and DeCaro, *Malcolm and the Cross*, 61–81.

114. R. A. Rogers, *Holy Piby*; Pettersburgh, *Royal Parchment*; Howell, *Promised Key*.

115. R. A. Rogers, *Holy Piby*, xv. On the connection between Athlicanism and Garveyism, see Sellers, "The 'Black Man's Bible.'"

116. Vinson, *Americans Are Coming*, 93.

117. R. A. Rogers, *Holy Piby*, xiii, 61.

118. Grant, *Negro with a Hat*, 384.

119. R. A. Rogers, *Holy Piby*, 61.

120. Ibid., 84.

121. Ibid., xiii.

122. Seraile, "Henrietta Vinton Davis"; N. Duncan, "'If Our Men Hesitate.'"

123. R. A. Rogers, *Holy Piby*, 64.

124. Ibid., 51.

125. Alexander Crummell, "The Destined Superiority of the Negro," in Oldfield, *Civilization and Black Progress*, 43–53.

126. Vinson, *Americans Are Coming*, 93–94.

127. R. A. Hill, *Dread History*, 18.

128. Pettersburgh, *Royal Parchment*, 5.

129. Ibid., 31.

130. Obeah is an African-derived religion practiced in Jamaica and other parts of the Caribbean. See Paton and Forde, *Obeah and Other Powers*.

131. Pettersburgh, *Royal Parchment*, 18, 79.

132. Ibid., 31, 47.

133. Ibid.

134. R. A. Rogers, *Holy Piby*, 27, 41, 71.

135. Pettersburgh, *Royal Parchment*, 47.

136. Ibid., 31. The modern Pentecostal movement, which emerged in the United States in the early twentieth century, was deeply African American in origin. See Wacker, *Heaven Below*; Yong and Alexander, *Afro-Pentecostalism*.

137. In some parts of the United States, however, including the Missouri Bootheel (an area stretching from southern Missouri to northern Louisiana), Pentecostalism readily coexisted with Garveyism *and* socialism. See Roll, *Spirit of Rebellion*. On Garveyism in this same region, see Rolinson, *Grassroots Garveyism*; and Hahn, *A Nation under Our Feet*, 465–76.

138. Quoted in R. A. Hill, *Dread History*, 24.

139. Pettersburgh, *Royal Parchment*, 25–26.

140. R. A. Hill, *Dread History*.

141. Howell, *Promised Key*, 20.

142. Ibid., 11.

143. Ibid., 5.

144. R. A. Hill, *Dread History*, 21–27.

145. Ibid.

146. H. Campbell, *Rasta and Resistance*; R. Lewis, "Marcus Garvey and the Early Rastafarians."

147. Howell, *Promised Key*, 3.

148. Ibid., 7.

149. Ibid., 21.

150. Post, "Bible as Ideology."

151. Luther, *Works of Martin Luther*.

152. Callahan, *Talking Book*, 49–82.

153. Murrell, Spencer, and McFarlane, *Chanting Down Babylon*.

154. Du Bois, *Black Reconstruction*.

155. On the Psalms in reggae, see Murrell, "Tuning Hebrew Psalms to Reggae Rhythms"; and J. Thompson, "From Judah to Jamaica."

156. On the struggle for women's equality in Rastafari, see Christensen, *Rastafari Reasoning and the Rasta Woman*.

157. Although overly crude, Howell's representation was not devoid of truth. There was indeed a mutually enabling relationship between Pius XI and Mussolini, both of whom came to power the same year, 1922. See Kertzer, *Pope and Mussolini*.

158. Howell, *Promised Key*, 7.

159. On the pan-African response to the Italian invasion, see Asante, *Pan-African Protest*; W. R. Scott, *Sons of Sheba's Race*; and Harris, *African-American Reactions to War in Ethiopia*.

160. Howell, *Promised Key*, 7.

161. "Stand up, stand up for Jesus, ye soldiers of the cross / Lift high his royal banner, it must not suffer loss / From victory unto victory, his army shall he lead / Till every foe is vanquished and Christ is Lord indeed."

162. Strang, *On the Fiery March*.

163. Jonas, *Battle of Adwa*.

164. Mao, *On Guerrilla Warfare*.

165. Larebo, *Building of an Empire*; McCann, *People of the Plow*.

166. T. Martin, *Poetical Works of Marcus Garvey*, 8.

167. W. R. Scott, *Sons of Sheba's Race*, 203–7; Grant, *Negro with a Hat*, 440–41.

168. Thus Garvey apparently played no role in the British-based formations that supported the Ethiopian cause, most notably the International African Friends of Ethiopia, later the International African Service Bureau, the leaderships of which included some of his notable black radical critics, such as George Padmore and C.L.R. James.

169. Stanley Crouch, "BLACKIE Speaks on Campus: A Valentine for Vachel Lindsay," in Baraka and Neal, *Black Fire*, 394.

170. Erskine, *From Garvey to Marley*, 116–29.

171. A small subset of Rastafarians never forgave Garvey for his barbs against Selassie. See Tafari, *Rastafari View*, 116.

172. Egbuna, *Destroy This Temple*, 17.

173. West, "History vs. Historical Memory," esp. 91.

174. Cyril Briggs, "American Neo-Colonialism," *Liberator* 1, no. 1 (January 1967): 17. Briggs's reference to "black nationalist" and "integration" trends in African American politics would have been an intervention in a debate sparked by a recently published and highly influential book by Harold Cruse, *The Crisis of the Negro Intellectual*. For an appraisal of the *Liberator,* the magazine in which Briggs's article appeared, and its role in U.S. Black Power, see Tinson, *Radical Intellect*.

2

"No Surrender"

Migration, the Garvey Movement, and Community Building in Cuba

FRANCES PEACE SULLIVAN

On February 13, 1921, officers of the Universal Negro Improvement Association (UNIA) in Marcané, Cuba, hosted a special gathering "so that the Negroes who were not yet members [could] come forth and join without delay." The evening entailed the usual elements of UNIA meetings, including opening remarks and a speech from the division president, a hymn and a prayer from the chaplain, and a talk from Secretary Scott. Then, Scott "kindly asked the ladies and gentlemen of whom were not yet combined in this association, to come at once and join for God's sake." Several speakers followed, praising UNIA president-general Marcus Garvey, his work, the organization, and its business ventures, including the Black Star Line. Finally, a young woman named Irene Richards stood up and told a story about her first days in Cuba. She showed the audience a UNIA membership certificate from the Santo Domingo division and explained that, upon arriving in Cuba, she had "first inquired if there was any society of the UNIA here." When she learned that, yes, there was, she felt "good and comfortable, for . . . if there wasn't any she [would have] had to move to another place where there was."[1] In other words, as she told her audience that night, Richards was so determined to remain connected to the organization that she based her migration decisions on the presence or absence of the association.

British West Indian migrants spread Garveyism across the Caribbean in the late 1910s and early 1920s. As Richards's story indicates, the organization was particularly important for those women and men who found themselves on the move. Garvey himself alluded to this phenomenon toward the end of his 1921 tour of the Caribbean and Central America. He told a large crowd in Panama City:

> During my last trip to Cuba, I saw nearly sixty to seventy thousand West Indians who had ran [sic] from the Panama Canal, from Bocas del Toro, from Costa Rica, from Nicaragua. Where next are you going? You cannot go back home except you are prepared for something—you cannot go back to Jamaica, or back to Trinidad, because your economic conditions at home are where you left them—the white man at the top. And the only way you can go back to your home, to your land, to your country, is to encourage that courage and spirit of true manhood. The next is to educate those who have never left home, who are still asleep deep down in their ignorance. . . . You have to give them a new religion and a new politics. Are you prepared for that?[2]

As Garvey acknowledged, his support in the Caribbean hinged in many ways upon the very act of movement. His organization was more popular among those hundreds of thousands of Caribbean women and men seeking economic opportunities away from home and laboring in sites of U.S.-led development than it was in his own homeland of Jamaica. Not unaware of their particular vulnerability (hence the notion of "running"), Garvey nevertheless argued that it was those well-traveled West Indians who were assigned the weighty task of educating their seemingly less enlightened countrymen, who had "never left home." He points to a strong correlation between migration and participation in the UNIA—between the disempowering experience of flight and the need for a mobile, diasporic organization.[3]

As Lara Putnam notes, "the UNIA was central to the British Caribbean overseas communities—and vice versa."[4] Receiving countries, including Cuba and Costa Rica, had more UNIA divisions than sending islands, such as Jamaica and Barbados.[5] British West Indian migrants were drawn to and spread the organization for several reasons, all suggested in the very name of the association. First, Garvey's *universal* message helped unite Caribbean men and women of different religions, classes, and home islands.[6] Garvey had sojourned in Costa Rica in 1910 and 1911, where he clashed with local West Indian elites whom he accused of classism and colorism, an experience he later recalled in his platform of race unity.[7] A West Indian immigrant to Cuba remembered, decades later, just how important this call for unity was:

[The UNIA] was a universal organization, and it made a kind of unity among the coloured people all over the West Indies. Because the negroes were divided. If your father could send you to school, or you could go to college, you would think that you were better than the rest of the negroes. . . . Garvey's movement came up and showed that you weren't better than me and I wasn't better than you . . . so it made a conscience throughout the West Indies.[8]

In close proximity in what Winston James has called "black contact zones," women and men from far-flung places found in the association a fruitful means of uniting across social differences.[9]

Second, the organization promoted *Negro* improvement. That is, it encouraged race-consciousness and race-pride organizing among women and men traveling a region increasingly dominated by American Jim Crow segregation and racialized labor subjugation.[10] As James explains, "black contact zones were often sites of shared suffering and black solidarity, congenial spaces for the development of black internationalism and Pan-Africanism. Not surprisingly, organizations such as the Universal Negro Improvement Association found ready adherents and recruits in such environments."[11] Finally, the UNIA was an *improvement association*, part of a panoply of mutual-aid and fraternal associations, masonic lodges, religious organizations, and scouting troops proliferating during what Putnam has called the "heyday of Christian civic enthusiasm and 'joining' that swept the British West Indian diaspora as it did North America."[12]

In his recent book on global Garveyism, Adam Ewing writes that "attempts to characterize Garveyism at a point along an ideological or political spectrum do not hold up to scrutiny: Garveyism was radical and some moments and reactionary in others, strident in some places and cautious in others."[13] Similarly, Marc McLeod has written that the movement "was not monolithic, but in fact adopted different forms in different countries."[14] A series of UNIA actions in Central America illustrate this claim. In 1919 the organization played a leading role in a major strike on the Panama Canal, with Garvey even sending a message of support and money to the striking workers.[15] Yet when UNIA representatives Henrietta Vinton Davis and Cyril Henry visited the Central American isthmus later that year, the United Fruit Company, which employed tens of thousands of Garvey supporters, concluded that the pair had no interest in launching a strike, gave workers a day off, and discounted rail transportation for those attending UNIA events. By the time Garvey traveled through the region in 1921 he had, as Robert Hill puts it, "retreated from radicalism."[16] Under pressure from the U.S. State Department, which threatened to deny Garvey a reentry visa, and the UNIA's financial precariousness, Garvey moderated his tone, cooperated with United Fruit, and claimed in Cuba, "I do not come here to interfere with the labor question or the political question where governments are concerned."[17] In short, rather than a set of ideological dogma with fixed perspectives on those questions that motivate much historical inquiry—especially questions about labor resistance and class consciousness (often contrasted with race and race consciousness), nationalism, or anticolonialism—the movement was, as Ewing puts it, a "method of mass politics."[18]

This essay takes a cue from Ewing's understanding of Garveyism as a "sustained project of network building" in order to shed light on the particular mechanics of that project in Cuba.[19] As Ewing suggests, Garveyism was about process as much as it was about substance. In this essay I explore what that process looked like in the Cuban case and in what ways it served the women and men who participated. Relying on close readings of the UNIA mouthpiece, the New York–printed Negro World, as well as documentary evidence from Cuban and American archives, I argue that, for West Indian women and men uprooted by British imperial decline and laboring in the "U.S.-Caribbean World," a core tenet and achievement of the UNIA was its particular portability and reliability.[20] While spreading a powerful message of black racial uplift, Garveyites built an association that afforded members concrete benefits measurable in their day-to-day lives. Specifically, it offered a degree of social capital in new homes—wherever those homes might be—and networks, thereby easing the impact of migration. In towns and cities this institutional infrastructure served to hold communities together despite the transience of members. Likewise, it assisted individuals on the move as they settled into new homes.

The Negro World, especially reports submitted to the paper from outpost divisions, was essential to this achievement. Garveyites did more than "imagine community" through their paper; they also built it, speaking directly to one another and reassuring each other that the organization would continue to buoy them in new destinations. In the UNIA, Garveyites built an organization that facilitated stability and network building all while, as Ewing clearly demonstrates, imbuing the everyday tasks of organizing with wider, world-historical significance.

I begin by providing historical context on the West Indian migration that made Garvey's movement so vibrant in the Caribbean basin during the late 1910s through the 1920s. Then I explore the portability, consistency, and community stability that Garveyites—particularly British West Indians—built through the UNIA in Cuba. In each of these sections I probe a particular set of sources to underscore the practical aims and purposes that, beyond the ambitious and long-term pan-Africanism Garvey promoted, shed light on individual involvement in the UNIA.

British West Indian Migration and the UNIA in Cuba

The past two decades have seen a proliferation of historical research into British West Indian migration in the late nineteenth and early to mid-twentieth centuries.[21] Migration away from the British Caribbean began immediately after emancipation in the 1830s, when women and men moved from Barbados to Guyana and Trinidad.[22] In the middle of the nineteenth century, the main thrust of movement was from the western Caribbean to Panama, where by the 1880s British Antilleans constituted a majority of workers on the canal and railroad projects.[23] The 1880s were also marked by economic decline in the eastern Caribbean, and laborers from the Leeward and Windward Islands, Barbados, and Trinidad traveled to northern parts of South America, including Brazil, Venezuela, Colombia, and the Guyanas.[24] These eastern and western migratory circuits converged when British Antilleans, especially Barbadians, built the Panama Canal, the construction for which took place under U.S. authority from 1905 to 1914. After completion of the canal, the Central American—and especially Costa Rican—banana plantations became major destinations for West Indian migrants, some of whom were directly contracted from the Canal Zone. By the late 1910s, New York had also become as a key destination, so much so that Caribbean immigrants and their children made up a quarter of Harlem's population by 1930.[25] As Putnam points out, in 1930, "nearly 300,000 strong, . . . the British West Indian diaspora was almost twice as large as the population of Barbados and fully six times that of Belize."[26]

Cuba entered this history largely in the late 1910s and early 1920s as a third major destination after the Canal Zone and Central American banana zones. Although British West Indians had been traveling to Cuba since the nineteenth century—on a clear day, one can see Jamaica from Santiago de Cuba— Afro-Caribbean immigration to the island took off significantly with a series of decrees exempting sugar workers from laws prohibiting "undesirable immigrants" starting in 1913.[27] During Cuba's wartime boom, tens of thousands of West Indian immigrants arrived every year. In all, over 140,000 British Antilleans arrived on the island between 1898 and 1938, many of whom had already sojourned elsewhere.[28] Most, though certainly not all, of these individuals were seeking to work—or had already been contracted for work—in the sugar industry, and the majority went to Camagüey and Oriente Provinces in the eastern part of the island, where sugar production had rapidly taken off under American corporation in the early twentieth century. Caribbean immigration slowed down only in the mid-1920s, when the Cuban government began issuing sugar quotas, and it stopped altogether with the Great Depression, when many foreign subjects returned home often destitute and in desperate circumstances.

While British West Indians were frequently lumped together (often as *jamaicanos* or the pejorative *jamaiquino*) by employers, officials, and the Cuban public, they were in fact an internally diverse group of women and men with major differences in terms of islands of origin, religion, employment, family lives, and more. Jorge Giovannetti disaggregates the population of *ingleses* in Cuba and uncovers distinct Cuban experiences among those migrants from Jamaica and those from the eastern Caribbean. For instance, Jamaican migrants received significantly more diplomatic support than their eastern Caribbean counterparts.[29] As Putnam points out, it would be a mistake to assume that all migrant experiences were essentially those of men employed by foreign capital and marginalized by their receiving societies.[30] Women like Irene Richards migrated throughout the Caribbean in large numbers, and many West Indians made their livings well beyond the purview of major sugar and fruit companies.[31] In Cuba, life beyond this framework of black labor/white capital often took place within British West Indians' rich civic associations. Everywhere they went, *ingleses antillanos* established churches, associations, fraternal societies, scouting troops, dime savings banks, sporting clubs, and more.[32] The UNIA was but one institution in this wide landscape of religious, fraternal, and uplift organizations. In Cuba, however, it was undoubtedly the most popular and interconnected West Indian association.

Thanks to the work of several scholars, we now have a fairly robust body of scholarship on the Garvey movement in Cuba.[33] One of the major threads of inquiry has revolved around the question of whether Afro-Cubans participated in the association. Early studies tended to take as their starting point Garvey's famous March 1921 meeting with Miguel Angel Céspedes, president of the elite

Afro-Cuban society, Club Atenas, when Céspedes declared that black Cubans "cannot conceive of having a motherland other than Cuba."[34] Some have interpreted the encounter as evidence that, in light of black participation in Cuba's wars of independence and subsequent legal protections for racial equality on the island, Garvey's race-first message clashed with Cuba's multiracial nationalism and failed to attract many Cubans.[35] With the working understanding that the Garvey movement was mainly a British West Indian phenomenon in Cuba, McLeod and Giovannetti have carefully investigated the UNIA's work as an "immigrant protection society" that pressured British diplomatic authorities to better serve the Crown's subjects in Cuba.[36] Garveyites, Giovannetti demonstrates, made strategic decisions about what elements of the UNIA program to stress in official documentation, sometimes omitting "Negro" and "African" from their organization's title and instead focusing on uplift and confraternity. He concludes that the UNIA served West Indians as "'an immigrant protection society' that operated mostly as a 'civil religion.'"[37]

More recently, scholars have revised the idea that Garveyism failed to attract black Cubans. Cespedes's comments, after all, only reflect the ideas of one, elite Afro-Cuban. McLeod has revisited his earlier work and detailed broader efforts Garveyites on and off the island made to reach Afro-Cubans and Haitians, by printing Spanish and French sections of the *Negro World*, singing the Cuban National Anthem and including Spanish-language speeches in UNIA meetings, and naming a Black Star Line ship after black Cuban independence hero Antonio Maceo.[38] In an update to his earlier work, McLeod reveals greater Cuban involvement than was previously recognized.[39] He points to a Havana-based Spanish-speaking chapter that sent its delegates across the island instructing members in the goals of the organization, and to the Cubans who took a leadership role in the organization.[40]

Similarly, Frank Guridy explores how black Caribbean immigrants successfully reached out to Afro-Cubans through performance and celebration in central Cuba, with the two groups joining causes on several occasions. He demonstrates that Afro-Cuban participation in the UNIA was so extensive by 1929 that Cuban president Gerardo Machado was alarmed and considered the UNIA a significant threat to his self-styled image as a promoter of racial harmony. Machado cracked down on the organization, closing several chapters, temporarily outlawing the *Negro World*, and prohibiting Garvey's entry to Cuba.[41] Guridy suggests that these restrictions were later lifted "presumably because the UNIA had been effectively neutralized."[42] The fact that many divisions in eastern Cuba dominated by British West Indians remained active through the crackdown confirms Guridy's argument that the Machadato was particularly interested in targeting those UNIA divisions with a sizable Afro-Cuban membership.[43]

The life trajectory of Eduardo Morales, who served as the UNIA's high commissioner to Cuba, illustrates the cross-cultural appeal of the UNIA and the transnational connections that characterized Garveyite activity. Born in Cuba but raised in Panama, Morales was a leader in both the UNIA and the United Brotherhood, key organizations in the 1919 Canal Zone strike. In a speech there, Morales claimed, "I am Panamanian but do not call myself one. . . . We should all be one and call ourselves negroes."[44] After the labor action was suppressed, Morales traveled along with fellow strike leader, William Preston Stout, to Cuba, where Morales was appointed high commissioner to Cuba, delivering speeches across the island and representing Cuba at UNIA conventions.[45] Morales's story exemplifies not only the UNIA's cross-cultural appeal but also the ways in which individuals participated in the institution in multiple locations with varying ideological emphases.

The first UNIA chapters in Cuba opened in 1919, as we know from reports on the enthusiastic reception received by the Black Star Line steamer *Frederick Douglass* in December 1919.[46] The August 1920 First International Convention of Negro Peoples of the World, which four delegates from Cuba attended, and early 1921 tours by UNIA chaplain-general Rev. George Alexander McGuire and by UNIA president-general Marcus Garvey himself also generated early enthusiasm for the movement.[47] Although we now have better appreciation of Afro-Cuban participation in the UNIA, British West Indians, according to McLeod, "were the heart and soul of Cuban Garveyism."[48] The majority of chapters were located in Camagüey and Oriente Provinces, where Afro-Caribbean migrants labored in the island's sugar industry and much of Garveyite energies were devoted to addressing the specific needs of the British West Indian community. When a 1920 crash in the sugar market brought many Afro-Caribbean immigrants to the brink of starvation, the UNIA provided food to destitute laborers and pressured the British diplomatic corps to address the needs of British subjects.[49] As McLeod points out, this material assistance likely boosted support for the organization, as a number of new UNIA chapters opened in 1922.[50] The organization continued to advocate for British West Indians throughout the 1920s by protesting, for instance, the required quarantine of Caribbean immigrants and Rural Guard abuse.[51] By the mid-1920s the island had over fifty UNIA divisions, more than any other country outside of the United States.[52]

There are several possible explanations for the UNIA's success in Cuba. In some respects the proliferation the UNIA on the island could be simply a reflection of Cuba's sizable British West Indian population. As Hill has pointed out, West Indians abroad "served as the key vectors in spreading the message of Garveyism, introducing it into whatever communities they reside in."[53] With British Antilleans numbering around 100,000 during the peak period of the Garvey movement, it should come as no surprise that the UNIA was popular on the island. The organization was also quite successful in other major West Indian destinations, such as Panama (with forty-seven divisions and two in the Canal Zone) and Costa Rica (with twenty-three divisions).[54] The Cuban location with the highest density of British Caribbean immigrants was the United Fruit Company town of Banes on the northern coast of Oriente Province, and it was there that one of the most successful and longest-lasting branches, Division 52, operated, and only closed after the Cuban Revolution of 1959.[55]

British West Indian immigrants had been bringing their rich organizational tradition along with a host of friendly societies and churches to Cuba since the turn of the century, yet it is the UNIA—and not, say, the Grand Order of Odd Fellows—that appeared in over fifty Cuban towns and cities.[56] This suggests that the UNIA had a special appeal on the island, and in fact Cuba presented several unique circumstances. On a basic level, Cuba was the most geographically spread out destination to which they migrated. Unlike the urban corridor of interconnected towns along the Panama Canal, unlike the relatively concentrated United Fruit Company banana plantations along the Atlantic coast of the Central American isthmus, and quite unlike Harlem, Cuban receiving towns were often geographically remote destinations with infrequent and irregular access between them.[57] As Ariel James has pointed out of Banes, communication between Banes and the American ports of New York, New Orleans, and Baltimore was more stable and regular than between Banes and the rest of Cuba.[58]

Without a singular urban center in which Afro-Caribbean migrants largely concentrated, the island was home to fewer mainstays of West Indian life overseas than places like Port Limón or the Canal Zone. There was not a specifically British West Indian newspaper in Cuba. In contrast, Limón, Bocas del Toro, and Panama City all boasted several locally printed, English-language papers with black readerships.[59] Readers in Cuba hoping to find black-run newspapers could turn to African American periodicals, such as the *Amsterdam News* and the *Chicago Defender,* but would not have found much in the way of news printed specifically with the black-immigrant-in-Cuba experience in mind. This could explain the fundamental importance the *Negro World* had in the lives of Cuba's West Indian residents and, in turn, the popularity the organization celebrated. Finally, as I discuss below, the portable, replicable, and predictable nature of the UNIA allowed it to flourish in a place where little else for black immigrants was reliable.

Rulebooks and Modules: Portability in Cuba's Garvey Movement

In the Provincial Government collection of the Archivo Histórico Provincial de Santiago de Cuba sits a rather dry associational record. Amid a thick file of papers typed and handwritten on thin, yellowing pages, this 1922 document stands out with its firm and evidently long-lasting stock, professional print quality, and blue ink. The thirteen-page booklet is the "Reglamento de la Asociación Universal Para el Adelanto de la Raza Negra" (Regulations of the Universal Negro Improvement Association), and it certifies that a division of the UNIA has been formed. The "Reglamento" spells out the aims of the association; responsibilities of officers; membership dues, requirements, and entitlements; and financial procedures. Specifics about individual division numbers, dates, locations, and officer names, however, were left blank by the printer and completed longhand, in this case, by Jermina Kelso, secretary of Division 52 in Banes, Oriente Province.

At first glance, this rulebook might disappoint the historian. After all, it offers nothing in the way of the day-to-day struggles UNIA members faced in this United Fruit Company town, how they maneuvered relationships with company and state, what the composition of their membership was like, or what drew members to the organization in the first place. Nor does it tell us about the personal lives of individual Garveyites, their origins, their families, their professions, or their disagreements.[60] When seen in a different light, however, the rulebook is compelling. With its good Spanish and blank spaces for particulars, it was clearly printed elsewhere for dissemination to local UNIA branches in order to assist in compliance with Cuban law requiring associations to register with the state, spelling out details about membership, dues, and leadership. The rulebook thus facilitated a legalization process that would have otherwise taken up the time and energies of UNIA members in typing, translation, and correspondence.[61] (Sure enough, the associational file is full of letters about missing information and forgotten signatures.) This document, then, speaks to the UNIA's particular characteristics as a replicable and portable institution.

While we know from research by Ewing and others, including contributors to this volume, that Garvey's message of black racial pride, uplift, and destiny— particularly "Africa for the Africans"—resonated across the globe, we also know that the Universal Negro Improvement Association was and remains the largest black organization in world history. Documents like the "Reglamento" raise important questions about the nuts and bolts of how exactly this particular organization spread, what concrete gains individuals attained by way of their participation, and how the association functioned in wider communities. "Ultimately the modular form of the UNIA was what made it readily portable, allowing its message to be diffused so widely," writes Hill.[62] The "Reglamento" suggests something of how that modular portability worked; the same rule-book, with different handwritten particulars, was used to register divisions in Guantánamo, Central Manatí, Jobabo, and Antilla.[63]

In Cuba, new UNIA chapters opened in several ways. Occasionally enthusiastic readers of the *Negro World* launched divisions of their own initiative, as did Cliffort Erlinton of the Palma Soriano mill town near Santiago de Cuba.[64] The paper certainly circulated widely in Cuba, as UNIA chaplain McGuire mentioned upon his return from Cuba and as West Indian immigrants recalled later decades.[65] On the whole, however, UNIA field-workers spread Garveyism to Cuban towns and cities. Some of these field-workers circulated internationally with the express aim of expanding the UNIA. Samuel P. Radway and Dave Davidson opened chapters in Costa Rica and in Panama before moving on to Cuba, where they spread the UNIA in the eastern part of the island.[66] In the mill town of Jobabo one Friday morning in early 1921, for instance, the two obtained permission from public authorities and began announcing a UNIA meeting from the town's busiest corner. They put up placards in Spanish and English and spread word about the meeting. By 7:30 that night, they claimed, they had gathered more than five hundred "Cubans, Haytians, and other West Indians, and a few Canadians" to whom they explained the aims and objectives of the UNIA. They thanked the "honorable gentleman, Mr. J. R. Bullard, general manager of the Jobabo Sugar Company, who is a friend of the Negro," suggesting a pragmatic working relationship with employers of black labor.[67] Some attendees enrolled, and after the whole process was repeated a second night, a new division was formed and officers elected.[68]

In March 1921, Garvey attempted to suppress Radway and Davidson's UNIA activities, claiming that "these men are not in very good standing with the [Negroes?] there, and they are only using the medium of the Negro World, to foist themselves upon the public in Cuba."[69] Garvey's instructions do not appear to have been heeded, however, as later that year Davidson helped form the People's Relief Committee, which in conjunction with the Santiago branch of the UNIA provided relief to destitute immigrants reeling from the 1920–21 crash. Additionally, Radway later published reports in the *Negro World*, including an article detailing troubles faced by immigrants in Cuba.[70] Radway and Davidson's rogue—or at least independent—efforts to spread the UNIA even without Garvey's consent suggest that the association sometimes took off as a result of deliberate measures taken by the parent body (pan-Caribbean tours by high officials), sometimes through collective efforts at the remote, local level (Erlinton's move to organize a branch in Palma Soriano), but very often thanks to field-workers who operated semi-independently and who took advantage of the UNIA's modular portability to spread the movement.

Garveyite leaders circulated through the Caribbean, sometimes working as organizers and sometimes serving in other capacities related to the UNIA.R.E. M. Jack, a schoolteacher from Saint Vincent, attended the 1920 UNIA convention in Harlem, where he was ordained an African Orthodox Church minister, before moving on to Cuba, Barbados, Saint Vincent, and back to the United States. Among his many activities during these travels, Jack headed a UNIA division in Saint Vincent, ministered to Cuba's West Indian population, and advised Garveyites on the construction of UNIA chapters.[71] His travels illustrate how the association's roles as a "civil religion" and as a "protection society" overlapped, as Giovannetti has written.[72]

Whereas figures like Radway, Davidson, and Jack traveled throughout the greater Caribbean, Arnold S. Cunning carried out his organizing efforts largely in Cuba. A Jamaican bookseller living in Banes, he served as a point person for UNIA activities in eastern Cuba. By 1920 he had become a major shareholder in the Black Star Line and a "liberal chaser of funds" for the Liberian Construction Loan, a funding endeavor geared toward the eventual construction of homes and industry in Liberia.[73] Cunning helped to organize several local divisions and restructure others struggling to remain afloat in the midst of economic turmoil and infighting. He also attended the 1920 UNIA convention in New York, where he signed the "Declaration of the Rights of the Negro Peoples of the World," as well as the 1921 UNIA convention, also in New York. His network

of contacts in New York and Cuba was so extensive that he organized Rev. Mc-
Guire's tour of Cuba, arranging for the him to make fourteen stops and serving as McGuire's personal secretary during his visit.[74] By 1926 he was the vice-
president of Division 52 in Banes.[75] After his years in Cuba, Cunning returned
to Jamaica, where he served as president for UNIA divisions in Harmony and
Saint Andrew.[76] Other field-workers included G. J. Molines, who was publicly
thanked in the *Negro World* for his travels and dedicated work organizing the
UNIA in the Punta Alegre region.[77]

Stories of local organizers like Davidson, Radway, Jack, Molines, and Cun-
nings often have been overshadowed in histories focused on Garvey himself
and his coterie of Harlem-based leaders. But it was these lesser-known figures
who carried out the hard work of carrying Garveyism with, as Ewing writes,
"impressive thoroughness to every corner of the 'Negro world.'"[78] Each of these
local and regional field-workers, whether operating under direct instructions
from Harlem or independently, would have found in the UNIA a relatively
straightforward and "modular" path to expansion. Those looking to form a division wrote to the parent body, submitted the appropriate funds, requested a
charter, and got to work.[79] Charter unveilings were always joyous affairs accompanied by processions, speeches, and music and attended by representatives
from nearby UNIA branches.[80]

Just as they traveled regionally to expand the organization to new places
and to celebrate openings, Garveyites in Cuba visited one another to aid in
ceremonial UNIA activities. Anniversary and Emancipation Day celebrations,
flag raisings, dedications, and other events almost always occasioned the arrival
of speakers and guests from regional UNIA chapters.[81] In each city and town,
women and men found familiar rituals, procedures, and rules. They also would
have established contacts and formed friendships that they could later deploy
when in need of assistance. Of Central America, Ronald Harpelle has written,
"British West Indian sojourners gathered at the Liberty Halls of the region and
relied on the organization as a support network as they passed through the region."[82] Similarly, in Cuba, West Indians used the UNIA to build networks that
sustained them in good times and bad.

Emerging out of a long tradition of friendly societies and mutual-aid associations, the UNIA was first and foremost a mutual-aid society. Members paid
dues toward sickness; as the "Reglamento" states, "It will be required that every
chapter and branch of the Universal Negro Improvement Association establish
a Mutual Aid Society to care for the sick of the Division."[83] UNIA membership

also included death benefits. When Mr. R. Hemmings, member of the Florida division, passed away in 1926, the UNIA chaplain performed his burial ceremony, and UNIA "officers and auxiliaries, including the legions and the Black Cross Nurses, were in the funeral procession."[84] When Luther Dixon fell to his death in a Camagüey sugar mill, representatives of several UNIA divisions in eastern Cuba attended his funeral.[85] On a happier note, Georgina Maynard from Santo Domingo married Samuel Mason of Antigua in February 1923 in the town of San Manuel, and their reception was hosted by Christiana Brown from Jamaica, all announced in the pages of the *Negro World*, which suggests that some or all participants were active in the UNIA.[86]

On these occasions, Garveyite ritual melded with broader social life, suggesting the extent to which the UNIA served not only as a mutual-aid society but as a community building institution. Cuban divisions hosted social and religious events—including parades, dances, feasts, Mothers Day celebrations, Easter services, and more, attended by immigrants and Cubans alike.[87] When twelve young women competed to be crowned "Queen of Ethiopia" in a 1926 Camagüey popularity contest, the victor earned over a thousand votes and each of the runners-up had more than eight hundred.[88] Because the typical division may have had from eighteen to a few hundred dues-paying members, the high number of votes in Camagüey suggests that many nonmembers joined in the creative celebration of diaspora and race pride.

The tradition of respectability captured by the Camagüey popularity contest suggests yet another important role the organization likely played in the everyday lives of members: to ensure and protect the respectability of women. As we know from stories like that of Irene Richards, women often migrated through the Caribbean of their own accord and, without labor contracts, were afforded a degree of autonomy. Women's events, such as such the Banes Mothers Day celebration in which women were advised to "educate your boys and girls and fit them for their future career so that they may be able when we are gone to marshal the cause to a glorious end," and women's auxiliary groups, such as the widely popular Black Cross Nurses, drew upon traditions of respectability and gendered uplift that were fundamental to UNIA culture.[89] The UNIA, then, offered newcomer women a means of quickly securing local connections, receiving vital information about boardinghouses and prospective employers, and affiliating themselves with an upright and widely respected local association.

"News and Views of UNIA Divisions": Ritual, Diaspora, and Consistency in the U.S.-Caribbean World

> Liberty Hall was crowded at the great mass meeting held by the Elia Division on Garvey Day. The meeting opened with devotional service conducted by Mr. A. J. Burrell, acting chaplain. The president then took the chair while the following program was rendered: Address by Mr. S. N. Knight; solo, Mr. S. C. Constable; Scripture reading by Mrs. A. W. Ricketts; address, Mr. C. B. McNeil; solo, Mr. A. G. Hunter; address, Mr. Charles Easey; selection by the choir, address by the president. The meeting closed with the singing of the "Ethiopian National Anthem."
>
> *Dora H. Stennett, "Elia, Camaguey, Cuba,"* Negro World, *April 11, 1925*

Garveyites across the globe contributed regularly to the *Negro World*, reporting the activities of their local outposts in a section titled "News and Views of UNIA Divisions," in which the above article appeared. Almost every report followed a similar format, detailing ceremonies conducted by Garveyites worldwide. Typically, "News and Views" contributions opened with a statement about the success of or excitement generated by a recent meeting. "The entire community seems to have caught the infection" created in the wake of a UNIA meeting, explained a writer from Las Minas.[90] Similarly, on Good Friday in 1925 the Jabitonico division "held a lovely service which was very successful."[91] Contributors then listed opening processions and speeches made by division officers (who were included by name), songs led by the choir or the chaplain (typically the UNIA hymn "From Greenland's Icy Mountains" or others from the UNIA catechism, such as "Onward Christian Soldier" and "Shine On, Eternal Light"), and any "distinguished visitors" from nearby UNIA divisions. Most meetings included oratorical and musical contributions from rank-and-file members, which were invariably introduced with "The following program was rendered" and described in entries such as "Solo by Miss Henry; Recitation by Master Sidney; address by W. M. Pitter."[92] Contributors also described any auxiliary group processions, officers elected, and sometimes local news. Most reporters noted that the meeting closed with the Ethiopian National Anthem, and ended their entries with a word of support for the "Honorable Marcus Garvey."[93] Sometimes contributors relayed a sense of the content of the speeches and addresses, though much more often they did not. "News and Views" reports drew upon a shared vocabulary and set of symbols to describe their rituals. Meetings were "called to order," auxiliary groups were "nicely clad in their uniforms, made from the colors The Red Black and Green," and speeches were "rousing," "eloquent," and "inspiring."[94]

Like the "Reglamento," the "News and Views" section can be a tricky source. Contributions are repetitive. One can read half a dozen entries before encountering tidbits suggestive of, say, Afro-Cuban membership (perhaps mentions of speeches delivered in Spanish) or of what ideological questions motivated local participants. Yet the "News and Views" section remains an invaluable source of information about what kinds of auxiliary groups different UNIA branches sponsored (Black Cross Nurses, African legions, schools, dime savings banks, marching bands, and more), which divisions were succeeding financially and which were struggling, which suffered a membership decline after the harvest and which weathered seasonal changes in labor.

"News and Views" articles can also be read for what Guridy has called "performing visions of the African diaspora."[95] As he explains, singing, elocution, and oratory were all central to UNIA membership. The use of visuals such as military-inspired uniforms, paraphernalia, and symbolism were central to the embodied practice of diaspora performed across cultural and linguistic barriers by Garveyites in Cuba.[96] "Despite their limitations," he writes, "the division reports in the *Negro World* provide glimpses of UNIA men and women *in performance*. . . . [W]e get a hint of how these Garveyites performed their membership in the African diaspora."[97] Certainly the vast majority of "News and Views" reports demonstrate the important role of performance in UNIA practices. Moreover, we can see that just as performances were certainly acts of diasporic belonging, so too was the process of writing and reading UNIA reports.

Sidney F. Lemelle and Robin D. G. Kelley have argued that black nationalism is a form of what Benedict Anderson calls "imagined community."[98] Anderson's conceptualization, although in many ways flawed with respect to Latin American nationalisms, offers a fruitful avenue of analysis for studies of Garveyism. He emphasizes the use of pageantry and symbols—such as a declaration of rights, an anthem, and a flag—in cohering a sense of nationalism. Rituals and events across the space of the nation, Anderson argues, occur at the same time, yet their participants may never meet, thereby forcing the work of *imagination* in conceiving a national community. Perhaps most importantly, he underscores of importance of "print capitalism," particularly newspapers, to nationalism. For Anderson, the "mass ceremony" of reading the morning paper is repeated across a contained space in a ritual shared between individuals who do not know one another but are confident they are sharing the experience.[99] We can similarly conceive of reading the *Negro World* as a form of "mass ceremony," but in this case the process is inverted; the *Negro World* transcends territorial boundaries. Indeed, it is precisely black exclusion from nation-states that makes the knowledge that others are engaging in the same ceremony so important.

As Putnam writes, "the international circulation of black-run periodicals, and their integration in communal discussion at multiple sites, generated a transnational black public."[100] Seen in this light, contributions to the "News and Views" emerge as rich sources not *despite of* but also *because of* their highly repetitive style. In other words, they suggest deliberate claims of participation in a diasporic community marked by the consistency of its symbols, rituals, performances, and even news style. The *Negro World* facilitated the cohesion of diverse and far-flung members of the British West Indian diaspora by sharing news about UNIA ceremony and ritual carried out *as such*. Mentions of the Ethiopian National Anthem, the "smart" uniforms of the Black Cross Nurses, and the Garvey movement's colors of red, green, and black remind readers that others whom they did not know were also holding Sunday-night mass meetings, monthly parades, and pageants.

Significantly, contributors and readers were reassured by the understanding that, should they have to pick up and leave in search of work, they might find a familiar and consistent organization awaiting them in their new destination, as did Irene Richards in Marcané, Cuba. As the written embodiment of the UNIA's international community and as a forum in which rank-and-file members communicated, then, the *Negro World* was the means through which readers and writers did more than *imagine* community; they constructed it in the pages of the paper.

Garveyites often spoke to one another in a general sense through the *Negro World*. In a report on the 1923 Mothers Day celebration in Banes a writer explained, "I desire to submit this report, which we trust may be a stimulant to other divisions in this Republic, as it is not possible for us always to visit other divisions in Cuba."[101] Similarly, a reporter from the Francisco sugar mill wrote, "Owing to the past silence of this division, it may be thought by the other divisions that we are sleeping. But we rise again to let the world know that we are silently, steadily carrying on the program, in spite of our adversities, opposition and sacrifices."[102] Offering a familiar narrative of perseverance in the face of obstacles, the author's somewhat defensive tone suggests that UNIA community belonging was intimately tied not simply to "putting the program over" but also to sharing news through the *Negro World*. The paper's function as forum for sharing diasporic, Garveyite experience was particularly important in Cuba, where it was the only paper specifically addressing the concerns of West Indian immigrants.[103] Garveyites also used the UNIA and its paper to share information about local conditions, as Radway's August 1921 "Report of Conditions Existing in the Cuban Republic" warned of the disastrous economic conditions prevailing in the wake of Cuba's sugar market crash and advised potential migrants not to leave home.[104]

Even though the *Negro World* was published in New York, it was read so widely in Cuba that UNIA members often spoke directly to one another through the paper. In 1923, Banes Division 52 made plans to host an organizational meeting for regional UNIA delegates, announcing in the *Negro World* that "all divisions in this province have been invited to send delegates and the delegates when assembled will hold a conference to devise plans for closer relationship among divisions and also better representation in the [upcoming international UNIA] convention." Included on the list of invitees are divisions in Santiago, Guantánamo, Miranda, Cueto, Cayo Mambí, Antilla, and San Gerónimo.[105] In another example, Morón Division 374 announced an Easter excursion in 1923, writing, "Seating capacity is limited, get your tickets at once."[106] The practice of listing by name individuals performing solos and recitations also served purposes beyond recognizing achievements and talents. Readers often wrote to the paper seeking information on the whereabouts of friends and family. One can easily imagine a reader in Harlem or Camagüey scanning the lists of "programs rendered" for news of loved ones.

Similarly, reading the UNIA's mouthpiece was an act of participation in an international, diasporic community, and Garveyites in Cuba often expressed a clear interest in receiving English-language news of the organization, of other divisions, and of global events. On his return from Cuba, Rev. McGuire claimed of Garveyites in Cuba, "They read the Negro World, mouthpiece of the association, more eagerly than it is read here in New York."[107] While he may have been exaggerating, men and woman in Cuba did read the paper avidly, occasionally aloud at mass meetings.[108] In their own letters to the editor and reports, this international readership frequently commented on the centrality of the *Negro*

World to their lives as West Indian migrants.[109] This was most clear in 1932 when the paper ceased publication. Several individuals from Cuba wrote to the editorial offices requesting simply that missing papers be sent to them quickly. Others, however, were explicit about the paper's role in their lives. Nathan A. Harison of the Francisco mill in central Cuba explained, "We feel quite out of place when we cannot get news of the Negro World. . . . I'll be glad to know that the only paper the Negro can read with satisfaction is still circulating."[110] Similarly, William Allen from the American colony at La Gloria on Camagüey's northern coast wrote, "When I can't get a *Negro World* to read I am sick."[111] In short, Garveyites considered the *Negro World* a crucial element of their lives as black men and women living far from home. Indeed, they used the New York paper to facilitate network building and community stability in Cuba.

Surmounting Obstacles, "Putting the Program Over," and Building Community in Cuba

Throughout the pages of the "News and Views" section, Garveyites in Cuba reported overcoming obstacles and persevering in the face of great difficulty. In a contribution titled "The UNIA in Camaguey, Cuba, Surmounts Difficulties," a member explained: "After a long and bitter struggle to prevent the disintegration which threatened during the last months of 1922 when the terrible economic depression that prevailed made the disbandment of the division a distinct probability, . . . [this branch has] come to life with renewed vigor and is prepared to climb the winding paths of progress with enthusiasm." The reporter concluded by thanking Camagüey members for their "dogged determination."[112] Similarly, in March 1923 a writer from Banes declared, "Conditions at present are very bad. Though the crop is on[,] wages [are] low and many of our members have had to travel a distance to earn a livelihood: hence the division has to suffer financially. But those of us who are left are still carrying on the work. It is an uphill task but the program must be put over."[113] This narrative of a dedicated cadre of members persevering despite difficulties, and of the UNIA surmounting the many obstacles of life in Cuba, is clearly designed to encourage readers and to celebrate the achievements of individual chapters. It is unsurprising to see heroic narratives in an associational mouthpiece. Criticism of the UNIA and of various individuals did, from time to time, appear in the paper, which makes the frequency of the celebratory narrative all the more noteworthy. Despite their propagandistic tone, then, these reports reveal a key role of the organization on the ground: building and maintaining a strong and consistent social and organizational infrastructure despite the many instabilities that marked immigrant life in Cuba, particularly unemployment and migration.

From the perspective of each mill town or city that hosted the UNIA, the association served to strengthen immigrant communities, even though the individuals who made up those communities were often transient, moving in and out in search of better prospects. In a 1923 Banner Day celebration in Jobabo, the division president gave a speech, explaining: "It is nearly two months since I left seeking a livelihood . . . but I am more than glad of the way the hall looks to me. It shows that you were not sitting waiting, but you were working for the improvement." Others in Jobabo were similarly proud to see the success of the division after their own absences: Miss Violet Smith was "glad to return to the division to see how it was going ahead," and other returnees praised the vice-president for how well he had "kept up" the division.[114] *Negro World* reports emphasized that, even in difficult times, parades continued, mass meetings were held, and members struggled against the odds to "put the program over."[115] In 1923, President Robert S. Blake wrote to the *Negro World* that Banes Division 52 put on a monthly parade despite the fact that "many of our male members have left this locality in search of employment" and that those still in town maintained a position of "no surrender." He concluded: "The race-loving Negroes of Banes have built up a lovely division. It's only for them to keep together."[116] To Blake, maintaining UNIA activities despite shifting community makeup was a chief responsibility of UNIA membership.

Much of the hard work of building and sustaining local community life fell to the women of the Garvey movement. While the Harlem leadership structure typically gave only those women positioned as Garvey's personal representatives prominent roles in the association, in Cuba women were often integrated into main leadership structures. Like Dora Stennett, who authored the "News and Views" contribution quoted earlier, women served as reporter or executive secretary, not simply "Ladies' Secretary," and as chairpersons at mass meetings, sports program organizers, and reporters to the *Negro World*.[117] It is likely that women had greater room to serve as leaders given the fact that many men traveled after the sugar harvests.[118] Most Garveyite women in leadership positions worked as domestic servants and were thus able to retain year-round employment and serve as backbones of local UNIA branches.[119]

From the perspective of individual migrants, the UNIA offered a means of retaining social capital and a sense of community even when traveling to unfamiliar towns and cities. Garveyites built a transnational association in which its mobile members would immediately find a welcoming group of men and women, a familiar set of rituals, and like-minded individuals in a new home. They knew this because they read the *Negro World* with its oft-repeated mentions of the Ethiopian National Anthem and "rousing" Sunday-night mass meetings. Irene Richards's insistence on settling in a town with a UNIA division highlights the association's importance to British West Indian women and men on the move.

In the early 1920s a man named J. J. Paul arrived in Guantánamo with no personal ties but who was familiar with UNIA rules and regulations, indicating he had participated in the organization elsewhere. According to a *Negro World* report, he found a welcoming home in the Guantánamo UNIA chapter and went on to serve as general secretary and associate secretary. In 1923, however, Paul once again found himself leaving town in search of employment and resigned his post. In a report to the *Negro World*, Paul's successor asked all UNIA members "to give Mr. Paul any assistance he may need," revealing a reasonable assumption that his friend and fellow Garveyite was likely to continue encountering *Negro World* readers and UNIA activities. The *Negro World* report on Paul's departure underscores the idea that affiliation was not only an effective way to build community and a means to work toward racial uplift but also an avenue to find "any assistance [one] may need" in a new home.

In short, involvement with the UNIA was most certainly about cohering ideologies of black racial uplift and redemption, but it was also a mechanism to accrue social capital through connecting to networks of known and unknown individuals in far-flung places.[120] The networks built through UNIA organizing and through the *Negro World* functioned to enhance the social capital of marginalized Afro-Caribbean immigrants living and working in a foreign and, more often than not, hostile land. Through the UNIA, as the "News and Views" section and its emphasis on perseverance demonstrates, West Indians in Cuba built and maintained a reliable community for women and men whose lives were characterized by fluctuation.

Conclusion

The ideological ambitions of Garveyism and its remarkable accomplishment in fostering a sense of race unity that would have lasting and far-reaching consequences are of the utmost importance in historical understandings of the Garvey movement. As Ewing illustrates in *The Age of Garvey*, one of the great successes of Garvey's movement was to imbue the day-to-day tasks of consciousness raising and organizing with a sense of larger significance. In this essay I have sought to consider some of these more mundane organizing mechanisms in the Cuban context, to explore the tools Garveyites used to build and share their organization, and to ask what immediate benefits members derived from participation in the Universal Negro Improvement Association.

Putnam writes that migrants used the UNIA and other associations "to cushion the risk and loneliness of an economic system built on extreme mobility."[121] Careful examination of the UNIA in Cuba, with particular attention to stories like those of Irene Richards and J. J. Paul, illustrates something of how this cushioning took place and in what ways the Garvey movement was perhaps exceptionally effective. Garveyites used the formal functions of the UNIA—mutual aid, consistent rules and rituals, news sharing—to enhance their own sense of stability. Richards and Paul found in the overall UNIA structure a reliable community with which they could affiliate in multiple locations, one through which they could enact familiar rituals and share in the values of race pride and racial uplift. Just as British West Indians in transit connected and established social network and communities through the UNIA even without personal ties to a particular locale, Garveyites in individual towns used the association to build a sense of stability despite the regular movement of members. West Indians in Cuba knew this was possible because they avidly read the *Negro World,* and contributors told them as much in a narrative of carrying on despite obstacles.

One of the Garvey movement's most remarkable achievements was the creation of a mass institutional framework and social network that offered portability, replicability, reliability, and consistency to its members. These achievements of UNIA activity can be gleaned if we take seriously the sources, however formulaic and repetitive, written and shared by Garveyites themselves. The formula and repetition of the rulebook, the "News and Views" reports, and the narrative of perseverance all emerge as subjects of analysis themselves rather than as entities to overcome or put aside. Through these sources we see how local organizers and rank-and-file UNIA members carried out their work and spread the Garvey movement's powerful messages of race pride and uplift.

Notes

1. "UNIA Marcane, Oriente, Cuba on the Upward March," *Negro World,* March 19, 1921. The UNIA constitution delineated clear distinctions between divisions (a group of seven or more people launching the association in a new city), chapters (additional UNIA groups in a city that already had a division), and branches (applied beyond the United States to the collection of divisions that fall under a dominion, provincial, or colonial charter required by local law). See "Constitution and Book of Laws, New York, July 1918," in R. A. Hill, *Marcus Garvey and Universal Negro Improvement Association Papers* [hereafter *MGP*], 1:256–57. These terms, however, are occasionally confused in original documents and in secondary literature. In this chapter, I have tried to replicate the language used in my sources.

2. "Speech by Marcus Garvey in Panama," *MGP*, 3:384–85.

3. This was not the only time Garvey criticized Jamaicans as "backward" and suggested that only those West Indians who had traveled, whether in search of employment or as part of the British West Indian Regiment serving in World War I, were better equipped to lead the race. See, for example, "Speech by Marcus Garvey," *Gleaner,* March 26, 1921, *MGP*, 3:280–81.

4. L. Putnam, *Radical Moves*, 17. Several scholars have pointed to correlation between British West Indian migration and the spread of the Garvey movement. See R. A. Hill, "General Introduction," *MGP*, 11:lxxxvi; and W. James, "Culture, Labor, and Race," 450–51.

5. There were 725 UNIA divisions in the United States and 271 divisions outside of the United States, with Cuba hosting the most (at least 52), followed by Panama (47), Trinidad (30), Costa Rica (23), Canada (15), and Jamaica (11). See T. Martin, *Race First*, 15–16. Trinidad a British West Indian territory was the only major exception to the pattern of the UNIA having more divisions in receiving societies than West Indian territories, and Trinidad was itself a migration destination.

6. R. Lewis, *Marcus Garvey*, 118; T. Martin, *Race First*, 24, 28–30; Harpelle, "Cross Currents," 65; L. Putnam, *Radical Moves*, 144.

7. Harpelle, *West Indians of Costa Rica*, 32–35; Chomsky, *West Indian Workers*, 203.

8. Garnes, "Marcus Garvey and the UNIA," 136.

9. W. James, "Culture, Labor, and Race," 450.

10. For a relatively recent study of racial practices in the United States' formal and informal empire in Central America, see Colby, *Business of Empire*. See also several key older works: W. James, *Holding Aloft the Banner*, especially chapters 1 and 3; Bourgois, *Ethnicity at Work*; Chomsky, *West Indian Workers*; and Harpelle, *West Indians of Costa Rica*. Perhaps the best-known—though certainly not the only—example of openly discriminatory racial practices in the region was the Panama Canal Authority's gold payroll for white employees and silver payroll for black employees, a system of formal segregation that extended to dining, living, and health facilities. See Conniff, *Black Labor on a White Canal*; Greene, *Canal Builders*; and Newton, *Silver Men*.

11. W. James, "Culture, Labor, and Race," 450.

12. L. Putnam, "'Nothing Matters but Color,'" 113.

13. Ewing, *Age of Garvey*, 6.

14. McLeod, "Garveyism in Cuba," 135.

15. For the Panama Canal strike, see Burnett, "'Are We Slaves or Free Men?'"; and Zumoff, "Black Caribbean Labor Radicalism."

16. R. A. Hill, "General Introduction," *MGP*, 11:lxxviii–lxxx.

17. Quoted in *MGP*, 1:lxxx. For a detailed account of the evolving relationship between the Garvey movement and employers of West Indian labor in Central America, see Harpelle, "Cross Currents." In addition to Hill's, Ewing offers excellent overviews of Garvey's "retreat from radicalism." See Ewing, *Age of Garvey*, 114–21; and Ewing, "Caribbean Labour Politics." I address the relationship between the UNIA and the United Fruit Company in "'Forging Ahead,'" 241–44.

18. Ewing, *Age of Garvey*, 6–7.

19. Ibid., 5.

20. Guridy, *Forging Diaspora*, 7–9.

21. Bourgois, *Ethnicity at Work*; Burnett, "'Are We Slaves or Free Men?'"; Chomsky, *West Indian Workers*; Corinealdi, "Envisioning Multiple Citizenships"; Watson, *Politics of Race in Panama*; Dalrymple, "In the Shadow of Garvey"; Giovannetti, "Black British Subjects in Cuba"; Giovannetti, "Elusive Organization of Identity"; Harpelle, *West Indians of Costa Rica*; R. A. Hill, "General Introduction," *MGP*, 11:xxxv–xc; W. James, *Holding Aloft the Banner*; Leeds, "Representations of Race"; L. Putnam, *Company They Kept*; L. Putnam, "Eventually Alien"; L. Putnam, "Borderlands and Border Crossers"; Pérez Nakao, "Inmigración jamaicana a Banes"; Pérez Nakao, "Inmigración españa, jamaicana, y árabe a Banes"; L. Putnam, *Radical Moves*; Watkins-Owens, *Blood Relations*; Zumoff, "Black Caribbean Labor Radicalism"; Chailloux Laffita and Whitney, "British Subjects y Pichones en Cuba."

22. Giovannetti, "Black British Subjects in Cuba," 40.

23. Newton, *Silver Men,* 47.

24. Giovannetti, "Black British Subjects in Cuba," 40–41; L. Putnam, "Eventually Alien," 279.

25. L. Putnam, "Eventually Alien," 282.

26. L. Putnam, "Nothing Matters but Color," 108.

27. For the early immigration of "nonspecified West Indians" and an overview of standard narratives of West Indian immigration to Cuba, see Giovannetti, "Black British Subjects in Cuba," 40–45.

28. Ibid., 42; Pérez de la Riva, "Cuba y la migración antillana," 11–12; McLeod, "Garveyism in Cuba," 136–37. It is important to bear in mind a few things about these figures. First, many Afro-Caribbean workers arrived annually in time for the sugar harvest and returned home after it completed, and thus were counted as having "arrived" multiple times. Second, immigrants likely arrived without being counted by immigration officials, sometimes through private company ports and sometimes as illegal migrants. McLeod writes: "According to the 1931 census, . . . 28,206 British West Indians had settled on the island. The actual number was probably even larger. The Jamaican Secretary for Immigration in Santiago, for example, reported that 'approximately 60,000 British West Indians alone resided in Cuba in 1930'" (ibid., 136).

29. Giovannetti, "Black British Subjects in Cuba," 3–5.

30. L. Putnam, "Borderlands and Border Crossers," 8.

31. For a thorough and compelling study of British West Indians living and working in Port Limón, Costa Rica, see L. Putnam, *Company They Kept.*

32. Charlton, "'Cat Born in Oven,'" 340–89; Giovannetti, "Black British Subjects in Cuba"; Giovannetti, "Elusive Organization of Identity."

33. Charlton, "'Cat Born in Oven,'" 371–83; Fernández Robaina, "Marcus Garvey in Cuba"; Bernardo García Domínguez, "Garvey and Cuba," in R. Lewis and Bryan, *Garvey*, 299–305; Giovannetti, "Black British Subjects in Cuba," 192–220; Giovannetti, "Elusive Organization of Identity"; Guridy, "Enemies of the White Race"; Guridy, *Forging Diaspora*, 61–106; R. Lewis, *Marcus Garvey*, 99–113; McLeod, "Undesirable Aliens"; McLeod, "'Sin dejar de ser cubanos'"; Sullivan, "Radical Solidarities"; Sullivan, "'Forging Ahead.'"

34. "Marcus Garvey, Moises de la raza negra expone al heraldo sus amplios planes sobre la futura República del África," *Heraldo de Cuba*, March 4, 1921, cited in McLeod, "'Sin dejar de ser cubanos,'" 79.

35. García Domínguez, "Garvey and Cuba"; R. Lewis, *Marcus Garvey*, 99–103; Rodríguez, "Marcus Garvey en Cuba." Several have synthesized this scholarship. See Guridy, *Forging Diaspora*, 82–85; and McLeod, "'Sin dejar de ser cubanos,'" 78–81.

36. Giovannetti, "Black British Subjects in Cuba," 111–40; McLeod, "Garveyism in Cuba." McLeod writes: "Rather than addressing more general working-class issues, Garveyism in Cuba met the specific racial and ethnic needs of British West Indian immigrants" (ibid., 153).

37. Giovannetti, "Elusive Organization of Identity," 3, 9–10, 14. In "'Forging Ahead'" I follow the lead of scholars such as Giovanetti and McLeod to explore the practical purposes that the UNIA served in the lives of its members and find that, in the United Fruit town of Banes, the association and the company came to a state of mutual acceptance, with the company tolerating the organization that performed much of the work reproducing the labor force that the company was unwilling to carry out. The notion that Garveyism should be thought of as "civil religion" was first articulated by Randall Burkett in *Garveyism as a Religious Movement*.

38. McLeod, "Garveyism in Cuba."

39. McLeod writes: "While the interpretation of Garveyism in Cuba as a movement dominated by British West Indian immigrants is accurate, such analysis tends to underestimate the potential appeal of Garveyism to black Cubans and overlooks the efforts of UNIA organizers to reach out to them" ("'Sin dejar de ser cubanos,'" 82).

40. Ibid.

41. Guridy, "Enemies of the White Race"; Guridy, *Forging Diaspora*, 61–106.

42. Guridy, *Forging Diaspora*, 105.

43. "Sociedad de instrucción y cultura 'Asociación Universal para el Adelanto de la Raza Negra División No 52 de Banes,'" Leg. 2452, Exp. 2, p. 155, Fondo Gobierno Provincial [hereafter GP], Archivo Histórico Provincial de Santiago de Cuba [hereafter AHPSC].

44. Burnett, "'Are We Slaves or Free Men?'"; Guridy, *Forging Diaspora*, 69–71. On another occasion he "exhorted his hearers to drop all insular selfishness and get together, . . . bury all 'Jamaicanism,' 'Barbadianism,' 'Panamanian-ism,' and all foolish names hurled at each other which were only keeping the race apart and giving its opponents the opportunity of further" oppression. See "D. H. OConnor, UNIA Colón Division," *MGP*, 11:502.

45. See Burnett, "'Are We Slaves or Free Men?'" 99; Guridy, *Forging Diaspora*, 69–71; and McLeod, "'Sin dejar de ser cubanos,'" 83.

46. "Capt. Joshua Cockburn to Marcus Garvey," Sagua la Grande, December 2, 1919, *MGP*, 2:157–58; "Capt. Joshua Cockburn to Marcus Garvey," Sagua la Grande, December 5, 1919, *MGP*, 2:61–62; "Report of UNIA Meeting," *Negro World*, March 6, 1920, *MGP*, 2:233.

47. Charlton, "'Cat Born in Oven,'" 371–73; McLeod, "Garveyism in Cuba," 137

48. McLeod, "Cuba," *MGP*, 11:clxxxix–cxcv.

49. Report "British Consulate, Santiago de Cuba, November 17th, 1921, submitted to the Colonial Secretary, Kingston," , Leg. 532, Exp. 12473, Fondo Secretaria de Estado, ANC; Giovannetti, "Black British Subjects in Cuba," 111–40; McLeod, "Garveyism in Cuba," 140–41.

50. McLeod, "Garveyism in Cuba," 141. This is confirmed with close examinations of multiple copies of the 1922 UNIA rulebook I address in the next section.

51. Marc C. McLeod, "Cuba," *MGP*, 11:clxxxix–cxcv.

52. Information on the precise number of divisions in Cuba varies. The UNIA's Central Division Records list 54 chapters and divisions in Cuba for a two-year period beginning in 1925. See "Divisions of the UNIA, 1925–1927," reel 1, box 2, A16, UNIA Central Division Records [hereafter UNIA-CDR], Schomburg Center for Research in Black Culture, New York Public Library [hereafter Schomburg]. , On the other hand, a police officer spying on the organization in Sagua la Grande, Cuba, repeatedly referred to the organization as having 55 chapters on the island. See Pedro Llanio, Comandante de Estado Mayor, a Capitán Ayudante de Distrito de Santa Clara, August 14, 1929, Leg. 77, No. 563, p. 68, Fondo Asociaciónes, Archivo Histórico Provincial de Villa Clara [hereafter AHPVC].

53. R. A. Hill, "General Introduction," *MGP*, 11:lxxi.

54. "Divisions of the UNIA, 1925–1927," reel 1, box 2, A16, UNIA-CDR, Schomburg. For a handy chart of international UNIA divisions, see T. Martin, *Race First*, 16.

55. Sullivan, "'Forging Ahead.'" For Jamaican immigration to Banes, see Pérez Nakao, "Inmigración jamaicana a Banes."

56. See the discussion of British Caribbean freemasonry in Cuba in Charlton, "'Cat Born in Oven,'" 347–55.

57. Marixa Lasso points to this "urban corridor" characteristic of Panama's geography in her current work on "The Lost Towns of the Canal Zone." I first learned of her exciting research during a lecture she delivered as a W.E.B. Du Bois research fellow with Harvard University's Hutchins Center on October 26, 2016.

58. A. James, *Banes*, 73.

59. L. Putnam, *Radical Moves*, 131–32.

60. "Reglamento de La Asociacion Universal Para el Adelanto de la Raza Negro División No 52 de Banes," July 3, 1922, Leg. 2452, Exp. 2, pp. 11–24, GP, AHPSC. With respect to possible disagreements, I am thinking here of Havana's associational registry, for instance, which details infighting between UNIA officers competing over election results. See, for example, "From the Sec de la Admon Provincial to Sr. Juez Correccional de Marianao," July 7, 1928, Leg. 306, Exp. 8892, Fondo Asociaciónes, ANC. . With respect to relationships with employers and the state, see the police reports Guridy found in Sagua La Grande in Guridy, "Enemies of the White Race."

61. Associational records in Cuba are often rife with exchanges between bureaucrats and club members about missing documents, failures to obtain the correct stamp, procedural technicalities, and so forth. The "Reglamento" clearly eases that process for those chapters which used it to inscribe in the Registry of Association. The origins of the "Reglamento" are unclear, though I suspect it was printed in Havana under the direction of High Commissioner Morales, who translated the "Ethiopian National Anthem," which appears on the booklet's final page. See "Reglamento," Leg. 2452, Exp. 2, pp. 11–24, GP, AHPSC.

62. R. A. Hill, "General Introduction," *MGP*, 11:lxxxv.

63. See "Reglamento," Leg. 2452, Exps. 2, 4, and 7, as well as Leg. 2497, Exp. 7, GP, AHPSC. It is likely that the rulebook appears in other collections that I have not visited.

64. "Distinguished Visit Paid to the Guantanamo Division, as Well as Others in Cuba by His Grace, Our Esteemed Chaplain General, Dr. George Alexander McGuire," *Negro World*, March 19, 1921.

65. "Dr. Alexander Given Ovation on Return," *Negro World*, March 19, 1921. Garnes quotes two informant memories of the *Negro World*: "A big, strong Black man called Mr. Newton sold us . . . the *Negro World*," and "The *Negro World* was Marcus Garvey's. We asked for new issues. In them we found everything, what Africans were doing and that stuff. It wasn't published here. It was made in the USA" ("Marcus Garvey and the UNIA," 139).

66. Of the pair in Panama, one contributor wrote from Port Pastellio that "under the burning rays of a tropical sun, the energetic field workers, Dr. S. P. Radway and Prof. Dave Davidson walked for two miles on the railroad to organize a branch of the UNIA." "Branch of the UNIA and ACL Formed at Port Pastellio," *Negro World*, March 19, 1921.

67. That Radway and Davidson went out of their way to thank the company manager is striking in light of the massacre of seventeen British West Indian laborers by Cuban soldiers during Cuba's Liberal Revolt in that very town. See Giovannetti, "Black British Subjects in Cuba." One can only speculate that West Indian workers and their advocates had learned to maneuver carefully in their dealings with company and state. I address this in "'Forging Ahead.'"

68. E. H. Hope Williams, "The UNIA Almost Encircles Island of Cuba," *Negro World*, March 6, 1921, 8; "Marcus Garvey to William H. Ferris, Literary Editor, *Negro World*," *MGP*, 12:423–25 n. 6; S. P. Radway, "Report of Conditions Existing in the Cuban Republic," *Negro World*, August 27, 1921, 7.

69. "Marcus Garvey to William H. Ferris, Literary Editor, *Negro World*," *MGP*, 12:423–25 n. 6. Many local organizers failed to send the parent body its proper dues. This is what Garvey may have been referring to when he deemed Radway and Davidson to be in "not very good standing."

70. S. P. Radway, "Report of Conditions Existing in the Cuban Republic," *Negro World*, August 27, 1921, 7.

71. This example is culled from various footnotes volume 11 of *MGP*. See Sullivan, "Review," 220.

72. Giovannetti, "The Elusive Organization of Identity," 14.

73. "Sociedad de instrucción y cultura 'Asociación Universal para el Adelanto de la Raza Negra División No 52 de Banes,'" Leg. 2452, Exp. 2, GP, AHPSC; "His Grace, The

Right. Hon. Chaplain General, The Rev. Dr. George Alexander M'Guire, Given Great Ovation on His Return from Cuba," *Negro World,* March 19, 1921, 1, 3.

74. *MGP*, 11:578–79 n. 7; "His Grace, The Right. Hon. Chaplain General"; Appendix IV, "Delegates to the 1921 UNIA Convention," *MGP*, 4:789; "Visit by Chaplain General to Guaro, Oriente, Cuba," *Negro World,* March 12, 1921; "Pleasant Times in Preston, Cuba," *Negro World*, February 19, 1921.

75. "Sociedad de instrucción y cultura 'Asociación Universal para el Adelanto de la Raza Negra División No 52 de Banes,'" Leg. 2452, Exp. 2, p. 49, GP, AHPSC.

76. Post, *Arise Ye Starvelings*, 417. For more on the Harmony division of the UNIA in Jamaica, see Nicole Bourbonnais's chapter in this volume.

77. "Spirit of Garveyism," *Negro World,* January 10, 1931, 4.

78. Ewing, *Age of Garvey*, 77.

79. Charlton, "'Cat Born in Oven,'" 374. An example from Panama gives a sense of this process. Edgar McCarthy, secretary of the Colón, Panama, branch, for instance, traveled to Cristóbal, Canal Zone, in February 1919 to open a new branch there. That month he wrote to the UNIA general-secretary in New York enclosing a list of sixty-one people who had already paid their dues. He enclosed a description of their successes thus far, including seven mass meetings, 115 new members enrolled, and the distribution of leaflets. Microfilm, M1440: Correspondence, RG 165: War Department, General and Special Staffs, United States National Archives, College Park, Maryland.

80. "Miranda, Cuba, Division 608, Unveils Its Charter—Event Very Impressive," *Negro World*, February 24, 1923; "Las Minas, Cuba," *Negro World*, May 25, 1925.

81. "Camaguey, Cuba, Elia No. 754," *Negro World,* January 10, 1925; "Miranda, Cuba, Division 608, Unveils Its Charter—Event Very Impressive," *Negro World,* February 24, 1923; *Negro World*, January 3, 1931, 3; "Sola Division," *Negro World,* January 17, 1931; "Spirit of Garveyism," *Negro World,* January 10, 1931, 4; "Camaguey, Cuba, Elia No. 754," *Negro World,* October 10, 1925; "The Camaguey Division Holds Inspiring Meeting," *Negro World,* August 25, 1923, 7.

82. Harpelle, "Cross Currents," 64.

83. "Reglamento," Leg. 2452, Exp. 2, GP, AHPSC.

84. "Florida, Cam. Cuba," *Negro World*, September 11, 1926.

85. "Death of a Beloved Member in Cuba," *Negro World*, January 10, 1925, 12.

86. "Wedding Bells in San Manuel, Oriente," *Negro World,* February 24, 1923.

87. "Pleasant Times in Preston, Cuba," *Negro World,* February 19, 1921; "Banes, Oriente, Cuba," *Negro World,* August 21, 1926; Robert Blake, "A Ringing Message from Banes, Oriente, Cuba," *Negro World,* April 14, 1923, 4; Small, "Remedios, Cuba," *Negro World,* August 21, 1926; A. E. Bridgeman, "Sola Division," *Negro World*, January 17, 1931, 3. See also Castillo Bueno and Rubiera Castillo, *Reyita*.

88. "Camaguey Div. Holds Unique Entertainment," *Negro World,* July 21, 1926.

89. R. G. Murray, "Big Day at Banes, Oriente, Cuba," *Negro World,* March 24, 1923, 4; Bair, "Pan-Africanism as Process."

90. "Las Minas, Cuba," *Negro World*, May 25, 1925.

91. "Jabitonico, Cuba," *Negro World,* May 9, 1925.

92. "Bartle, Orte, Cuba," *Negro World,* April 11, 1925.

93. The examples are almost too numerous to cite. Any given "News and Views" sec-

tion will repeat this format in several contributions. Consider, for just one example, the "News and Views" page from August 21, 1926, which included six contributions from Cuba.

94. "Miranda, Cuba, Division 608, Unveils Its Charter—Event Very Impressive," *Negro World*, February 24, 1923; "Ciego de Avila, Guey, Cuba," *Negro World*, April 11, 1925.

95. Guridy, *Forging Diaspora*, 105.

96. Ibid., 91–96.

97. Ibid., 90.

98. Lemelle and Kelley, *Imagining Home*, 7; B. Anderson, *Imagined Communities*, 24–25.

99. Anderson, *Imagined Communities*, 35. Lara Putnam also highlights Anderson's "evocative image of the of the reader of the daily paper of national circulation." See *Radical Moves*, 127.

100. L. Putnam, *Radical Moves*, 126.

101. "UNIA in Cuba Celebrates Mother's Day," *Negro World,* April 14, 1925.

102. "Central Francisco, Cuba," *Negro World,* May 16, 1925.

103. L. Putnam, *Radical Moves*, 131.

104. S. P. Radway, "Report of Conditions Existing in the Cuban Republic," *Negro World*, August 27, 1921, 7.

105. Blake, "All's Well in Banes, Oriente, Cuba," *Negro World*, May 26, 1923, 9.

106. *Negro World,* March 17, 1923, 10, quoted in Charlton, "'Cat Born in Oven,'" 376. Lara Putnam also cites Charlton in *Radical Moves*, 131.

107. "Dr. Alexander Given Ovation on Return," *Negro World*, March 19, 1921.

108. "Guantanamo, Cuba," *Negro World*, January 10, 1925.

109. An example from the Dominican Republic further illustrates this point. "A Young Dominican with Proper Race Spirit," the headline explained, praised the *Negro World* for keeping readers abreast of news that concerns black men and women in a letter to the editor. *Negro World*, January 17, 1925. Similarly, a contributor from Spanish Honduras praised the paper as "one of the most effective weapons which can be used by the Negroes against the so-called superior race of today" and claimed that it was widely read and well received in his town. "A Greeting from Spanish Honduras," *Negro World,* March 12, 1921.

110. Letter from Nathan A. Harison, Central Francisco, Camaguey, Cuba, December 21, 1932, reel 1, A33–36, "Negro World Correspondences," UNIA-CDR, Schomburg.

111. Letter from William Allen, La Gloria Camaguey, Cuba, January 4, 1933, "Negro World Correspondences," reel 1, A33–36, Schomburg, UNIA-CDR, Schomburg.

112. Jones, "The UNIA in Camaguey, Cuba, Surmounts Difficulties," *Negro World,* May 26, 1923, 7.

113. R. G. Murray, "Big Day at Banes, Oriente," *Negro World*, March 3, 1923.

114. Sydney F. Hugh Miller, "Memorial Banner Day for Division, 323," *Negro World*, April 28, 1923, 7.

115. R. A. Martin, "Florida Division," *Negro World,* May 5, 1923, 8.

116. Blake, "A Ringing Message from Banes," *Negro World,* April 14, 1923, 4.

117. For the North American leadership structure, see Bair, "True Women, Real Men," 155. For examples of an integrated leadership structure, see "Ingenia, Rio Canto," *Negro*

World, September 5, 1925; "Santiago, Cuba," *Negro World,* May 19, 1925; R. H. Bachelor, "Garvey Relief Cantata Is Staged by Division #164, at Guantanamo," *Negro World,* September 8, 1923, 7; and Dora Stennett, "Elia, Camaguey, Cuba," *Negro World,* August 21, 1926.

118. McLeod, "Garveyism in Cuba," 146–47.

119. See "Sociedad de instrucción y cultura 'Asociación Universal para el Adelanto de la Raza Negra División No 52 de Banes,'" Leg. 2452, Exp. 2, GP, AHPSC, for several documents listing the officers, their names, and their professions in Banes.

120. "UNIA & ACL, Div. 164 Guantanamo, Cuba," *Negro World,* February 24, 1923. The author writes: "Mr. Paul is a young gentleman who when you come to the UNIA & ACL knows nothing about personal friendship, but knows that the laws and rules of the association must be carried out."

121. L. Putnam, "Nothing Matters but Color," 123.

3

"The Second Battle for Africa Has Begun"

Rev. Clarence W. Harding Jr., Garveyism, Liberia,
and the Diasporic Midwest, 1966–1978

ERIK S. MCDUFFIE

Rev. Clarence W. Harding Jr. looked determined. It was August 1977 in Monrovia, the capital of the West African nation of Liberia. Wearing a boubou and kufi, the Chicago-born Harding led a parade of the Universal Negro Improvement Association (UNIA) down one of Monrovia's main thoroughfares. During a pause in the procession, he carefully inspected twenty dashiki-adorned Liberian members of the UNIA's medical battalion.[1] Charismatic and austere, Harding was the president of the Monrovia-based Metropolitan Division of the UNIA. The UNIA was a global Pan-African movement founded by the Jamaican black nationalists Marcus Garvey and Amy Ashwood Garvey in Kingston, Jamaica, in 1914.[2] At its peak in the early 1920s, the UNIA was the largest black protest movement in history. The organization claimed six million members in the United States, Canada, the Caribbean, Central America, Africa, Europe, and Australia.[3] The UNIA understood itself as a provisional government in exile committed to building self-reliant black institutions, an independent Africa, and a global black empire capable of protecting the rights and dignity of the African-descended everywhere. Marcus Garvey's call for race pride, pan-African solidarity, and black self-determination galvanized black people across the diaspora, not the least Clarence Harding.[4]

At this day's parade in Monrovia, Harding was flanked by two uniformed and helmeted soldiers of the Universal African Legion (UAL), the UNIA's paramilitary force, first established in 1919.[5] The medical battalion stood at attention as he reviewed them. This event demonstrated his passion for building the UNIA, advancing Garveyism, and serving the needs of the Liberian people.

From his arrival in Liberia from Chicago in May 1966 through the late 1970s, Harding played a pivotal role in leading the UNIA in Liberia and across the continent. In early 1966, Thomas Harvey of Philadelphia, president-general of the UNIA, conceived the Africa Project. Inspired by the longtime Garveyite dream of redeeming Africa and by the emergence of more than twenty African nations since 1960, the purpose of the Africa Project was to rebuild the UNIA on the continent and provide organizational support "for the liberation and restoration of Africa for the Africans at home and abroad."[6] The initiative was to be based in Monrovia. Harvey appointed Harding as the UNIA high commissioner of Africa and sent him to Liberia. Harding enthusiastically accepted this charge.[7] Under his leadership, the Africa Project emerged as the most successful UNIA-led initiative on the continent during the organization's entire history. The program touched the lives of thousands of Liberians and had an impact on liberation struggles across the continent. Well respected both by young, college-educated militants and by everyday indigenous working-class people in Monrovia and beyond, Harding remained in Liberia until his untimely death in 1978. He is buried in Monrovia. His story remains largely unknown.[8]

This chapter examines the encounters of Clarence Harding in Liberia and across Africa from the mid-1960s through the late 1970s. Tracing his journey to the continent expands the geographic, analytical, and temporal scope of the study of Garveyism, Africa, and the black world by revealing the history of what I call the "diasporic Midwest." I use "diasporic Midwest" as an empirical and theoretical framework to extend the study of the African diaspora by tracing the significance of the American heartland as a center of black transnational political activism, to appreciate the gendered contours and paradoxes of pan-African movements, and to chart a genealogy of global black freedom struggles through Garveyism. The diasporic Midwest encompasses the American industrial heartland, a region that includes states north of the Ohio River between the Appalachians and the Rocky Mountains, as a single yet complex geographic, political, historical, and discursive formation linked to Africa, the black diaspora, and the world. Garveyism provided a powerful vehicle for black urban midwesterners such as Clarence Harding to forge transnational linkages with peoples of African descent everywhere.[9]

The distinguishing feature of midwestern Garveyism was its ability to build long-lasting, grassroots political and cultural formations committed to global black freedom. Local, regional, and global forces converged in the American heartland to make it a transnational epicenter of black protest. Beginning in the early twentieth century, Chicago, Cleveland, and Detroit emerged as sites of the most advanced industrial manufacturing on the planet. From the 1910s through the 1960s, millions of black people from the U.S. South and beyond migrated to the urban Midwest in search of good-paying jobs in automobile factories, steel mills, and stockyards. This new world of mass production, urbanization, and consumer capitalism, together with the growing radicalization of black people globally during World War I, transformed the lives of recently arrived black migrants in Cleveland, Chicago, and Detroit.[10] Blacks in these cities enjoyed political rights and economic opportunities they could find nowhere else. Unlike in the Jim Crow South, black midwesterners could vote. They earned incomes higher than their counterparts anywhere else. These cities were centers of militant labor organizing. Black midwesterners came to see unionization as critical to their struggle for full freedom and racial justice.[11] They founded dynamic cultural institutions committed to racial uplift. At the same time, black urban midwesterners encountered virulent racial oppression in these new urban industrial settings.[12] World War I, the Depression, World War II, and decolonization fundamentally challenged white supremacy and the geopolitical status quo across the globe.[13]

These local and global developments explain the militancy and endurance of Garveyism in Chicago, Cleveland, and Detroit that propelled the transnational work of Harding in Liberia. UNIA divisions (locals) in these cities remained some of the largest and most active locals in the transnational Garvey movement into the 1970s. A large portion of the UNIA's male rank and file in these cities worked in heavy industries, whereas the vast majority of Garveyite women toiled backbreaking hours as domestics in the homes of white women.[14] Although Harding did not work industrial jobs, he lived in black midwestern communities whose social relations and militancy were profoundly shaped by factories. Given their location in the industrial heartland, midwestern Garveyites with their comfortable incomes were uniquely positioned to support the transnational work of Harding in West Africa.[15]

Further, calling attention to the diasporic Midwest through Harding's work rethinks and extends the geographic and temporal scope of Garveyism. His activism redirects the study of Garvey movement in the United States from coastal cities such as New York and New Orleans, which were linked to maritime economies and migrations, and from the rural Jim Crow South.[16] Harding's activism demonstrates the importance of cities such Chicago, Cleveland, and Detroit in leading the transnational UNIA. The industrial character of these cities cultivated a distinctive militant working-class and internationalist perspective that propelled Garveyism. Similarly, Harding's life in Liberia sheds new light on Garveyism in Africa. Recent work on Garveyism on the continent tends to focus on the 1920s and 1930s, with special attention to the Garvey movement in southern, central, and eastern Africa. In doing so, this work overlooks the ways Garveyism shaped West African life and politics after Garvey's death in 1940.[17] Calling attention to these connections counters the common perception of the American heartland as provincial, and challenges the traditional view that frames the influence of Garveyism and the UNIA on Black Power organizations and African decolonization of the 1960s and 1970s from the perspective of its rhetorical and organizational legacy.[18] Harding's activism in Liberia illustrates the concrete ways the UNIA survived as an organization, attempted to navigate the political landscape of a postcolonial African state, and revitalized Garveyism through movement and institution building on the continent during the era of African decolonization.

Harding's work also illustrates the interconnections between what historian Mary Rolinson has called "grassroots Garveyism," that is, the organizational work UNIA leaders and activists performed at the local level to achieve global black freedom, with the transnational dimensions of the Garvey movement explored in recent work by the historian Adam Ewing.[19] "View[ing] Garveyism not as an ideology but as a method of organic politics," Ewing stresses how the power of Garvey movement rested in its ability "to join a vast, expanding, and dazzling project of diasporic connectivity and international organization."[20] This description fits Harding's transnational activism in West Africa.

The framework of the diasporic Midwest, an intersectional approach focused on the connections among race, gender, sexuality, and class, sheds important light on the gendered contours of Garveyism through Harding's activism in Liberia. Reflecting the times, the UNIA adhered to prevailing, socially constructed ideas about the alleged "natural" roles of women and men in the public and private spheres. Viewing gender roles in hierarchal and complementary terms, men were to be, the UNIA charged, husbands and fathers who provided for and protected their families, and women were to be faithful wives, nurturing mothers, and caretakers of the home. This gender ideology created unique space within the UNIA for women to voice their issues and to lead the struggle for racial uplift. At the same time, the Garvey movement promoted masculinism. This outlook equated black freedom with the redemption of black manhood and required the subordination of women to male leadership. Ultimately, black men held the reins of power within the Garvey movement.[21] Like other twentieth-century black male spokespersons across the African world, Harding and other UNIA male officials often adhered to this masculinist and patriarchal view. This stance often equated black liberation with black manhood redemption, shrouding the unique oppressions facing African-descended women.

Examining the history of the diasporic Midwest through the journeys of Harding to West Africa sheds light on the paradox of Garveyism, namely, its tendency to understand African liberation in "civilizationist" terms. Garvey believed that the diaspora had a moral obligation to civilize allegedly backward indigenous African societies.[22] Although he embraced a more modern view of pan-Africanism, one that looked to the continent as a source of revolutionary inspiration, Harding and some of his colleagues never fully dispensed with civilizationism.

Telling the story of Harding's work is a difficult task. Harding neither wrote an autobiography nor penned articles. However, archival collections of UNIA records in the United States contain scores of correspondences by and photographs of him. Tracing Harding's life through archival material in Liberia is especially challenging. Archivists in the Center for National Documents and Records (National Archives) in Monrovia have yet to discover materials related to Harding. The repository recently reopened to the public after being closed for years following the bloody civil war (which ended in 2003) in this West African nation. Combatants destroyed and looted millions of pages of documents from the repository. In order to fill this gap, I have conducted interviews in Monrovia with his associates who worked with him during the 1970s. Still, many questions may never be answered about his work in West Africa. What is certain is that his journeys to the continent demonstrate the significance and mixed results of Garveyism in advancing African liberation, the gendered contours and paradoxes of pan-Africanism, and the transnational political connections between the Midwest and West Africa during the 1960s and 1970s.[23]

Harding's Early Years

Coming of age in Chicago, a city with a rich history of diasporic struggle, prepared Harding for his work in Liberia during the 1960s and 1970s. Biographical information on Harding's early years is scarce. He was born in Des Moines,

Iowa, around 1919. His father was from Illinois and worked as a mail carrier, a respectable job within the African American community. His Iowa-born mother apparently did not work outside the home. What is clear is that he moved at a young age with his parents to Chicago and grew up in the predominantly African American South Side neighborhood.[24] From its very beginning, Chicago was a diasporic city. Its first permanent non-native inhabitant was Jean Baptiste Point du Sable, a fur trader who is believed to have been born in Haiti.[25] During the nineteenth century Chicago emerged as a center of abolition, of the Underground Railroad, and for emigration movements to Africa. By the early twentieth century it boasted the second-largest black urban population on the planet. African Americans from the South came to the city to escape Jim Crow and to acquire good-paying jobs in the city's booming stockyards, steel mills, and railroads. The city's black population exploded from 44,103 in 1910 to 109,458 in 1920. Blacks lived in the highly segregated, densely populated, underserved South Side. African Americans regularly encountered violence from the police and from white civilians.[26] The Chicago Race Riot of 1919 left thirty-eight people dead, more than five hundred injured, and hundreds homeless.[27] These local events, together with the global political and economic crisis immediately following World War I, radicalized blacks in and laid the groundwork for Garveyism to take root in Chicago.

The midwestern metropolis constituted a key site in the transnational UNIA from the 1920s onward. Garvey—along with several of his leading lieutenants—visited Chicago numerous times in the years during and immediately after World War I. The UNIA president-general referred to the Windy City a UNIA "stronghold" for its staunch support for African redemption.[28] At its height in the early 1920s the UNIA division on Chicago's South Side claimed eighteen thousand members, making it the second-largest Garveyite local in the world behind Harlem. The *Negro World*, the official newspaper of the UNIA, with its global circulation, regularly featured articles about Chicago.[29]

Beyond the UNIA, black nationalism thrived in numerous political, cultural, and religious formations in the Windy City from the 1920s onward. Black male industrial workers and female domestic laborers comprised the bulk of many of the organizations. The religiously unorthodox Moorish Science Temple of America, founded by Noble Drew Ali and headquartered in Chicago, lauded Garvey and drew from the ranks of the UNIA. Similarly, the Nation of Islam, established in Detroit in 1930 and later headquartered in Chicago, claimed Garvey as one of its progenitors. The Nation of Islam produced Malcolm X, the preeminent U.S. black nationalist of the post–World War II period, who was born in Omaha and reared in Lansing by Garveyite parents.[30] The Peace Movement of Ethiopia, founded in 1933 by Mittie Maud Lena Gordon, a former member of the Chicago UNIA, emerged as the largest African American emigration movement during the Depression.[31] Garveyites moved into the Communist Party, trade unions, mainstream black religious organizations, and electoral politics in the Windy City.[32] Drawing from the resources and freedom dreams of their largely working-class constituency, these formations endured for decades and left indelible marks on black life in Chicago and beyond.

The midwestern metropolis was hardly the only city in the heartland where the Garvey movement thrived during the early and mid-twentieth century. In the 1920s, UNIA divisions in Detroit, Cincinnati, and Cleveland counted thousands of members, many of whom worked in factories. The Midwest was the home to several key leaders of the transnational UNIA. James R. Stewart of Cleveland, who joined the Garvey movement in 1919, succeeded Marcus Garvey in 1940 as the UNIA president-general. Stewart moved the organization's headquarters to Cleveland. He eventually emigrated to Liberia. John Charles Zampty of Trinidad, who first met Garvey in 1912 in Panama, made his way to Detroit, worked in the auto industry, and served as the UNIA auditor general from the 1920s onward. Charles L. James of Antigua headed UNIA locals in Gary and Chicago before becoming president-general of the UNIA in 1978. Chicago UNIA leader Elinor White gained the trust of Garvey in the 1930s and remained a fixture in the movement through the 1960s. Later in life, Harding would work with many of these figures.[33]

Harding cut his political teeth in black nationalist movements in Chicago. His parents were staunch Garveyites, although no evidence has been found to indicate whether they met Garvey. In the 1940s, Harding participated in Chicago-based black nationalist movements committed to racial justice. By the 1960s he served as president of Chicago UNIA Division 401 and gained the trust of UNIA president-general Thomas Harvey, based in Philadelphia. The membership of Division 401 paled in comparison to the glory days of the Chicago UNIA of the 1920s, but it still counted about two dozen active die-hard members. Outside of the UNIA, Harding ministered in the Kenwood United Church, a politically active black church on the South Side affiliated with the politically progressive, multiracial United Church of Christ. When he departed for Liberia in May 1966, Harding had acquired a reputation as a skilled grassroots activist and committed Garveyite leader.[34]

The UNIA and Liberia, 1919–1964

Harding's sojourn to Liberia was part of a long history of African American journeying to the West African republic dating to the early nineteenth century. Formerly enslaved African Americans and their descendants who desired to be free first arrived in what is now Liberia in 1822, with emigration continuing after the country gained independence in 1847. Prominent nineteenth-century black nationalists such as Edward Wilmot Blyden of Saint Thomas and Alexander Crummell of the United States championed emigration to Liberia. They saw the nation as critical to the redemption of Africa. However, all was not rosy in Liberia.[35] Although they came in pursuit of freedom, Americo-Liberians, as settlers and their descendants from the diaspora came to be called, established a settler-colonial state that ruthlessly subjugated the indigenous population. Black settlers embraced a civilizationist impulse that viewed indigenous people as inferior and backward.[36]

Despite these paradoxes, blacks in the diaspora continued to see Liberia as a symbol of freedom into the twentieth century. Garvey identified this West African republic as the fulcrum for worldwide African liberation. In 1919 he announced his intention of eventually moving the UNIA's headquarters from New York to Liberia. During the1920s he sent four delegations of UNIA representatives to the West African nation to negotiate a deal with the Liberian government. Garveyism generated some interest among Liberians. Gabriel M. Johnson, the mayor of Monrovia, headed the UNIA division in the Liberian capital, formed by 1924. The local counted about one hundred members, most of whom were elite Americo-Liberians.[37] The division was short lived. It shut down after the falling out between the Liberian government and Garvey over the country's agreement with the U.S.-headquartered Firestone Rubber Company, marking the end of the UNIA's major activities in West Africa during the interwar years.[38] In the coming years, Garvey continued to advocate emigration to Liberia following his deportation in 1927 from the United States for mail fraud. In the 1930s he worked with avowed white supremacists such as Theodore Bilbo, a U.S. senator and staunch segregationist from Mississippi, and the author Earnest Sevier Cox in support of African American emigration to Liberia. The three men's belief in racial separatism explains how these apparent foes found common ground. Garvey passed away in June 1940. Ironically, the self-declared "Provisional President of Africa" never set foot in Liberia or anywhere else on the continent.[39]

Although Garvey failed to realize his vision of relocating the UNIA's head-quarters to Liberia, Garveyites from the diasporic Midwest loomed large in building the transnational UNIA in the West African republic during the post–World War II years. James R. Stewart of Cleveland was the most promi-nent UNIA leader to pursue emigration to the West African republic during the 1940s and 1950s. Originally from Mississippi, Stewart moved to Cleveland, where he became one of Garvey's closest lieutenants. Soon after Garvey's death, Stewart succeeded him as the president-general of the UNIA and moved the group's headquarters from Harlem to Cleveland. In 1949 he emigrated to Liberia with his wife and children.[40] There is no evidence indicating whether Clarence Harding met James Stewart before he left the United States.

By repatriating to and relocating the UNIA's headquarters to the continent, Stewart achieved what Garvey had only dreamed: championing African re-demption from the continent. In the coming years, Stewart attempted to revi-talize the transnational UNIA from the West African nation as the continent moved toward decolonization. Befriending Liberian president William V. S. Tubman, Stewart established a UNIA-run commercial farm in Gbandela, a re-mote village located 110 miles northeast of Monrovia. Organizing three interna-tional UNIA conferences in Gbandela in 1950, 1954, and 1958 was his crowning achievement in Africa. More than fifty delegates—mostly from the U.S. Mid-west—as well as President Tubman and several Liberian officials attended these gatherings. Members of the Cleveland UNIA, many of whom worked in the city's steel mills, played a vital role in financially supporting the conferences and Stewart's work in Liberia.[41] Personally, Stewart found living in Liberia to be an emancipatory experience. Free from the racism and government harassment he had known so well in the United States, he lived happily with his wife, Goldie Stewart, on the UNIA-operated farm in Gbandela. He passed away in Liberia in 1964. Fittingly, he was buried in Gbandela.[42]

Despite several important achievements, Stewart's work was not without its paradoxes. Like Garvey and most black male leaders of his time, Stewart un-derstood freedom in highly gendered terms. Equating black liberation with the redemption of black manhood, Stewart's masculinist vision often overlooked the special oppressions faced by African-descended women. Stewart also sub-scribed to a civilizationist vision that equated freedom with westernization and modernization. He neither learned Kpelle, the indigenous local language spo-ken where he lived in Liberia, nor wore African clothes. His staunch racial es-sentialism led him to correspond with the prominent white-supremacist writer

Earnest Sevier Cox and to endorse colonization schemes backed by hard-core white racists. In addition, Stewart—like Garvey—was a staunch anticommunist. The Cleveland Garveyite believed that capitalism provided the path toward black liberation. Living in a remote Liberia village, advocating a narrow black nationalism, and espousing anticommunism isolated Stewart from burgeoning freedom movements across the African world.[43] At the same time, the organizational weakness of the UNIA and internal rivalries within the transnational Garvey movement prevented Stewart from rebuilding the Garvey movement into a powerful global force.[44] Consequently, the UNIA in Liberia never grew into a mass movement during the 1940s and 1950s. Rather, it largely comprised Stewart and his loyalists from the American heartland who repatriated to Liberia. The mixed results of his work did not prevent Garveyites from continuing their work in Liberia. In the coming years, Garveyites continued to look to Liberia as a site for freeing black people around the world. Clarence Harding was at the forefront of these efforts.

The Africa Project and the Metropolitan Division

The activism of Clarence Harding in Liberia represented a new chapter in the history of Garveyism in the West African republic and continent. Unlike the UNIA's previous initiatives in Liberia led by James Stewart, Clarence Harding's project found success in the West African nation in building a sustained mass Garvey movement composed mostly of indigenous and poor African people from the mid-1960s through the late 1970s.[45] Harding's work demonstrates the transnational linkages between the diasporic Midwest and the continent through Garveyism and illustrates the concrete ways the UNIA built an oppositional movement that attempted to negotiate the complex political terrain of Liberia during the most radical phase of African decolonization.

The UNIA high commissioner of Africa had never before traveled to the continent when he landed at Roberts Field outside of Monrovia on May 11, 1966. No UNIA division operated in Monrovia upon his arrival to the West African republic. And there is no evidence that Clarence Harding ever contacted Goldie Stewart and the small community of midwestern Garveyites in Gbandela. Although he initially planned to live in Liberia for only a short time, Harding remained there for twelve years and carried out his most important life's work.[46]

Harding came to Liberia at an exciting and complex moment in the history of this West African nation and the continent. By the late-1960s, Africa counted more than twenty-five independent states, and armed struggles against Portuguese colonialism in Guinea-Bissau, Cape Verde, Angola, and Mozambique had gained momentum. The Organization of African Unity (OAU), founded in 1963 in Addis Ababa, Ethiopia, pledged support for decolonization and greater cooperation between African states.[47] The winds of change that swept across the continent affected Liberia, and by the late 1960s a new generation of Liberians became increasingly dissatisfied with the country's underdevelopment and the growing authoritarianism of William Tubman, who died in office in 1971. Vice-President William R. Tolbert Jr. succeeded Tubman. Initially, Liberians were hopeful about Tolbert, an Americo-Liberian who pledged democratic reforms and economic development. Internationally, Tolbert pursued a new foreign policy more in line with the changing times. Liberia forged closer diplomatic relations with militant West African states such as Guinea, headed by anticolonial champion Sékou Touré. Despite Tolbert's progressive overtures and a promising start, Liberia remained an undemocratic society and a U.S. client state. U.S. cold warriors saw Liberia as an important bulwark against Soviet influence in Africa. Given these realities, Tolbert, like his predecessor, pursued a foreign policy that did not fundamentally challenge U.S. interests on the continent. Tolbert failed to implement democratic reforms or to lift the country out of grinding poverty. By the late 1970s, antigovernment demonstrations made up largely of poor urban youth shook Monrovia. In 1980, Samuel K. Doe, an indigenous Liberian and army officer, led a military coup that overthrew and killed Tolbert. Although he initially enjoyed broad-based support, Doe became increasingly dictatorial. His rule plunged the country into years of conflict.[48] Globally, Garveyism enjoyed a resurgence of interest among a new generation of African-descended militants during the 1960s. Black Power activists searched for their ideological forebears. They looked to Garvey, Garveyism, and the UNIA.[49] It was within this context that Harding worked on behalf of the UNIA in Liberia and across the continent.

Taking organizing skills he had acquired as a UNIA leader and community activist in Chicago, Harding began building a broad-based Garvey movement in Liberia the moment he set foot on the continent in May 1966. Within days of his arrival, he met prominent church leaders and William Tolbert (it is unclear whether Harding and Tolbert met again). Although he forged connections with Liberian elites, the UNIA high commissioner of Africa concentrated his efforts on working with the urban masses of Monrovia. By July 1966 he established a UNIA chapter in the capital that came to be known as the Metropolitan Division. At its peak in the 1970s the local counted around four hundred members, most of whom were indigenous working people. Mr. Allison P. Tarlue, an indigenous Liberian from the countryside, headed the Metropolitan Division. His encounters while clerking for a racist white merchant in Monrovia led him to Garveyism prior to Harding's arrival to West Africa. Tarlue was critical to recruiting young, working-class indigenous Liberians into the division. As in Chicago and other cities around the world where the UNIA remained active, the Metropolitan Division regularly staged parades and held mass meetings. The local also operated a cafeteria and health clinic in the Liberian capital, underscoring the UNIA's concern for the survival and well-being of African people. Outside of Monrovia, Harding in the summer of 1966 established divisions across Liberia and in Abidjan, Ivory Coast, as well as a short-lived commercial farm in the Liberian countryside.[50]

By the end of 1966, Harding was optimistic about the UNIA's future in Liberia and Africa. This sentiment was evident in his December 1966 letter to UNIA officials and members across the continent. He noted that several African nations had gained their independence from European colonial rulers in recent years. However, political independence did not bring full freedom and economic autonomy to African people. He wrote: "Exploitation of human and material resources, of Africa continues, inter-racial deceit and chicanery lashes the black man wherever he may dwell." Despite these challenges, he was convinced that forces committed to African liberation were gathering. Emphasizing that "the second battle for Africa has begun," he argued that the UNIA and Garveyism would play a pivotal role in restoring the "ancient glory of this great land." In the coming years, Harding attempted to put these words into action.[51]

The Marcus Garvey Memorial Institute
and Sojourning across Africa

Harding's establishment of the Marcus Garvey Memorial Institute (MGMI) in the Liberian capital represented the most significant accomplishment of the Africa Project in building a grassroots movement committed to uplifting ordinary African people. Founded in 1966 by Harding, the MGMI was an independent elementary and secondary school run by the UNIA. At the time, the MGMI was the only school in the world operated by the UNIA. Harding was the school's principal. Located in a three-story modern building in a busy, commercial section of Monrovia, the MGMI enrolled more than five hundred students from seven African countries per year by the early 1970s. Children, adolescents, adults, and soldiers took courses at the school. Most students worked full-time. Given these realities, the MGMI offered night classes to accommodate its students' busy schedules. The MGMI employed professional teachers who possessed or were completing their college degree. Although the Liberian government provided some funds, the bulk of the school's revenue came from student tuition and contributions from the UNIA's parent body in the United States.[52]

The MGMI built a grassroots Garvey movement that disseminated Pan-Africanism to the urban masses of Monrovia. Students embraced the school's mission and respected Harding. Lauding the UNIA high commissioner of Africa for bringing "a great change in the lives of many Liberians, especially the common man," one student wrote, "the Garvey Memorial Institute is not just a mere school but it is a center for brotherhood, uniting young men and women both spiritually and socially. . . . [T]hey are brought up to date with the progress of the race and the problem confronting black people everywhere around the world."[53] He was right. The MGMI provided a quality and affordable education in a nation where most people did not go to school. It cultivated the values of Pan-Africanism, self-determination, and community in its students. The school's graduation ceremonies occurred in a church sanctuary adorned with the red, black, and green tricolor African liberation flag conceived by Garvey in 1920, and was filled with proud students dressed in white caps and gowns.[54] Most students did not join the UNIA. For Harding, instilling the principles of Garveyism among young people was far more important than building a partisan organization.[55]

Looking beyond Liberia, Harding traveled across Africa to advance the Garveyite cause and to build the UNIA. In 1967 he received an invitation from Boubacar Diallo Telli, a Guinean diplomat and co-founder of the OAU, to discuss the UNIA and its role in African contemporary affairs at the OAU headquarters. Telli arranged meetings of Harding with President Joseph Mobutu of the Democratic Republic of Congo (DRC) and Kenyan president Jomo Kenyatta in Kinshasa and Nairobi, respectively. Mobutu and Kenyatta received Harding like a visiting head of state. Both African presidents shared their admiration for Garvey with Harding and welcomed the formation of UNIA divisions in their respective nation. Harding also journeyed to Addis Ababa, Ethiopia, where he addressed a one-day OAU conference on the UNIA and its relation to African decolonization. Representatives from fourteen states attended the gathering. They agreed to support the UNIA program for African redemption.[56]

Like most previous UNIA-led efforts in West Africa, Harding's attempts to build the Garvey movement in the DRC and Kenya, as well as to shape OAU policy, were never realized. The UNIA apparently never established permanent divisions in the DRC or Kenya, and little sustained action seems to have come out of the OAU conference on the UNIA. The long-standing organizational weakness of the UNIA, together with the lack of resources and ideological divisions among African nations, helps explain these results. Harding never again traveled across the continent. He would focus his efforts in liberating Africa from Liberia.[57]

The Movement for Justice in Africa

Although he was unable to revitalize the UNIA at the organizational level across the continent, the MGMI through Harding's leadership emerged as a crucial site for disseminating the principles of Garveyism to a new generation of African militants and for building mass opposition to the Liberian government during the most radical moment in African decolonization. This work was most evident in Harding's collaborations with the Movement for Justice in Africa (MOJA). Togba-Nah Tipoteh, a young radical professor who earned his PhD in economics at the University of Nebraska and who taught at the University of Liberia, a hotbed of militancy, formed MOJA in 1973. Initially, the group was composed mostly of University of Liberia students committed to supporting African liberation in the Portuguese colonies of Guinea-Bissau, Angola, and Mozambique, as well as to ending white-minority rule in South Africa and Rhodesia (Zimbabwe). By the late 1970s, MOJA developed a working-class base, advanced revolutionary nationalism, and called for democracy in Liberia. The group eventually established chapters across West Africa, including Gambia and Ghana. Given its politics, MOJA emerged as one of the main opposition groups to the Tolbert administration.[58]

Harding was critical to MOJA's success. The group regularly held organizational and public meetings at the MGMI. The Chicago Garveyite often attended MOJA meetings, but he never joined the group. He was not interested in participating in local partisan politics. His primary focus was to uplift ordinary Liberians. Still, Harding enjoyed working with and mentoring young people. He befriended Amos Sawyer, who became the executive of MOJA in the late 1970s and by the end of the decade he had become the leading spokesperson of mass opposition in Monrovia to the Tolbert administration. In 1979 he ran for mayor of Monrovia. Fearing his militancy and grassroots support, the Tolbert administration canceled the election. In the following decades, Sawyer remained a major political leader in Liberia, serving as president of the Interim Government of National Unity from 1990 through 1994.[59]

Sawyer's political awakening illustrates the importance of the diasporic Midwest in cultivating African radicalism during the Black Power era. Sawyer was born in 1945 in Greenville, a small coastal town located 150 miles from Monrovia. His family hailed from the continent and the diaspora. He graduated with a bachelor's degree from the University of Liberia in 1966. As a college student, the young Liberian had no plans of becoming a full-time militant. His life changed when he came to the United States in the late 1960s and studied political science at Northwestern University in Evanston, Illinois, outside of Chicago. It was as a graduate student at Northwestern that he was first introduced to Garveyism and learned about Harding's work in Monrovia. Peers invited him to a UNIA meeting in Chicago. This meeting changed his life. At this gathering, veteran Garveyites informed Sawyer about Harding, and encouraged the young Liberian to contact the UNIA high commissioner of Africa when he returned home. Sawyer followed their advice.[60]

After returning home, Sawyer accepted a teaching job at the University of Liberia and contacted Harding. They became close. Looking back, Sawyer remembered Harding as a "very wonderful man" who dedicated his life to the uplift of common people and African liberation. Harding practiced what he preached. He lived a spartan life. Although Sawyer did not join the UNIA, Harding played an important role in nurturing his Pan-African outlook. For Sawyer and other young African radicals, Harding represented a connection to Garvey and an earlier generation of black militants. Impressed with the MGMI, Sawyer and several MOJA members taught at the school for free. In 1978 Sawyer instructed future military coup leader Samuel K. Doe, who at the time was in his late twenties and was an enlisted army soldier. Doe apparently joined neither MOJA nor the UNIA, and he did not publicly credit the MGMI for shaping his politics after he came to power. But it seems possible that his education at the MGMI played a role in prompting his call for grassroots democracy and Pan-Africanism during the early years of his rule.[61]

Harding's work with MOJA highlights the ways the UNIA high commissioner of Africa from Chicago navigated the growing political crisis in the West African republic. The Tolbert administration grew increasingly uneasy with MOJA and the UNIA as mass opposition mounted. Liberian authorities surveilled the MGMI, MOJA, and the Metropolitan Division.[62] Harding suspected that the Garvey movement in Monrovia was being watched by the police and that the government placed informants within the UNIA. The Metropolitan Division developed a secret code to evade government surveillance.[63] Authorities never arrested Harding or Sawyer, but the government jailed some MOJA activists who taught at the MGMI following violent antigovernment protests in Monrovia in 1979 that came to be known as the "Rice Riot."[64] Harding's fear of government repression might explain his decision not to formally join MOJA or openly participate in partisan politics. He surely knew that criticizing the Liberian government might have led to his deportation or imprisonment. What is for sure is that Harding's work helped to foment opposition against the Tolbert government.

In addition to helping to build opposition to the Tolbert administration, the Garvey movement in Monrovia under Harding's leadership defied the Liberian government through sending troops and material support to armed struggles against Portuguese colonialism in nearby Guinea-Bissau and Mozambique in southern Africa. For African nationalists everywhere, armed struggle against Portuguese colonialism symbolized the determination of Africans to break the shackles of the last remaining European colonial empire on the continent. In 1970 the Metropolitan Division formed a "battalion" of the Universal African Legions. The UAL was independent of the Liberian military. In 1972 the Liberian UAL lost two soldiers in action against Portuguese forces in Mozambique. These two fallen soldiers became heroes both to Harding and to young militants in Monrovia.[65] The UAL's decision to deploy troops to Mozambique contrasted with the policy of the Liberian government, which did not send soldiers to Guinea-Bissau or Mozambique. In this regard, Liberian policy did not significantly differ from U.S. foreign policy toward Africa, which supplied Portugal with arms used against African insurgents. The Liberian government did not jail Harding or UAL soldiers for their activities in support of African liberation movements. Given mass support in Monrovia for armed liberation struggles across the continent and the growing unpopularity of the Tolbert administration, Liberian rulers seem to have tolerated the Garvey movement's military actions in Guinea-Bissau, Angola, and Mozambique. At the same time, these activities probably contributed to growing state surveillance of Harding, the UNIA, and MOJA.[66]

What is certain is that Harding's close proximity to radical pan-African militants in Monrovia positioned his politics to the left of his predecessor James Stewart, as well as to the left of some UNIA officials in the United States and

Liberian rulers. Upon his arrival to Liberia, Harding embraced a civilizationist stance. In an October 1966 letter to UNIA president-general Thomas Harvey, Harding lamented that Liberian workers apparently lacked "discipline" and "badly" needed outside supervision from repatriated diasporan blacks.[67] In the coming years he increasingly put his faith in young Africans and revolutionary nationalist movements for liberating the continent. This was evident in his willingness to collaborate with MOJA and his strong support for radical African nationalists such as Amílcar Cabral, the brilliant Third World Marxist leader of the Partido Africano da Independência da Guiné e Cabo Verde (African Party for the Independence of Guinea and Cape Verde). The assassination in January 1973 of Cabral in Conkary, Guinea, at the hands of black agents working for Portugal infuriated Harding.[68] In a report to Harvey, Harding called Cabral's assassination a "foul deed," placing the ultimate blame for his death on Portugal and the United States.[69] Harding neither became a Marxist nor disavowed emigration, but unlike Stewart, he never promoted anticommunism. Plus, there is no record of correspondence between Harding and white supremacists in the United States, whereas Harvey and other U.S.-based UNIA officials continued to collaborate with white supremacists who believed colonization was in the best interests of blacks and whites.[70] The politics of the UNIA high commissioner of Africa were more in line with prevailing political currents among militant African liberation movements than with Stewart, who had emigrated to Africa immediately after World War II and Liberian authorities. Above all, Harding's location on the continent and collaborations with militants during the most radical phase of African decolonization reveal how he—unlike Garvey and Stewart—was able to build a mass opposition movement that provided concrete support for African independence through armed struggle.

Still, Harding shared much in common with his predecessors, namely, their masculinist understanding of African liberation. In one report he wrote: "For as long as Black Men Fight for Freedom in Angola, Mozambique, Rhodesia, and the Union of South Africa, our work is not done."[71] His statement reflected the invisibility of women in the formal leadership of the Monrovia UNIA. While men held the reins of power within the organization, women actively participated in the Monrovia UNIA. They performed community service in the Black Cross Nurses, the UNIA auxiliary that carried out similar duties as the Red Cross. Black Cross Nurses fed the poor and provided much needed health services in West Point, Monrovia's large and sprawling slum. Women enrolled in the MGMI and gained visibility in MOJA, most notably Philomena Bloh Sayeh, who later became the director-general of the Center for National Documents and Records Agency in Monrovia.[72] In the United States, Garveyite women played a vital role in sustaining the Africa Project. Jean Slappy, a Philadelphia-based Garveyite and daughter of Thomas Harvey, chaired the African Redemption Committee, the UNIA body charged with supporting the Africa Project. Elinor White, a longtime Chicago UNIA official, worked with Slappy and corresponded with Harding's staff in Monrovia.[73] While men dominated the formal leadership of the Monrovia UNIA, women on both sides of the Atlantic were crucial to the Africa Project.

Garveyites from the diasporic Midwest played an important role in supporting Harding's transnational activism in Liberia. The UNIA's membership by the 1970s had significantly declined globally, including in the U.S. industrial heartland. Still, UNIA divisions in Detroit, Cleveland, and Chicago, composed largely of well-paid industrial workers, remained some of the most active and influential locals in the worldwide Garvey movement. The enduring significance of the Midwest to the transnational UNIA was apparent in the region's support for Harding's work in Liberia. The Detroit UNIA, headed by longtime Garveyite and retired autoworker Charles Zampty, was critical to bankrolling the cash-strapped MGMI. In fact, Zampty complained to Thomas Harvey that the Detroit UNIA disproportionately bore the responsibility of financing Harding's work in Liberia.[74] Veteran Garveyites Charles James and Elinor White assisted in fund-raising in midwestern divisions for the Africa Project.[75] In 1973 James toured West Africa and met with Harding during his stay in Liberia.[76] The U.S. heartland of midwestern Garveyites also offered non-financial aid to the Africa Project. Cleveland Garveyites sent more than five hundred medical items to Harding, which were then shipped to Guinea-Bissau.[77] From Monrovia, Harding kept up with news about his Garveyite colleagues in Chicago.[78]

If Harvey influenced young African militants, then his encounters on the continent also affected the Garvey movement in the diaspora. U.S.-based UNIA officials sent reports about Harding's work in Liberia to divisions across the United States, Canada, and the Caribbean. Harding occasionally returned to the United States, where he spoke at UNIA events about his work on the continent. In September 1966 he spoke at a UNIA mass meeting in Brooklyn. Members of the Montreal UNIA traveled down from Canada to hear him. Harding also addressed a UNIA-sponsored event in Philadelphia. He surely helped them to gain fresh insight into the global dimensions of African liberation from a Garveyite who was working on the front lines of this global struggle. Living in Liberia transformed his life. While he apparently never learned indigenous languages, he came to regard Africa as his home. He often wore African clothes and interacted comfortably with local people. Indeed, Harding's work in Liberia illustrates the impact of continental Africans on the diaspora.[79]

Harding's untimely death (he was in his late fifties) in 1978 due to a fall he sustained in Monrovia, together with the 1980 coup in Liberia, ended the UNIA's Africa Project. Given his love for Africa, Harding was buried in Monrovia. Garveyites in Liberia and the United States mourned his loss. In Monrovia, his comrades staged an elaborate memorial for him.[80] His passing marked the end of sustained UNIA activity in Africa. Harding was unsuccessful in revitalizing the organization globally, and he espoused a patriarchal politics. However, the Africa Project touched the lives of thousands of indigenous working people in Monrovia, affected national Liberian politics, and had an impact on anticolonial struggles across the continent. His experiences as a community activist and UNIA leader in Chicago prepared the ground for his work in West Africa. Garveyites from the industrial American heartland were critical to sustaining Harding's work, underscoring the connections between the diasporic Midwest and West Africa.

Conclusion

The encounters of Clarence Harding in Liberia constitute a remarkable and fascinating story. Coming of age in the American heartland and in a Garveyite family, he took the lessons he had learned as a UNIA leader and community organizer in Chicago with him to Liberia in 1966. In Monrovia he led the Africa Project, the most successful UNIA initiative on the continent following Garvey's passing. From the moment he arrived in Liberia until his death in 1978, Harding built a vibrant oppositional grassroots movement in Monrovia composed largely of working indigenous people and college-educated militants committed to the Garveyite principles of race pride, Pan-Africanism, and self-determination. Shrewd and dedicated, he skillfully navigated the complicated and growing political crisis of a postcolonial African state. Although his work ultimately failed to resuscitate the transnational UNIA, Harding's efforts had a direct impact on Liberian life and politics, as well as liberation struggles across the continent. The Midwest proved to be a key base of support for his transnational work on the continent. Living and agitating in West Africa transformed his life. He shared lessons that he learned in Africa with his colleagues in the United States.

Harding's life and transnational activism reveal the broader importance of the diasporic Midwest to the multidirectional flow of people, politics, and ideas across the twentieth-century African world. Centering the industrial Midwest provides a lens for appreciating the diverse geographic locales where black people forged transnational political linkages in less-studied regions of the African world. Harding's activism in West Africa requires African Americanists and diaspora scholars to appreciate the global impact of midwestern industrial cities such as Chicago, Cleveland, and Detroit in shaping the history of the black world through Garveyism. For the study of West Africa, Harding's activism highlights the resonance of Garveyism in the region into the period of decolonization. His work in Liberia also shows how African liberation movements had an impact on Garveyism, prompting him to dispense with the civilizationist outlook his predecessors and even some of his contemporaries continued to embrace. At the same time, Harding's masculinist framings of black liberation speaks to the need for scholars to interrogate the gendered contours of Pan-Africanism.

Lastly, Harding's work in Liberia contains important lessons for realizing the full freedom of the African-descended everywhere in our contemporary moment. The African world remains in crisis. Resurgent white supremacy, globalization, mass incarceration, HIV/AIDS, climate change, and growing intra-racial tensions threaten the very survival of African-descended people. Harding surely could not have envisioned that the African-descended today would face such an existential crisis in light of the strides toward freedom black people globally made during this Chicago-born Garveyite's lifetime. The UNIA and the Garveyism movement contained their limitations and paradoxes. However, the Garvey movement also produced activists such as Rev. Clarence W. Harding who were passionately committed to liberating African people everywhere. Harding took the principles of Marcus Garvey seriously, adapting them to fit a changing a world and to build a mass movement for African liberation. Above all, everyday African-descended men, women, and children from Chicago to Monrovia and beyond inspired him. What a remarkable legacy to follow.

Notes

1. The original name of the organization was the Universal Negro Improvement and Conservation and African Communities (Imperial) League. However, the group later came to be known as the Universal Negro Improvement Association–African Communities League and then the Universal Negro Improvement Association–African Communities League (August 1929) of the World. For consistency, I will refer to the organization as the UNIA. T. Martin, *Race First*, 6, 18.

2. In this chapter I use the term "Pan-Africanism" to describe organizations and movements such as the UNIA that expressly committed themselves to forging global unity among African-descended people and for fighting for their freedom. I use the term "pan-Africanism" to describe a range of movements and beliefs that frame African descendants on the continent and in the diaspora as one people who share a common history and destiny, as well as a commitment to liberation and human dignity. For more discussion see Shepperson, "Pan-Africanism and 'Pan-Africanism.'"

3. The exact size of the UNIA's membership is difficult to quantify. It seems likely that the organization inflated the size of its membership. T. Martin, *Race First*, 13–16.

4. Issa, "The Universal Negro Improvement Association"; McDuffie, "'A New Day Has Dawned,'" 75–76, 97–103.

5. R. A. Hill, *Marcus Garvey and Universal Negro Improvement Association Papers* [hereafter *MGP*], 2:19–20; "Annual Inspection and Review—August 1977," photo, box 19, folder 27, and Allison P. Tarlue (Monrovia) to Thomas W. Hardy [hereafter TWH], July 3, 1966, box 12, folder 3, both in Universal Negro Improvement Association Records, Stuart A. Rose Manuscript Rare Book and Archives Library, Emory University, Atlanta, Georgia [hereafter UNIA Records Rose Library]; Amos Sawyer, interview with author, January 11, 2016, Monrovia, Liberia.

6. TWH form letter, September 18, 1967, box 12, folder 3, UNIA Records Rose Library.

7. Ibid.; Clarence W. Harding [hereafter CWH] to TWH, May 14, 1966, box 12, folder 2, UNIA Records Rose Library.

8. Amos Sawyer, interview with author, January 11, 2016; McDuffie, "'A New Day Has Dawned,'" 75–76, 97–103.

9. McDuffie, "'A New Day Has Dawned,'" 76–77.

10. Drake and Cayton, *Black Metropolis*; R. Bush, *We Are Not What We Seem*, 88–93; Baldwin, *Chicago's New Negroes*.

11. Bates, *Making of Black Detroit*.

12. Hine and McClusky, *Black Chicago Renaissance*; Phillips, *AlabamaNorth*, 98–126, 161–89.

13. N. P. Singh, *Black Is a Country*.

14. Stein, *World of Marcus Garvey*, 229.

15. McDuffie, "'A New Day Has Dawned,'" 76–78.

16. To date, Kenneth Jolly's insightful biography of UNIA leader William L. Sherrill of Detroit is the only monograph on midwestern Garveyism. However, the book focuses on Sherrill and Detroit, overlooking a community of Garveyites across the heartland who were actively involved in forging transnational linkages with Africa from the 1920s through the 1970s. Jolly, *"By Our Own Strength."*

17. Ewing, *Age of Garvey*; Vinson, *Americans Are Coming*; *MGP*, vol. 10.

18. Lauck, *Lost Region*, 1–12.

19. Rolinson, *Grassroots Garveyism*; Ewing, *Age of Garvey*.

20. Ewing, *Age of Garvey*, 6, 7.

21. For discussions of women and gender in the UNIA, see Taylor, *Veiled Garvey*; Blain, "'We Want to Set the World on Fire'"; Leeds, "Toward the 'Higher Type of Womanhood'"; N. Duncan, "Efficient Womanhood"; and Bair, "True Women, Real Men."

22. Adeleke, *UnAfrican Americans*.

23. McDuffie, "Garveyism in Cleveland."

24. United States Census 1920: https://familysearch.org/ark:/61903/1:1:MDM7-NVT; United States Census 1930: https://familysearch.org/search/collection/results?count=20&query=%2Bgivenname%3AClarence~%20%2Bsurname%3AHarding~%20%2Bresidence_place%3AChicago~%20%2Bgender%3AM%20%2Brace%3ABlack&collection_id=1810731 (both accessed April 11, 2016); Reed, *Black Chicago's First Century*.

25. Dolinar, *The Negro in Illinois*, xxx, 2–5.

26. Ibid., 14–143; Reed, *Black Chicago's First Century*, 9, 10, 22; McDuffie, "Chicago, Garveyism."

27. Tuttle, *Race Riot*, 242.

28. *MGP*, 3:164.

29. *Negro World*, October 24, 1925, 6, and June 20, 1925; McDuffie, "Chicago, Garveyism"; McDuffie, "Garveyism in Cleveland."

30. McDuffie, "Diasporic Journeys of Louise Little."

31. Blain, "'Confraternity among All Darker Races.'"

32. Gellman, *Death Blow to Jim Crow*.

33. Mayor's Inter-racial Committee, *Negro in Detroit*, section XI, page 7; Smith-Irvin, *Footsoldiers*, 36–55, 64–72; M. N. Duncan, *Survey of Cincinnati's Black Press*, 75; McDuffie, "'A New Day Has Dawned,'" 80; McDuffie, "Chicago, Garveyism," 134, 140.

34. *Atlanta Daily Worker*, February 26, 1947; *Chicago Defender*, September 21, 1965; Amos Sawyer, telephone conversation with author, November 22, 2014; McDuffie, "'A New Day Has Dawned,'" 97–98.

35. Clegg, *Price of Liberty*; J. Campbell, *Middle Passages*; Sundiata, *Brothers and Strangers*, 23–29; Blyden, *Christianity, Islam, and the Negro Race*; Moses, *Alexander Crummell*.

36. Sundiata, *Brothers and Strangers*, 48–96; J. Campbell, *Middle Passages*, 226–67.

37. *MGP*, 10:152–54, 176–78; Sundiata, *Brothers and Strangers*, 31–41.

38. The U.S. government and Firestone Rubber Company, which established a massive plantation in the country in 1926, pressured Liberian officials to break ties with the UNIA. *MGP*, 10:152–54, 176–78; Sundiata, *Brothers and Strangers*, 15–47; C. B. James, *Garvey*, 177–291.

39. Fitzgerald, "'We Have Found a Moses'"; Hedlin, "Earnest Cox and Colonization." Garvey's collaborations with Bilbo and Cox were not the first time Garvey had worked with white supremacists. During the early 1920s he met with the imperial wizard of the Ku Klux Klan. T. Martin, *Race First*, 344–58.

40. Roberta Stewart Amos, telephone conversation with author, January 25, 2013.

41. Minutes of the Eleventh International Convention of the UNIA, Gbandela, Liberia, West Afica, October 1–21, 1950, Sara R. Isaac Collection, box 21, folder 1, Charles

L. Blockson Collection, Temple University, Philadelphia, Pennsylvania; Conference attendees of the 1954 gathering included C. M. Tolbert of Cleveland, James Bennett of Youngstown, Lillie Mae Gibson, the UNIA's international organizer, and Margaret Davis of Cleveland, who emigrated to Liberia with Stewart's family and served as the president-general's loyal secretary until his death. Minutes of the Twelfth International Convention of the UNIA, Gbandela, Liberia, 1954, box 15, folder 56, UNIA Records Rose Library; Minutes of Thirteenth International Convention of the UNIA, Gbandela, Liberia, August 1958, Wahab Collection, box 4, folder 6, Charles H. Wright Museum of African American History, Detroit, Michigan; Roberta Stewart Amos, telephone conversation with author, February 11, 2014.

42. McDuffie, "Garveyism in Cleveland"; McDuffie, "'A New Day Has Dawned,'" 85–92.

43. Stewart was hardly the only prominent Garveyite who collaborated with white supremacists during the post–World War II years. Amy Jacques Garvey, who began corresponding with Earnest Sevier Cox in the 1920s, continued to exchange warm letters until his death in 1964. Amy Jacques Garvey to Earnest Sevier Cox, December 14, 1925, and December 17, 1964, box 2, folder 6, and box 15, folder 5, Earnest Sevier Cox Papers, David M. Rubenstein Rare Book and Manuscript Library, Duke University, Durham, North Carolina; McDuffie, "'A New Day Has Dawned,'" 91.

44. In 1951 the UNIA split into two rival organizations, both of which claimed be the legitimate UNIA. Critics of Stewart, who had organized the Rehabilitating Committee in 1943, had long accused him of theft and of abandoning the principles of Marcus Garvey. At a conference of the Rehabilitating Committee in Detroit in August and September 1951, the group renounced Stewart as a thief and dictator, declared his office "null and void," and announced itself as the "legitimate" UNIA. The group elected Thomas Harvey as its new president-general. Detroit served as the temporary headquarters of this UNIA faction. In 1953 the group elected William L. Sherrill of Detroit, a veteran Garveyite, as its president-general and moved the headquarters to Philadelphia. "A Proclamation by the Universal Negro Improvement Association 1929 of the World," n.d. [ca. November 1951], box 15, folder 53, UNIA Records Rose Library; Jolly, *By Our Own Strength*, 187–202.

45. TWH, "UNIA Launches Five Point African Program," box 12, folder 2, UNIA Records Rose Library.

46. CWH to TWH, May 14, 1966, box 12, folder 2, UNIA Records Rose Library; McDuffie, "'A New Day Has Dawned,'" 97–98.

47. Birmingham, *Decolonization of Africa*.

48. D. E. Dunn, *Liberia and the United States*, 6–7, 87–137; Sirleaf, *This Child Will Be Great*, 1–6.

49. The resurgence of interest in Garveyism was due in no small part to the work of Amy Ashwood Garvey and Amy Jacques Garvey, Garvey's first and second wives, respectively, who were leading Pan-African thinkers in their own right. See Jacques Garvey, *Garvey and Garveyism*; T. Martin, *Amy Ashwood Garvey*; Vincent, *Black Power*; and McDuffie, "'A New Day Has Dawned,'" 98.

50. CWH to TWH, May 14, 1966, and Benny J. Whitefield to Elinor White, June 24, 1966, both in box 12, folder 2, UNIA Records Rose Library.

51. CWH to the Presidents, Officers and Members of all West African Divisions of the UNIA, December 1966, and CWH to TWH, December 8, 1966, both in box 12, folder 2, UNIA Records Rose Library.

52. Isaac Mialo to TWH, March 15, 1971, box 12, folder 7, and CWH to John Vincent, September 27. 1972, box 12, folder 8, both in UNIA Records Rose Library; Amos Sawyer, e-mail to author, November 14, 2014.

53. David K. Franklin, "History of Marcus Garvey Memorial Institute," March 1972, box 19, folder 410, Dabu Gizenga Collection on Kwame Nkrumah, Moorland Spingarn Research Center, Howard University, Washington, DC.

54. Graduating Class of 1978, MGMI, Monrovia (photograph), box 19, folder 28, UNIA Records Rose Library; Amos Sawyer interview with author, January 11, 2016.

55. Amos Sawyer, telephone conversation with author, November 24, 2014; McDuffie, "'A New Day Has Dawned,'" 99.

56. CWH to TWH, September 25, 1967, and CWH to Arnold L. Crawford, September 27, 1967, both in box 12, folder 3, UNIA Records Rose Library.

57. De Witte, *Assassination of Lumumba*.

58. Togba-Nah Tipoteh, interview with author, January 11, 2016; "Movement for Justice in Africa (MOJA)," in D. E. Dunn, Beyan, and Burrowes, *Historical Dictionary of Liberia*, 237–38; D. E. Dunn, *Liberia and the United States,* 92; Amos Sawyer, e-mail to author, November 15, 2014.

59. Amos Sawyer, interview with author, January 11, 2016; "Sawyer, Amos Claudius," in D. E. Dunn et al., *Historical Dictionary of Liberia*, 293.

60. Amos Sawyer, interview with author, January 11, 2016; "Sawyer, Amos Claudius," in D. E. Dunn et al., *Historical Dictionary of Liberia*, 293.

61. Amos Sawyer, e-mail to author, November 15, 2014; John Stewart and Emmanuel Moses, interview with author, January 13, 2014, Monrovia, Liberia.

62. John Stewart and Emmanuel Moses, interview with author, January 13, 2014; "Secret Message Codes," box 18, folder 28, UNIA Records Rose Library.

63. Secret Message Codes, box 18, folder 28, UNIA Records Rose Library; Amos Sawyer, interview with author, January 11, 2016.

64. Sirleaf, *This Child Will Be Great*, 86–90; John Stewart and Emmanuel Moses, interview with author, January 13, 2014.

65. It is uncertain how UAL fighters traveled to southern Africa. They apparently traveled there independently of the Liberian government. Roberta Stewart Amos, telephone conversation with author, January 25, 2013; John Stewart, telephone conversation with author, October 21, 2014; CWH to Arnold J. Crawford, April 12, 1968, box 12, folder 4, and CWH to John Vincent, September 27, 1972, box 12, folder 8, both in UNIA Records Rose Library.

66. Roberta Stewart Amos, telephone conversation with author, January 25, 2013; John Stewart, telephone conversation with author, October 21, 2014.

67. CWH to TWH, October 23, 1966, box 12, folder 2, UNIA Records Rose Library.

68. Carlos Pinto Santos, "Amilcar Cabral: Freedom Fighter," trans. John D. Godinho, https://libyadiary.wordpress.com/2011/01/01/amilcar-cabral-freedom-fighter (accessed July 24, 2018).

69. CWH to TWH, February 5, 1973, box 12, folder9, UNIA Records Rose Library.

70. Charles W. Connelly Jr. to TWH, May 26, 1969, and TWH to Charles W. Connelly Jr., June 21, 1968, both in box 12, folder 5, UNIA Records Rose Library.

71. CWH, "A Special Message to All West African Divisions of the UNIA" (July 1966), box 12, folder 2, UNIA Records Rose Library.

72. Amos Sawyer, telephone conversation with author, November 24, 2014; Philomena Bloh Sayeh, interview with author, January 8, 2016, Monrovia.

73. Jean Slappy to Elinor White, Raymond Kelly, Solomon Fitzhue, and Oquine Jackson, October 14, 1966, and Benny J. Whitefield to Elinor White, June 24, 1966, both in box 12, folder 2, UNIA Records Rose Library.

74. J. Charles Zampty to TWH, May 5, 1970, and TWH to CWH, November 30, 1968, both in box 12, folder 8, UNIA Records Rose Library, box 12, folder 8.

75. Thomas W. Harvey to Charles L. James, September 6, 1965, and Thomas W. Harvey to Elinor White-Neely, September 6, 1965, both in box 12, folder 1, UNIA Records, Rose Library.

76. TWH to CWH, October 24, 1973, and CWH to TWH, November 14, 1973, both in box 12, folder 9.

77. CWH to TWH, November 14, 1973, box 12, folder 9, UNIA Records Rose Library.

78. CWH to TWH, January 23, 1968, box 12, folder 4, UNIA Records Rose Library.

79. Alma Golden form letter to Brooklyn UNIA membership, August 8, 1966, Alma Golden, Secretary of Brooklyn UNIA, to her co-workers, September 28, 1966, TWH to Agatha Holland, UNIA Commissioner for Jamaica, September 17, 1966, and TWH, "Parent Body Bulletin" (October 1966), all in box 12, folder 2, UNIA Records Rose Library; E. J. Tucker (Montreal) to TWH, March 7, 1968, box 12, folder 3, UNIA Records Rose Library.

80. Slappy to Clarence Harding Sr., July 6, 1980, box 13, folder 10, UNIA Records Rose Library; John Stewart and Emmanuel Moses, interview with author, January 13, 2014; Amos Sawyer, interview with author, January 11, 2016.

4

Marcus M. Garvey and Joseph A. Craigen

Collaborations and Conflicts

RONALD J. STEPHENS

This essay is a local (and micro-) study of global Garveyism with a focus on what Erik S. McDuffie calls the "diasporic Midwest."[1] It explores the clash between global Garveyism and local Garveyism by investigating the practice of Garveyism on the ground. My specific focus is on Joseph Alexander Craigen, the executive secretary of the Detroit chapter of the Universal Negro Improvement Association and African Communities League (UNIA-ACL) and a leading UNIA official. Craigen maintained a professional relationship with Marcus Garvey from 1919 to 1931 but was sometimes in disagreement with Garvey's top-down leadership and management style. McDuffie's case study, which focuses on the political activities of Clarence Harding in the black diaspora of the Midwest, is instructive because it illuminates the ways in which Garveyism served as "a powerful vehicle for black urban midwesterners" such as the Caribbean-born Craigen "to forge transnational linkages with peoples of African descent everywhere."[2] It also enables scholars to better understand how the practical operation of the UNIA—despite Garvey's efforts to establish a clear chain of command—encouraged the creation of local centers of power. Craigen was able to establish influence as a local division leader because of the organizational tools offered to him by the UNIA. But this influence also came to be viewed as a threat by Garvey and led to Craigen's split with the president-general during the Sixth International Convention of the Universal Negro Improvement Association of the World, in 1929.

The essay has three objectives. First, it explores Garvey's rise to power as a global leader, his influence in Michigan, and his professional relationship with highly ranked leaders of the Detroit division. Second, it examines Craigen's rise to power within the ranks of the Detroit division as well as through his personal relationship and professional association with Garvey as high commissioner of five midwestern states and as a ranking member of Garvey's Committee of Presidents. The Detroit division of the UNIA was one of the largest divisions in the nation, second only to headquarters in Harlem, New York. Third, it examines Craigen's split with Garvey, which resulted from a series of pointed arguments, conflicts, disagreements, and bad judgments that materialized during the disastrous Sixth International Convention. The essay concludes by following Craigen's career beyond his formal association with the UNIA, demonstrating the manner in which the mass movement was sustained in the United States during the 1920s and continued to reverberate not only within the parameters of the UNIA itself but in the activities of talented men and women who gained a political education in the organization and left their mark in nationalist, pan-African, civil rights, professional, political, and labor organizations in the decades that followed.

The UNIA in Michigan

Garvey's UNIA and its "philosophy of race first, self-reliance, and nationhood captured the imagination of the black world after he moved headquarters from Jamaica to Harlem in 1918."[3] Garvey had a vision, and he persuaded the masses that he could free them. Much attention has been devoted to the ways in which he failed, but as Garvey scholars Randall K. Burkett, Tony Martin, and J. A. Rogers have each observed, the ways in which Garvey succeeded, both domestically and globally, are far more fascinating. In a candid 1915 discussion about black rights in Jamaica, published in the *Jamaican Times*, Garvey declared his intention to rescue the race.[4] A decade later he was hailed an international hero who had mobilized black men and women throughout the world, and whose leadership had lifted his people.

By 1919 the UNIA had a large following in Michigan, particularly in Detroit, which was home to about 4,000 black citizens. The city experienced a period of growth from 1910 to 1930, facilitated by World War I, during which the black population rose to more than 120,000. Employers needed black workers to fill labor jobs, and this led many African Americans in the South to relocate to Detroit, as they were seeking employment during the first wave of what became known as the Great Migration. During this period, middle-class leaders of the NAACP and the Urban League endeavored to help with the recent migrants. Hundreds of black workers found employment in Henry Ford's factories with the assistance of Rev. Robert Louis Bradby of Second Baptist Church of Detroit, who was recognized as the dean of African American pastors during the period and also president of Detroit's branch of the NAACP. He served as "the guiding hand in helping newcomers get adjusted to city life and to see that they were placed in jobs."[5] The migration of thousands of African Americans to the city also engendered growing racial divisions between whites and blacks. In 1925, for example, the State of Michigan charged Ossian Sweet, a black physician, with murder after he and others used a shotgun to kill a white man who was part of a mob trying to force Sweet and his family to leave their newly purchased house, which was centrally located in a primarily segregated white neighborhood.[6]

Detroit, as Judith Stein notes, "with its impoverished public and political life and its economic opportunities, advertised business solutions to all problems."[7] Most Garveyites, like most of the city's African Americans at the time, eschewed active involvement in Detroit politics, choosing instead to invest their energy in the UNIA.[8] The Detroit division of the UNIA did not officially organize until after the First International Convention of the Negro Peoples of the World, which convened in Harlem from August 1 to August 31, 1920. Among the delegates, attending this convention was Rev. A. D. Williams, who returned to Detroit ready to organize. John Charles Zampty recalled how Williams returned to the city carrying "a red, Black, and green flag," patrolling the streets of Detroit with others to organize the Detroit division.[9]

Because of the Detroit division's rapid growth, Garvey, during his first visit to the city, saw it as a critical local node that would be important to the organization's goals. As the chapter grew from its founding in 1920, Zampty, Leonard Smith, and later Joseph Craigen—each a central figure within the Detroit division—became involved in the work of the parent body in New York and became intimately connected to Garvey. Zampty, who was born in Belmont, Port-of-Spain, Trinidad, was Garvey's traveling secretary, auditor general of the UNIA, and at one point executive secretary of the Detroit division. The two men had first met "after a series of jobs that took [Zampty] from Trinidad to Nigeria, West Africa," to Colón, Panama in 1912. Garvey built connections through Zampty during his 1916 visit to Detroit, making the city one of the important sites for his organizational tours to increase memberships, as he did when he returned a second time in June 1919. During each of these and other trips, Garvey sought "to meet with black leaders to raise money for the [Black Star Line]."[10] Garvey would tour Detroit on at least four other occasions. It was during his last visit, in 1925, after speaking tours in Colorado and California, that Garvey received a telegram the morning of February 5, 1925, advising him to return to New York because the U.S. Circuit Court of Appeals had upheld the mail fraud conviction.

The Detroit division of the UNIA had a large membership.[11] As Judith Stein informs us, by March 1925 the rolls had grown in numbers and influence in the city:

> The division made its political debut in 1925 when it endorsed the maverick Charles Bowles for mayor. Bowles's strength was among disaffected, native-born members of the petite bourgeoisie, the same social strata that nurtured the Klan, which also backed Bowles. The elites of Detroit, black and white, supported the incumbent, Mayor John W. Smith, who was re-elected with the ballots of most blacks who voted. Republican politics alone yielded apathy, not political alternatives. Bowles's platform of efficiency, municipal growth, economy, and law and order was no different from the elite's blueprint for good government.[12]

The division also prospered economically. As early as August 2, 1924, the Detroit division's president, Fred E. Johnson, announced at the fourth UNIA convention that the seven-thousand-member body had become a power in the city and had organized affiliated chapters in suburban areas around Detroit.[13] By 1927 the division had assets worth $50,000 (approximately $682,000 in 2014 dollars), mostly property. "The Detroit division had businesses of all types," noted Craigen. "We had laundries, restaurants, shoe shine parlors, drugstores, and we even had theaters under the auspices of the UNIA."[14] The wealthy and politically powerful Charles Coles Diggs Sr., who founded and operated Detroit's House of Diggs Funeral Home,[15] which was established in 1921 and recognized as Michigan's largest mortuary, led the Detroit division's board of trustees, which managed the division's assets.[16]

The Detroit division was extremely successful in expanding the visibility of the UNIA throughout the state of Michigan.[17] Anna Reese, recording secretary of the division, wrote in a May 22, 1927, report that "we [the Detroit division] are working to get Michigan organized for the UNIA." Leonard Smith (1927–31), president of the Detroit division and acting commissioner for Michigan, "followed up by issuing a statement on behalf of Detroit's recruitment campaign to all divisions and chapters of the UNIA in the state of Michigan, asking them to increase their membership in addition to proposing the discussion of ways and means of expanding while increasing our activities in this state." Essentially, Johnson, Zampty, Smith, and Craigen were successful in organizing the different Michigan divisions.[18]

Like urban Detroit, the small population in northern rural Yates Township in Lake County, Michigan, began to increase during the New Negro Movement era. The rural suburban all-black community of Idlewild, Michigan, like the Black Belt midwestern cities of Detroit and Chicago, had served as the venue where leading African American spokespersons could keep abreast of changes and troubles within the midwestern states and the nation to discuss issues relevant to African American life, culture, and history.[19] The fact that the Idlewild UNIA division was located in an all-black town underscored the UNIA's emphasis on race pride, economic development, nationhood, and self-reliance. Although the Garvey movement had begun to fragment and decline by the late 1920s in some areas of the country, the UNIA-ACL doctrine of race first continued to spread throughout Idlewild.

The Idlewild division was organized in 1927, two years after Garvey's last visit to Detroit. In 1925, after a failed appeal of his conviction on the charge of mail fraud, Garvey was summoned to return to New York. He left Detroit by train for New York and was immediately arrested upon his arrival. He would spend the next two years and nine months in an Atlanta federal penitentiary. Thousands of letters poured into the White House, and in response to the public pressure to release Garvey, President Calvin Coolidge transferred him to New Orleans and pardoned him on November 18. Two weeks later, on December 2, Garvey was set to sail for Jamaica aboard the steamship *Saramacca*. More than five thousand dedicated supporters wanted to see him sail off, among them Craigen and Rev. Albert Glen Taylor of the Brooklyn, New York, division. Prior to Garvey's departure, organizational responsibilities were reassigned. Under Craigen's leadership and Garvey's instructions, Taylor was appointed to serve as the president of the new Michigan division in Idlewild.[20] By representing both Detroit and the general national membership, maintaining an intimate and positive relationship with members of the Paradise Gardens subdivision in the Idlewild community, and having been designated one of Garvey's most trusted associates, Craigen was to attend to a variety of emerging domestic and international concerns in Garvey's absence.[21]

The Idlewild division was unique because it was founded the same year Garvey was deported. Craigen was secretary of the Detroit division at the time and he helped the Idlewild division to flourish during the late 1920s rather than the early 1930s. Some Idlewilders, who were attracted to Garvey's philosophy of race pride, unity, and self-reliance and were actively engaged in other Michigan divisions, claimed that Garvey toured and delivered an address in Idlewild in 1929. Interviews were conducted with several respected Idlewild residents who were children at the time; one of them claimed he saw and heard Garvey deliver a speech at the Idlewild Community Hall on Broadway Avenue, now the site of the Idlewild Historic Cultural Center. Efforts to verify these claims met with little success. This suggests Garvey would have visited the resort two years after his deportation to Jamaica from New Orleans in early fall of 1927. Typically, however, although there were many imposters roaring about, Garvey's aides were charged with making such speeches and performing other duties on his behalf. Craigen was born in a region of the Caribbean where people of African descent spoke with a similar accent, dialect, and language structure and grammar. He was also the Detroit division's general secretary and executive secretary, and it appears that he might have delivered the speech in Garvey's absence. His profile fits Garvey's mannerism, height, accent, skin complexion, and level of education. Moreover, it is very unlikely that Garvey secretly entered the country and risked being caught, arrested, and imprisoned. However, recall during Garvey's deportation that Craigen's appointment was to serve as one of the leaders to run the international organization. Joining him years later, Zampty would own and operate a small real estate company in Idlewild, and Craigen would acquire and develop property to build a cottage and the Casa Blanca Hotel.

Craigen and Garvey's Collaborations

Joseph A. Craigen was a proud professional Caribbean-born Detroiter and a dedicated Garveyite. "Joe," as he was commonly called, was noted for his leadership. Those who knew Craigen and respected his opinions were impressed with his foresight and courage and admired his strong sense of honesty and sincerity."[22] Like other former Detroit Garveyites such as Charles Diggs Sr., John Charles Zampty, Elijah Poole (aka Elijah Muhammad), and Ed Vaughn, Craigen focused "on building new black middle- and working-class networks." Craigen, a native of Guyana (formerly British Guiana), was born to Robert Craigen and Louise Beete on April 5, 1896.[23] He graduated from Temperance Collegiate Institute and Queen's College in Georgetown, Guyana.[24] After finishing secondary school and earning a degree at Queen's College,[25] Craigen migrated to the United States to work as a Spanish interpreter for the Navy Department at Muscle Shoals, Alabama.[26] In 1918 he relocated to Detroit, where he resided in an area of the city known as Black Bottom.[27] Having worked several years in Detroit automobile factories, Craigen joined the Detroit division of the UNIA, served as the division's executive secretary, and eventually became UNIA high commissioner for Wisconsin, Michigan, and Minnesota. At one point he was considered one of Garvey's most trusted aides.[28] As Craigen moved up the ranks to become a highly respected black midwestern diasporic UNIA leader, he acquired a reputation as a loyal supporter, rising leader, and an outspoken challenger to matters pertaining to Garvey's leadership, management practices, and decision making.

Like Garvey, Craigen believed that black people in the West should "redeem their motherland Africa, to create a government for Negroes, of Negroes and by Negroes, so they can be protected everywhere."[29] Though a loyal Garveyite, Craigen did not shrink from questioning Garvey's judgment. During the UNIA's Second International Convention of the Negro Peoples of the World at Liberty Hall in Harlem, in New York, in August 1921, for example, Craigen joined Boston chaplain Rev. George A. Weston and other delegates in opposing Garvey's request for legislation that would grant him power over all UNIA and Black Star Line steamship corporation finances.[30] At the fourth convention, at Liberty Hall in Harlem on August 5, 1924, Craigen reported on the economic conditions in Detroit, stating it was "the second greatest division of the association, second only to New York," and that the economic situation in Detroit was far better than in the average city because the Ford plants employed blacks "on equal terms with whites." Craigen told the delegates that the Detroit division was "on the upgrade" and was "determined to stand by the cause to the last man and to the last dollar."[31] However, there were many cases of discrimination, because the supervisors did not carry out what company owner Henry Ford "wills to the letter," and blacks were "victims of prejudice and discrimination."

Craigen in March 1926 had also been one of four conveners of an emergency UNIA-ACL convention held in Detroit, at which Craigen's and the chapter's continued loyalty to Garvey and his principles of racial redemption were reaffirmed.[32] He was also one of a committee of five leaders to visit with Garvey

Figure 4.1. While on board the SS *Saramacca*, Marcus M. Garvey stands on deck December 2, 1927, before sailing back to Kingston, Jamaica, with (*from left to right*) Joseph A. Craigen, executive secretary, Detroit division; Sylvester V. Robertson, president, Cleveland division; Marcus M. Garvey; Ernest B. Knox, Garvey's personal representative; William Ware, president, Cincinnati division; and Dr. J. J. Peters, president, New Orleans division. Arthur P. Bedou, Photographer. Courtesy of Xavier University Library, Special Collections Division.

aboard the *Saramacca* at New Orleans on December 2, 1927, minutes before his departure.[33] In January 1928, while residing in Jamaica, Garvey appointed six high commissioners as district leaders to help bring about "a thoroughly-organized Negro Race within the United States ready to take their part alongside the organized Negroes in other parts of the world." As commissioner for Wisconsin, Michigan, and Minnesota,[34] Craigen was sent to Florida as the UNIA-ACL parent body's special representative to arbitrate disputes and to assist with organizational membership drives. In February 1928, Craigen was arrested in Miami after entering a property dispute between Garveyites and supporters of

Laura Kofey, a former charismatic UNIA organizer who had founded a rival group. Advised to investigate Kofey, Craigen claimed to have known her when she was a member of the Detroit division in the early 1920s.[35] On March 8, 1928, Kofey was assassinated in Miami. Two UNIA members were indicted; Craigen managed their defense, and they were eventually acquitted. He also successfully employed emotional appeals in the *Negro World*, the UNIA newspaper, to collect funds. Craigen suggested that Kofey "came to her death at the hands of some of her own followers who turned on her after finding out she was robbing them."[36] By November 1928, Craigen was a member of a planning conference consisting of UNIA high commissioners and representatives of major divisions for the Sixth International Convention of the Negro Peoples of the World, while Garvey was traveling in Toronto, Canada,. Nine months later, Craigen was one of three Michigan delegates to attend and participate in the month-long August 1929 Sixth International Convention of the Negro Peoples of the World under the auspices of the UNIA of the World convention in Kingston.[37] After the departure of Detroit president Fred Johnson, who had left the convention following a vicious depute with Garvey, Garvey recognized Craigen and Rev. Albert Glen Taylor, the newly elected president of Idlewild Division 895, as two of three progressive delegates.[38] A member of the Miami UNIA African Legion later recalled that legion members shared memories of saving Craigen's life one "dreadful December night in 1917 in New York's Liberty Hall."[39]

Craigen Splits from Garvey

Indeed, the year 1929 represented an important period in the UNIA's history as the organization's internal conflicts spilled out into the open after Garvey publicly announced that "race traitors" were leading the UNIA to bankruptcy. Over the years, Garvey had publicly broken with several prominent followers: Amy Ashwood Garvey, his first wife and co-founder of the UNIA; Rev. James W. H. Eason, "Leader of the American Negroes"; and Kofey. But now, exiled in Jamaica, Garvey did not have the same leverage within the organization to reassert unquestioned control. When conflict erupted during the Sixth International UNIA Convention in Kingston in August 1929, the resulting fallout dealt a significant blow to the organization. Garvey's conflict with Craigen at the convention, which emerged over what Craigen felt was Garvey's mismanagement of the UNIA, ultimately disrupted and ruined their relationship.

The tensions emerging among various factions within the UNIA had been rising since Garvey's deportation, which compromised his control over the American wing of the organization. Garvey described the controversy with his American opponents—local UNIA leaders—as dreadful, stating: "One J. A. Craigen who style himself as Executive Secretary of the U.N.I.A. in Detroit, and William Ware, who has connected with the Organization as President of the Cincinnati Division, along with J. J. Peters and Leonard Smith of Detroit, also President of the Detroit division, have, since the rising of the Convention in Jamaica in 1929, been most viciously carrying on a propaganda to discourage the loyalty of the Division of the Organization, that would not otherwise entertain a thought of being disloyal to the Parent Body and the cause." This charge initiated the organizational split, as Garvey continued to announce the formation of the unincorporated UNIA-ACL of the World. The new organization, he indicated, would be headquartered in Kingston and would serve as a rival parent body to the original UNIA, Inc., in New York.[40]

This breach apparently further intensified tensions between Garvey and Craigen during the 1929 convention, when Craigen joined others in questioning Garvey's desire to dominate the UNIA. Craigen and several other local leaders from the Midwest also sided with E. B. Knox, Garvey's personal representative, who objected to Garvey's decision to move headquarters from New York to Kingston. In August 1929, Garvey had formed the unincorporated Universal Negro Improvement Association and African Communities League of the World illegally to reassert and maintain control of the organization. Knox and his allies had reasoned that money raised in the United States "should remain here in the States, where it would have some protection."[41] In response to this argument, Garvey, according to historian Robert A. Hill, "dismissed Knox from his elected second-in-command position in the preceding spring of 1930, a break which showed the total collapse of his ability to control the direction of the American wing of the organization from his distant Jamaican base."[42] Garvey had learned of Knox's plans to call "a conference of all the presidents of the movement," so he declared the Chicago convening was unauthorized. In a telegram to Harold G. Saltus, the business manager of the *Negro World*, on May 12, 1930, Garvey reiterated this point and appointed "Madame M.L.T. DeMena as the parent-body representative to America." Describing Knox's plans for the conference as an act of subversion, Garvey pushed for a new centralized administrative system that would limit New York's power and influence. This suggestion would also lead Craigen to break ties with Garvey.

In April 1931, Craigen and Garvey ended their relationship bitterly when they publicly charged one another with corruption. Craigen claimed in a circular that Garvey had improperly used funds from U.S. divisions to purchase property in Jamaica. On April 11, Garvey published a letter in the *Negro World* in which he denounced Craigen and several other UNIA leaders as "villains and rascals" and claimed that they were responsible for the UNIA's financial woes, due to their alleged mishandling of its affairs during his imprisonment. A week later, on April 19, Craigen replied to Garvey's accusations at a public meeting held in Liberty Hall in Detroit.[43] As Hill reports, "Craigen responded to this denunciation by Garvey with a savage counterattack cataloging in great detail the criticisms and dissatisfaction of the American opposition" in an article entitled, "A Partial Answer to Marcus Garvey," listing nineteen reasons "why the U.N.I.A. is split all over the world" and directing blame at the "Self-Styled President-General of the UNIA."[44] Craigen first argued that Garvey "morally killed, and connived to physically kill every intelligent young man who became associated with him in the U.N.I.A. when they refused to further carry out his criminal investigation." When Garvey accused Ware, Craigen, Peters, Smith, Haynes, and Toote as enemies of the UNIA, Craigen responded stating Garvey had become "a semi-maniac" and had "willfully lied to the delegates in Toronto, Canada, about buying a new printing plant in London, England," adding, "where he would print the daily *BLACKMAN* newspaper, when in fact the Printing Plant he did buy with American Dollars was over twenty years old and was bought from a friend of his in Jamaica." He said that Garvey did not understand the rule of law, since "the new U.N.I.A. is not recognized in the courts of this country."[45] The charges leveled by Craigen would ultimately have a lasting impact on Garvey's reorganizational plans as he was leaving Jamaica to relocate in England. Continuing his efforts to overcome issues and problems created by himself, Garvey's influence as a top-down leader based upon the hierarchical structure and management style he had attempted to implement was slowly fading. Unlike William Le Van Sherrill, who split with Garvey in 1926 "but later repaired his relationship with him,"[46] Craigen broke ties with Garvey completely in 1931. Garvey organized the Seventh International Convention in Jamaica, focusing on the "centenary of West Indian Slave Abolition," in 1934, and the eighth in Toronto in 1938. Moreover, when he traveled to Windsor, Canada, in September 1937 to speak with "representatives from associate organizations such as the Peace Movement of Ethiopia"[47] during the Eighth International Convention at a church, Craigen was not on the platform.[48]

Craigen Looks Back and Moves Forward

Craigen was a lawyer and labor adjudicator by profession with interests in Detroit politics. A year before the split with Garvey in 1931, Craigen was elected a constable from the Seventh Ward. A year later he became a court clerk for Wayne County Circuit Court Judge Guy A. Miller, "a position he held until he was appointed deputy State labor commissioner in 1937." While serving the county in this capacity, Craigen also attended the Detroit College of Law in 1932, where he participated in the debate team throughout his career as a law student. During the time of this participation, he became co-captain of the intercollegiate debating champions.[49] An imposing figure and impressive debater, Craigen was one of only a few students of African descent to attend the college. Graduating in 1936, Craigen was among an impressive list of graduates and aspiring alumni of the college. After graduation, Craigen pursued an interest in politics, which would benefit every organization he would belong to for the remaining years of his career. A few years later, while practicing law, Craigen's appointment as a deputy registrar for the Probate Court by Judge Patrick O' Brien[50] was upgraded by former Michigan governor Frank Murphy to allow him to serve as the state's workmen's compensation commissioner, "a position he held until his death." He was nominated during the Truman administration for an appointment as a federal judge, and although U.S. Attorney Thomas P. Thornton got the position,[51] the announcement did not disrupt Craigen's momentum as he joined the Detroit chapter of the Kappa Alpha Psi Fraternity, Inc.

An active member of the Kappa Alpha Psi Fraternity, Inc. and the Michigan State Bar Association, Craigen was elected to the second-highest national office in Kappa Alpha Psi, as senior grand vice polemarch, in 1937 and 1938. In maintaining this leadership capacity Craigen joined a small group of representative citizens to encourage all "race voters" to pressure Congress to pass an anti-lynching bill and other legislation pertaining to black rights.[52] However, due to the outbreak of World War II, the fraternity and its national leaders did not hold its yearly Grand Chapter Convention in 1942. Rather, the grand polemarch convened with other members of the board of directors and a few key political members on December 11 and 12 in Chicago to conduct other pressing business of the fraternity.[53] One of those called upon to attend the meeting to honor Chicago congressman William Dawson for being "reelected to Congress for a fourth time in a Democratic landslide" was Craigen.[54] Craigen was encouraged to serve the national body of the fraternity in 1948 as a member of the

DEBATING

Left to Right—Standing:
M. H. Shillman, Joseph A. Craigen.

Left to Right—Seated:
H. J. Hoshner, Coach Charles H. Lockwood.

Figure 4.2. Standing (*left to right*) are debate co-captains Morris H. Shillman and Joseph A. Craigen and seated (*left to right*) are H. J. Hoshner and Coach Charles C. Lockwood, Detroit College of Law debate team. From the 1936 *Detroit College of Law Yearbook*.

Grand Board of Directors, an elected office he retained through 1951.[55] By 1956, Craigen served as the National Chairman of the Housing Commission. He also served as a board member of the Detroit branch of the NAACP.[56] Besides supporting King as the symbolic leader of the civil rights movement in Detroit and throughout the nation, Craigen became one of the first African Americans to hold various positions within the city and the state.

Figure 4.3. UNIA leaders of the African Diaspora of the Midwest are standing (*from left to right*) William Sherrill, Harold Bledsoe, Thomas Drum, William L. Dawson, Emmett Cunningham, and Joseph A. Craigen, November 20, 1948. From the UNIA papers at the Manuscript, Archives and Rare Book Library, Emory University.

Serving the charitable nonprofit fraternity organization nationally, Craigen was equally active locally as he led the Detroit Alumni Chapter as polemarch from 1941 through 1948 in consecutive terms (the only member to do so in the history of the Detroit organization). He was elected to this position again in 1957 and 1958. As such, Craigen was responsible for securing the purchase of the chapter's fraternity house in 1945. Consulted several times years later by other chapter leaders, Craigen was asked to assist in obtaining their houses, and the Detroit chapter of the NAACP asked him to serve as chairman of their "Fight for Freedom" drive in 1954. "Joe, as he was nicknamed, was noted for his leadership. Those who knew Craigen and respected his opinions were impressed with his foresight and courage and admired his strong sense of honesty and sincerity."[57] The former president of the Michigan Bar Associa-

Figure 4.4. Craigen dancing with fellow Detroit Idlewilder Dottie Rose, ca. 1950. Courtesy of Dottie Rose.

Figure 4.5. Sitting on the sandy beach of Idlewild Lake is Craigen with Ann Peake (*far right*) and behind her, her sister Dottie Rose, along with other African American women, ca. 1950. Courtesy of Dottie Rose.

tion was also a member of the Detroit Caribbean Club and a founding officer of the Detroit Idlewilders Club.

A respected legal mind, Craigen, through contacts he had established in the city, was one of the founders of the Detroit Idlewilders Club, Inc.[58] Joining a group of colleagues and friends from Chicago, Cleveland, Detroit, Indianapolis, and Saint Louis in 1952, who had been frequent summer vacationers in Idlewild, Craigen participated in several discussions regarding the organizing of several Idlewilders city-clubs. In Detroit, Sunnie Wilson during a casual meeting at the Mark Twain Hotel motioned to organize the chapter. A week later, a small group of Detroiters, which included Craigen, Joseph and Velma Branam, Clarence Brown, Winola Burch-Conway, Isola Graham-Winburn, Sunnie Wilson, and Judge Lucile Alexander-Watts, formulated some plans to organize the Detroit Idlewilder's Club.[59] At the special meeting called in the home of the Branams, who were "successful owners of the Golden Dairy Milk company," Sunnie Wilson was elected president, Craigen vice-president, *Michigan Chronicle* columnist Isola Graham-Winburn secretary, "and Joseph Branam treasurer."[60] The club pledged "to aid and support charitable and civic endeavors and to promote social entertaining and recreation."[61]

Prior to acquiring the Idlewild clubhouse property and a meeting place in Detroit, the club "gathered at various members' homes until increasing membership prompted us to gather at the Mark Twain and Garfield Hotels."[62] However, in 1954 the club acquired some property in Idlewild, and according to Wilson, "I financed the purchase of the Detroit Idlewilders clubhouse from a doctor out of Chicago. Afterward, I turned it over to the organization. Each member owns a share of the clubhouse." While Wilson was responsible for the purchase of the clubhouse, Craigen purchased a set of vacant lots across the road so that members from the four other city-clubs and their guests could park their automobiles.[63] Inside the clubhouse, members sporting glittery suits and gowns and summer wear would dance the night away. Craigen had an active social life, and always spent his leisure time in the company of young beautiful women.

The Detroit activist attorney and political insider may have disagreed with Garvey's management style, but he never fully abandoned his Garveyite roots. It is unclear how long Craigen had ties to the Idlewild community. His relationship with the community dated as far back as from 1929 to 1931 when he helped to organize fourteen different Michigan UNIA divisions, including Idlewild, while serving as executive secretary of the Detroit chapter. However, it does appear that Craigen's relations in Idlewild during the 1950s through repeated and friendly interactions with Lela G. Wilson, who served as vice lady president of the Idlewild UNIA-ACL division 895 from 1929 to 1931, were extremely positive. Besides making this connection, Craigen purchased property in Idlewild after the war, and he vacationed there annually.

Detroit and Chicago vacationers enjoyed a wide variety of leisure and recreation activities in Idlewild. During the period after World War II, a stay in Idlewild was an adventure to every African American consumer from the war veteran, policy racketeer, motorist, professional, and average factory worker. The location was accentuated by the availability of mom-and-pop grocery stores, gas stations, hotels, motels, rental cottages, all-night diners, and after-hours clubs. Michigan tourism and a bad loan repayment deal during this era of black institution building had inspired Craigen to make an investment in the hotel business in Idlewild. Besides owning an Idlewild cottage at the time of his passing in 1962, Craigen was legally one-third of a partnership in the ownership of the Casa Blanca Hotel. He was also a man who knew how to host some of the swankiest indoor and outdoor summer parties, which always included an impressive list of distinguished guests. Dignitaries such as Detroit congressman Charles Diggs Jr.,[64] Chicago congressman William Dawson, Detroit's Recorder Court judge Harold Bledsoe, Michigan senator Charles Roxborough, and funeral home founders James T. Cole and William Stinson frequently attended them. Idlewild socialites Elizabeth Ann Hawkins, Maryellen Wilson, and Dorothea Rose and her sister Ann Peats did too. So as America was transitioning from a wartime economy to a peaceful one in the fall of 1950, black elites were gathering at Craigen's cottage during the Labor Day weekend. Marion Campfield, staff writer for the *Chicago Defender,* characterized the crowd attending Craigen's private cottage parties as a "Who's Who from everywhere."[65]

Craigen's summer home was a showpiece. Known as the Craigen Inn,[66] it was the space where guests such as Fleetwood McCoy of Detroit were entertained with the latest recordings by African American musicians, artists, and "cocktails for out-of-town visitors." Prior to organizing this celebratory gathering, two-thirds of the section of the vacated property Craigen owned consisted of undeveloped land until a hotel was built and completed in 1950. The hotel operated for approximately twenty years with single rooms on the first, second, and third floors. Advertisements frequently appeared in the *Negro Travel Guide and Green Book* by Woolsey Coombs of the Casa Blanca

Figure 4.6. Craigen is standing at the front gate of the Craigen Inn, Idlewild, Michigan, ca. 1950. Courtesy of Ronald J. Stephens.

Hotel and Phil Giles of the Giles Hotel, who sought to cater to an emerging black middle-class clientele. The property where the Casa Blanca Hotel sits was originally purchased by Craigen. The hotel itself was built and owned by W. C. Coombs, a middle-class building contractor from Detroit who was born in the West Indies. As early as 1945 Craigen had sold a third of the property he purchased to Woolsey and Ivy Lee Coombs. Both Craigen and Coombs were from the British Caribbean. Craigen was from Guyana and Coombs was from Jamaica. Coombs built the hotel in 1949 and opened it for business in 1950.

As Idlewild marched into the last two decades of the ladies and gents' era, where the men wore suits, alligator and Stacy Adams shoes, white shirts, and black silk ties, and the ladies wore long silky gowns, gold and diamond jew-

Figure 4.7. The Casa Blanca Hotel, Idlewild, Michigan, ca. 1950. Courtesy of John Meeks Sr.

elry, and mink coats, the Casa Blanca accepted guests during the summer months and on weekends. Guests paid seven dollars per person per day to stay at the hotel. They shared bathrooms. It was common for five hundred people to be turned away due to overbookings over a typical Fourth of July weekend. The Casbah Cocktail Lounge and the small dining room on the lower level were popular locations for guests. By the summer of 1956 the Casa Blanca served choice liquor, including beer and wine, and advertised menus of delectable meals in an exquisite dining salon.[67] Guests with advanced reservations for accommodations were assured rooms.[68]

However, as guests began booking rooms, the deal went bad as Coombs refused to pay Craigen the balance owed. Craigen, who had lent Coombs an additional eight thousand dollars to complete the building, responded to a handwritten letter by Mrs. Coombs regarding the failed business deal and arrangement. "As far as I am concerned there is no misunderstanding," he wrote. "It is simply a matter of business and we should not lose any friendship about it although nine times out of ten when you lend people money, there is always a falling out when time comes to be paid. . . . I was only helping your husband out after he got himself in a jam. You remember him telling me that if he got $8,000.00 he could finish the Hotel. I got him the money."[69] Craigen's documentation of the events surrounding the six-month loan, which came with a promissory note for full payment to be made in one year, was not honored. In Craigen's mind, this note would provide Coombs with adequate time to build the hotel and open for operation. However, after more than two years of nonpayment from Coombs and the fact that the hotel was not finished,[70] Craigen told Mrs. Coombs that one third of the interest in the ownership of the hotel belonged to him. "Now, for the papers that I drew up for you to sign giving me 1/3 interest, I want you to know that I didn't approach your husband to make the bargain, he approached me and suggested that I buy 1/3 interest at that time for $15,000.00 and that we would get together and finish it."[71] Craigen had serious doubts about the manner in which Coombs was managing the establishment as a businessman, and he wanted to supervise the daily operations of the hotel.[72] By insisting on some protection from this investment, Craigen argued that the current management of the hotel was threatening its successful operation as a popular lodging facility.[73]

Conclusion

From his own plot of land in Idlewild, Joseph Craigen was able to live out the Garveyite ideals of racial uplift, property ownership, and self-reliance. Along with fellow Caribbean-born Detroit Garveyites John Charles "Papa" Zampty and Woolsey Coombs, he was able to incorporate black nationalist ideas into the history, development, and sustainability of Idlewild.

Throughout the 1950s, Craigen, Zampty, and Coombs thus pursued the work of global Garveyism on a local scale. Zampty, for instance, owned his own summer cottage and also managed and operated a "Homesite" Realty Company.[74] During the 1960s and 1970s he worked to link the black nationalist politics of the 1920s to the insurgent politics of Black Power and Pan-African nationalism.[75]

When Craigen passed away on June 21, 1962, in Burton Mercy Hospital, at the age of sixty-six, he had not been a member of the UNIA for more than three decades. And yet from his organizational beginnings in the UNIA he had built a dazzling career as a politically active Detroit attorney, as a representative of the Detroit NAACP, as a Michigan referee and judge, and as a prominent member of the Idlewild community. These career paths were not reducible to, but were inextricably bound with, the work he started as a Garveyite in the diasporic Midwest. At his funeral, on June 25, 1962, a standing-room-only crowd filled St. Matthews Episcopal Church to pay their final respects.[76]

Acknowledgments

I am indebted to the pioneering scholarship of Garvey scholars Robert A. Hill, Tony Martin, Judith Stein, Richard W. Thomas, Rupert Lewis, and Paul Lee. I wish to thank Peter A. Bermel, Joseph Dorsey, Ligia Aldana, Carol Ann Dennis, Leonard Harris, and Adam Ewing for commenting on early drafts of this essay.

Notes

1. See McDuffie's essay in this volume, "'The Second Battle for Africa Has Begun': Rev. Clarence W. Harding Jr., Garveyism, Liberia, and the Diasporic Midwest, 1966–1978." See also McDuffie, "Chicago, Garveyism"; McDuffie, "Garveyism in Cleveland"; and McDuffie, "'A New Day Has Dawned.'" McDuffie uses the term "'diasporic Midwest' as an empirical and theoretical framework to extend the study of the African diaspora by tracing the significance of the American heartland as a center of black transnational political activism, to appreciate the gendered contours and paradoxes of pan-African movements, and to chart a genealogy of global black freedom struggles through Garveyism" ("'Second Battle for Africa,'" 90).

2. McDuffie, "'Second Battle for Africa,'" 90.

3. Paul Lee, "Garveyism in Michigan: The Early Years," *Michigan Citizen*, September 1–7, 2000, A8.

4. Marcus Garvey, "Mr. Garvey Sends a Message, Entitled Any Nigger Is a Nigger: A Letter from Marcus Garvey," *Jamaica Times*, July 8, 1916, reprinted in Robert A. Hill, "Some Impressions of America, What He Is Aiming For," New York City, May 24, 1916.

5. R. J. Stephens, *Idlewild*, 63; Babson, *Working Detroit*.

6. See Sugrue, *Origins of the Urban Crisis*. Sweet was acquitted of all charges.

7. Stein, *World of Marcus Garvey*, 230.

8. Ibid., 231.

9. Smith-Irvin, *Footsoldiers*, cited in Lee, "Garveyism in Michigan," A8.

10. Lee, "Garveyism in Michigan." Lee adds that this visit was during the summer and not the spring, as Stein suggested.

11. Smith-Irvin, *Footsoldiers*, quoted in Lee, "Garveyism in Michigan."

12. Stein, *World of Marcus Garvey*, 230.

13. R. J. Stephens, "Garveyism in Idlewild," 44. Charters for UNIA divisions were granted upon the successful application of seven or more citizens of a community. Once a division had been organized in a city like Detroit, subsequent applicants from the area were granted charters to form a chapter and were supervised by the local division. See Article 1, Sections 4 and 5, UNIA Constitution and Book of Laws, in R. A. Hill, *Marcus Garvey and Universal Negro Improvement Association Papers* [hereafter *MGP*], 1:256–257.

14. Lee, "Garveyism in Michigan." In 2014 that number would have been adjusted to approximately $682,000 due to inflation.

15. See Charles C. Diggs, Sr. & Charles C. Diggs, Jr., "The Business of Black Death in Detroit," courtesy of the *Michigan Chronicle,* November 4, 1950, and available at https://tbobdid.wordpress.com/the-need-for-black-undertakers/undertakers-in-detroit/diggs/. See also Richard Pearson. "Charles Diggs Dies at 75," *Washington Post,* August 26, 1998, B06. After leaving the organization he became involved first in Republican politics and then changed affiliations to the Democratic Party in 1932. Diggs was also an early organizer for the establishment of Black Democratic Clubs in Detroit.

16. R. W. Thomas, *Life for Us*, 196.

17. Records reveal that the UNIA in Michigan consisted of fourteen branches: Albion, Ann Arbor Branch, North Detroit, Flint, Halfway, Hamtramck, Idlewild, Jackson, Kalamazoo, Macomb, Pontiac, Quinn Road, River Rouge, and Ypsilanti.

18. In the *Negro World,* July 16, 1927, the Detroit division issued a statement under Smith's presidency, stating that "each division and chapter is expected to have a representative" (7) attend a designated Michigan Day. The Schomburg Center for Research in Black Culture, New York Public Library, owns an incomplete set of index cards with the division names by location as well as the charter number and other data from 1926 to 1928.

19. R. J. Stephens, *Idlewild*. During the 1929 International Convention a major split occurred between Garvey, then of Kingston, and the New York division of the UNIA, in which Division 895 was renumbered and designated Division 126 by March 1930.

20. See *MGP*, 7:472, 962. A. G. Taylor was listed as a representative of the Idlewild division. The Idlewild Resort Company founded Idlewild in 1912. By 1915 the company recruited middle-class African American professionals to promote the community and held its first excursion for African Americans. By the late 1920s, Idlewild was the place to be if you were an African American. Some leaders in Idlewild were determined to preserve it as an autonomous black town, and they found Garveyism as an important source to do so.

21. See *MGP*, 3:688. He served as a delegate of the 1921 UNIA Convention (*MGP*, 3:787–78). See also R. J. Stephens, "Garveyism in Idlewild," 44.

22. See "Final Rites Held for Joe Craigen," *Michigan Chronicle,* June 30, 1962,1A; and Crump, *Story of Kappa Alpha Psi,* 343.

23. See certificate of death from the Michigan Department of Health Vital Records

Section with the local file number 8945. Craigen died on June 21, 1962, in Wayne County, Michigan, at Burton Mercy Hospital in Detroit. He was sixty-six years old.

24. See Knowles, *International Encyclopedia of Higher Education*; and International Association of Universities, *International Handbook of Universities* (Basingstoke, UK: Palgrave Macmillan, 1946–49), which notes that Guyana (formerly British Guiana) became constitutionally independent on May 28, 1966.

25. Higher education had begun in October 1963 at the University of Guyana. Prior to that the university had been housed at Queen's College. See Knowles, *International Encyclopedia of Higher Education.*

26. Obituary of Joseph A. Craigen, *Detroit Free Press,* June 23, 1962.

27. See the *Detroit City Directory* for 1936–37, 1940, 1953–54, and 1957 regarding Craigen's legal address in Detroit.

28. *MGP,* 7:xliii, 134 n. 8, 460; Lee, "Garveyism in Michigan." Paul Lee is an independent researcher and the director of Best Efforts, Inc., in Highland Park, Michigan.

29. *MGP,* 7:168.

30. *MGP,* 3:692–93 n. 3.

31. *MGP,* 5:661–62.

32. Cronon, *Black Moses,* 139; *MGP,* 7:458–59, 468.

33. T. Martin, *Race First,* lxvii, 6 n. 1, 14; *MGP,* 7:lxvii, 6 n. 3, 14; Cronon, *Black Moses,* 143.

34. *MGP,* 7:88.

35. *MGP,* 7:133, 134 n. 8, 169.

36. *MGP,* 7:141–42, 166–67 n. 1, 170.

37. R. J. Stephens, "Garveyism in Idlewild"; *MGP,* 7:313–14 n. 1, 316, 318 n. 4, 341, 448, 962.

38. *MGP,* 7:316, 318 n. 4, 341, 448, 962; "Rev. A. G. Taylor Speaks," *The Blackman,* August 3, 1929, 5. See also "Fourteenth Business Session of Negro Peoples of the World, Held at Edelweiss Park Yesterday Morning," *The Blackman,* August 31, 1929, 5. During his term as president, Taylor not only helped to increase the division's visibility locally, nationally, and internationally but also helped to outline a strategic plan and vision to increase the membership and carry the division for the next six years. By the end of his term, the Idlewild division was an active black nationalist organization.

39. *MGP,* 7:134 n. 8.

40. *MGP,* 7:lxxi–lxxii.

41. *MGP,* 7:xl–xli, 411 n. 1, 448.

42. R. A. Hill, *The Black Man,* 11.

43. *MGP,* 7:lxxiv, 458–60, 462, cited in Lee, "Garveyism in Michigan."

44. R. A. Hill, *The Black Man,* 11. Hill adds: "*The Black Man* [magazine] represents the final political testament and legacy of the once widely-acclaimed leader of the world's first, and still the only, international mass movement among people of African descent. It began publication in December 1933, in Jamaica, the island of Garvey's birth, which had become, paradoxically, the land of his imposed exile after his deportation six years earlier from America, the epicenter of his movement's once phenomenal strength" (5).

45. Ibid., 12. Hill writes that "while undoubtedly many of these accusations were

slanderous and speculative, several of them struck at very sensitive areas with telling effect" (12).

46. Lee, "Garveyism in Michigan."

47. R. Lewis, *Marcus Garvey*, 91.

48. *MGP*, 7:781, cited in Lee, "Garveyism in Michigan."

49. *The Forum, 1934–35* (published by the Senior Class of the Detroit College of Law, Detroit, Michigan), 126. This particular debate team was known as the "know no defeat team." The team was led by veterans M. H. Shillman, Joseph A. Craigen, and George J. Schreiber. Regarding Craigen's appointment as a federal judge ten years later, see also "Petitions Ask Negro Judge: J. A. Craigen Urged for Federal Bench," *Detroit News*, November 3, 1948; "Negro Urged as U.S. Judge," *Detroit Free Press*, December 19, 1948; and "Now Is the Time for a Judge," *Michigan Chronicle*, November 13, 1948, 8.

50. "Names Craigen," *Michigan Chronicle*, June 14, 1939, 4. A caption notes that Craigen "is the first Negro to hold such a position in the state."

51. "Appointment of Atty. Creates Disappointment," *Michigan Chronicle*, January 22, 1949, 1 and 4.

52. "Detroit Citizens Organize National Pressure Movement," *Chicago Defender*, August 6, 1938, 4.

53. "Kappa Officials Map War Time Program: Pledge All-Out Aid to Government," *Chicago Defender*, December 19, 1942, 6.

54. Photo, *Chicago Defender*, November 20, 1948, 4.

55. "Kappa Alpha Psi Brothers at 39th Convention," *Chicago Defender*, January 7, 1950, 4. See also "Official Delegates to 28th Annual Conclave of Kappa Alpha Psi," *Chicago Defender*, January 14, 1939, 7.

56. Four years prior to this appointment with the NAACP, Craigen served as "deputy workmen's compensation commissioner for Detroit." "Craigen Reinstated to Commissioner Post," *Chicago Defender*, March 15, 1952, 4.

57. R. W. Thomas. *Life for Us.*

58. Wilson, *Toast of the Town*, 134.

59. R. J. Stephens, *Idlewild*, 95.

60. Wilson, *Toast of the Town*, 134.

61. Ibid.

62. Ibid.

63. R. J. Stephens, *Idlewild*.

64. Charles C. Diggs Jr. was born in Detroit in 1922. His father, Charles C. Diggs Sr., was elected Michigan's first black senator in 1936 and served the state until 1944. In 1951, Diggs Jr. succeeded his father in the state senate, becoming the first African American congressional representative from Michigan, a position he held for twenty-five years. During his tenure he helped found the Congressional Black Caucus and became chairperson of the House District Committee.

65. Campfield, "Socialites Enjoy Labor Day at Idlewild Resort," *Chicago Defender*, September 16, 1950, 8.

66. Kenneth Davis, *Idlewild Yearbook for 1959* (Idlewild, Michigan, 1959), 20.

67. R. J. Stephens, *Idlewild*.

68. Joseph A. Craigen to Woolsey Coombs, March 18, 1952, in author's private collection.

69. Joseph A. Craigen to I. Coombs, May 4, 1949, on *State of Michigan Workmen's Compensation Commission,* Lansing, Michigan, letterhead, in author's private collection.

70. Ibid.

71. Ibid.

72. Ibid.

73. Ibid.

74. Davis, *Idlewild Yearbook for 1959,* 6.

75. *MGP,* 7:316, 318 n. 4, 341, 448, 962.

76. Craigen's obituary was published on June 23, 1962, in two of Detroit's leading newspapers, the *Detroit News* and *Detroit Free Press.*

5

Our Joan of Arc

Women, Gender, and Authority in the Harmony Division of the UNIA

NICOLE BOURBONNAIS

When Mr. Cunning announced "the fire-brand speaker," and
brought back memories of the Convention with a small lady
mounted on a grey horse, that seemed every inch to him, Joan
of Arc, the crowd went cheering wildly, and kept on calling for
Madam de Mena.

"Mr. Johnson Speaks to Harmony Division," New Negro Voice,
March 14, 1942

In the early 1940s, Maymie L. T. Aiken (aka Madam de Mena) was a crowd
favorite at meetings of the Harmony Division of the Universal Negro Improvement Association (UNIA) in Kingston, Jamaica. She knew how to work the
room, a skill cultivated over nearly two decades traveling the United States,
Central America, and the Caribbean on behalf of the organization. Born Leonie
Turpeau in Louisiana in 1879, she was first exposed to the UNIA while living in the predominantly Afro-Caribbean community of Bluefields, Nicaragua,
with her first husband, local Creole activist Francis H. Mena. Returning to the
United States after the couple's divorce, "Madam de Mena" would rise through
the ranks of the organization, accompanying Marcus Garvey and his second

wife, Amy Jacques Garvey, on speaking tours, serving as international organizer, editing the *Negro World,* and helping organize the 1929 UNIA convention, where she rode horseback through the streets of Kingston in full military attire, leaving an indelible impression on the city's inhabitants (as evident in the quotation above). By the time she settled down in Jamaica in 1935 with her new husband, Jamaican labor activist Percival A. Aiken, Madam de Mena (now referring to herself as "Maymie Aiken") was one of the organization's most recognizable figures.[1]

Scholars have long noted the high rate of women's participation in the Garveyite movement, but leaders like Madam de Mena have remained, until recently, "little more than a footnote" in the history of the UNIA.[2] This may reflect, in part, the marginalization of Garveyite women by the organization itself. As Barbara Bair has pointed out, although women held executive positions in the various "Ladies Auxiliaries" of the UNIA, these positions were subservient to male leaders; the organizational structure was "not separate and equal but separate and hierarchical."[3] Marcus Garvey's philosophical tracts also embraced a "proudly masculinized language that fetishized Victorian gender norms, celebrated the reclamation of a fallen manhood, and relegated women to the roles of nurturer, mother, helpmate, and guardians of racial purity and nationhood."[4] Furthermore, Garvey's speeches and writings condemned single motherhood, interracial marriage, illegitimacy, and birth control, thereby encouraging the surveillance of black women's bodies and behavior by protective male leaders in the name of the race struggle. Scholars have thus argued that Garveyites were "progressive in their stance against white supremacy yet reactionary in relation to the internal organization of black communities."[5] As Michael O. West and William G. Martin put it, Garveyism "would not have been confused with feminism."[6]

Attempts to impose a strict order on gender and sexual relations were not, of course, unique to Garveyism. Temperance, social purity, and moral reform movements flourished throughout the early-twentieth-century Atlantic world and cut across racially defined communities. As Michele Mitchell argues, the anxiety of black reformers surrounding sexuality and reproduction at this time must also be seen in the context of mainstream discourses, which cast black men and women as deviant parents and sexually immoral/accessible; high infant and maternal mortality rates that plagued black families; and poor socioeconomic conditions, which generally made individual and collective livelihoods perpetually insecure.[7] In this context, it is not hard to understand why some women might have found Garvey's emphasis on family order and validation of black women's purity, dignity, and importance as mothers appealing.[8] But the UNIA also attracted a number of women who stretched the "race mother" trope to its limits (or eschewed it altogether), both in their forceful personas and their engagement with feminist movements also spreading around the Atlantic world in the early twentieth century. Leaders like Madam de Mena and Amy Jacques Garvey traveled widely, delivering fiery oratories on behalf of the UNIA and becoming powerful leaders in their own right; female UNIA members commented on politics and raised contemporary debates over suffrage, gender roles, and women's leadership in the transnational *Negro World* as well as local Garveyite newspapers. A group of women even seized the floor of the 1922 UNIA convention to protest their subordinate status.[9] These efforts could spark vehement reactions, and some of the UNIA's most prominent female leaders found themselves censored or pushed out of the movement as a result of such activism.[10] Focusing on local chapters in Jamaica in the early 1930s, however, Honor Ford-Smith argues that Garveyite women were sometimes able to effectively carve out spaces within the organization to put forward their own concerns, while also using the oratory and argumentation skills they honed within the UNIA to push for feminist causes in other forums. If the UNIA itself was not feminist, she argues, it could still serve as a kind of "feminist training ground."[11]

Whether or not one sees the UNIA as a space for women's empowerment or feminist expression, of course, depends in part on when, where, and at whom you look. As with most social movements, there could be a considerable gap between the speeches and philosophical writings of Garvey and the interpretations of those who followed him; individual chapters of the UNIA were also embedded in shifting local contexts that inevitably shaped the way the transnational organization operated in practice. Focusing on the local level thus allows us to see the "cracks, contradictions, and absences through which participants grasped alternative meanings and enacted them."[12] Our understanding of gender dynamics in ideology and practice also depends on how one defines and situates the concept of "feminism." As Ula Taylor argues, if Amy Jacques Garvey's writings do not fit neatly with the ideology of today's mainstream liberal feminist movements, Jacques Garvey and other Garveyite women could be seen as putting forward a kind of "community feminism," focused on the "uplift" of the community over individual rights yet feminist in the way it "discerns the configuration of oppressive power relations, shatters masculinist claims of women as intellectually inferior, and seeks to empower women by expanding their roles and options."[13] Rhoda Reddock defines a "feminist" broadly as "someone who manifests an awareness/consciousness of the subordination of women and seeks actively to change it," thus encouraging us to recognize that "there might be different starting points for conceptualising the causes of this subordination and, by extension . . . differences in the solutions proposed and acted upon."[14] This scholarship pushes us to move beyond a characterization of the UNIA as *either* sexist *or* feminist, to consider a more nuanced set of questions, such as, What opportunities did the UNIA provide for women, and what kinds of feminist critiques were raised in UNIA spaces? Which aspects of gender roles and relations were up for debate, and which were seen as nonnegotiable? How were these conversations shaped by Garvey's ideology and the organization's structure, on the one hand, and the particularities of the local context and individual personalities, on the other?

This chapter uses the Jamaican Garveyite weekly *New Negro Voice* to submerge us in the world of the Harmony Division of the UNIA in early 1940s Kingston, in order to think through these questions in the context of one particular time and place. I focus on the years from 1941 to 1943, when the paper was edited first by Z. Munroe Scarlett (July 26–October 4, 1941) as the *Negro Voice,* then taken over by T. A. Kitchener (October 4, 1941–October 23, 1943) and renamed the *New Negro Voice* (with Kermit Henderson as coeditor from October 4 to November 1, 1941). The weekly editions during this period ran from approximately eight to ten pages and included detailed descriptions of meetings of the Harmony Division and events at Kingston's Liberty Hall, along with myriad news articles, editorials, poems, and short stories written (or at least compiled) primarily by local Garveyites. As such, the paper provides us with a window into the practical participation of local actors and the exchange of ideas and action within the movement during these years.

I begin by providing some background on the Harmony Division and the *New Negro Voice* (placing it within the context of the decline of the UNIA and the rise of Jamaican labor, nationalist, and feminist movements), before focusing on the participation of women and gender dynamics within the organization. The patriarchal structure and binary gender roles outlined by scholars certainly appear here in vivid form. But the pages of the *New Negro Voice* and the meetings of the Harmony Division also seem to have provided space for alternative visions of gender roles and critiques of women's subordination put forward by both female *and* male Garveyites who valued women's broader activities outside the home, argued that women's full equality was pivotal to the future of the race, and praised Jamaican women's political leadership. Similarly, alongside images of the nurturing, caretaking "race mother" or patriarchal "race man," the sources highlight other means of status-claiming within the organization that were more gender neutral, based on a member's militarism, sense of justice, level of commitment to the organization, practical contribution to the cause, and, above all, skill at oration and ability to hold an audience. These principles could empower women to speak their mind and exercise their creativity and intellect on a public stage; it also allowed women like Aiken to exercise considerable authority at Liberty Hall and beyond.

This authority did not, however, go unchallenged, and some feminist critiques proved more controversial than others. In the second half of the chapter I explore the dilemma created by a debate over birth control that split the leadership of the Harmony Division along more conventional gender lines. Aiken and several other Garveyite women supported access to contraceptives for poor black women; prominent male leaders admonished them for defying Garvey's teaching and promoting "race suicide." The debate suggests that, at least for some members, certain aspects of Garvey's ideology were less flexible in practice than others: in particular, those aspects that privileged women's control over their bodies/lives or transgressed dominant sexual mores. But the objections of prominent men did not, in this case, silence those who felt otherwise. Bolstered by the strength of the Jamaican feminist community at this particular historical moment and by her personal conviction, Aiken became even *more* explicitly activist following the birth control debate and used her authority to push for a series of Women's Nights which powerfully subverted the structure of weekly meetings. Her experience suggests that formal power and patriarchal privilege could not always trump the authority that came from commitment to the cause and oratory skill; the widespread popularity of these nights also further illustrates the support for women's leadership among both Garveyite men and women. In the early 1940s Harmony Division, at least, Aiken may well have gotten the last word.

"Garveyism Is Again Taking the Island by Fire": The Harmony Division and the *New Negro Voice* in the early 1940s

Kingston holds a special place in the history of the UNIA; it was here, after all, that Marcus and Amy Ashwood Garvey founded the first chapter in 1914 and began to outline the organization's pan-Africanist message of race pride, self-reliance, and community uplift. Although the locus of the movement shifted to the United States for most of the following decade (as Garvey promoted the cause from UNIA headquarters in New York), Jamaican chapters continued to work on the local scale. These efforts were boosted by Garvey's return to Jamaica in 1927 with his second wife, Amy Jacques Garvey, and the decision to hold the 1929 convention in Kingston, which culminated in an elaborate parade through the city. Scholars have noted a marked decline in UNIA activities after Garvey's departure in 1935 for London and his worsening health,[15] but Jamaican activists proved unwilling to let the movement fade away with its leader. On the contrary, in 1938, S. U. Smith (proprietor of the Liberty Club) and several other Garveyites took it upon themselves to resuscitate Kingston's Harmony Division chapter, once again holding weekly meetings at the local Liberty Hall.

On July 26, 1941, editor Z. Munroe Scarlett launched the *Negro Voice* to both report on and contribute to this revival. Casting itself as the official organ of the Harmony Division and the "mouthpiece of the U.N.I.A. in the West Indies,"[16] the *Negro Voice* outlined "Our Duty" to "work as never before to place UNIA in [the] position Garvey intended it to occupy, to hold in view always the Redemption of Africa and Uplifting of Our Noble Race."[17] The paper also announced plans to raise money for a bust of (recently deceased) Garvey and to support Garvey's widow and two children, domiciled in Jamaica since the late 1930s.[18] In the second edition, Munroe announced a membership drive, calling on readers to join the Harmony Division or create their own divisions with support from established commissioners.[19] Although it is hard to track readership, letters to the editor came in from across the island, praising the *Negro Voice* for helping cement "the true spirit of brotherhood" and "giving to the masses of this country a paper of their own."[20] Letters from abroad also suggest an international audience, and in November 1941 the paper claimed to have 378 subscriptions from Central America and 516 from the United States.[21]

The paper included lengthy descriptions (usually a full broadsheet, sometimes with speeches transcribed) of weekly meetings, giving us an idea of both the structure of the Harmony Division's work and the activities of Liberty Hall more generally. As in the past, meetings usually ran from around 8:00 to 10:00 on Sunday nights and featured a mix of sermons, recitations, musical performances, and speeches. Liberty Hall revived its standing as a social and cultural center,[22] hosting several small businesses and a lunchroom where workers could get "native dishes" at "very low prices,"[23] while also airing radio broadcasts and holding weekly dances made affordable for "the hundreds of our poorer group who could find no place of amusement."[24] The Harmony Division also revived the long tradition of pageantry and performance that had made the UNIA famous.[25] A "Rally of Red Black and Green" held on December 28, 1941, for example, included a procession of prominent members dressed as Garveyite personalities and various Ethiopian royalty, who took to the stage "in real Hollywood fashion" and kept the crowd "roaring with laughter" from 8:00 to 10:30 p.m.[26] These performances also spilled out into the streets. Members of the Harmony Division organized a mock "attack" on Greenwich Town on June 14 in which officers planted the flag, sang the battle hymn of the UNIA, and stormed the city "not in the physical fashion" but rather through an explanation of the aims and projects of the UNIA. Although a heavy downpour led them to retreat to the Ethiopia Spiritual Mission, by 6:00 p.m. the city had reportedly "surrendered and asked that a branch of the U.N.I.A. be set up there without delay."[27]

Coverage of the organization in the *Negro Voice* (renamed the *New Negro Voice* in October 1941 under the editorship of T. A. Kitchener) was overwhelmingly positive. Reporters praised how Liberty Hall was "once more one of the leading educational centres"[28] and claimed that street meetings held by UNIA speakers reached audiences of five to six hundred people.[29] Rallies at Liberty Hall were reportedly so full that at times they had to set up loudspeakers outside for those who could not get in;[30] at one meeting, the reporter claimed that "there was not a vacant flight of steps on the staircase. People sat on both adjoining fences, on the roofs of houses, and some were even seen in a nearby tree."[31] Of course it is possible that some of these numbers were exaggerated, as the *New Negro Voice* attempted not only to *document* but also to *produce* the image of a powerful, united black community.[32] But one cannot doubt the spirit of enthusiasm running through the paper, which announced triumphantly in November 1941: "There is every indication that Garveyism is again taking the Island by fire."[33] Describing a meeting in December of that year, a reporter further remarked that the atmosphere "reminded one of the glorious days, when the late Mr. Garvey could sway and spellbound his audience with his thrilling and deep-rooted lectures on the Redemption of Africa," and noted how the audience "cheered and cheered as the speakers and musical artistes delivered the goods."[34]

But if the paper connected itself to a glorious past, it would also have to contend with a present that was markedly different from the heyday of the UNIA in the 1920s and early 1930s. This was a Jamaica, after all, still in the aftershock of a widespread labor rebellion that shook the island in 1938, revealed the power of the masses to disrupt British colonial rule, and spurred a wave of unprecedented mobilization, including the creation of the island's first island-wide labor union (the Bustamante Industrial Trade Union) and the first nationalist political party (the People's National Party under Norman W. Manley). Critiques of colonialism, racism, and class inequality took center stage as commentators of all stripes debated the island's future in meetings of trade unions, citizens associations, social clubs, and local branches of political parties.[35] The rebellious climate in Jamaica, coupled with the wider activist fervor and sense of urgency characterizing the late 1930s/early 1940s on a global scale, "made available (temporarily) social and discursive spaces hitherto defined as unspeakable or nonexistent."[36] This included heated debates over family life, birth control, and women's status that spilled out from newspapers and lecture halls onto street corners.[37]

Black women inspired by anticolonial, pan-Africanist, and international feminist movements alike seized on the opportunities presented by this moment to inject their voices into discussions of Jamaica's future. In 1937, Maymie Aiken had joined local activists Amy Bailey, Ina Bailey, and Eulalie Domingo to create the Women's Liberal Club (WLC), calling on Jamaican women to foster national spirit, take an interest in local and world events, study "negro history," and advance the status of Jamaican women socially and politically.[38] Moving beyond the white-elite-dominated suffragette and ladies "charity work" organizations of the previous decades, the WLC sought to combine a critique of race, class, and gender inequality. Shortly after the labor rebellion, the WLC organized the island's first cross-racial "Women's Conference," featuring speeches by Jamaica's leading female social workers, teachers, and reformers and attended by some fifty women of diverse backgrounds. The conference manifesto (published in the mainstream *Daily Gleaner* and presented to the island's governor) demanded equal rights for women, full participation in political decision making, an expansion of social services, and access to birth control in state medical clinics. The conference ended by launching the political campaign of teacher Mary Morris-Knibb, who would go on to become the island's first elected female politician, marking a historic moment in the history of Jamaican women's activism.[39]

Although its primary goal remained the promotion of Garveyite philosophy and the construction of a pan-Africanist movement, the *Negro Voice* could hardly avoid engaging with these local developments. And indeed, interspersed between excerpts from Garvey's philosophical tracts, tales from African history, and "Ethiopian News" shorts tracking contemporary developments in Africa, one can find articles assessing local government reports, publicizing meetings of other Jamaican organizations, drawing attention to labor activism, and promoting the work of the People's National Party.[40] The paper also dedicated considerable space to the questions surrounding women, gender, and sexuality occupying the island's attention at the time. This is perhaps unsurprising considering the active participation of women in the UNIA, including many of those at the forefront of women's activism like Amy Bailey and Maymie Aiken. Indeed, as we will see below, the local division proved relatively open to women's leadership and supported several of the demands of contemporary women's rights activists.

"She Must Say Something": Women's Participation and Gender Politics in the Harmony Division

As elsewhere, women were involved in a variety of activities within the UNIA: attending weekly meetings, engaging in organizational work, providing financial support. When the Harmony Division launched a "million penny drive" to purchase Liberty Hall, women featured regularly on the list of top collectors, and on June 26, 1943, Adina Spencer was honored for being the top collector for three consecutive weeks.[41] Other women helped distribute the *New Negro Voice* both at home and abroad. After receiving a copy of the paper that had been addressed to her (recently deceased) husband in the Canal Zone, for example, one Florence Bright ordered two hundred copies to distribute and assured the editor that "as his wife and co-worker I am still doing my part on behalf of the service that we have both pledged to render to our Race."[42] Women were also present onstage at Harmony Division meetings every week, whether delivering recitations, performing music, or as featured speakers. Occasionally, they were in the majority. This can be seen, for example, in the program for a meeting on September 21, 1941, outlined by the paper as follows:

Chorus by the Rising Star Singing Co

Recitation by Master Porter

Negro Spiritual by the Rising Star Singing Co

Solo by Mrs. E. Levy

Recitation by Mrs. T. McPherson

Solo by Mrs. S. Brown

Short address by Madam DeMena Aiken

Anthem by the Rising Star Singing Co

Mandolin solo by Mr. L. Noble

Solo by Miss Hewie

Short address by Miss Amy Bailey

Negro Spiritual by the Rising Star Singing Co

Solo by Little Miss Thompson

Solo by Mrs. McCreath

Short address by Mr. E. E. Whyte

Solo by Miss Leon

Duet by Mrs. Brown and Mrs. McPherson

Solo by Little Miss Thompson

Anthem by the Rising Star Singing Co.

Chairman's closing remarks.[43]

The fact that the program was so heavily dominated by women went unremarked on by the *Negro Voice*, perhaps providing evidence of the ease with which women were incorporated on the platform.

The assertiveness of these women as financial providers, performers, speakers, and newspaper distributors contrasts sharply at some points with the privileging of male activism in many of the *New Negro Voice*'s articles, editorials, and letters. Writers frequently gendered "the Negro" as male or referred to the "Negro man" directly as the key actor, calling on *him* to "Awake to newness of Life, [and] Work STRENUOUSLY and CO-OPERATIVELY for TRUE EMANCIPATION."[44] Both men and women repeated this emphasis on male leadership in their discourses before the Harmony Division. A speech by the late Garvey's second wife, Amy Jacques Garvey (domiciled on the island since the late 1930s), for example, argued: "The Negro will have to begin to use his brain. Get out of the rut you are in. Think that what other men have achieved you can achieve. You must show the world that you can work systematically. . . . Stand square on your feet like a man and act properly."[45] Articles, letters, and speeches also at times relegated women to a nurturing, caretaking role in the domestic sphere, calling on them "to do all in their power to bring up their children in a proper manner so that they may be able to take an active part in the emancipation of the Negro race."[46]

But the *New Negro Voice* also highlighted other ways of gaining prominence and authority within the movement that did not center as neatly around the elevation of militarized masculinity or the fulfillment of binary gendered destinies. Some called for men to adopt characteristics traditionally associated with femininity, such as compassion and care. One article lamented, for example, that "in some of our Institutions we have men at the head of them who are absolutely void of the human touch, whose hearts are vacant as far as human love and justice is concerned."[47] A short story by Randolph Williams, published in several installments in 1941, also championed a male hero (Mr. Stanford Stapleton) who would not have fit comfortably within the militarized male divisions of a Garvey parade. Described as a "small and nimble"[48] homeless man who dresses in rags and sleeps regularly on a park bench, Stapleton earns the respect of onlookers through his strong sense of justice and his organizational skills as he rallies the community to defend a man who is wrongfully arrested. Stapleton also comes to be known as "chief of all the speakers";[49] Williams describes how his passion for justice "welled up in him, reached his head and found an exit in his mouth out of which it rushed in bold fiery oratory."[50] These principles were also stressed in other articles and editorials, as both male and female members of the Harmony Division were praised for their commitment to the cause, sense of justice, and speeches delivered in a "fiery manner"[51] which "kept the audience spell bound."[52]

Historians have, of course, recognized the strength of these principles in the past, noting that for Garveyites "integrity" was seen "not as a reflection of education, or profession, or wealth, or ancestry, but as something conferred by one's investment in the principles of the organization, and by one's sacrifice and toil for the race."[53] But scholars have rarely drawn attention to the fact that these means of status-claiming were relatively gender neutral, accessible to both male and female followers, and could sometimes trump the fulfillment of gendered roles. Of course it should be stressed that these were *relatively* gender neutral; in societies deeply shaped by gender inequalities nothing is totally gender neutral. Gender norms that denigrated women's intellect, poor women's double burden of working both outside and within the home, as well as preexisting biases toward masculine styles of leadership and speaking may well have given men a leg up from the outset; indeed, scholars have noted that women in other UNIA chapters sometimes had difficulty being recognized from the floor by men who presided over UNIA meetings.[54] But the considerable number of women who *did* find a platform within the Harmony Division suggests the barriers were perhaps lower than in other spaces where power was more dependent on financial wealth, social position, or access to education. Consider, for example, the case of Miss V. Warren, who stepped onto the platform at Liberty Hall for the first time in late September 1941. Warren noted that she had never given an address in public before but that the UNIA "impressed her so much that she must say something."[55] Her address was brief, summarized by the reporter for the *New Negro Voice* thus: "In her work or at play she can think of nothing else but the U.N.I.A. and it surprised her to know that there are so many people who are just going about who do not take such a noble movement seriously."[56] Within a few months, Warren had gained status and recognition as an "ardent member of the Harmony Division"[57] who spoke regularly and also exercised her creative talents as an actress in UNIA plays.[58]

Several female members also gained status as some of the Harmony Division's finest speakers. The division's first lady vice president, Miss D. Payne, was known to give "stirring" speeches,[59] and Jamaican activists Amy Bailey and Alma LaBadie were billed as "forceful" speakers.[60] Amy Jacques Garvey's occasional attendance at Harmony Division meetings and UNIA-organized excursions in the early 1940s was used as a selling point in advertisements,[61] speaking to her popularity as a figure in the movement. Indeed, if she had faced some pushback for her assertiveness in the United States,[62] the *New Negro Voice*'s consistent praise for her exhilarating speeches (even when they attacked the work of UNIA men) suggests a level of comfort with her leadership. As a report after one meeting noted: "Mrs. Garvey after her long silence excelled herself, a flash of the 'old fire' seemed to have returned to her especially for the occasion."[63] During her speech at the fourth anniversary of the Harmony Division, the *New Negro Voice* reported, "deathly silence pervaded, while the fiery little figure put forth words of truth."[64]

Maymie "Madam de Mena" Aiken, the Harmony Division's most frequent female speaker in the early 1940s, also held considerable authority within the organization through her long-standing commitment to the cause and strong elocution skills. Indeed, Aiken appears to have played as prominent a role as many of the more formal leaders, at least in the structure of weekly meetings and UNIA events. She sat on the platform alongside the official executive and was the division's installing officer, appearing in regalia to officially welcome new members to the organization. Aiken also arguably had greater sway over public opinion than did many of her colleagues. She was a central speaker more often than some of the formal leaders of the movement, and her popularity is highlighted repeatedly by the *New Negro Voice*, which referred to her as "our little Joan of Arc"[65] and recorded numerous speeches delivered "in her usual brilliant manner."[66] As discussed further below, she also had the power to shape the agenda of weekly meetings and served on key commissions within and outside of the organization. Indeed, although she might have technically been subservient to the male leadership structure, one gets the sense that the average meeting attendee might well have thought Aiken was in charge.

Aiken had long used her platform within the movement to explicitly encourage Garveyite women to "line up for women's rights" and break out of the narrow gender roles promoted by some of her peers.[67] She embodied this activism in her own persona, choosing, for example, to ride horseback in military regalia at the Kingston convention in 1929; as Adam Ewing notes, she would have cut a stark contrast to the other featured woman on the parade, a gowned "Queen."[68] Aiken also took a key position in the Harmony Division's "attack" on Greenwich Town in June 1942 as head of the Motor Corps Division,[69] a "militarized" auxiliary headed by a woman brigadier general (with training in military tactics and automobile repair). While the Motor Corps has not received as much attention from gender scholarship as the more traditionally feminine Black Cross Nurses (who, incidentally, appear very rarely in the pages of the *New Negro Voice*), the ease with which members accepted (more than that, *adored*) their militarized female leader suggests a certain degree of flexibility in gender roles and ideology.[70]

Indeed, numerous members of the Harmony Division seem to have interpreted the role of "race Mother" to extend beyond the home and the position of nurturing supporter. When the *New Negro Voice* held a competition in December 1941 calling on youth to write an essay on the topic of "Why Should We Read the 'New Negro Voice,'" the winner was thirteen-year-old Shirley E. James of Pilgram, Claremont, who wrote: "I would like to get to a university and have an education as the white man's daughter. The New Negro Voice has started the road to reach all these objectives."[71] A letter from the Canal Zone by Dulcie Payne also imagined an assertive role for women within the movement: "We want our names to be written indelibly on the pages of History, that our children yet unborn, when they see our footprints they can call us blessed. If we can read of a Joan of Arc, a Florence Nightingale, why we as women can't do the same?"[72] Payne's invocation of *both* Florence Nightingale *and* Joan of Arc suggests that the average Garveyite woman might have seen both the caretaking role of the Black Cross Nurses and the forceful, militarized leadership embodied by Madam de Mena as potential paths in service of the movement. Indeed, scholars have noted in passing that Garveyite women in other places and times also invoked the image of Joan of Arc and spoke of themselves as "self-sufficient women warriors,"[73] suggesting the broader appeal of women's militarized leadership among the organization's female members.

Several male Garveyites also spoke out in favor of broader opportunities for women and their leadership in spheres beyond the home. An editorial (presumably by Kitchener) documenting the advances made by women globally during World War II spoke approvingly of women who were not "merely keeping the home fires burning" but also "in helmets, overalls, furnace goggles, aviator suits, nurse's aprons, doctor's smocks and laboratory uniforms, women risking their lives daily in the occupied countries."[74] The *New Negro Voice* also doled out praise for Mary Morris Knibb's work on the Kingston and St. Andrew Corporate Council. As one letter to the editor noted, within a short period of time Morris Knibb had managed to get things moving on a number of problems to which "these men councillors" had "blinded their eyes" in the past.[75] The Harmony Division as a whole also appears to have offered practical support for women's careers. Miss Iris Patterson was honored by the division for her "unflinching career,"[76] and efforts were made by Mr. Thoywell-Henry of the Harmony Division to have a book of her poems published.[77] Poet and radio personality Una Marson was also described by the *New Negro Voice* as "Cleopatra No. 2"[78] and praised by the paper for being "not only an outstanding woman of the age but . . . also worthy of being considered one of those Negroes who deserves the wholehearted sympathy of everyone who traces an ancestry to Africa."[79] In the early 1940s Harmony Division, then, praise for motherhood and family life did not necessarily entail a disavowal of women's creative and political pursuits.[80]

In addition to praising women's leadership in a range of spheres, the *New Negro Voice* also drew attention to some of the powerful barriers and intense struggles shaping black working-class women's daily lives. An exposé on the Maternity Hospital, for example, lambasted the dire conditions under which poor women were forced to deliver their children,[81] a story on female street vendors called for better conditions at the Jubilee market,[82] and several editorials called out men who would attack "young women and women of advanced age" who "have to toil for their livelihood and after a hard day's task are compelled to face the nerve-racking ordeal of being robbed, molested and sometimes criminally assaulted by these ruthless criminals."[83] An editorial on "Women and Labour" also lamented the low wages for women workers, calling for "a fair day's pay for a fair day's work."[84] As the editor argued: "If any country should reach its highest peak, there should be the greatest respect and consideration paid to its women. Until this is done you can expect but very little in its progress."[85]

In these articles, *New Negro Voice* writers and readers invoked a wider discourse popular among both women's activists and nationalist reformers in the early twentieth century, which posited women's status as a "barometer of civilization."[86] As scholars have pointed out, this discourse at times came shrouded in a paternalistic language of protection;[87] indeed, pieces on sexual harassment in the *New Negro Voice* sometimes called specifically on *men* to uplift and defend women against those who would "destroy the virtue of womanhood."[88] But holding up women's status as a quintessential aspect of community well-being and racial/national advance also created space for the kinds of discussions noted above, calling attention to the structures constraining women's reproductive and productive lives and providing support for women's political engagement, creative endeavors, and careers beyond the home. The *New Negro Voice* also praised women who took defense into their own hands, not only rhetorically but in practice. This is perhaps most vividly illustrated in the paper's front-page coverage of a 1942 mugging of Miss Jeanette Clarke, vice-president of the Harmony Division. The journalist reported: "Miss Clarke, who displayed great bravery, gave the intruder a smashing blow on the right jaw, staggering him, and chased him until he was apprehended by an ARP Special Constable, and taken to the Hannah Town Police Station."[89] Clearly, the paper was not only interested in projecting an image of delicate femininity, but also recognized the real-life militant women in their midst.

The Limits of Ideological Flexibility? The Birth Control Debate Comes to Liberty Hall

If the *New Negro Voice* appears more progressive in its approach to a number of women's issues than we might assume, the paper's staff (and Garveyite men who attended Harmony Division meetings) attempted to draw the line more sharply on the issue of birth control. As noted above, several women active in both the Women's Liberal Club and the UNIA (including Maymie Aiken and Amy Bailey) had come out in favor of expanding access to birth control at the Women's Conference in February 1939. The friction this caused within the organization from the outset is evident in a letter published in the mainstream *Daily Gleaner* on August 28 of that year, penned by J.A.G. Edwards, a union activist and prominent UNIA member. Edwards wrote:

> I am indeed greatly disappointed in seeing Mrs. P.A. Aiken, popularly known in the U.N.I.A. as Madam de Mena, championing Birth Control.... Whilst I always hold Madam in high esteem, and still regard her as a lover of the race, . . . [h]ow in the name of goodness can any far-sighted Negro Leader agree to the practice of Birth Control within the race to-day as it stands, when the only power the Negro can boast of to-day is his power in numbers, even though, maybe 60% of them are half-starved.[90]

Edwards closed by noting his hope that "Madame will again reflect, because I genuinely feel that she means well, but she is too anxious to get relief for the suffering people."[91]

Undeterred, Aiken defended her position forcefully in a letter to the *Gleaner* a week later that highlighted the threat to women's health of frequent childbearing and unsafe abortions "undertaken in a vain attempt to end an unwanted pregnancy,"[92] while also lamenting the undue suffering experienced by children whose parents were unable to maintain them. She stated the case simply and forcefully:

> Through Birth Control Clinics, the women of Jamaica will secure the necessary knowledge, so easily obtained by those who are able to pay private physicians. Many women will acquire a general knowledge of the care of their bodies . . . which would be a great contribution to family welfare. Why not give a fair chance to every child that is born; and the right to every woman of voluntary parenthood?[93]

Aiken also expressed her surprise to see Edwards attacking birth control "from a racial standpoint," when "Birth Control is not practised by any particular race group, but is a representative institution started to benefit humanity in general."[94] Aiken closed her letter by claiming that "nearly every woman who is a mother will agree that the subject of Birth Control is of very little interest to the selfish man,"[95] thus blatantly calling out the gendered double standard underlying a discourse that called on women, specifically, to sacrifice personal health and reproductive control toward the collective cause.

As the *New Negro Voice* did not begin publication until 1941, it is hard to know how this conflict played out within Liberty Hall in 1939. But the issue would come to a head more visibly in a January 16, 1942, meeting of the Harmony Division that again pitted Garveyite men against women. Social worker Alma LaBadie had been invited to speak on "The Rocking of the Cradle," a subject, the paper stressed, of "vital importance" to all.[96] Before a crowd that reportedly numbered one thousand, LaBadie covered a range of topics, from education to the lack of support for single mothers. Unleashing her frustration with gender relations,[97] LaBadie lamented how

> our men go out and hatch children, while they just grow up to enter the Penitentiary. It is due to lack of self-respect for our women. . . . If a woman wants to have a baby, see that the man makes provision for the support therefore, and afterwards if they wanted one hundred children, let them have them, provided he can continue to support them. . . . [But] [o]ur aim should be for not a million negroes, but the quality negroes, especially here in Jamaica.[98]

LaBadie's apparent promotion of birth control provoked an immediate uproar among the crowd, prompting Aiken to step in to defend her colleague and restore order. As the *New Negro Voice* reported, Aiken had not planned to give an address, but "during the course of the former speaker, there seemed to have been a few persons who did not agree with all she had to say, and she did not approve and would not tolerate even that slight misbehaviour on the platforms of the Universal Negro Improvement Association."[99] Aiken discussed her own experiences seeing women abandoned with their children and reaffirmed LaBadie's core narrative: "Get quality, respect the women of the race."[100] The next speaker, St. William Grant, who was an active Garveyite in New York prior to his return to Jamaica, affirmed his respect for Aiken but then launched into a long "Anti–Birth Control" rant. As the *New Negro Voice* recorded: "He claimed that Mr. Garvey was no advocate of birth control, and if he were alive he would not support it. As a true Garveyite he was not in accord with it."[101]

Invoking Garvey was obviously meant to put an end to the conversation. Yet Grant seems to have felt the need to bring it up again at the next meeting of the Harmony Division, at which he proclaimed himself "one hundred per cent anti-birth control" and continued: "I defy any man or woman, married or unmarried, belonging to the U.N.I.A. or not to talk birth control. I will declare war on God himself to talk birth control while I am around."[102] The *New Negro Voice*'s staff also joined in the anti–birth control brigade. On January 31 the paper published an editorial titled "Birth Control or Extermination of the Blacks—Which?" confirming the paper's "unqualified denunciation" of birth control, as an affront against Christianity and a harbinger of "race extinction."[103] Two editorials in March of that year affirmed the paper's opposition to attempts to "decrease the population of the blacks" through "Birth Control, or vicious abortions."[104] J.A.G. Edwards also devoted several of his "As I See the Negro World" columns in the *New Negro Voice* to lambasting birth control, calling on "the Negro Mother" to instead "gird her loins with more Christian fortitude and deep love for her children to the point of seeing them properly educated in the schools of the land, while playing her part eminently at home in giving the necessary home culture and training."[105]

A number of different elements seem to have shaped this reaction. Although they might appear extreme, the *New Negro Voice* writers' concerns over malicious attempts to promote "race extermination" were not completely unfounded. The early twentieth century had seen the rapid spread of eugenics campaigns transnationally calling for "better breeding" policies, including the involuntary sterilizations of select populations in Europe, North America, and beyond; in most cases, those deemed "unfit" and targeted for sterilization were poor, working-class, and/or ethnically marginalized populations.[106] Plans for compulsory sterilization fairly explicitly targeted at the black working classes had also reached local legislatures in Bermuda, Barbados, and Jamaica in the late 1930s and early 1940s.[107] Although public outcry and popular mobilization ensured that these proposals were promptly abandoned, politically conscious Jamaicans remained justifiably concerned about the birth control movement. But the *New Negro Voice* also opposed efforts to incorporate contraceptives into public health services on an explicitly *voluntary* basis, calling on "Negro Voters of Jamaica" to press legislators to abandon one such bill in 1942.[108] Columns in the *New Negro Voice* also suggest a deeper anxiety over the possibility of sex without reproduction, whether voluntary or not. For some it was an affront to Christian morals; for others it was a betrayal of the gendered demands of the Garveyite movement, expressed in their most conservative and rigid form. If Garveyite ideology could at times be more flexible in practice than we assume (as illustrated by scholars and my own discussion above), we must recognize that for some proponents on some issues, there was no space for maneuver allowed.[109]

Indeed, the *New Negro Voice*'s staff appears to have been decidedly unable to entertain the arguments put forward by their female colleagues, resorting instead to personal attacks that represent a low point in the history of gender relations within the organization. Shortly after LaBadie's speech at the UNIA, an editorial in the paper argued that several prominent black advocates were being used "as tools to spread the Birth Control Propaganda," adding: "These ladies of brains, 99 1/2 per cent of whom never had a child, and know not of a mother's love, fail to realize that they are ringing the death knell of race-destruction."[110] Edwards called out Amy Bailey and the Women's Liberal Club explicitly, arguing that the WLC should "avoid making themselves childishly sympathetic in thoughts and acts, because such childish sympathies tend more to destroy our Race" and suggesting that they were being misled by white women. Edwards also drew on discourses of paternalism, posing the question: "Miss Bailey, wouldn't you be real happy in having, say, ten under nourished, and physically underfed black brothers to defend your Ladyship when attacked by an intruder than not having any one at all?"[111]

Responses in the paper suggest a mix of views among Garveyite personalities and *New Negro Voice* readers. A number of letters to the editor supported the position of the paper, calling birth control a false panacea for the island's problems and/or highlighting the Bible's call for the people to "go forth and multiply."[112] But the paper also gave voice to dissenting opinions. A letter by the anonymous "Sympathizer," for example, called on the editors to recognize a distinction between "murder control" and preventative birth control, which was "necessary for a happy home."[113] Of course, it is difficult to know what the average reader or the average attendee at the Harmony Division meetings thought about the matter, but I would not assume that the opposition of St. William Grant and the *New Negro Voice* staff would necessarily trump the support of Aiken, LaBadie, and others. The *New Negro Voice* was a powerful but not a hegemonic force in shaping public opinion; St. William Grant also faced criticisms for misusing his platform and at one meeting was actually kicked out of Liberty Hall for being disruptive.[114] Aiken, on the other hand, appears to have held fairly universal respect; as evident above, even those who disagreed with her were careful to express their continued admiration for her. Indeed, it might well be that the anti–birth controllers' flurry of response was a reflection of the very real authority Aiken held in the organization, and her power to sway public opinion: in this case, away from Garvey's strict philosophy surrounding birth control.

The resistance of these men certainly did little to dissuade black women activists from their work. Alma LaBadie was energized rather than discouraged by the negative reaction to her speech before the UNIA, relating in a letter shortly afterward her plans to give 180 similar talks across the island to black lodges— "especially women's lodges"—to ensure that they were all made "Birth Control conscious."[115] Amy Bailey was similarly unfazed, recalling in later interviews how she skilfully faced down an objector who accused her of bringing in a white woman to "kill off black people."[116] In doing so, these women vividly illustrated how the skills of elocution learned in the UNIA could be put toward feminist causes, as argued by Ford-Smith.[117] But continuing on with the *New Negro Voice* past this moment of heightened tension also suggests that these same women continued to see the UNIA as a fruitful space for women's rights activism. Bailey continued to speak before large UNIA crowds, featured at the Empire Day Celebration in 1943 and at several Women's Nights organized by Aiken over the course of 1942 and 1943.[118] Indeed, in the year following LaBadie's January 1942 speech, Aiken appears to have asserted herself—and her women's rights agenda—within the organization even *more* prominently than before.

Seizing the Space: Women Occupy Liberty Hall

Aiken's activism within the organization in the aftermath of the birth control conflict took a variety of forms. In February 1942 she started a "Women's Column" in the *New Negro Voice* that ran regular features on "the history of the achievements of women,"[119] including women such as Mary McLeod Bethune, Madame C. J. Walker, Marian Anderson, and Sojourner Truth. Although many of these appear to have been copies of articles from the *Negro World* with some commentary by Aiken,[120] they portrayed a clear message that women had a prominent role to play in "the new social order of the future whether that place be in the home or whether it be in the professional or business world."[121] An article titled "Women in Next Peace Conference," for example, both challenged gender stereotypes and argued in favor of parity in leadership. The (unknown) author argued that "while I have no patience with the idea that women are nobler, finer, and more spiritual than men and that they will purify government, I do believe that women have a definite contribution to make which has too long been overlooked" and called for women and men to be represented at government and international conferences on "a fifty-fifty basis."[122]

Aiken also organized a series of Women's Nights that incorporated some of the island's most prominent women's activists; these were enthusiastically supported by the *New Negro Voice* and attended by both men and women. The first, held in September 1942, was presided over by herself and the Harmony Division's lady president, Miss Davis, with speeches by Councillor Mary Morris-Knibb and Amy Jacques Garvey, among others. As the *New Negro Voice* explained to readers: "The women feel that men have been officiating too much, and they are not being given enough say in the management of the affairs. . . . The men are going to be quiet, and see how the ladies will carry through."[123] The conference was touted by the paper as a "wonderful success"[124] and received a favorable review in a letter to the editor: "Never in the history of [the] UNIA of Kingston, can we recall a better spent night. . . . I now say that we men had better brush up or the ladies are going to lead us to a victorious end during and after this present conflict."[125]

The event was such a "banner night" that another was organized for November 29, with guest chair Edith James (a well-known social worker) and talks by Marjorie Stewart, Ina Bailey, and Amy Jacques Garvey.[126] The *New Negro Voice* reported that the event was a "brilliant gathering" as "the women members of the Harmony Division U.N.I.A., putting the men in the background, presented their audience with the 'Women's night' when they promised to put the 'devil on the run,' the long awaited treat that was appreciated by the thousands who attended."[127] James stressed the importance of children having black female role models and called on women to "be emancipated" from inferiority complexes and realize that "they should have faith in themselves for whatever a man can do women are capable of doing the same and more."[128] Stewart spoke on the need for more opportunities for girls and the importance of cooperation, while Jacques Garvey finished with a talk on "Women's place in the world." She noted that although "50 years ago a woman's place was her home but as time evolved and the years rolled on women's place has evolved with them," before ending with a more conservative Garveyite gender vision: "We respect and love our men; we want to look up to them, and we want to hold their hands and help them on, not only in Jamaica but the world at large."[129] The meeting reportedly ended "amidst shouts of 'Long may they (women) live.'"[130]

Rather than reflecting a single, coherently progressive vision of women's rights and status,[131] the Women's Nights thus became a space for the expression of a variety of visions on the movement and women's roles within and beyond it.[132] At a Women's Night on July 18, for example, the evening began with a discourse by the assistant secretary, Miss Marshall, on the history of leadership by women in the UNIA, leading into a more conservative speech by one Mrs. Brown on the need for the "woman's touch" in the home, followed by a powerful discourse by Amy Bailey that openly critiqued the elevation of black women based solely on ideas of traditional femininity. Bailey questioned: "Why is it that the Negro men are not proud of their Negro women, and the only time the other fellow will learn to respect our women is when we treat our women folk as if they were queens like the other race."[133] She pointed out that Mary Magdalene had been "one of the greatest outcasts of those days" and argued that "whatever a woman's station is in life she should be treated with respect; if they have to sell us our fish or vegetables etc., they should be treated with respect."[134]

Women in the UNIA thus both played into and pushed at the edges of the gender roles outlined by some members of the movement, and by their society more generally. In the process, they asserted their right to occupy the space of the UNIA and direct it toward their concerns, however defined. The Harmony Division's willingness to accommodate these demands, along with the enthusiasm of the *New Negro Voice*, suggests that male members of this UNIA branch recognized that right, even if they did not always like what women had to say. Unlike in other places and times, the organization of Women's Nights also does not seem to imply a cordoning off of women into a confined space in an attempt to marginalize their demands. The nights were organized by Aiken explicitly with the pretense of subverting the patriarchal order of the organization, men appear to have attended them en masse, and Garveyite women continued to play a prominent role in the organization outside of these nights. In August 1942, for example, Aiken was the first person nominated for a UNIA commission,[135] and she continued to speak regularly at general meetings on other issues (such as the role of Africa in the movement, the "Laws of god compared with the laws of Nature," and the Atlantic Charter).[136] Aiken also created a business called the Garment Hospital, which was run out of the Liberty Club and provided employment for "needy women" in clothes repair,[137] thus attempting to combine her political message with practical efforts to empower women financially. The endeavor was roundly supported by the *New Negro Voice*, which implored its readers in September 1943: "Have you helped by sending in clothes?"[138]

Conclusion

On October 23, 1943, the *New Negro Voice* assumed a new managing editor, the well-known Jamaican activist W. A. Domingo. The change in management led to a considerable change in tone and style, as Domingo shortened the paper to just four pages of brief news with occasional editorials; as a result, it is difficult to follow through the debates and the internal dynamics of the Harmony Division in the detail provided above. Several articles focused on plans to buy the Liberty Club, which appear to have fallen through in late 1943, as the thirty-eight hundred pounds required for purchase was deemed too expensive, although the Harmony Division eventually acquired a property at 133 Orange Street for a lower figure.[139] Occasional references also suggest that the prominence of women within the movement did not die. Indeed, Aiken recuperated from an illness just in time to help open the new headquarters,[140] and she continued to give further speeches met, predictably, with "thunderous applause."[141]

Aiken's legacy within the Harmony Division provides a vivid illustration of the ways in which assertive Garveyite women challenged the limits of patriarchy and paternalism. But tracing the story of women and gender in the *New Negro Voice* also suggests that Aiken was not alone in pressing the issue. Through the pages of this weekly, the movement appears more receptive to some feminist principles than we might expect. Indeed, this is not only a story of women battling male patriarchal authority and ideology, but also a story of men supporting women's leadership and participation in the movement beyond the role of caretakers and helpmates. It is a story of gender ideologies that could be rigid at times for some actors (particularly surrounding the issue of women's bodily autonomy) but more fluid and open for others, providing space for feminist critique and activism not only beyond, but also *within*, Liberty Hall.

Of course, it may well be that the Harmony Division in the early 1940s is a deviation from the norm or a genuine outlier. Undoubtedly, the strength of the feminist movement in Jamaica at this moment and the particularly forceful presence of Madam de Mena were critical factors in opening up the space discussed here. But letters to the *New Negro Voice* from other areas, as well as references in other scholars' work, suggest that the imagery of Joan of Arc reached well beyond Jamaica; it is possible that the conversations about gender invoked by this symbolic figure and the authority of women leaders also stretched beyond this time and place, and will be revealed through further examinations of local chapters and individual Garveyite women. We may find that in fact the image of Joan of Arc held even more appeal than that of the Black Cross Nurses among Garveyite followers, some of whom may well have "confused Garveyism with feminism": or rather, recognized that the organization's core principles, strong women leaders, and openness to engaging with debates over women's status could provide space for alternative imaginings of what Garveyism meant, or could become, for women.

Acknowledgments

I would like to thank the participants of the Global Garveyism symposium for their comments and suggestions on the paper on which this chapter is based; Keisha N. Blain, Ronald J. Stephens, and Adam Ewing for their additional written feedback on the first draft; and Ula Y. Taylor and Lara Putnam for their advice and encouragement.

Notes

1. Madam de Mena's biography has recently been reconstructed by Courtney Morris, including a correction to the prevailing assumption that Aiken was Afro-Nicaraguan by birth. See Morris, "Becoming Creole, Becoming Black."

2. Ibid., 173.

3. Bair, "True Women, Real Men," 154. See also Mitchell, *Righteous Propagation*, 225–26.

4. Ewing, *Age of Garvey*, 150.

5. Leeds, "Toward the 'Higher Type of Womanhood,'" 19. On this contradiction, see also Blain, "'We Want to Set the World on Fire,'" 204; Satter, "Marcus Garvey," 67; Macpherson, "Colonial Matriarchs," 523; Parker, "Sex at a Crossroads"; and Mitchell, *Righteous Propagation,* 220–24.

6. Michael O. West and William G. Martin, "Contours of the Black International: From Toussaint to Tupac," in West, Martin, and Wilkins, *From Toussaint to Tupac*, 12.

7. Mitchell, *Righteous Propagation*.

8. Ibid., 58. See also Satter, "Marcus Garvey," 48; and Bair, "True Women, Real Men," 159.

9. See Taylor, "'Negro Women,'" 104–5; Blain, "'We Want to Set the World on Fire'"; Ewing, *Age of Garvey,* 153; Parker, "Sex at a Crossroads," 209–11; and Mitchell, *Righteous Propagation,* 226–28.

10. See, for example, Bair, "'Ethiopia Shall Stretch Forth Her Hands'"; and Parker, "Sex at a Crossroads."

11. Ford-Smith, "Unruly Virtues of the Spectacular," 32.

12. Ibid., 22.

13. Taylor, "'Negro Women,'" 105.

14. Reddock, "The First Mrs. Garvey," 60.

15. Hart, *Towards Decolonisation*, 128.

16. "Mass Meeting of Harmony Division Sunday 20th July 1941," *Negro Voice,* July 26, 1941, 6.

17. "Our Duty," *Negro Voice,* July 26, 1941, 4.

18. Ibid.

19. "Special Membership Drive," *Negro Voice,* August 2, 1941, 6.

20. H. B. Lawson, letter to the editor, *Negro Voice,* July 26, 1941, 4.

21. "*New Negro Voice* Circulation," *New Negro Voice,* November 22, 1941, 7.

22. On the role of Liberty Halls as social and cultural centers, see Ewing, *Age of Garvey,* 149; and Beverly Hamilton, "Marcus Garvey and Cultural Development in Jamaica," in R. Lewis and Bryan, *Garvey,* 87–111.

23. *New Negro Voice,* October 17, 1942, 1.

24. "Kingston Liberty Club," *New Negro Voice,* July 18, 1942, 7; see also "UNIA Conference Ends," *New Negro Voice,* August 8, 1942, 1; and "Liberty Club—Formerly Liberty Hall, 76 King St," *New Negro Voice*, November 1, 1941, 5.

25. On this tradition, see Ford-Smith, "Unruly Virtues of the Spectacular"; and Hamilton, "Marcus Garvey and Cultural Development in Jamaica."

26. "Rally Attracts Large Crowd," *New Negro Voice,* January 3, 1942, 5.

27. "Harmony Division Impress Audience," *New Negro Voice,* June 20, 1942, 8.

28. "UNIA Activities—Harmony Division," *Negro Voice,* August 16, 1941, 6.

29. "Harmony Division," *New Negro Voice,* November 22, 1941, 6. "Harmony Div. UNIA Blazes Trail," *New Negro Voice*, December 6, 1941, 1.

30. See, for example, "Rally Attracts Large Crowd," *New Negro Voice*, January 3, 1942, 5.

31. "Unprecedented Crowd Enjoy Rally of the Colours," *New Negro Voice*, January 31, 1942, 3.

32. As Ford-Smith argues, UNIA performances provided a "pedagogy of nation," a way to imagine a strong united community that did not yet exist in recognized form ("Unruly Virtues of the Spectacular," 23–24). We might see the *New Negro Voice* acting in a similar capacity.

33. "Crowd Cheer UNIA Speakers," *New Negro Voice,* November 22, 1941, 2.

34. "Harmony Div. UNIA Blazes Trail," *New Negro Voice,* December 6, 1941, 1.

35. For broad overviews of these developments, see Hart, *Towards Decolonisation;* Post, *Arise Ye Starvelings*; and Bolland, *Politics of Labour.*

36. Gregg, *Caribbean Women,* 49. See also Blain, "'We Want to Set the World on Fire,'" 196–97, on the 1940s as a "moment of possibilities" more broadly.

37. See Altink, *Destined for a Life of Service*; L. Putnam, "Global Child-Saving"; Bourbonnais, *Birth Control;* and Vassell, "Voluntary Women's Associations in Jamaica."

38. Honor Ford-Smith, "Women and the Garvey Movement in Jamaica," in R. Lewis and Bryan, *Garvey,* 81.

39. "Women Deal with Big Problems," *Daily Gleaner,* February 28, 1939, 10; Vassell, "Voluntary Women's Associations in Jamaica," 34.

40. On support for the People's National Party within the *New Negro Voice,* see Hart, *Towards Decolonisation,* 129.

41. "Miss A. Spencer Tops Million Penny Drive," *New Negro Voice,* June 26, 1943, 6. I believe this is the same Adina Spencer who played a prominent role in the labor movement in Jamaica.

42. Florence Bright, letter to the editor, *Negro Voice,* August 30, 1941, 4. See also G. M. Manning, letter to the editor, *Negro Voice,* August 16, 1941, 6; and Leanora Dobson, letter to the editor, *Negro Voice,* September 20, 1941, 4.

43. "UNIA Activities—Harmony Division," *Negro Voice,* September 27, 1941, 6.

44. "Our Weekly Message: Be Prepared," *Negro Voice,* August 2, 1941, 1. For another vivid example of this stress on men and redeemed manhood, see H. A. Palmer's poem "The Negro's Need," *Negro Voice,* August 23, 1941, 7.

45. "Mrs. Amy Jacques Speaks at Liberty Hall on Garvey's Day," *Negro Voice,* September 6, 1941, 6.

46. "UNIA Activities—Harmony Division," *Negro Voice,* August 16, 1941, 6.

47. "Human Misfits," *New Negro Voice,* May 29, 1943, 2.

48. Randolph Williams, "Mr. Stanford Stapleton: Gentleman?" *Negro Voice,* July 26, 1941, 3.

49. Randolph Williams, "Mr. Stanford Stapleton: Gentleman?" *Negro Voice,* August 2, 1941, 7.

50. Randolph Williams, "Mr. Stanford Stapleton: Gentleman?" *Negro Voice,* August 16, 1941, 3.

51. "UNIA Activities—Harmony Division," *Negro Voice,* August 16, 1941, 6.

52. "St. Andrew Division Notes," *Negro Voice,* September 27, 1941, 6.

53. Ewing, *Age of Garvey,* 149.

54. See Bair, "'Ethiopia Shall Stretch Forth Her Hands,'" 45; and Parker, "Sex at a Crossroads," 206.

55. "UNIA Mass Meeting," *New Negro Voice,* October 4, 1941, 6.

56. Ibid.

57. "Harmony Division," November 1, 1941, 6.

58. Ibid. See also "New Members Take Oath to Serve Race," *New Negro Voice,* December 13, 1941, 2; and "Harmony Division Notes," *New Negro Voice,* March 20, 1943, 5.

59. Robert Sterling, letter to the editor, *New Negro Voice,* January 10, 1942, 4.

60. "Miss Badie to Speak," *New Negro Voice,* January 17, 1942.

61. See, for example, "Bus Excursion to Montego Bay," *New Negro Voice,* November 8, 1941, 1.

62. See Taylor, "'Negro Women,'" 118–19.

63. "Marcus Garvey's 54th. Birthday Celebrated at Liberty Hall," *Negro Voice,* August 23, 1941, 6.

64. "4th Anniversay Harmony Division," *New Negro Voice,* April 11, 1942, 2.

65. "Harmony Division Makes Presentation," *New Negro Voice,* February 14, 1941, 7.

66. "UNIA Activities—Harmony Division," *Negro Voice,* September 27, 1941, 6.

67. Ewing, *Age of Garvey,* 158. See also Erik S. McDuffie, "'[She] devoted twenty minutes,'" 221–22.

68. Ewing, *Age of Garvey,* 158.

69. "Harmony Division Impress Audience," *New Negro Voice,* June 20, 1942, 8.

70. Michele Mitchell recognizes the militarized nature of the Motor Corps but points

out that they were still subservient to the male Universal African Legions (*Righteous Propagation,* 226). While this may be true, I still think the symbolism of the position is important, especially when embodied by an authority like Aiken.

71. "1st Prize Essay Competition: Why Should We Read the 'New Negro Voice'" by Shirley E. James, 13 years, Pilgram, Claremont," *New Negro Voice,* December 27, 1941, 6.

72. Dulcie Payne, letter to the editor, *Negro Voice,* August 16, 1941, 8.

73. Bair, "'Ethiopia Shall Stretch Forth Her Hands,'" 50; Ewing, *Age of Garvey,* 157.

74. Editorial, "Allied Women Work, Fight with Men in Common Struggle on Axis," *New Negro Voice,* April 18, 1942, 4.

75. Letter to the editor, *Negro Voice,* September 6, 1941, 7.

76. "Miss Iris Patterson Honoured," *New Negro Voice,* March 20, 1943, 6.

77. Letter to the editor, "Miss Patterson's Poems," *New Negro Voice,* May 16, 1942, 7.

78. Letter to the editor, "An Appreciation of the Race," *New Negro Voice,* February 28, 1942, 4.

79. Libra, "On the Scales," *New Negro Voice*, February 14, 1942, 4.

80. This stands in contrast to Mitchell's findings in *Righteous Propagation,* 229.

81. "My Experinece in the Maternity Hospital," *New Negro Voice,* December 5, 1942, 4–5.

82. "Women Vendors Appeal to Lady Huggins," *New Negro Voice,* October 9, 1943, 1.

83. "Hooliganism Must Go," *New Negro Voice,* July 18, 1942, 4. See also "Women Threatened?" *New Negro Voice,* August 21, 1943, 6.

84. "Woman & Labour," *New Negro Voice,* October 31, 1942, 4.

85. Ibid.

86. Reddock, "The First Mrs. Garvey," 61.

87. See, for example, Mcpherson, "Colonial Matriarchs"; and Leeds, "Toward the 'Higher Type of Womanhood.'"

88. Law Abiding Citizen, letter to the editor, *New Negro Voice,* August 1, 1942, 4.

89. "Harmony Division Vice President Robbed," *New Negro Voice,* October 24, 1942, 1.

90. J.A.G. Edwards, letter to the editor, *Daily Gleaner*, August 28, 1939, 12.

91. Ibid.

92. Maymie L. T. Aiken, letter to the editor, "Birth Control," *Daily Gleaner,* September 8, 1939, 10.

93. Ibid.

94. Ibid.

95. Ibid.

96. "Miss Badie to Speak," *New Negro Voice,* January 17, 1942.

97. On anger as a motivating force for women's activism, see Taylor, "'Negro Women,'" 116–19.

98. "Miss Badie to Speak," 5.

99. "Over One Thousand Flock Liberty Hall," *New Negro Voice,* January 24, 1942, 5.

100. Ibid.

101. Ibid.

102. "Unprecedented Crowd Enjoy Rally of the Colours," *New Negro Voice,* January 31, 1942, 2.

103. Editorial, "Birth Control or Extermination of the Blacks—Which?" *New Negro Voice*, January 31, 1942, 4.

104. "Garvey's Prophecy Revealed: Underlying Birth Control Is the Fear of Increased Population (?)," *New Negro Voice,* March 21, 1942, 8; see also "Child Murder . . . or Birth Control?" *New Negro Voice,* March 28, 1942, 1, 8.

105. J.A.G. Edwards, "As I See the Negro World," *New Negro Voice,* April 4, 1942, 3.

106. For a review of eugenics programs transnationally, see Bashford and Levine's *Oxford Handbook of the History of Eugenics.*

107. See Bourbonnais, *Birth Control,* chapter 1.

108. "Birth Control or Extermination of the Blacks—Which?" 4.

109. This observation fits with Mitchell's contention that reproduction and sexuality were "particularly fraught" among black activist circles in the early twentieth century. *Righteous Propagation,* 11.

110. "Birth Control or Extermination of the Blacks—Which?" 4.

111. Ibid., 2.

112. Adrian Holdsworth, letter to the editor, "Against Birth Control," *New Negro Voice,* February 21, 1942, 4; S. P. Radway, letter to the editor, "Scores Birth Control," *New Negro Voice,* April 4, 1942, 4; Sidney R. Mills, letter to the editor, "Agrees with MR. Lowe," *New Negro Voice,* April 4, 1942, 4; (Miss) Betsie Lamb, letter to the editor, *New Negro Voice,* July 25, 1942, 4.

113. Sympathizer, letter to the editor, *New Negro Voice,* February 7, 1942, 4. A few months before LaBadie's talk, the paper had also published an article that called on man to "space his family legitimately and rightmindedly." Rev. Cowell Lloyd, "Christmas Message," *New Negro Voice,* December 20, 1941, 6.

114. "Harmony Division Holds Meeting," *New Negro Voice,* March 21, 1942, 2.

115. Alma LaBadie to Miss Farquharson, n.d., 4/108/1348, May Farquharson Collection.

116. "Amy Bailey: Great Family Planning Pioneer," *JFPA News,* December 1970, 6, found in J2235, NLJ, National Library of Jamaica, Kingston.

117. Ford-Smith, "Unruly Virtues of the Spectacular," 32.

118. "Empire Day Celebration," *New Negro Voice,* May 22, 1942, 3.

119. "Women's Column," *New Negro Voice,* February 21, 1942, 7.

120. On recirculation and reprinting as a means to build a broader African American community, see Zackodnik, "Recirculation and Feminist Black Internationalism," 439–40.

121. "The Negro Girl Who Enters College," *New Negro Voice,* March 14, 1942, 3.

122. "Women's Column," *New Negro Voice,* April 25, 1942, 2. The column appears to have been taken over by one Martin Henry Williams in July 1942, retitled "Famous Women Past and Present," (July 18, 1942, 5), and then "Famous Men and Women Past and Present" (August 8, 1942, 3).

123. "Harmony Division Will Have Women's Night," *New Negro Voice,* September 12, 1942, 1.

124. "Women's Night Wonderful Success," *New Negro Voice,* September 19, 1942, 6.

125. Letter to the editor, "UNIA Ladies Admirer," *New Negro Voice,* September 26, 1942, 5.

126. "Women's Night," *New Negro Voice,* November 28, 1942, 1.

127. "Women's Night a Brilliant Gathering," *New Negro Voice,* December 5, 1942, 2.

128. "Monster Crowd at Joint Meeting," *New Negro Voice,* December 5, 1942, 5.

129. Ibid., 6.

130. Ibid.

131. As Joy James notes: "Liberal, radical, and revolutionary black feminisms are often reductively presented as ideologically unified and uniformly 'progressive,'" thus glossing over the significant differences in their attitudes toward institutional power and revolutionary goals. Joy James, "Radicalizing Feminism," in J. James and Whiting, *The Black Feminist Reader*, 244; see also McDuffie, "'[She] devoted twenty minutes,'" 221.

132. In this sense, the women's nights played a similar role to the *Negro World*, as outlined by Blain in "'We Want to Set the World on Fire.'"

133. "Woman's Night a Big Success," *New Negro Voice*, July 24, 1943, 2.

134. Ibid., 6.

135. "UNIA Commission to Be Appointed," *New Negro Voice*, August 15, 1942, 1.

136. See, for example, "Harmony Division Holds Meeting," *New Negro Voice*, October 17, 1942, 2; "UNIA Will be Reorganised in Spanish Town," *New Negro Voice*, October 17, 1942, 5; "Speakers Laud Marcus Garvey," *New Negro Voice*, June 26, 1943, 2.

137. "Garment Hospital" advertisement, *New Negro Voice*, July 18, 1942, 3.

138. "Liberty Club Activities," *New Negro Voice*, September 5, 1942, 6.

139. "Harmony Division Explains," *New Negro Voice*, November 13, 1943, 1.

140. "Harmony Div. Activities and Notes," *New Negro Voice*, December 11, 1943, 1.

141. "Harmony Division Activities," *New Negro Voice*, March 11, 1944, 2.

6

"The Language of Freedom"

Garveyite Women, Diasporic Politics, and Pan-African Discourses of the 1940s

KEISHA N. BLAIN

In a 1945 article titled "The Language of Freedom," pan-Africanist leader Amy Jacques Garvey emphasized the fundamental role of freedom in civil society. "All through the ages," she explained, "men and women, answering their inner urge, have dedicated their lives to the cause of freedom." "Human Freedom, whether it be on the hands or the minds," she added, "reconstructs lives, re-builds homes and families, resuscitates a people, a Race, and lifts their standard to the level of progressive, striving people."[1] Her comments underscored black nationalist women's call for universal emancipation at a moment when people of African descent throughout the globe were being denied full citizenship and human rights. Against the backdrop of World War II, Jacques Garvey called on black men and women to fight for their freedom, joining a vast diasporic community of black intellectuals and activists confronting global racism, impe-rialism, and colonialism. Like Jacques Garvey, several other Garveyite women intellectuals and activists used their writings and speeches to openly condemn European colonialism and to call for black political self-determination and eco-nomic self-sufficiency during the 1940s.

This essay explores the political ideas of black nationalist women based on their writings in several newspapers of the 1940s. It shows how women in the Universal Negro Improvement Association (UNIA), from diverse backgrounds and writing from various locales, promoted a global black liberationist vision and added distinctive voices to discourses surrounding pan-Africanism—the political belief that African peoples, on the continent and in the diaspora, share a common past and destiny. Maintaining cultural and racial bonds with Africans throughout the diaspora, these women skillfully used the black press—on local, national, and international levels—to endorse anticolonial politics, challenge global white supremacy, and counter negative images and stereotypical depictions of African history and culture. Yet, while committed to that mission, these women also embraced imperialist and civilizationist views that promoted some of the same ideals they rejected. Examining the largely overlooked writings of Garveyite women in the United States and other parts of the globe captures the richness and complexities of black nationalist women's ideas and activism during the twentieth century.

By exploring Garveyite women's political writings during the 1940s, this essay builds upon, yet extends beyond, the current literature on black nationalism and black radical politics.[2] Since the publication of Mark Matthew's 1979 article on Amy Jacques Garvey and the *Negro World*, a number of scholars—Honor Ford-Smith, Ula Y. Taylor, Tony Martin, and Barbara Bair, among them—have offered key insights into how the UNIA provided a platform for women activists to engage in national and global black politics during the 1920s.[3] Much of this work, however, has focused on a handful of prominent women in the movement. This essay joins a recent and ongoing scholarly effort to center the writings of rank-and-file Garveyite women and thereby excavate the political histories of black women activists who have been marginalized in the literature on black nationalism.[4] It also captures the continued salience of black nationalism as a driving force in black women's politics during era that historians have largely overlooked.[5]

Shifting focus from scholarly narratives on pan-Africanism, which generally emphasize the contributions of men, this essay offers new insights into how black women engaged pan-Africanist politics and discourses during the 1940s. Joining the scholarly works of Ula Y. Taylor, Asia Leeds, and others, this essay highlights the tensions, complexities, and contradictions of these women's ideas and shows how their political visions were both consistent with and contradictory to those of black male intellectuals and activists of the period.[6] The essay broadens the discourse on pan-Africanism during the 1940s by departing from historical accounts that privilege the story of the Fifth Pan-African Congress, held in Manchester, England, in 1945.[7] Centering black nationalist women's writings in this period reveals that the Fifth Pan-African Congress, while a major development in the period, was by no means the only locus of pan-Africanist activity during the 1940s. To the contrary, black women found a space in the black press to articulate visions of pan-African unity and to mobilize against racial discrimination, colonialism, and imperialism.

Garveyism and Black Politics during the 1940s

The 1940s was an era of significant transformation in the lives of black men and women across the United States and other parts of the globe. The outbreak of World War II, more than any other development during this period, marked a turning point in global history.[8] Concerned about the future of millions of people of color across the globe whose lives would be greatly affected by the war, black activists across the diaspora amplified their efforts to end global racism, imperialism, and colonialism.[9] On the home front, many black Americans were ambivalent about supporting American military aspirations given the persistence of racial violence, disenfranchisement, and Jim Crow segregation. A. Philip Randolph's plan for a March on Washington (1941) and the Double V campaign (1942), which called for an end to fascism abroad and Jim Crow at home, exposed the racial grievances concerning U.S. foreign policy.[10] These developments coincided with the formation of the Congress of Racial Equality (CORE), a multiracial political organization that helped to launch the modern civil rights movement and the second wave of the Great Migration, in which an estimated one million black southerners relocated to the North and West.[11]

For black women, the 1940s was an era of hope and possibility marred by the persistence of racial and gender inequality. When the United States entered World War II on December 8, 1941, women entered the labor force in record numbers to replace the men who had gone to battle. Certainly, the rapidly expanding labor force improved socioeconomic conditions for many black women, who comprised 600,000 out of one million black workers during World War II.[12] A significant number of black women who entered the army—an estimated four thousand—joined the Women's Army Corps (WAC), and more than three hundred became members of the Army Nurse Corps.[13] Notwithstanding the significance of these opportunities, black women's experiences during the 1940s were shaped by racial and gender discrimination. On the war front, African American WACs were relegated to segregated living quarters and endured, on a daily basis, gender and racial prejudice in an army dominated by white male officers.[14] In the workplace, black women encountered a racialized and gender-based hierarchy that consistently placed them at the bottom.[15]

Amid the socioeconomic upheavals of this era, many black men and women turned to the UNIA as a significant site for political engagement. Established in Jamaica in 1914 by Marcus Garvey, with the assistance of Amy Ashwood, the UNIA attracted millions of followers in more than forty countries around the world. These men and women embraced Garveyism—Garvey's race-based philosophy centered on black pride, political self-determination, economic self-sufficiency, and African redemption (from European colonization). Building on the ideas of earlier black leaders, including the Tuskegee Institute founder Booker T. Washington, pan-Africanist Martin Delany, and African Methodist Episcopal (AME) bishop Henry McNeal Turner, Garvey advocated a militant response to global white supremacy, calling on people of African descent to assert their political agency.[16]

Significantly, the UNIA functioned as a political incubator in which many black women became politicized and trained for future leadership. Garveyism provided a sense of empowerment, and within the UNIA women found opportunities to serve in a variety of both public and private roles.[17] Unlike women in many other race organizations, such as the National Association for the Advancement of Colored People and the National Urban League, women in the UNIA were "well integrated into the movement's structure" and constitution.[18] According to historian Ula Y. Taylor, the organization "went beyond carving out an auxiliary niche for women by developing a system in which each local division elected a male and female president and vice president."[19] In this way the UNIA provided a space for some women to maintain visible leadership positions. In the immediate aftermath of Garvey's arrest, imprisonment, and deportation from the United States to Jamaica during the mid-1920s, a host of factors, including financial difficulties, fragmentation, sexism, and ethnic tensions, facilitated a significant decline in UNIA membership.[20]

Garveyite Women's Writings during the 1940s

Despite the internal tensions in the UNIA, Garveyism as a movement and as an organizing tool, remained salient during the 1940s and beyond.[21] In the aftermath of Garvey's death in June 1940, black men and women in the United States and throughout the African diaspora held fast to many of Garvey's teachings. In July 1942, Ethel Collins, a Jamaican-born Garveyite residing in Cleveland, Ohio, published an article in the *New Negro World* in which she emphasized the continued influence of Garvey's ideas among black activists and intellectuals across the globe.[22] "Garvey is not dead, for he lives in the Hearts of men," she explained. "He believed the Negro capable of controlling his own destiny," she continued, "and he sought to ... liberate the Negro from the shackles of political and economic slavery, and from domination of imperialism in Africa." Articulating a militant anticolonial vision, Collins went on to emphasize the need for black men and women to assume the mantle of Garvey's leadership: "His spirit goes marching on, and shall not rest, until AFRICA IS FREE."[23] Mrs. J. P. Giddings, UNIA commissioner of Virginia, expressed similar sentiments in a 1942 editorial in which she emphasized Garvey's continued influence. "Although our dear leader has gone in the flesh," Giddings explained, "he can never really die here in the state of Virginia." "The name of Garvey seems to be on almost every tongue."[24]

For Giddings and many other black women activists and intellectuals, Garvey's memory was especially significant not only because of the influence of his ideas but because of the crucial role the UNIA played in their lives during this period. In the UNIA, these women, often from working-class backgrounds, found a space in which to challenge global white supremacy and to agitate for universal black liberation. While they were not oblivious to the class dimension of their political struggle, Garveyite men and women generally eschewed Marxism and had little interest in leftist organizations. In contrast to activists in the U.S. Communist Party and other leftist organizations of the period, activists in the UNIA promoted black capitalism as a way to bolster the economic standing of people of African descent.[25] Similar to other black nationalist organizations of the period, including the Nation of Islam (NOI), activists in the UNIA advocated racial separatism, black pride, political self-determination, and economic self-sufficiency. In contrast to members of the NOI, however, UNIA members promoted pan-Africanism, embracing a global vision of black liberation and diasporic cooperation.[26]

This vision would be reflected in Garveyite women's writings during the 1940s. Writing in *The African: The Journal of African Affairs*, the official periodical of the Harlem-based Universal Ethiopian Students' Association, Amy Jacques Garvey articulated a vision of pan-African unity. "The ties of blood that bind us transcends all national boundaries," she argued. "The differences of languages and dialects are being overcome as all of us are learning the language of freedom." "As Africans at home and abroad," she continued, "we join hands across the Oceans of the world. We pool our brains and our resources, slender though they may be, and TOGETHER we fulfill the high calling of our Creator, 'to live as brave men and to die as heroes.'"[27] Like many other black activists and intellectuals during this period, which historian Penny Von Eschen has described as a "diaspora moment," Jacques Garvey viewed the World War II era as a pivotal moment for black men and women in the diaspora to confront global white supremacy and secure their economic and political freedom.[28]

In August 1941, President Franklin D. Roosevelt and Prime Minister Winston Churchill introduced the Atlantic Charter, which laid out a set of principles meant to guide the Allied powers toward peace and stability.[29] The document declared that Roosevelt and Churchill would "respect the right of all peoples to choose the form of government under which they will live." While the charter "appeared to be the United States' and Britain's pledge to correct the injustices of the past and create a much more humane order," it excluded people of color.[30] Though Roosevelt later insisted that the charter's provision should include colonized nations, the lack of consensus on the issue underscored the persistence of the twentieth-century global color line that marginalized the needs and concerns of people of color.[31] Despite its limitations, the Atlantic Charter galvanized black activists in the United States and abroad. For people of color, including millions living under the heel of colonialism in Africa, Asia, and the Caribbean, the charter represented a pivotal development and became an organizing tool around which activists across the diaspora began to mobilize.[32]

Like Jacques Garvey, several other Garveyite women during this period took to pen and paper to openly challenge global racism, imperialism, and colonialism. Reflecting nineteenth-century black nationalist discourse, these women emphasized the notion of African redemption, calling for the complete liberation of Africans and peoples of African descent from racism, European colonization, and global imperialism.[33] As colonial rule spread throughout Africa, Garveyite women were at the center of an international pan-Africanist movement, aimed at securing universal black liberation and "redeeming" the continent. Writing in the *New Negro World*, Garveyite Lucy Lastrappe, a Georgia native who had joined the New York–based Garvey Club in 1931, emphasized the notion of "African redemption" as one of her guiding principles. As Lastrappe explained in a 1942 article, "My work has not been easy and I've had my bitters and sweets, but I love my work and love the principles of the Universal Negro Improvement Association. . . . I have had some good and bad times but I'm still working in the Cause of African Redemption, and . . . I want my work to be an inspiration to some girl or boy to take up the work and carry on until Africa is redeemed."[34] Lastrappe's comments underscore how African redemption was a central component of Garveyite philosophy.

Throughout the 1940s, Garveyite women writers also sought to "counter [the black] experience of cultural and temporal dispossession, and to furnish the black American community with a usable past."[35] Rejecting the negative images and stereotypical depictions of black history and culture that dominated mainstream mass media, women wrote articles that emphasized African beauty and exalted the nobility of African civilizations. In an editorial titled "Arise," Adelia Ireland, a Garveyite residing in St. Louis, Missouri, reminded readers of their rich African heritage: "We are the Sons and our Father left us a great heritage, for in the days of old, there were Kings and Princes. They had a civilization. . . . The City of our Forefathers was traveled by Cesar, and who can forget Hannibal, who scalled [sic] the Alps and marched on Rome. His Nobility shall never die."[36] Subscribing to a romanticized view of precolonial Africa, Ethel Collins expressed similar sentiments: "Stand beneath the colossal Pyramid of Egyptian civilization from the books of the dead. Walk along the banks of the Niger and listen to the solemn voice of Nineveh's ashes and Babylon's decay; they all tell that the Black Sons of Ham gave to the World its civilization."[37]

Similar to earlier black nationalists, women embraced the philosophy of Ethiopianism, using biblical verses as a prophetic reminder of inevitable black redemption.[38] Reflecting Ethiopianist discourse of the eighteenth and nineteenth centuries, women writers for the *New Negro World* endorsed the belief that the "redemption" of Africa, the complete liberation of peoples of African descent, was divinely ordained. As Mrs. J. P. Giddings expressed it, "Let us ask Him to hasten the day the Princes shall come out of Egypt, and Ethiopia shall stretch forth her hand to God; let us tell Him that we know now that our house is occupied by strangers, but are willing to take a chance to fight, yes even die, for a part of His house that He gave to the Black Race."[39] Ethel Collins agreed, urging readers to hold fast to Psalm 68:31: "Princes shall come out of Egypt, and Ethiopia shall stretch out her hands unto God." "We have accomplished much . . . through Unity of purpose," she added, "but we shall not stop . . . for there is much more to be done to reach our objective."[40] Collins's statements, along with those of Giddings, illustrate how women drew upon earlier pan-Africanist traditions to formulate their political ideas during the 1940s.

For many Garveyite women during the World War II era, black emigration was a viable step toward hastening the redemption of Africa. Echoing the sentiments of earlier black nationalist thinkers—Martin Delany, Edward Blyden, and Henry McNeal Turner, among them—Garveyite women writers during the 1940s championed black emigration, arguing that Africa is the homeland for people of African descent. In a 1942 article published in the *New Negro World*, Collins advocated emigration to West Africa as the ultimate solution to African redemption. "We want the right to have a country of our own . . . Africa is the legitimate, moral, and righteous home of the Black peoples of the world," Collins argued. Insisting that people of African descent needed to "create their own destinies" and build the "culture and civilization of their own," Collins emphasized the importance of reclaiming Africa: "We of the Universal Negro Improvement Association have made up in our minds to work for the restoration of human liberty and the land of our fathers."[41] Elaine Cooper, secretary of the UNIA's division in Montreal, Canada, expressed similar sentiments, arguing that "Negroes should be more determined today than they have ever been, to protect their own interests." Emphasizing the need for black men and women to establish their own nation, Cooper implored black men and women in the diaspora to "realize that the time is coming when every man and every race must return to its own 'vine and fig tree.'"[42]

Although Cooper did not offer concrete details on exactly how people of African descent would establish an independent black nation-state, other black nationalist women writers during this period expressed their vision for how this could be achieved. Josephine Moody, an activist residing in Ohio, called for an immediate overthrow of the global white power structure. Reflecting the ethos of the New Negro Movement, Moody called for a militant and urgent response to global white supremacy.[43] "The bleeding wound of Africa is wide open," Moody argued, "and the nations of the world keep the wound from healing, and we, the Negro must be our own physician to effect a healing of that wound." The liberation of Africa, Moody continued, would only come by force: "We want to set the world on fire, we want freedom and justice and a chance to build for ourselves. And if we must set the world on fire . . . we will, like other men, die for the realization of our dreams."[44] Eustance G. Campbell, a Garveyite activist residing in Newark, New Jersey, expressed similar sentiments in a 1942 editorial in which she decried white supremacy and called for an immediate response from black activists across the globe. "There is no time to lose," she explained, "There is a lot of work to be done. We can't wait until the War is over to be free; the time is now, right now."[45]

Similar to Marcus Garvey, and Edward Wilmot Blyden before him, Campbell drew inspiration from the Zionist movement for Jewish self-determination.[46] During the 1940s, as news of the Holocaust spread across the globe, Zionist groups attempted to secure international support for the creation of a Jewish state. Campbell insisted that black men and women, like Jews, deserved support, and specifically, an army of their own: "Don't you see what the White Race is doing? He is speaking about giving the Jews an Army in Palestine, then, where will OUR Army be[?]" Emphasizing the urgency of the situation, Campbell implored "Brothers and Sisters of the African Tribe" to join the struggle for black liberation and political self-determination. "This is the only chance we have," she explained, "and if we let this chance pass us, we will not get it again for a thousand years more."[47]

Like other pan-Africanists during this period, including Kwame Nkrumah, Garveyite women openly condemned colonial rule in Africa and championed political self-determination as a right for all people of color. The principle of self-determination, which first gained significant currency in mainstream political discourse during World War I, became a driving force behind black nationalists' activism during the 1940s.[48] Writing from her base in Montreal, Elaine Cooper reminded black men and women in the diaspora of the importance of self-determination, especially in the social climate of the 1940s: "This is the day of racial activity, when each and every group of this human family must exercise his own initiative and influence in its own protection. . . . Nationhood is the only means by which a people can completely protect itself. Nationhood is the highest ideal of all peoples."[49] At a moment when race leaders like W.E.B. Du Bois were calling on African Americans to join the war effort to improve their political standing in the United States, Cooper and other Garveyite women during this period used their writings to endorse the creation of a black nation-state elsewhere. For these women, the call for nationhood emerged from a practical desire to build a better life for themselves and their children. Dissatisfied with the slow pace of change in the United States, Edith Allen, a Garveyite activist residing in Ohio, emphasized the need for a black nation-state and criticized those who failed to embrace this vision. In response to the lynching of a black man in the state of Georgia, Allen argued that black people could escape racial terror if only they were willing to leave the country. "We cry we are not going to Africa," she asserted, "but, my friends, I ask you would such treatment continue if we had a country of OUR OWN?"[50]

Significantly, Garveyite women's writings during the 1940s also shed light on their contradictory political ideas. While these women envisioned black emigration as a means of bolstering black political and economic autonomy, they also subscribed to a civilizationist view of Africa that was characteristic of nineteenth-century black nationalist thought.[51] Indeed, these activists laid claim to African land and envisioned relocation to West Africa as an opportunity to control and Americanize native Africans. Their perspectives illustrate how, as feminist theorist E. Frances White argues, black nationalism "can be radical and progressive in relation to white racism and conservative and repressive in relation to the internal organization of the black community."[52] On the one hand, black nationalists were deeply committed to pan-Africanism as a "direct response to the imperialist annexation of Africa and Eurocentrism."[53] On the other hand, they subscribed to a civilizationist view of racial uplift that mirrored the same practices they rejected. Reflecting the imperialist aspirations of these activists, Florine Wilkes, a frequent writer for the *New Negro World*, declared in a poem, "No man shall successfully rule my people, / But a man who looks like me."[54] Wilkes's statement underscores what literary scholar Stephanie Batiste describes as the "uneven, inconclusive, and sometimes contradictory" nature of "black manifestations of imperial discourses."[55]

Similar to Wilkes, Amy Jacques Garvey championed universal black liberation while endorsing policies that would undermine the sovereignty of African nations. Much like her late husband, Jacques Garvey endorsed racial uplift ideology and thought little about the ramifications of black emigration to West Africa. Imagining that black activists would receive full support from African leaders, Jacques Garvey called on blacks during the mid-1940s to "answer [Africa's] crying needs by taking advantage of every opportunity in the Western World to fit yourself for service in her rehabilitation." "'To thine own self be true.' Enlist now for service," she added.[56] Jacques Garvey, like other black nationalists, laid claim to African land and envisioned relocation to West Africa as an opportunity to control and "modernize" native Africans. These views shed light on her civilizationist outlook—one that was characteristic of other black nationalists during this period. Yet, Jacques Garvey's perspectives stood in direct contrast to those of pan-Africanist Paul Robeson and other black intellectuals in the Council on African Affairs, who eschewed racial uplift ideology and argued that Africans would liberate themselves.[57]

Jacques Garvey's civilizationist ideas stood side-by-side with her pan-Africanist vision. During the mid-1940s she was also working tirelessly to bring the Fifth Pan-African Congress to fruition. The congress, held in Manchester, England, in 1945, was arguably the most significant of the series of pan-African events held during the twentieth century. After the first (1900) Pan-African Conference, led by Trinidadian lawyer Henry Sylvester Williams in London, four Pan-African Congresses followed between 1919 and 1927—three in Europe and one in the United States. The Fifth Pan-African Congress, scheduled for 1945, was organized by Trinidadian journalist George Padmore with the assistance of Kwame Nkrumah and W.E.B. Du Bois.[58] Du Bois had invited Jacques Garvey to serve as the congress's co-convener. Although she could not afford travel expenses to England, she did much of the legwork for planning the event in the months preceding it. Among other things, she offered detailed suggestions on crafting the invitation letter for the significant gathering and insisted that black women be included in the program.[59] In so doing, she called attention to the male-dominated tradition of the Pan-African congresses and sought to use her influence to include women's voices during the planned session.

To some extent, her goal would be realized—if only partially. Although Jacques Garvey could not attend the Fifth Pan-African Congress, her archrival, Amy Ashwood—Marcus Garvey's first wife who helped to establish the UNIA in 1914—attended the event as one of only two women speakers on the program. In addition to chairing the congress's first session, Ashwood provided a report to attendees in which she argued that women's voices and concerns should not be absent from pan-Africanist movements and discourses. "Very much has been written and spoken of the Negro," Ashwood remarked, "but for some reason very little has been said about the black woman." "She has been shunted into the social background to be a child-bearer," Ashwood added. "This has been principally her lot."[60] Her comments echoed Jacques Garvey's concerns.

Although Jacques Garvey was physically absent from the Fifth Pan-African Congress, she used her writings to endorse pan-Africanism, appealing to blacks under colonial rule to "be prepared educationally and scientifically to strike a blow for their own freedom."[61] Writing in 1944, she condemned the ideology of white supremacy, reminding readers that "even 'backward peoples' have minds . . . and sooner or later these primitive minds . . . will rise to superhuman strength, and build for themselves a 'Heaven of Hell.'"[62] While acknowledging the challenges facing people of African descent across the globe—who were "treated as serfs, second rate citizens and objects of exploitation"—Jacques Garvey expressed optimism that "these sacrifices . . . will be compensatory in the perennial struggle of Africa's people, at home and abroad, for the right to rise without hindrance to their full stature as men, and to control and direct their own destiny."[63] Echoing the rhetoric of self-determination, Jacques Garvey insisted, "Liberty is a synonym of independence and self-government. And only when we too have created the states, built the nations and erected the governments comparable to those of other men, can we honestly hope to erase the stigma of inferiority."[64]

Her words captured the essence of pan-Africanist thought—a critique of imperialism and a demand for black political rights. Above all, her statements captured what she referred to as the "language of freedom."

Conclusion

An examination of Garveyite women's writings during the 1940s shows how black nationalist women promoted a global black liberationist vision and added distinctive voices to discourses surrounding pan-Africanism. During a period of much turmoil and political instability, Garveyite women from various parts of the African diaspora used their writings in several black newspapers to endorse anticolonial politics and self-determination and to challenge global white supremacy. At the same time, these women often embraced imperialist and civilizationist views that promoted some of the same ideals they rejected. By exploring Garveyite women's political writings during the 1940s, this essay enriches our understanding of black nationalism and black radical politics. It captures the richness and complexities of black nationalist women's ideas and sheds new light on rank-and-file Garveyite women, revealing how these women activists and intellectuals engaged pan-Africanism during the 1940s. In so doing, it deepens our understanding of twentieth-century African American history, women's history, and the history of the modern African diaspora.

Notes

1. A. Jacques Garvey, "The Language of Freedom," *The African*, May–June 1945, 10.

2. In this essay I use the term "black radical" to describe individuals who challenged the status quo on the basis of race (or ethnicity), gender, and/or class and advocated revolutionary social changes. While there is no denying that black radical activists maintained conservative views on various issues including gender politics, they maintained a radical perspective as it relates to anti-racist and/or anti-capitalist politics. See W. James, *Holding Aloft the Banner*, 292 n. 1. On the black radical tradition, see Robinson, *Black Marxism*.

3. These works include Matthews, "'Our Women and What They Think'"; Honor Ford-Smith, "Women and the Garvey Movement in Jamaica," in R. Lewis and Bryan, *Garvey*, 73–83; Taylor, *Veiled Garvey*; Adler, "'Always Leading Our Men'"; Seraile, "Henrietta Vinton Davis"; and N. Duncan, "Efficient Womanhood."

4. See Bair, "'Ethiopia Shall Stretch Forth Her Hands'"; N. Duncan, "Princess Laura Kofey"; and Blain, "'We Want to Set the World on Fire.'" Also see Blain, *Set the World on Fire.*

5. Historians of black nationalism typically focus on the rise and fall of Garvey and the UNIA during the 1920s or on Black Power of the 1960s and 1970s. These works include T.

Martin, *Race First*; R. Lewis, *Marcus Garvey*; Stein, *World of Marcus Garvey*; P. E. Joseph, *Waiting 'Til the Midnight Hour*; and Ogbar, *Black Power*.

6. See Blain, Leeds, and Taylor, "Women, Gender Politics, and Pan-Africanism."

7. See Geiss, *Pan-African Movement*; Shepperson, "Pan-Africanism and 'Pan-African-ism'"; Padmore, *Pan-Africanism or Communism*; and T. Martin, *Pan-African Connections*.

8. Polenberg, *War and Society*; Brandt, *Harlem at War*; Wynn, *African American Experience*.

9. Von Eschen, *Race against Empire*; Meriwether, *Proudly We Can Be Africans*.

10. Bynum, *A. Philip Randolph*. On the "Double V" campaign, see R. James, *Double V*. On the March on Washington, see Lucander, *Winning the War for Democracy*.

11. Grossman, *Land of Hope*.

12. Honey, *Bitter Fruit*, 2.

13. Ibid. On African American women in the WAC, see B. L. Moore, *To Serve My Country*; and Earley, *One Woman's Army*.

14. Buckley, *American Patriots*, 295–304.

15. K. T. Anderson, "Last Hired, First Fired," 84.

16. Rolinson, *Grassroots Garveyism*, 24–47.

17. Bair, "True Women, Real Men"; Satter, "Marcus Garvey"; Ford-Smith, "Women and the Garvey Movement in Jamaica."

18. Taylor, *Veiled Garvey*, 44. Although women were well integrated into the UNIA, the constitution did not guarantee *equal* participation in the organization.

19. Taylor, "Street Strollers," 158.

20. McDuffie, "Garveyism in Cleveland," 173. McDuffie's article offers the most comprehensive examination of Garveyism in Ohio. For other scholarly works on the impact of Garveyism in the U.S. Midwest, see Jolly, *"By Our Own Strength"*; Christian, "Marcus Garvey"; and R. J. Stephens, "Methodological Considerations."

21. See Ewing, *Age of Garvey*; and Vinson, *Americans Are Coming*.

22. Modeled after the *Negro World*, the official periodical of the UNIA, the *New Negro World* was established by James R. Stewart, Garvey's successor, in 1940.

23. Ethel M. Collins, "A Tribute to the Late Honorable Marcus Garvey," *New Negro World*, July 1942, 7.

24. J. P. Giddings, "Have I a Place in My Father's House?" *New Negro World*, March 1942, 13.

25. R. Bush, *We Are Not What We Seem*.

26. Adi and Sherwood, *Pan-African History*; Olisanwuche, *Pan-Africanism*.

27. Amy Jacques Garvey, "Africans at Home and Abroad," *The African*, October 1945, 14.

28. Von Eschen, *Race against Empire*.

29. Brinkley and Facey-Crowther, *Atlantic Charter*.

30. C. Anderson, *Eyes off the Prize*, 17.

31. Von Eschen, *Race against Empire*, 25–26; On the global color line, see Du Bois, *Souls of Black Folk*; Marable and Agard-Jones, *Transnational Blackness*.

32. C. Anderson, *Eyes off the Prize*, 17.

33. Drake, *Redemption of Africa*.

34. "Mrs. Lucy Lastrappe's History," *New Negro World*, October 1942, 7.

35. Dubey, *Black Women Novelists*, 25.

36. Adelia Ireland, "Arise," *New Negro World*, July 1942, 16.

37. Collins, "Tribute to the Late Honorable Marcus Garvey," 7.

38. Moses, *Golden Age of Black Nationalism*, 156–57; Shepperson, "Ethiopianism and African Nationalism"; Drake, *Redemption of Africa*; Moses, *Afrotopia*, 26–27.

39. J. P. Giddings, "Have I a Place in My Father's House?" *New Negro World*, March 1942, 13.

40. Ethel M. Collins, "Liberty," *New Negro World*, January 1942, 8.

41. Ibid.

42. Elaine Cooper, *New Negro World*, January 1942, 13. On Garveyism in Canada, see Marano, "'Rising Strongly and Rapidly.'"

43. Huggins, *Harlem Renaissance*; D. L. Lewis, *When Harlem Was in Vogue*; Baker, *Modernism and the Harlem Renaissance*; Ogren, "What Is Africa to Me?"; Baldwin, *Chicago's New Negroes*; Curwood, *Stormy Weather*; Chapman, *Prove It on Me*; Baldwin and Makalani, *Escape from New York*.

44. Josephine Moody, "We Want to Set the World on Fire," *New Negro World*, January 1942, 4.

45. Eustance G. Campbell, "Wake Up Negro," *New Negro World*, July 1942, 20.

46. R. A. Hill, "Black Zionism."

47. Campbell, "Wake Up Negro," 20.

48. Manela, *Wilsonian Moment*.

49. Elaine Cooper, *New Negro World*, January 1942, 13. On Garveyism in Canada, see Marano, "'Rising Strongly and Rapidly.'"

50. Edith Allen, "Ga. Prisoner Chained to Tree," *New Negro World*, October 1941, 8.

51. Adeleke, *UnAfrican Americans*; Moses, *Alexander Crummell*.

52. E. F. White, "Africa on My Mind," 76–77.

53. B. Bush, *Imperialism, Race, and Resistance*, 14.

54. Florine Wilkes, "Our Condition," *New Negro World*, March 1943, 9.

55. Batiste, *Darkening Mirrors*, 258.

56. Amy Jacques Garvey, "Where Are My Children?" *The African*, June 1946, 11.

57. Robeson, *Here I Stand*, 33–35. See also Von Eschen, *Race against Empire*.

58. Geiss, *Pan-African Movement*. There has been much scholarly debate concerning Nkrumah's role as well as Du Bois's role in organizing the conference. For these varying perspectives, see Hooker, *Black Revolutionary*; D. L. Lewis, *W.E.B. Du Bois: The Fight for Equality*; Nkrumah, *Ghana*; Sherwood, *Kwame Nkrumah*.

59. Taylor, *Veiled Garvey*, 165–70.

60. Amy Ashwood Garvey, speech given to the Manchester Pan-African Congress, October 19, 1945, in Padmore, *History of the Pan-African Congress*, 52.

61. Amy Jacques Garvey, "Be Prepared," *The African*, May 1946, 12.

62. Amy Jacques Garvey, "Adversity + Courage = Advantages," *The African*, November–December 1944, 4.

63. Ibid.

64. Amy Jacques Garvey, "The Language of Freedom," *The African*, May–June 1945, 10.

7

"Hidden" in Plain Sight

Toward a History of Garveyite Women in South Africa and the Increased Visibility of Africa in Global Garveyism

ROBERT TRENT VINSON

In 1926, a Zulu named Wellington Buthelezi told transfixed Africans in South Africa a fascinating tale. He claimed to be an "American Negro" known as Dr. Butler Hansford Wellington and that he had left his medical practice in Chicago to spread the word that the United States, the most powerful nation on Earth, was led by a "mighty race of black people overseas, dreaded by all European nations," who made "locomotives, ships, motor cars, airplanes and mighty weapons of war."[1] Taking advantage of the exalted status of black Americans among many South Africans, "Dr. Wellington" claimed to be one of forty American Negroes sent to initiate a takeover of South Africa. According to Wellington, Britain's king George V had promised South Africa to them as compensation for American intervention in World War I, but South African prime minister James Hertzog refused to let these diasporic blacks come back to Africa. Waving pictures of Universal Negro Improvement Association (UNIA) leaders Marcus Garvey and Henrietta Vinton Davis, Wellington prophesied that "Gen." Garvey would lead a fleet of airplanes carrying African American troops to establish a black-led, modern South Africa. They would strike with flaming balls of charcoal against whites and Africans alike who did not belong to Garvey's UNIA and would dump the infidels into the sea, an apocalyptic vision of liberation that African UNIA member Julia Ghu "like[d] very much."[2]

Wellington was one of many blacks in 1920s and 1930s South Africa who indigenized Garveyism through as many as twenty-four official and unofficial South African UNIA chapters. Garveyism also flourished in non-UNIA institutions such as the leading African political organization, the African National Congress (ANC), the leading black trade union, the Industrial and Commercial Workers Union (ICU), and in South African churches like the House of Athlyi and the African Orthodox Church, both with strong ties to American and Caribbean blacks. Wellington's UNIA exploded in segregationist South Africa, where a white minority ruled over mostly landless, impoverished, and politically disenfranchised Africans, a country Garvey regarded as "the worst spot in the world for Negroes; worse than the Southern States of America."[3] The Wellington movement reflected the anger and disillusionment of blacks worldwide with global white supremacy. Wellingtonites organized under the UNIA banner because they shared Garvey's broad goals of African independence, black economic and educational advancement, religious autonomy, cultural pride, and racial unity. Based in the remote, rural Transkei region of South Africa, Wellingtonites connected their local struggles against their political subordination, deepening poverty, landlessness, and lack of control over their religious and educational institutions to the UNIA, the largest black-led movement in world history, which had over a thousand divisions in forty-three countries and more than a million followers around the world. As the UNIA posed a significant challenge to the United States and European colonial governments in Africa and the Caribbean, so too did the Wellington movement to South Africa's white-minority regime.

Beginning with Garvey's second wife, Amy Jacques Garvey, a pioneering generation of Garvey scholars painstakingly reconstructed this global movement, vividly illustrating Garvey's stunning achievement in building the largest black-led movement in world history. These scholars demonstrated the lie of Garvey's contemporary rivals and many subsequent chroniclers, namely, that the UNIA was a massive but ultimately buffoonish sideshow relegated to being a curious footnote in standard narratives of black history. Reflective of the tremendous growth in the study of the African diaspora and black internationalism in the last twenty-five years, more recent Garvey scholars have expanded the chronologies and geographies of Garveyism beyond an American-centered focus on Garvey and the 1920s UNIA. Studying Garveyism as a set of ideologies and practices not necessarily under the formal UNIA banner, these scholars have recovered the histories of rank-and-file and female Garveyites and explored the gendered dynamics of the movement in the United States, the Caribbean, and Central America.[4] Yet with few exceptions, studies of Garveyism in Africa lag behind in this developing historiography.[5] Even more so, while there have been a number of studies of Garveyite women throughout the African diaspora, similar studies of African Garveyite women remain almost nonexistent.[6] While several scholars have recovered the histories of South African Garveyism, comparatively little attention has been paid to the central role of Garveyite women in these ubiquitous movements from the 1920s into the 1940s.[7] There are also virtually no detailed studies of either prominent individual women or women's organizations within African nationalist historiography before 1948, much of which is focused on the ANC, South Africa's leading anti-apartheid organization and current ruling party.[8] Thus this chapter not only fills a gap by centering African women's politics in early nationalist historiography but also offers a rare example of non-ANC nationalist politics, suggesting too that this rural organizing, while important in its own right, may have also been foundational to apartheid-era women's rural politics.

Studies of the Wellington UNIA movement invariably focus on Wellington's charismatic, mercurial "American Negro" identity and his apocalyptic prophecies of American Negro liberation. Yet this understandable fascination with "Dr. Wellington" has rendered invisible the African Garveyite women who organized and sustained the movement's greatest achievement: the hundreds of African-led Garveyite churches and schools established in the 1920s and 1930s. Focusing on the former Transkei region of South Africa, this article is an initial attempt to recover the overlooked histories of Garveyite women in South Africa. It aims to move women from the margins to the center of this mass movement, propelling forward a "grassroots Garveyism" as ideology and a "method of organic mass politics."[9] African women in the Transkei indigenized global Garveyism to further their objective of African self-determination, particularly in their political, religious, and educational lives. Regarded as apolitical tribal "natives" by government officials and as legal minors and social children by both black and white men, Garveyite women adopted transnational "American" identities to assert themselves as political actors, moving freely throughout the country to prophesy "American Negro" deliverance and to organize UNIA churches and schools.

"You Strike a Woman, You Strike a Rock": Women's Political Activism in the Transkei

The transnational nature of the "Americans" was a significant challenge to a South African government that sought to "retribalize" Africans as native subjects with no political or economic rights. The Transkei region of South Africa was a vast territory of more than sixteen thousand square miles divided into twenty-seven districts. In a system further codified by the 1927 Native Administration Act, government power flowed downward from the secretary of native affairs, based in Pretoria, through the chief magistrate, who resided in the Transkeian capital of Umtata. The chief magistrate oversaw the twenty-seven individual magistrates, one for each district. Trained lawyers, magistrates administered and enforced civil law, distributed land, and monitored the government-appointed chiefs and subchiefs, known as headmen, who collected taxes from their fellow Africans. The scarcity of police power (about 242 white policemen and 176 African constables) to monitor one million Africans meant that the enforcement and administration of government laws, directives, and desires depended largely on the administrative and judicial talents of headmen, clerks, and interpreters, with some reliance on the missionaries, traders, teachers, and others in civil society who supported and upheld state rule.[10]

The 1925 Native Taxation and Development Act exemplified the onerous taxation on Africans, who received no parallel increase in government services, including monies to fund and staff white-controlled schools for African youth.[11] High commodity prices and drought conditions contributed to widespread starvation and malnutrition. Africans were able to express grievances only through their headmen, whose status, livelihood, and privileged landholdings depended on their administration and enforcement of these same unpopular government regulations. Because men were the primary labor migrants to work year-long contracts in faraway cities, and other men died from mining-associated diseases such as tuberculosis, African women were the majority of rural residents and thus bore the brunt of the lack of arable land, the high taxes and commodity prices, and other discriminatory state policies. Thus it is of little surprise that they would also likely be the majority of the "American" movement that so electrified the Transkei.[12]

Indeed, Wellington's movement built upon earlier, women-led organizing in the region. Long before his arrival, mostly Christian African women in the Herschel district organized as Amafelandawonye (we shall all die together), "making the trouble" by protesting high taxes and food prices and boycotting white mission churches and schools.[13] The Herschel magistrate lectured African men to "control their women and to call off the boycott of the schools," and enjoined the female store boycotters to "devote your time to the care of your homes which is your proper province."[14] These women also joined black-led churches such as the African Methodist Episcopal Church (AME), where "hundreds of women attended [the] meetings and services."[15] The AME had established itself in South Africa in 1896, after African Christians broke away from white-controlled missions and created independent black-led churches. These African Christians were known as "Ethiopian" largely because they viewed the biblical Ethiopia as a synonym for Africa and as a historical site of an ancient black Christian nation. Ethiopians interpreted Psalm 68:31, "Princes shall come out of Egypt and Ethiopia shall stretch forth her hands unto God," as a prophecy that Africans would regain their independence. These ideas were amplified when, in 1896, Ethiopia defeated Italian whites and maintained its independence even as European powers colonized the rest of Africa.[16]

Wellington's prophecies also built upon circulating beliefs of imminent Garveyite American Negro deliverance spearheaded by women prophets. In 1923, Nonteta, a female herbalist and prophet, forecast that "American Negroes are coming who will cut the throats of the Europeans."[17] She preached black unity to overthrow white supremacy and ordered African children out of government churches and schools, a model later replicated by Wellington. Her followers hoped that "the Americans would free us. As oppressed people, we always had hope that we would be released."[18] Also in 1923, the prophet Josephina promised that God's word had appeared to her through lightning bolts and visions, and she foretold a Garvey-inspired apocalypse that would bring "a plague of locusts [with] the heads of human beings and tails like scorpions." Although Josephina disappears from the historical record by the time of Wellington's arrival in the Transkei, Nonteta's movement flourished, even after state officials confined her to a psychiatric hospital in Pretoria, where she died of stomach and liver cancer in 1935. Wellington visited Nonteta in Pretoria, forging a brief alliance with one of her daughters and other followers.[19]

Wellington inaugurated his movement in the midst of this unrest, billing himself as a medical doctor who specialized in "diseases of women and children" and falsely claiming to be an AME minister.[20] Influenced by a West Indian, Ernest Wallace, who had established two UNIA branches in nearby Basutoland and one in the Transkei district of Mount Fletcher, Wellington established his own UNIA chapters in Herschel and in adjoining Transkeian districts such as Tsolo, Qumbu, and Mount Fletcher. Wellingtonites wore red, black, and green membership badges that pledged to "pull down the British Empire," painted their houses black, and slaughtered pigs, white goats, and white fowl, supposedly necessary acts to prompt American Negro deliverance. As in UNIA chapters around the world, Wellington's chapters had women's divisions and female officers and a decidedly religious quality.[21] Meetings opened with prayers and the singing of "Nkosi Sikelel' iAfrika" ("God Bless Africa").[22] Wellington opened one UNIA meeting, with seventy-five women and twenty-five men present, with a two-and-a-half-hour sermon. According to one observer, his frequent prayers explained why "on the womenfolk he has made a big impression."[23]

Wellington's movement focused on African self-determination, particularly control of their churches, schools, and political institutions. Women dominated his African Christian Church, which by 1930 claimed two hundred individual churches, with names like "Mount St. Garvey's." These African-led churches pledged allegiance to the UNIA, not the South African government, and allowed blacks to conduct marriage ceremonies according to their own customs and to avoid the burdensome fees, documentation, and other requirements demanded by the state and European ministers.[24] One unnamed African widow and UNIA member hosted one of these churches at her *kraal* (homestead).[25] The Qumbu UNIA chapter had an Umanyano (women's prayer group) church, which included women from right across the Basutoland border.[26] One white missionary, B. W. Semple, concerned about his congregants defecting to UNIA churches, stormed into an Umanyano to discover seventy women attending to church business. When he threatened to report them to the authorities, the women surrounded him, dancing and singing "Nkosi Sikelel' iAfrika" while they "brandished sticks and umbrellas in the best heathen style." They taunted him, promising to draw away his remaining parishioners, and Semple beat a hasty retreat, lamenting this "intolerable situation."[27] For these women, religion and politics were not separate categories, but part of an organic, grassroots movement that would reverberate across the Transkei.

By 1928 the Amafelandawonye-Wellington alliance formed about twenty women-led separatist "Amafela" schools, prompting some mission schoolteachers like Kiddy Jokazi to leave their posts and lead an American school.[28] In October 1927, twenty-seven women were jailed and sentenced for closing white-run schools, whereupon angry women in the courtroom gallery raised such a commotion that additional armed police units rushed in to restore the peace. At Wellington's February 1927 trial, at which the government enjoined Wellington's own father to testify to his son's Zulu origins, a crowd of fifteen hundred, mostly women, converged on the courtroom. The alarmed Qumbu magistrate contacted the South African Police, because "where large gatherings of natives take place, and especially when these are attended by women, it is always necessary to guard against the spontaneous action." A few years later, this same magistrate noted that "women, chiefly widows . . . [were the] principle [*sic*] offenders" in these political clashes.[29] The Amafelandawonye informed magistrates that they would pay their UNIA membership dues instead of state taxes and refused to submit to mandated vaccinations.

In one of several violent confrontations, Wellingtonites killed an African constable in Qumbu district during a failed police attempt to arrest a UNIA organizer. Predominantly female Wellingtonites in a raucous crowd of about 150 people forcibly freed two arrested "American" teachers by throwing sticks and stones at an African constable and Headman James Msi. Eventually the resident magistrate jailed twenty-two women, including Anne Zibi, and five men, sparking a flood of angry telegrams from Wellington and his wife, Esther Wellington. The American school continued to operate. Perhaps reflecting their leadership position, Anne Zibi and an unnamed female accomplice received the harshest sentences of fifteen pounds or three months' hard labor.[30] The Tsolo police reported Africans "sharpening their assegais for war" and "very unruly" Africans "all armed with sticks"; they protested Wellington's arrest and followed the constable all the way to the "Police Camp at Sulenkama."[31] They threatened Tsolo magistrate Edgar Lonsdale, ominously alluding to the 1881 murder of another magistrate, Hamilton Hope, who was killed by Africans resisting colonial rule.[32] Like the Amafeladonwye, other Wellingtonites targeted traders who charged high commodity prices, promising that "the neck of old Mr. Newman at the Tinana store is to be cut and his blood given to Dr. Wellington to drink, the Americans will then take the store."[33]

The Wellington movement also attracted government headmen like Edward Zibi, who was disillusioned because the government did not recognize him as chief. When the state stripped Zibi of his headmanship and landholdings and banished him from Mount Fletcher, "American" women, wearing black dresses and white aprons adorned with badges and ribbons, protested to Mount Fletcher magistrate Welsh that they did not "want anybody else but Chief E. Zibi."[34] Though government officials were well aware that "the women are taking a leading part" in politics,[35] Welsh deliberately excluded them in a meeting to discuss who would replace Zibi as headman. But they persisted in their protests and continued to hold UNIA concerts to support the American schools.[36] Edward's mother, Anne Zibi, also was a leader of a Tsolo UNIA chapter, which regularly sent monthly dues and fees to the UNIA parent body. This UNIA chapter also clashed with the police, as when a white policeman attempted to arrest the Wellington leader Enoch Mbijana (claiming to be an "American Negro" named John Mackay) for allegedly assaulting a non-UNIA African. Mbijana swept into

Tsolo district with numerous female followers and "singing and drilling children." An estimated forty UNIA members wielding sticks and assegais resisted police attempts to arrest Mbijana. In the ensuing melee, an unnamed female Wellingtonite died and the policeman shot Mbijana before another UNIA supporter, Xesibe Hloma, shot and killed an African policeman.[37]

Education for Liberation: The American Schools

Since the mid-nineteenth century, government-sanctioned, white Christian missions controlled African education with a curriculum that presumed white superiority and prepared students for positions within the colonial framework as teachers, clerks, ministers, interpreters, or other government employees. Thus, African-controlled education had deep political implications. In the late nineteenth century, many "Ethiopian" Africans who had left white missions linked with the AME primarily because of the promise of black-controlled schools. The AME eventually established schools in Cape Town and Evaton, outside Johannesburg, and between 1894 and 1925 as many as four hundred black South African students studied at American universities, particularly black schools such as Hampton, Tuskegee, Wilberforce, Lincoln, and Howard. Founded in 1903 and modeled after Tuskegee, Ohlange Institute was an independent coeducational boarding school led by future ANC president John Dube with an all-black female and male staff, including two African American women, Julia Cele and Katherine Blackburn. The prospect of Africans controlling their own educational destinies frightened many whites. Fearful that black American universities were inculcating dangerous ideas of freedom and equality to African students, in 1915 the South African government established the white-led University of Fort Hare to keep Africans in the country. In 1921, with Ohlange teetering on bankruptcy (significantly, to cut costs, they stopped taking female students but kept enrolling male students), the Department of Native Education in Natal took control of the school, installing a white principal and forcing Dube out.

In this context, the Wellington UNIA sought education for liberation, not subordination within the colonial state. Their "American" schools of the 1920s and 1930s represented one of the few sustained examples of independent African educational models in South African history. By 1930, Wellington claimed to have approximately 180 schools and asserted that thousands of African children had left their mission schools to attend them. A relative lack of documentation makes these numbers virtually impossible to verify, but we do have some cursory information about these schools. In an argument that anticipated South Africa's black consciousness movement of the 1970s, which protested the material and psychological damage of Bantu education on Africans in apartheid South Africa, Wellington railed against African children being indoctrinated with ideas of black inferiority in schools:

> In schools you are taught to say Boss to any white man young or big all the same. Your names are Jim, John, George, Jack, etc. I am working very hard for the liberation of my race, because these houses you see which you call schools are, in reality, prisons. . . . [T]here is a curtain between the child and real education. . . . [A]llow me to open a school for you, not a jail.[38]

Despite undercapitalization, insufficient buildings and trained teachers, and overt hostility from the government, missionaries, and non-UNIA Africans, the American schools were an extraordinary attempt to create viable alternatives to white-controlled religious and educational institutions.[39] Women administered these schools, some of which featured female or male teachers exclusively teaching children of the same sex. The American schools held fund-raising concerts and charged UNIA members a monthly fee to pay teacher salaries and defray costs.[40] At least some UNIA schoolchildren had books and pamphlets explaining UNIA aims and objectives.[41] Although American schools used the same books as the government schools, they ultimately sought to import American textbooks, hoping that "the children would be taught something far different to what they are being taught now."[42] Former ANC secretary-general Walter Sisulu, Nelson Mandela's political mentor, attended a Wellingtonite school; his mother was a UNIA teacher. Sisulu remembered that African cultural values had infused the curriculum. The "Americans" prayed to "the God of Mtirara, or Langalibalele," not to "the God of Abraham, Isaac and Jacob, because they were white."[43]

In 1926, Wellington organized a church and "university," St. Welford Universal Industrial College, at government headman Edward Zibi's homestead in Mount Fletcher district.[44] Edward's mother, Anne Zibi, also known as "Ma Wellington," helped establish the school and led it at least until the late 1930s. St. Welford attracted mostly female teachers and children from neighboring Tsolo district. It was a two-room schoolhouse with an adjoining multipurpose building used as sleeping quarters, dining room, and additional classroom.[45] Most "American" teachers, such as Mina Lobanga, had no professional training, though St. Welford had former mission schoolteachers, including Gretha Jokazi, and Marian and Gertrude Matchanda.[46] St. Welford also drew students away from government schools.[47] Another former mission teacher, Emily Malindi, also hosted an American school at her kraal.[48]

St. Welford provided boarding opportunities for young women pursuing their education, and the movement included female teachers and interpreters who saw practical benefits to joining Wellington. In February 1927, St. Welford comprised sixty students, "mostly young girls."[49] UNIA children's choirs, composed of girls and boys, performed at monthly UNIA concerts to raise funds for the schools. Instead of the standard "God Save the King" salute sung in schools throughout the British Empire, the UNIA children sang "God Bless Dr. Wellington" and "Nkosi' Sikelel' iAfrika."[50] Calling themselves "Americans" and "carrying banners with the Stars and Stripes of America," the UNIA children derided their non-UNIA peers as "Englishmen" and attacked them with sticks. With their elders, UNIA youth burned the houses of non-UNIA Africans and surrounded the homes of others, singing, "let us go to the country of the black people in America . . . we are waiting for the Americans to come to Africa."[51]

In March 1927 the government cracked down on St. Welford, revoking Zibi's headmanship and allotted lands and convicting four teachers, including Gretha Jokazi and Marian and Gertrude Matchanda, along with fourteen schoolchildren, for entering Mount Fletcher without a pass.[52] Yet the "Americans" persisted, moving St. Welford to the kraal of Pieter Sidlayi. The exasperated magistrate acknowledged that there was no law against private institutions and that he was powerless to "arrest its progress."[53] African mission teachers such as Lydia Genu complained steadily about their declining student enrollments and pressed the government to pass new laws to ban the American schools.[54] The "Americans," they lamented, recognized the UNIA, not government officials, as their political authority. Perhaps such complaints prompted UNIA members to continue their aggressive posture against non-UNIA Africans, with one loyalist begging Tsolo magistrate Lonsdale for permission to carry a gun, since "the followers of Wellington are very much against me, so much so that I fear, if they could get the chance of doing the bodily harm, they would gladly do it."[55] When government officials tried to close other American schools that were causing drastic declines in white mission school enrollment, UNIA women confronted the officials with "assegais and sticks as though the enemy approached" and turned the tables by closing several white-run schools with boycotts and intimidation.[56]

"Women on the Loose"

Women utilized the Wellington movement to gain greater political power and freedom of action and movement, breaking free of the expectations of both black and white men that they stay within male-dominated households as wives, daughters, and mothers focused on agricultural work and child-rearing. Long-distance labor migration and cattle herding were both gendered male. Women who traveled freely, unbounded by patriarchal control, were a source of great anxiety for some white and non-UNIA African men and women concerned about losing their patriarchal and generational grip on these women.[57] UNIA women like Gretha and Kiddy Jokazi and Flora Tungata taught in the American schools but also traveled throughout Natal and the Eastern Cape with Wellington as political organizers and interpreters (to maintain his American identity, Wellington feigned ignorance of African languages).[58] A "Mrs. Flatella" had been a student, then a teacher, at an American school. She also left the Anglican Church, her home, and her family to become an itinerant preacher, promising, "the Americans are coming. They are going to take over."[59] Wellington traveled with "prophets, nine women and six men." One unnamed woman left her homestead to follow Wellington, saying that she was an "interpreter for a commander of God."[60] In 1929, "young women" accompanied Wellington to visit the followers of Nonteta, by now held by government authorities at Weskoppies asylum in Pretoria.[61] African police attempting to arrest Wellingtonites were astonished by the "many young native girls" who "came dancing and singing round about our horses."[62] Thus, Garveyite women used the UNIA as a site of refuge from troublesome domestic situations and a site of confrontational public protest and politics.

Wellington's opponents attempted to delegitimize the political activism of these women, and the UNIA, by implying that Wellington and his male lieutenants were engaged in immoral and illicit behavior with the "choirs of young girls" who traveled with him.[63] Opponents also accused male Wellington lieutenants such as UNIA African Christian Church leader Joubert Mnqibisa of consorting with "girls and women," but ultimately the Herschel magistrate admitted grudgingly that they were "probably a sort of committee," political actors in their own right.[64] Long after the government banned Wellington from the Transkei in 1927, women carried the movement forward, hosting meetings at their kraals in which women often made up the majority.[65] Throughout the 1930s in Mount Fletcher, Anne Zibi continued to host "American" churches and schools at her kraal, where she also provided her son Edward with refuge after the government revoked his lands.[66] Mrs. Sophie Zibi, most likely married to Edward, was the first lady president of the Mount Fletcher UNIA and headed St. Welford.[67] The unnamed wife of Mnqibisa, who also had ties with African American Baptists, was a teacher at the American school they hosted in their Tsolo home.[68] In the late 1930s, Wellington used the Queenstown home of Miss Leonorah Silwane as his mailing address.[69]

Women school administrators may have tried to shield precious monies and maintain some autonomy from Wellington, whose unpredictable behavior was matched by his constant demands for money, though he failed to deliver the promised American textbooks or regularly pay his teachers. This included his largely female staff at his other "university" located in Edendale, Natal. On one occasion he chastised both Anne Zibi and "a female President of the Union named Sobopa" for not attending his meetings and sending funds and school reports to other UNIA officials instead of to him.[70] Wellington was also physically and verbally abusive to women. One UNIA school administrator, Tibora Nyangane, left her post, claiming that Wellington had physically assaulted her.[71] Wellington also accused unnamed UNIA women of being like "the lady of Samson," modern-day Delilahs "bought with silver and gold" and killing "their own lands." Referring to the same-sex relationships that sometimes developed between men and "boy wives" in the all-male migrant worker hostels in South African cities, Wellington declared, "I would rather be those boys in Johannesburg who pretend to be ladies whereas they are men than be a lady."[72]

There was also some internal dissension between younger female teachers and students' parents about marriage protocols. The teachers wanted American schools to certify marriages, while the parents criticized this plan as too similar to white mission practices and preferred traditional marital arrangements that only required parental consent. It is not clear how this dispute was resolved, but it is also clear that Wellington upheld some patriarchal norms. He discriminated against UNIA women, proposing that they could not marry non-UNIA men, although UNIA men were free to marry non-UNIA women, since such women would supposedly follow the lead of their husbands and become UNIA members as well.[73] While it is not clear how UNIA women responded to Wellington's edict, some of these internal problems might have contributed to the closing of Wellington's Tylden school in 1934, followed two years later with the government declaring American schools to be illegal.[74] Noting "there are lawful private schools in the U.S.A.," Wellington demanded to government officials that St. Welford be reopened, though as we have already seen, Anne Zibi continued to operate that school.[75]

But despite the school closures, the Wellington UNIA continued apace. In the late 1930s, Qumbu UNIA secretary Elizabeth Semekazi linked this remote rural district to global Garveyism, writing and reading all correspondence to and from Garveyites in America and South Africa and to Garvey himself. Elizabeth's husband, Lutoli, was UNIA president, but he, like UNIA chairwoman Julia Magagamela, was illiterate. Considered by colonial officials to be "one of the worst agitators in Qumbu," Elizabeth had been a UNIA schoolteacher in the late 1920s.[76] From Elizabeth's pen flowed the clarion call of freedom: "Come ye Africans to liberate us . . . under Marcus Garvey's flag," "come at once so that God's work may be done and finished . . . liberating Africa and . . . proclaiming the new Kingdom." "They tremble when they hear of the coming of the King the Hon. General President Marcus Garvey."[77] Adorned with the UNIA flag, the Semekazi homestead, named "Liberia," hosted this local UNIA chapter, which they named the Liberian Division. As Drosilah Mgobozi complained, Qumbu UNIA members felt "sore at the hardships imposed upon us by payment of taxes and dipping of cattle and are agitated by these hardships."[78]

During World War II, this continued UNIA activity forced the chief magistrate to authorize Transkeian magistrates to enforce wartime emergency regulations against UNIA sympathizers.[79] Such concerns followed government resolutions in 1936 and 1937 to ban unauthorized UNIA meetings, churches, and schools in Tsolo,[80] but Tsolo UNIA members continued to operate their "American Association Schools and Churches."[81] Even as South Africa officially entered World War II as part of the British Empire fighting against Nazi Germany and its allies, Manyose Macamba, a UNIA woman characterized by government officials as "the present moving spirit" of the Qumbu UNIA, still sought outside deliverance from a foreign power strong enough to defeat the British. Reflecting the desperation that many Africans felt as they suffered under the yoke of colonial oppression, Macamba promised imminent liberation from none other than Adolf Hitler, who would kill the British-supported oppressors of Africans.[82]

Conclusion

Of course, women associated with Garveyism were not just in the Transkei. Women were officers and members of the Cape Town UNIA chapters. A joint UNIA, ANC, and Cape Indian Council political rally protesting the government's proposed extension of the hated pass laws to women invited Indian nationalist and poet Sarojini Naidu to speak.[83] After listening to a Garvey speech on gramophone, she declared that "this program as laid down by your leader, Marcus Garvey is the only solution to the emancipation of the Africans."[84] Naidu and her Cape Town Garveyite hosts linked together the nationalist struggles of South Africans, Indians, Egyptians, and the Irish.[85] Minnie Bhola, leader of the Women's Section of the Western Cape ANC, toured South Africa with the ANC leader James Thaele, a Garveyite, urging African women to establish local ANC women's chapters. The government honored her efforts by making her the first woman it charged under the Native Administration Act (1927), designed partially to corral Garveyite-influenced black politics. Speaking at Port Elizabeth and Basutoland, Freda Adams, billed as the first African woman astronomer, mirrored Garvey's Afrocentric assertion that modern civilization had its origins "among the blacks" and praised Garvey for his vision of African redemption, also saying, "the picture is as clear to me at this hour as our daylight." She argued that Africans must develop their own powerful governments to prevent lynchings and other forms of racism. Taking out a picture of Garvey and directly addressing headmen, she demanded, to deafening applause, that they support Garvey "in his effort for a free and redeemed motherland—Africa."[86] In the pages of the *Negro World,* Freda's sister Gertrude concluded her description of a Port Elizabeth UNIA meeting, "Long live the UNIA and ICU."[87] In Namibia, the Lüderitz UNIA featured the Black Cross Nurses, who sang songs such as "Garvey Is Calling" and "Ethiopia, Land of Our Fathers."[88] Writing to the pro-Garvey South African newspaper, *African World*, Ethel Humphrey encouraged South African women to fight like the Old Testament figure Deborah, who had led Israel into battle. Humphrey concluded with her own battle cry, "Onward with the Black African Empire!"[89]

In the Transkei, Wellington's meteoric rise and subsequent fall—a narrative arc applied to Marcus Garvey by some scholars—has garnered most of the limited attention devoted to the work of the UNIA in the region. By 1929, shackled by government bans, imprisonment, infiltration of his organization by African constables and informants, and by his fiscal foibles—Wellington had disavowed his American identity and his unfulfilled prophecies of American Negro liberators. The attention given to Wellington has obscured the reality that it was Garveyite African women who were the backbone of the UNIA movement in the Transkei, particularly in the hundreds of American churches and coeducational schools with a mostly female student body. Before, during, and after the heyday of Wellington, Garveyite women responded to colonial misrule by organizing UNIA chapters, churches, and schools to reflect their vision of self-determination, for their race and for themselves.

African women in the Transkei localized global Garveyism, shaping it to facilitate their freedom dreams and their fervent desires to educate their children for liberation, not subordination. Women like the Amafeladonwye organized before, during, and after Wellington's brief sojourn in the Transkei, leading boycotts of white churches, schools, and trading stores. Fiercely defending UNIA institutions and personnel, these women stormed courthouses, prevented police from arresting their colleagues, and burned down the houses of their political opponents. Though dismissed by men as apolitical legal minors and social children, these women used the UNIA as a vehicle to empower themselves as political actors with freedom of action and movement. While indigenizing global Garveyism, they connected their remote rural UNIA chapters to other Garveyites in South Africa and the United States and to Garvey himself in England. In short, without the central role of women, the Wellington UNIA would have been little more than a fleeting episode in South African history, a curious story about the meteoric rise and fall of a fake American Negro.

Uncovering the histories of Garveyite African women fills a gap in the outstanding recent scholarship on South African women across the nineteenth and twentieth centuries.[90] These women and the schools that they built and sustained also add to the exciting new directions in South African education historiography.[91] In contrast to the patriarchal notions of both white and African men, these "American" Christian women led politico-religious rural movements informed by rebellious rumors and apocalyptic prophecies of liberation from South African segregation and apartheid.[92] Their story adds to extant scholarship on the centrality of women's political organizing in rural South Africa.[93] Similar to Ula Taylor's notion of "community feminism," wherein deeply political Garveyite women both sustained established gender roles and challenged men's attempts to marginalize them, South African Garveyite women exhibited a "public motherhood" that propelled them to the political center in the Transkei. Defying their supposed status as social children and legal minors, Garveyite women's public politics was an extension of their private domestic identities as wives and mothers.

Above and beyond Wellington's American identity and apocalyptic prophecies, these African women indigenized diasporic Garveyism to local African contexts. With "American" identities that raised their status above the subordinated category of "native," these Garveyite women sustained the "American" movement by exhibiting the maternal authority and responsibility not only to create independent churches and schools to empower their children but also to protest material hardships that were obstacles to maintaining economically stable homes and communities.[94] While an important story in its own right, the story of how African Garveyite women translated apocalyptic prophecies and rumors into a robust political, religious, and educational movement during the interwar years may have informed apartheid-era female-led rural rebellions stoked by Christian prophetic rumors.[95] Lastly, while studies of South African women have increased in recent years, few feature children as political actors. The story of the "American" Garvey movement is more than Wellington's prophecies and the prominence of women; it also offers tantalizing glimpses of the politicization of schoolchildren decades before the well-known 1976 Soweto school uprisings. In short, the seemingly male-dominated UNIA, with the mercurial Wellington attracting most of the attention, was actually a female-centered organization. In addition to the exciting recent scholarship on African women-led organizations such as the Daughters of Africa, the National Council of African Women, Zenzele, the Bantu Women's League, and Umanyano prayer unions, scholars must also consider how African Garveyite women too were part of this rich tradition of female-based organizations in segregationist South Africa.

Likewise, the remarkable recent scholarship of women in the Garvey movement in the Americas and the Caribbean has illuminated new depth and dimension to the study of Garveyism in those regions. Notwithstanding pioneering and excellent previous work, recovering the history of African Garveyite women is the pathway to recovering the history of African grassroots Garveyism as ideology and method. This article is only an initial exploration into this vitally important but inexcusably neglected topic. This exploratory piece demonstrates that careful attention to source material—even archival documents generated almost solely by white and African men—reveals heretofore hidden histories of African women's activism and, in turn, heretofore hidden histories of grassroots African Garveyism. Despite the UNIA rallying cry of "Africa for the Africans," studies of Garveyism often use Africa and Africans as obligatory reference points to tell stories of black people outside of Africa. The history of the African diaspora begins in Africa, not just as an obligatory launching point to study black people outside of Africa but to explore ongoing connections between black peoples.[96] Notwithstanding the multiple African diasporas *within* Africa, the global phenomenon of Garveyism illustrates the ongoing, multilayered engagement of Africa and Africans with the black diasporic world. Excavating the histories of African women's political activism will reveal new horizons and histories of "Global Garveyism," studies that truly integrate the study of Africa and Africans into the fields of black internationalism and the African diaspora, thereby illuminating the contours of a "Global Africa."[97]

Notes

1. W. D. Cingo, "Native Unrest," *Kokstad Advertiser*, September 30, 1927.

2. Julia Ghu to Native Constable Ndzunga, March 21, 1927, NTS 7602 file 26/328 part 1, National Archives of South Africa Cape Town Depot [hereafter NASA, CT].

3. Marcus Garvey, "Whites in South Africa Want Social Equality with Colored," *Negro World,* November 5, 1921, 1.

4. The last ten years have seen a veritable renaissance in Garvey studies, with an emergent generation of scholars pushing the field in exciting new directions. The introduction to this volume provides a representative sample of this new scholarship.

5. For African Garveyism, see Ewing, *Age of Garvey*; Vinson, *Americans Are Coming*; McDuffie, "'A New Day Has Dawned'"; Sundiata, *Brothers and Strangers*; West, "The Seeds Are Sown"; Pirio, "The Role of Garveyism"; Okonkwo, "Garvey Movement in British West Africa"; and Olusanya, "Notes on the Lagos Branch."

6. See Adler, "'Always Leading Our Men'"; Bair, "Renegotiating Liberty"; Bair, "'Ethiopia Shall Stretch Forth Her Hands'"; Bair, "True Women, Real Men"; Blain, "'We Want to Set the World on Fire'"; Blain, *Set the World on Fire*; N. Duncan, "Efficient Womanhood"; Leeds, "Toward the 'Higher Type of Womanhood'"; Macpherson, "Colonial Matriarchs"; Tony Martin, "Women in the Garvey Movement," in R. Lewis and Bryan, *Garvey*, 67–72; Richard Newman, "'Warrior Mother of Africa's Warriors of the Most High God': Laura Adorkor Kofey and the African Universal Church," in Newman, *Black Power and Black Religion*, 131–45; Satter, "Marcus Garvey"; Taylor, "Intellectual Pan-African Feminists"; Taylor, "'Negro Women'"; and Taylor, *Veiled Garvey*. One exception is Bair, "Pan-Africanism as Process."

7. Vinson, *Americans Are Coming*; Vinson, "'Sea Kaffirs'"; Kemp and Vinson, "'Poking Holes in the Sky'"; Bradford, *Taste of Freedom*; R. A. Hill and Pirio, "'Africa for the Africans'"; Edgar, "Garveyism in Africa."

8. For a strong articulation of this problem, see Healy-Clancy, "Women and the Problem of Family."

9. Ewing, *Age of Garvey*; Rolinson, *Grassroots Garveyism*.

10. Edgar, "New Religious Movements," 165.

11. The 1925 act required all married men to pay thirty shillings per wife annually to satisfy the "hut" tax, and livestock owners had to pay a tax of between six pence and one shilling per cow. Additionally, all unmarried and/or landless men paid an annual poll tax (or general rate) of one pound, ten shillings, which often equaled a month's pay for individual Africans.

12. Evans, *Bureaucracy and Race*, 176; Mears, "Study in Native Administration"; Brad-

ford, *Taste of Freedom*, 220; Redding, *Sorcery and Sovereignty*; Landau, *Popular Politics*; Crais, *Politics of Evil*.

13. *Cape Times*, March 14, 1926.

14. J. F. Herbst, Secretary for Native Affairs, to Chief Native Commissioner, March 17, 1926, Herschel file, 2/SPT file N1/9/2, NASA, CT; Beinart and Bundy, *Hidden Struggles*, 237.

15. *Umteteli wa Bantu*, May 8, 1926.

16. The first independent African churches were the Thembu Church (1883); a Lutheran Baptist church (1883); a Lutheran Bapedi church (1889); the African Church (1890); the Zulu Mbiyana Congregational Church (1891); the African Native Church (1892); and the Ethiopian Church (1893).

17. Statement by Sinon Maneli, Headman Ngcabassa location, King Williams Town, May 15, 1923, South African Police files (SAP), box 41, NASA, CT.

18. Edgar and Sapire, *African Apocalypse*, 31. In the 1850s, Nongqawuse, a fifteen-year-old Xhosa girl, proclaimed that Xhosa ancestors would rise from the dead to liberate her people from the encroaching British as soon as the Xhosa killed their cattle and destroyed their granaries. Her prophecies drew some power from false rumors that a black country had recently defeated the British in the Crimean War. See Peiries, *Dead Will Arise*, 72.

19. Edgar and Sapire, *African Apocalypse*, 31–32, 117. Locusts are central to the eighth plague in the story of the plagues of Egypt (see Proverbs 30:27). In Revelation, locusts with scorpion tails and human faces torment unbelievers for five months when the fifth trumpet sounds. The book of Joel is written in the context of a recent locust plague. Magistrates wanted locusts cleared because swarms could strip fields and damage crops. Other Africans claimed that the locusts would have iron heads.

20. This claim of specialization was on Wellington's stationery. See B. H. Wellington to Secretary for Native Affairs, August 3, 1925, NTS 7603 file 26/328, NASA, CT.

21. "St. Booker Washington Memorial University College Calendar, 1930," and Wellington to Edward Zibi, June 16, 1937, NTS 7602 file 26/328, NASA, CT.

22. Composed in 1897 by Enoch Sontonga, this hymn became a liberationist anthem in segregationist and apartheid South Africa. Previously adopted by Zimbabwe, Zambia, and Namibia as their national anthems, reflecting the pan-African solidarity that united the broadly similar struggles against southern African colonialism, it is currently part of the national anthem in South Africa and Tanzania.

23. Statement by Philip Payn, March 12, 1927, and Police Report, April 12, 1929, NTS 7602 file 26/328, NASA, CT.

24. Umtata Police Report, July 6, 1932, and Lady Grey constable to Aliwal North Commandant, January 29, 1929, NTS 7602 file 26/328 part 4, NASA, CT; SAP Sergeant to SAP District Commandant, December 19, 1927, 1/MFE (Mount Frere District), box 8/1/14, file 2/12/4, NASA, CT.

25. Edgar Lonsdale, Tsolo Magistrate, to Chief Magistrate, September 21, 1938, NTS 7602 file 26/328 part 4, NASA, CT.

26. For a history of Umanyanos in South Africa, see Deborah Gaitskell, "Devout Domesticity? A Century of African Women's Christianity in South Africa," in Walker, *Women and Gender*, 251–72.

27. B. W. Semple to Qumbu Magistrate, November 28, 1927, JUS 1/18/26, NASA, Pretoria.

28. Beinart and Bundy, *Hidden Struggles,* 253; Herschel Magistrate to "Mr. Norton," December 9, 1927, and Corporal Sigenu to Herschel Magistrate, October 4, 1928, 2/SPT, file N1/9/2, NASA, CT.

29. Qumbu Magistrate to Chief Magistrate, February 14, 1927, and January 29, 1929, NTS 7602 file 26/328 part 1, NASA, CT.

30. Affidavit of African Constable E. Ndaba, April 17, 1936, and Hartmann to Chief Magistrate Rufus Fyfe-King, May 18, 1936, NTS 7602 file 26/328 part 4, NASA, CT; South African Police Deputy Commissioner to South African Police Commissioner, June 5, 1936, NTS 7605 file 26/328 part 3, NASA, CT.

31. Affidavit of Ernest Woon, March 17, 1927, and Affidavit of Robert John Waldeck, March 10, 1927, NTS 7602 file 26/328 part 2, NASA, CT.

32. Tsolo Magistrate Edgar Lonsdale to CM Welsh, July 19, 1927, and Statement of Eliezer Mnguni, January 31, 1929, NTS 7602 file 26/328, NASA, CT.

33. Affidavit of Ida Ndibibala, December 10, 1928, NTS 7602 file 26/328 part 2, NASA, CT. Chief Lutshoto of neighboring Tsolo district reportedly told followers that store prices for mealies would drop from 14/- to 5/-. J. P. Casteling to Lonsdale, March 7, 1927, NTS 7602 file 26/328 part 2, NASA, CT.

34. Members of the UNIA and ACL to Welsh, September 23, 1927, 1/MTF, box 7/16, file 2/9/1, NASA, CT.

35. E. G. Lonsdale, Tsolo Magistrate, to Chief Magistrate, June 11, 1927, andDecember 29, 1929, NTS 7602 part 1(A) file 26/328 (A), NASA, CT.

36. Welsh to Chief Johannes Zibi, stamped October 4, 1928, and Welsh to Chief Magistrate, October 27, 1928, CA 1/MTF 7/16 file 2/9/1, NASA, CT.

37. South African Police Major to South African Police Commissioner, February 1, 1929, JUS 188 file 2/62/14 part 2, NASA, CT; Acting Tsolo Magistrate to CM Welsh, January 14, January 28, 1929, 1/TSO 5/1/21, NTS 7602 file L11, NASA, CT.

38. Undated statement by N. A. Mazwai, NTS 7602 file 26/328 part 4, NASA, CT.

39. Edgar Lonsdale, Tsolo Magistrate, to Chief Magistrate, June 11, 1927, NTS 7602 file 26/328, NASA, CT; Robert Edgar, "African Educational Protest in South Africa," in Kallaway, *Apartheid and Education,* 186–87; Nqamakwe Magistrate A. L. Barrett to Chief Magistrate, October 6, 1927, and undated report of N. A. Mazwai, NTS 7603 file 26/328 part 4, NASA, CT.

40. Native Corporal Sigenu to Herschel Native Commissioner, October 25, 1933, NTS 7602 file 26/328 part 1 (A), NASA, CT.

41. Statement by Julius Matsiyana, May 16, 1927, NTS 7602 file 26/328, NASA, CT.

42. Statement by African Constable Joel Mbalo, September 7, 1927, SAP/15/79/26, NASA, CT.

43. Walter Sisulu, interview by the author, April 26, 1998, Cape Town; 47th Annual Report of the South African Missionary Society (1928), cited in Edgar, "African Educational Protest," 187.

44. Statement by Walter Bourquin, November 25, 1926, 1/MTF 7/16 file 2/9/1, NASA, CT.

45. Detective Sergeant to Queenstown Resident Magistrate, April 17, 1930, NTS 7602 file 26/328 part 2, NASA, CT.

46. Unsigned letter to Chief Magistrate Robert Welsh, April 9, 1927, CA 1/MTF 7/16

file 2/9/1; Tsolo Police Sergeant F. Malan to Tsolo Resident Magistrate Edgar Lonsdale, April 22, 1927, CA 1/TSO 5/1/18 file 2/16/4; R. D. Nortje to Welsh, March 12, 1927, and Welsh to Lonsdale, March 16, 1927, both in CA 1/TSO 5/1/18 file 2/16/4; South African Police to Lonsdale, April 22, 1927, 1/SPT Herschel file; Native Corporal Obed Sigenu to Herschel Resident Magistrate, October 3, 1928, 1/TSO 5/1/18 file 2/16/4. For the Jokazi's, see R. D. Nortje, SAP, to Mount Fletcher Magistrate, March 12, 1927, and Lionel Harris to Tsolo Magistrate, February 10, 1927, both in 1/TSO 5/1/18 file 2/16/4, NASA, CT. The Jokazis and the Zibis were perhaps the two most actively involved "American" families. Brothers James and Joseph Jokazi were both Tsolo headman, and Joseph's children attended American schools. Thomas Jokazi's kraal was the site of another American school.

47. Nortje to Welsh, March 12 and March 15, 1927, NTS 7602 file 26/328, NASA, CT.

48. Statement by Giwu Ngqingili, May 10, 1927, NTS 7602 file 26/328 part1, NASA, CT.

49. Ernest Woon, SAP Deputy Commissioner to South African Police Commissioner, February 25, 1927, NTS 7602 file 26/328, NASA, Pretoria. A cursory list of student compiled by a policeman in February 1927 indicates that twenty-seven of the thirty-seven children were girls. See E.J.H. Preston, SAP Constable, to the Mount Fletcher Magistrate, February 24, 1927, 1/MTF 7/16 file 2/9/1, NASA, CT

50. Affidavit by Ncanywa Giyose, Nqamakawe, May 27, 1927, NTS 7602 file 25/328, NASA, Pretoria; Statement by Jackson Magadla, May 26, 1927, NTS 7602 file 25/328, NASA, Pretoria; Affidavit of E. Browning, June 27, 1927, CA 1/TSO 5/1/18 file 2/16/4, NASA, CT.

51. Affidavit of Richard Welsh, May 13, 1929, NTS 7602 file 26/328, NASA, Pretoria; Affidavit of Philip Payn, March 12, 1927, CA 1/TSO 5/1/18 file 2/16/4, NASA, CT; Lonsdale to CM Welsh, February 15, March 19, 1927, CA 1/TSO file 5/1/18, NASA, CT; Report of South African policeman Killie Tile, February 24, 1927, CA 1/TSO file 5/1/18, NASA, CT; Affidavit of Lonsdale, March 12, 1927, CA 1/TSO file 5/1/18, NASA, CT.

52. E. A. Williams for B. H. Wellington to the Minister of Justice, June 22, 1936, NTS 7602 file 26/328 (A), NASA, Pretoria; Welsh to CM Welsh, July 5, 1927, CA 1/MTF 7/16 file 2/9/1, NASA, CT. For the mostly female composition of teachers and students, see Welsh to SAP, April 7, 1927, and Welsh to SAP, April 11, 1927, CA 1/MTF 7/16 file 2/9/1, NASA, CT.

53. MTF Magistrate Welsh to Chief Magistrate, July 5, 1927, CA 1/MTF 7/16 file 2/9/1, NASA, CT.

54. Lydia Genu to Lonsdale, August 15, 1927, CA 1/TSO 5/1/18 file 2/16/4, NASA, CT.

55. Bushula Makalima to Edgar Lonsdale, Tsolo Magistrate, August 29, 1927, NTS 7602 file 26/328, NASA, Pretoria.

56. C. C. Harris to Engcobo Resident Magistrate, November 10, 1927, 1/ECO (Engcobo District), file 6/1/99, NASA, CT. Wellington followed this lead by warning that he would expel UNIA members who allowed their children to attend Government schools. "Extracts from Report Taken on the 6th Day of July, 1932, at Umtata," NTS 7602 ile 26/328 part 1 (A), NASA, CT.

57. For earlier examples of young women leaving domestic homesteads elsewhere in South Africa, sometimes to escape unwanted marriages or to alleviate intergenerational tensions with their parents, see Carton, *Blood from Your Children*; and Healy-Clancy, "To Control Their Own Destiny"; Lauren V. Jarvis, "Gender, Violence and Home in

the Nazareth Baptist Church, 1906–1929," in Healy-Clancy and Hickel, *Ekhaya*, 107–30; Cabrita, *Text and Authority.*

58. Report of N. A. Mazwai, January 15, 1929, NTS 7602 file 26/328 part 1(A); NASA, Pretoria; Statement by Elizier Mguni, January 31, 1929, NTS 7602 file 26/328 part 4, NASA, Pretoria.

59. Amanda Kemp, interview with "Sister Bertha" of the Anglican Mission, St. Cuthbert's Tsolo, February 25, 1997, in Kemp, "'Up from Slavery,'" 295.

60. Unnamed author to William Sidlai, within correspondence from the Mount Fletcher Magistrate to the Chief Magistrate, December 11, 1928, NTS 7605 file 26/328 part 2, NASA, Pretoria. The pattern of young women leaving their homesteads to become part of the Wellington movement mirrored the phenomenon of young females going to mission stations to become Christians and to secure a Western education. See, for example, Redding, "Women as Diviners," 385–88.

61. "Dr. Wellington," *Imvo Zabantsundu*, January 15, 1929.

62. Statement by Constable Adriaan Mathys Venter, February 4, 1927, 1/MTF, box 7/16, file 2/9/1, NASA, CT.

63. Examples include "Dr. Wellington," *South African Outlook*, June 1, 1927; "Dr. Wellington," *Imvo Zabantsundu,* January 15, 1929; SAP officer James Coombs to the SAP District Commander, January 18, 1927, and James Coombs, SAP Qumbu, to SAP District Commandant, January 18, 1927, NTS 7602 file 26/328, NASA, Pretoria.

64. Herschel Magistrate to "Mr. Norton," March 1, 1926, and Muthi Hlomendlana to Herschel Magistrate, February 3, 1928, 1/TSO 5/1/18 file 2/16/4, NASA, CT.

65. South African Police Sergeant (name unintelligible) to South African Police District Commandant, March 17, 1929, and Statement by James Siwundhla, C. Dlepu, and V. G. Mandonde to Qumbu Resident Magistrate, February 11, 1929, 1/TSO 5/1/18 file 2/16/4, NASA, CT.

66. R. D. Nortje, SAP statement, May 13, 1929, JUS 920 file 1/18/20 part 17, NASA, Pretoria; Mount Fletcher Magistrate to Chief Magistrate, June 16, 1937, NTS 7602 file 26/328 part 4, NASA, Pretoria.

67. Wellington to Mrs. Sophie Zibi, in MTF Magistrate to Chief Magistrate, June 25, 1936, NTS 7605 file 26/328 part 3, NASA, Pretoria.

68. Sterkspruit Native Commissioner to Tsolo Magistrate, November 1, 1946, CA 1/ TSO 5/1/133 file N1/9/3, NASA, CT. Joubert's uncle, Timothy Mnqibisa, was an AME minister who involved himself in Herschel's Amafela and UNIA politics. For more on Mnqibisa, see J. Campbell, *Songs of Zion*, 321–27.

69. See, for example, Wellington to Minister of Justice, November 8, 1937, and Wellington to Department of Native Affairs, November 16, 1937, NTS 7602 file 26/328 part 4, NASA, Pretoria.

70. "Extracts from Report Taken on the 6th Day of July, 1932, at Umtata," and Wellington to "Mrs. Zibi," n.d., both in NTS 7602 file 26/328 part 1 (A), NASA, Pretoria.

71. "Extracts from Report Taken on the 6th day of July, 1932 at Umtata," NTS 7602 file 26/328 part 1 (A), NASA, Pretoria. This account simply notes that Wellington reprimanded Nyangane and does not interrogate her charge of physical assault by Wellington.

72. Report of N. A. Mazwai, January 29, 1929, NTS 7602 file 26/328 part 4, NASA, Pretoria.

73. "Extracts from Report Taken on the 6th day of July, 1932 at Umtata," NTS 7602 file 26/328 part 1 (A), NASA, Pretoria.

74. Labuschagne, Detective Sergeant, SAP, to SAP District Commandant, January 15, 1934, NTS 7602 file 26/328 part 1, NASA, Pretoria.

75. E. A. Williams for B. H. Wellington to Minister of Native Affairs, November 4, 1936, NTS 7602 file 26/328 part 1 (A), NASA, Pretoria. Wellington was seeking 200 pounds in compensation for fines and legal fees when the government officials arrested and convicted the Mount Fletcher teachers and students.

76. Trial Transcript of Lutoli Semekazi and James Ghazu, NTS 1681 file 2/276 part 2, NASA, Pretoria; D.W. Semple to Frank Doran, Qumbu Magistrate March 28, 1927, and Doran to Deputy Commissioner of Police, December 30, 1927, NTS JUS file 1/18/26, NASA, Pretoria.

77. Semekazi to Ghazu, January 4, February 11, and May 4, 1938, NTS 1681 file 2/276 part 1, NASA, Pretoria.

78. Trial Transcript of Lutoli Semekazi and James Ghazu-Affidavit of Drosilah Mgobozi, 14 August 1938, and Qumbu UNIA meeting minutes, July 31, 1938, NTS 1681 file 2/276 part 1, NASA, Pretoria.

79. Paul Gulwa to Marcus Garvey, March 8, 1938, in author's possession. I would like to thank Robert Edgar for sharing these letters, which he collected from Paul Gulwa in 1974.

80. R. Fyfe King to Transkeian Magistrates, November 30, 1939, CA 1/NKE 58, NASA, CT; United Transkeian Territories General Council, 1936, Minute 114: March 30, 1936, NTS 7605 file 26/328 part 3, NASA, Pretoria.

81. Paul Gulwa to the Department of Native Affairs, August 9, 1938, October 4, 1938, NTS 7602 file 26/328 part 4, NASA, Pretoria.

82. Qumbu Magistrate to the South African Police Commissioner, May 4, 1942, NTS 7602 file 26/328 part 4, NASA, Pretoria.

83. Vinson, *Americans Are Coming*, 97.

84. "Mrs. Naidu, Noted East Indian Poetess, at Great U.N.I. A. Mass Meeting in Cape Town, South Africa, Lauds Principles and Leadership of the Association," *Negro World*, May 17, 1924, 2; Van der Spuy and Clowes, "'A Living Testimony.'"

85. *Negro World*, June 20, 1925.

86. "What We Need Here in Africa Is a Government of Our Own," *Negro World*, July 5, 1930, 3.

87. Gertrude A. Adams, "Port Elizabeth Welcomes Home One of Its Sons," *Negro World*, July 2, 1927, 2.

88. R. A. Hill, *Marcus Garvey and Universal Negro Improvement Association Papers*, 9:204.

89. *African World*, October 17, 1925.

90. For one classic work, see Walker, *Women and Resistance*. For more recent scholarship, see Hassim, *Women's Organizations*; and Gasa, *Women in South African History*. For recent historiographical surveys of the field, see Healy-Clancy, "Women and the Problem of Family"; Berger, "African Women's Movements"; and Erlank, "Current State of South African Scholarship."

91. Healy-Clancy, *World of Their Own*; Magaziner, *Art of Life in South Africa*; Vahed and Waetjen, *Schooling Muslims in Natal*.

92. There were similar prophetic movements in other parts of Africa before Garveyism. For an East African example, see M. Wright, "Maji Maji."

93. See, for example, Redding, *Sorcery and Sovereignty*.

94. For the term "public motherhood" see Semley, *Mother Is Gold*; Semley, "Public Motherhood in West Africa." For its use in South Africa see Healy-Clancy, "Family Politics." I borrow the phrase "legal minors and social children" from Redding, "Legal Minors and Social Children."

95. Redding, "'Maybe Freedom Will Come from You.'"

96. Gomez, *Exchanging Our Country Marks*; Sweet, *Recreating Africa*; and Thornton and Heywood, *Central Africans, Atlantic Creoles*.

97. See Hodgson and Byfield, *Global Africa*.

8

Popular Pan-Africanism

Rumor, Identity, and Intellectual
Production in the Age of Garvey

ADAM EWING

In early June 1931, in Northern Rhodesia's (now Zambia's) Luapula Valley, tantalizing reports traveled through several Lunda villages predicting the imminent arrival of African American liberators. "It is being widely accepted and believed that large numbers of American negroes are coming to the country very soon who will drive out the present European residents," reported the district commissioner at Kawambwa, J. B. Thomson. The Americans, it was said, would "initiate a more benevolent system of administration by suspending all Taxes for a period of four years and teaching the people mechanical arts[,] the practice of which will quickly raise them to the economic standard of Europeans."[1]

The people responsible for generating the rumors, as Thomson knew from experience, were followers of the Watchtower movement, an independent African religious sect derived from the American-based Watch Tower Bible and Tract Society. Since 1923, when Watchtower preacher George Kunga began exhorting mine workers in Bulawayo, Southern Rhodesia (now Zimbabwe), to prepare for the triumph of the "black races" over the British "Goliath," rumors about black American liberators had followed the routes of Watchtower proselytizing across the Rhodesias.[2] As I have argued elsewhere, the emergence of these rumors in 1923 and 1924—accompanying a third wave of subversive Watchtower revivalism in central Africa—were a reflection of the spread of Garveyite ideas and information into the region during the same period.[3]

In the years following World War I, Jamaican-born activist Marcus Garvey's message of race pride, diasporic unity, and African liberation was carried by sailors, emblazoned on press clippings, and whispered by agents and organizers stationed in metropolises and outposts throughout the black world. By the mid-1920s, Garvey's Harlem-based organization, the Universal Negro Improvement Association (UNIA), had established hundreds of divisions in Canada, the United States, throughout the greater Caribbean region, and in western and southern Africa.[4] Where the organization was banned—as it was in the Rhodesias—supporters of Garvey's message established front organizations, corresponded furtively with Garveyites in South Africa and the United States, and pursued a nation-building program of "quiet and peaceful penetration" while awaiting a more opportune moment to reveal their anticolonial intentions.[5] Garveyism energized and gave shape to a number of local and regional projects, from labor unions in the British Caribbean to culture clubs in Cuba to African nationalist organizations like the National Congress of British West Africa and the African National Congress in South Africa.[6] And in the years following the decline of the UNIA, Garveyites gravitated into other organizational vessels and gave shape to the nationalist, pan-Africanist, labor, and civil rights contests of the Depression and post–World War II eras.[7]

But alongside these projects—and with far more unpredictability and volatility—Garveyism surfaced again and again in Africa as a device for popular politics making. Rumors and millennial predictions of black American liberators—closely following the introduction of Garveyite organizers and information into a region—were spread not only through British Central Africa but across vast stretches of the subcontinent: among followers of the prophet Simon Kimbangu's anticolonial revival in the Belgian Congo (Democratic Republic of the Congo); among Herero Christians in South West Africa (Namibia); and in the Eastern Cape among followers of "American Negro" Dr. Butler Hansford Wellington (aka Zulu-born Wellington Butelezi), who prophesied that on the appointed day "General Garvey" and his army of black Americans would rain balls of burning charcoal on whites and nonbelievers from warplanes.[8] Outside of Africa, as scholars have demonstrated, popular enthusiasm for Garveyism was often guided by prophetic, eschatological, and ecstatic interpretations of the movement's spread and growing influence, whether among members of Harlem's "mystical religious underground," rural Garveyites in the Missouri Bootheel, members of the far-flung circum-Caribbean migratory sphere, or adherents of the Rastafarian movement.[9]

Tracing the story of organizational Garveyism presents a challenge. Despite the invaluable work of Robert A. Hill's Marcus Garvey and Universal Negro

Improvement Association Papers Project, the archives remain scattered across the world. But it also encourages us to search for familiar benchmarks: the rise and fall of institutions; the exploits of movement leaders; the articulation of intellectual and oppositional discourses. The informal mechanics of Garveyism's spread, by contrast, encourages us to think expansively and creatively about the movement's resonance. It makes little sense to label Watchtower adherents "Garveyites." Indeed, local admirers of Garvey condemned the Watchtower movement, and Garvey himself disavowed the type of millennial fervor practiced by Watchtower proselytizers.[10] But the spread of Garveyism was nevertheless useful for Watchtower preachers. In formulating their language of defiance, these preachers drew on Watch Tower liturgy as well as local and regional discourses and belief systems. But the "myth of the black American liberator"—a diasporic vision of political upheaval that promised to shift the balance of power against the colonial state—offered what Karen Fields has called "a luxuriant symbolic language in which to think about African liberation" and with which to win converts and mobilize followers.[11] As elsewhere, in other words, Garveyism's global spread was utilized and transformed by local practitioners in dynamic and often unexpected ways.

Recently, Lara Putnam has challenged scholars of transnational history to move beyond "uncovering the existence of connections in the past" to historicizing connection.[12] Examining intellectual exchanges across borders and oceans does not get us very far if we do not explain how those exchanges mattered *in place* and *within communities* (rather than among a small circle of mobile intellectuals). And the celebration of diasporic routes only tells us so much if we do not also examine how the transmission of ideas also shaped—and was shaped by—existing and frequently oppressive relations of power. This calls attention to the ways in which extra-national ideologies and identities are produced "from the bottom up" and by regular folk. And it turns our attention to the types of knowledge production utilized by Watchtower preachers—rumor and prophecy, and other modes of communal address: modes that might allow us to track the transmission, transformation, and utility of intellectual production in the communities we study. Indeed, during the interwar period the intellectual production of "Garveyism" was generated most expansively, and most subversively, from below, and within frameworks of popular knowledge production. Following the spread of Garveyism as rumor and prophecy helps us track the breadth and depth of the movement's influence. It helps us understand precisely why white authorities across the colonial world viewed Garveyism with such paranoia and concern. And it invites a larger rethinking of the trajectories of pan-Africanism as a political device—and about the parameters of the black global imagination more broadly.

The "Madness" of Marcus Garvey

During the UNIA's heyday, Garvey's critics in the black intelligentsia pointed to the more popular elements of his appeal with varying degrees of amusement, dismissiveness, and alarm.[13] Amid the pageantry and euphoria of the UNIA's First International Convention of the Negro Peoples of the World, in 1920, W.E.B. Du Bois declared that Garvey was a "demagogue" who attracted "the lowest type of Negroes," and confidently predicted that his movement would "collapse in a short time." Chandler Owen and A. Philip Randolph, editors of the socialist journal *The Messenger*, complained that Garvey was "either a fool or a rogue," an "ignoramus" who was appealing to his followers "through their emotional nature" and who lacked "the scientific type of mind necessary to lead a big movement."[14] When these types of predictions proved wildly wrong, Garvey's African American opponents launched a desperate campaign to have Garvey, as Du Bois succinctly put it, either "locked up or sent home."[15] George Padmore, expressing the mood of the Communist International, declared "the struggle against Garveyism" to be "one of the major tasks of Negro toilers in America and the African and West Indian colonies."[16] In South Africa, meanwhile, Davidson Don Tengo (D.D.T.) Jabavu, the moderate South African educator and activist, was left grumbling about the "attractiveness of the program" among "our illiterate people," easy victims to Garvey's propaganda and "the magic motto, 'Ama Melika ayeza' (The Americans are coming)."[17]

In the decades since, scholars have been similarly repelled by what they view as a profound anti-intellectualism at the heart of Garveyism's appeal. Garvey's first biographer, E. David Cronon, argues that Garvey sold "an unrealistic escapist program of racial chauvinism" to "the ignorant black masses." Judith Stein likewise argues that the "methods and visions" of the UNIA were shaped by "the fatalism of the powerless" and "the utopias of hustlers and charlatans." David Levering Lewis views Garveyism as "little more . . . than pageantry and incantation" and without "a sober program." Paul Gilroy perceives a "profound kinship" between Garvey's race-conscious politics and the "fascist political movement of the period in which it grew."[18]

In many other places, as Steven Hahn observes, scholars briefly summon

Garvey and the UNIA to serve as foils, to be quickly "marginalized, dismissed, or derided." Hahn attributes the enduring silence on Garveyism in the American academy to the power of a prevailing "liberal integrationist framework" that emphasizes African American connections to—rather than alienations from—the nation-building project of the United States.[19] But the silences also speak to a profound discomfort with Garvey's methods and to an axiomatic belief that Garveyism was, at its root, impractical. Unlike the brilliant Du Bois and the patient technocrats of the National Association for the Advancement of Colored People, or the innovative black radicals aligned with the Communist International, or the beleaguered workers and farmers who would give root to the "long civil rights movement," Garveyism is reduced to an emotional, spectacular, but necessarily short-lived oddity—"the proverbial comet," writes Stephen Tuck, "who lit up the sky before crashing to earth."[20] In other places, Garveyism's impact is noted, only to be quickly set aside for more serious discussions. In his recent work on pan-Africanism and communism, Hakim Adi acknowledges that "Garveyism remained a major influence in the United States, in Africa and throughout the African Diaspora during the 1920s and 1930s," but only after first complaining that Garvey's ideas "contained many contradictory elements"; that the UNIA "did not provide any programme to realize [its] demands" and "engaged in "dubious economic schemes"; and that by the mid-1920s the UNIA was "increasingly divided and weakened." As in much of the recent work on interwar black communism, Garveyism exists as an aggravating but shadowy foil, its ability to capture the attention of the masses deemed counterproductive but also not much examined.[21]

The black global imagination—whether pan-Africanism or *négritude* or radical internationalism or another form of diasporic consciousness—is traditionally rendered as an intellectual project that adheres to (or itself crafts) the contours of Western humanism and is voiced by erudite, cosmopolitan elites.[22] Scholars rightly marvel at the audacity and ingenuity of their subjects' "freedom dreams"—their far-sighted articulations of national liberation, gender equality, anti-racism, cultural pluralism, economic freedom, sexual liberation, environmental justice—and bestow attention on those activists whose perspectives are most innovative, most discordant with their own, dark times, and typically most in line with our current values and aspirations.[23] Du Bois, one of the great thinkers of the twentieth century, slinger of devastating rhetorical arrows, academic soothsayer, is lavished with attention. Marcus Garvey, perceived to be an unapologetic promulgator of retrograde racialist politics, a shameless propagandist, prone to demagogic tendencies, has been a harder sell.

But what if we insist that the black global imagination be located not in the aspirations of exceptional intellectuals but in the communities where ordinary people worked, socialized, and negotiated daily configurations of power and privilege? What if we insist that "freedom dreams" not only inspire small cadres of activists and nascent political aspirations but also mobilize people to action, inspire people to see in those dreams something that is meaningful and productive in their own lives? Garveyism's success as a popular politics—and more to the point, its intellectual valence as a tool for popular politics making—should remind us to be wary of formulations that ascribe too much power to the polished and published ideas of "Great Men and Women of Thought." It should recall Michel Foucault's critique of the Weberian notion of methodological individualism: that our individualism is constituted by our social embeddedness in relations of power; that the relationship between intellectual thought and political production is produced among and within competing communities of power.[24] It calls our attention away from the intellectual brilliance of Du Bois and reminds us that during the era in which Du Bois and Garvey competed for attention it was Garveyism that worked its way into the warp and woof of black communities and, just as importantly, into the dynamic confrontations between those communities and the guardians of white supremacy.

There are good historical and political reasons for scholars of African diaspora history to celebrate their subjects' embeddedness in familiar modes of discursive rationality. When E. Franklin Frazier denied Melville Herskovits's insistence that African cultural artifacts survived the Middle Passage, or when Carter G. Woodson criticized the exuberance of rural black religious expression, or when Garvey's critics dismissed him as a buffoonish West Indian outsider, they were making strategic claims about black rationality—and by extension, about black humanity—that cut against the racial logic of white supremacy.[25]

But the idea that discursive "rationality" can or should be viewed as something easily distinguished from modes of thought deemed to lack standard structures of reason—folk belief, rumor, faith, sorcery—creates distressing blind spots. It evinces a type of binary thinking at the core of the Enlightenment project to posit enlightenment/reason/civilization as the measurable opposite of darkness/irrationality/savagery: a "Here" and an "Elsewhere"; a West and its "Savage slot."[26] As Foucault has illustrated, and as more recent scholars like Veena Das, Jean and John Comaroff, Randall Styers, and Stephan Palmié have argued, the belief in a rational Western modernity requires its own kinds of magical thinking.[27] Modernity was less a distinct mode of thought than a political stance, a system of belief that cloaked itself in universalism and in doing so constructed the "nonmodern," the stigmatized non-European "other," as well as the boundaries of the rational and the irrational. When, in the twentieth century, Western scholars set out to rethink the intellectual worlds of non-Western peoples, they concluded that belief systems that had been previously derided had a functional, rational utility. But more recently, as scholars have noted the persistence of non-rational behaviors and modes of thought in the era of so-called globalization, they have wondered if that earlier formula might not be reversed—that rather than ascribing rational utility to non-Western modes of thought, we might be better served recognizing the pretensions of our own claims to rationality, and unsettling the very premise undergirding rationalism itself.[28]

The reflexive claim to rationality also creates blind spots because it implicitly ascribes agency to the progenitor of the great idea—the Du Bois—rather than to those who receive and shape it. This perspective has been convincingly challenged by subaltern scholars, who argue that political consciousness among the masses does not derive from cleverly formulated words promulgated by erudite elites or intellectuals but from, in Ranajit Guha's words, the "negative condition of their social existence."[29] Disempowered communities understand the terms of their oppression quite well; it is shifting ideas about the opportunity to defy power, rather than shifting belief systems, that rouses people to action. What is important in the spread of ideas is not their precise revolutionary message but the practice of their transmission and the translation of their meaning into popular idioms. If this is true, then in seeking the utility of intellectual production we should be paying less attention to the personal beliefs and articulations of the Du Boises and Garveys of the world and more to the capacity of their work to generate intellectual production from below. And we need to find ways to access not only the intellectual texts produced by social movements but the dynamics of group belief and conversation by which ideas travel, transform, and take flight.

And this draws our attention to the prophetic, magical, affective, and ecstatic forms of belief that propelled and elevated Garveyism. Garveyites spread a series of broad beliefs: a view of the "Negro race" as an ancient category of belonging with a glorious history and a glorious future; a prophetic belief that Africa is the God-given homeland of the Negro people; and an argument that the redemption of Africa was a precondition to racial justice for Negroes both "at home and abroad," that the fates of all members of the race were inextricably bound. These propositions were easily carried around the world, both because they were familiar and because they offered great latitude for local activists and communities to populate them with their own meaning and to direct them creatively to their own political needs. Rather than dictating action, they engendered community building, identity construction, and political debate. And this in turn invited action, both from black communities and by the guardians of global white supremacy.

Tracking Garveyism at the sites of its enactment indeed supports some of the most dynamic theoretical work on the concept of an African diaspora. We have come a long way in the decades since Paul Gilroy provocatively and influentially suggested the "black Atlantic world" as a unit of analysis and intercultural exchange.[30] New work has forgone a discussion about roots and routes to examine the production of diaspora in localities, within communities, and *in place*. This is because, as Tina Campt observes, the African diaspora is "less a concrete geographical trajectory than a set of relations constructed actively by communities for specific purposes toward particular ends." The black Atlantic is, in J. Lorand Matory's words, "an identity option, and a context of meaning-making, rather than a uniquely bounded, impenetrable, or overdetermining thing." It offers what John Lonsdale describes as a "changing moral arena of political debate." Diasporic identity, argues Kesha Fikes, is produced through "diasporic practice" and "instantiations." And it is articulated not merely by diasporic communities but "under constrained circumstances" and within modes of governmentality. For all of its global reach and emancipatory potential, in other words, diaspora acquires resonance at the site of its use; its power arises not from its transcendence of extant geography and power relations but from its capacity to engage communities in conversations and debates about identity, politics, and the parameters of the possible.[31]

Scholars of rumor, gossip, sorcery, and other forms of popular knowledge production have likewise noted the manner in which these types of speech acts are produced within "teams." They represent "opinion-in-formation." They are "tentative, groping, and unedited." They are "in process."[32] Rumors and popular religious practices, like diaspora, create, as Karin Barber puts it, "webbed discourses" that are both wide in their range and detailed in their local applications.[33] The political power of these systems comes not from a single speech act but from the capacity of an idea to acquire wide-ranging purchase as a genre that allows general understanding across space and specific articulation and differentiation within space. It lives so long as it offers a mechanism for group debate, negotiation, and belief.[34] These forms of knowledge production, in other words, give us access to socially produced, and socially embedded, intellectual production. It allows us to study ideas not at the moment of their creation but in their deployment within extant relations of power. It proposes a method of intellectual production in which the author "makes" politics only as a symbol—as a Black Moses, for example. Because as Roland Barthes argues, "To give a text an Author is to impose a limit on that text, to furnish it with a final signified, to close the writing."[35] Social texts contain no such limits.

A Rising Tide of Color

In their compelling effort to map the intellectual history of "black internationalism," Michael O. West and William G. Martin observe that the fear and alarm engendered by Garveyism among "the guardians of empire" following World War I recalls the paranoia and reaction generated by the Haitian Revolution, the first successful slave rebellion in the Americas. Like the "common wind" that carried news from Haiti back and forth along the dense circuits of Afro-diasporic communication, news of Garvey's Harlem mobilization—and the smaller mobilizations across the "Negro world"—was carried on the lips of sailors, spread widely by the transatlantic black press, and transported along migration networks throughout the Americas and across sub-Saharan Africa. Like the Republic of Haiti, which promised refuge to escaped slaves, Garveyism gave black internationalism "a return address"—an organizational apparatus within which to mobilize the scattered descendants of Africa. But during an era of vocal and mobilized white supremacy, and an era of resurgent colonial power in Africa, organizational apparatuses were fragile and often fleeting. Garveyism derived its power and its menace less from its infrastructure—its cash-strapped shipping lines, its quixotic colonization schemes, its numerous but often lightly populated UNIA divisions—than from its influence as "metaphor," as "archetype," as inspiration. Like the Haitian Revolution, Garveyism was a "pan-African potter's clay" that "could be molded any which way," at times to explosive effect.[36]

If we look past the modern sophistication of Garvey's movement—its deployment of racial and national identification, its celebration of industrial empire-building, its brilliant utilization of propaganda and the press—we are confronted with popular imaginaries not indifferent from those generated by the founding of the Black Republic. Just as the example of Haiti—and rumors of Haitian assistance—engendered insurrectionary mobilizations in Virginia, Louisiana, South Carolina, Cuba, and Barbados, stories of Garvey's rise in the United States, and the UNIA's relentless promotion of a complementary narrative of rising, global anticolonialism mobilization, inspired new narratives of possibility throughout sub-Saharan Africa. Just as rumors served as "instruments of political debate and mobilization" during the era of slavery, Garveyism's popular transmission offered "vocabularies of agency" with which communities could rethink the terms of their disempowerment.[37]

And just as New World slave rebellions tended to erupt during moments of imperial rivalry, the backdrop for Garveyism's emergence was the catastrophic immolation of the Great War. The fighting left millions dead, empires shattered, Europe in financial collapse, and colonial subjects, people of color, and workers newly mobilized. "The white race rests its claim to superiority on the frankly materialistic ground that it has the guns, soldiers, the money and the resources to keep it in the position of the top-dog and to make its will go," observed Hubert Henry Harrison, progenitor of the New Negro movement that Marcus Garvey would so successfully catalyze. With the "fratricidal strife" destroying the very resources upon which this superiority was built, the world's "colored majority" could "find consolation" for the "agony and bloodshed . . . in the hope that when this white world shall have been washed clean by its baptism of blood, the white race will be less able to thrust the strong hand of its sovereign will down the throats of the other races." True to Harrison's prediction, protests, anticolonial mobilizations, strikes, and rebellions erupted across Asia, the Middle East, Africa, and the Americas. From every corner of the globe, observers wondered if the global color line had forever escaped its bounds, if white supremacy was imperiled, if new and more terrible wars for racial domination lay ahead. "The majority races cannot be eternally coerced into accepting the sovereignty of the white race," warned Harrison. "If the white race is willing, then, there will be such blood-shed later as this world has never seen."[38]

The vague menace of a "rising tide of color" engendered concern among the architects of empire in Africa. During the grueling and devastating East African Campaign, a British intelligence officer, Captain J. E. Philipps, had detected discomfiting evidence that the war was cultivating a climate that raised the specter of "a violent Pan-African upheaval." "In the course of the war there has been an unprecedented mixing of representatives of almost all the black races of Africa,"

Philipps observed. Nigerians and "Gold Coast natives" were meeting Hausa porters, "Cape boys," Zulus, and Matabele. "'Liberal' ideas from the Cape and Sierra Leone," and tenets of the Ethiopian Church in Rhodesia, South Africa, and Abysinnia, "have been discussed over the camp fires and a good deal of rather vague political generalization has been implanted in minds ill-adapted to digest the matter or to use it properly." Philipps worried about the galvanizing effect of the war's hardships, the reliance on—and arming of—Africans to fight the European war, and the psychological impact of "the killing of white by black." Mostly, he worried about "the doctrine of 'Africa for the Africans.'" "For the first time in Eastern Africa has arisen a conscious feeling of the possibilities of a black Africa," warned Philipps. "And what the native *thinks* is being done in this direction is invariably more dangerous than the actual action which gives rise to it."[39]

Philipps believed that the emergence of a widespread pan-African movement after the war would require "some outside influence" (he guessed "political Islam"). It is not surprising, then, that when Garveyism reached western and southern Africa in 1919, with its message of African rebirth, unity, and self-determination, colonial officials reacted with alarm. French authorities made possession of the UNIA's official organ, the *Negro World*, punishable by death in Dahomey and five years' imprisonment elsewhere, arguing that its propaganda was "more dangerous than rifles." By the end of 1922 the *Negro World* had been officially banned or was "strictly controlled" by governments throughout the British colonies. Rumors of Garveyist-engineered uprisings, or of wild alliances between Garveyites and communists, pan-Islamists, and anticolonialists of all stripes, enlivened official fears. In 1923, when the American explorer Hermann Norden trekked across the Belgian Congo, he was shocked to discover how seriously Belgian officials viewed Marcus Garvey and his (by then defunct) Black Star Line, and how they pressed him for "other details of that mad dreamer's plan to win the continent back for its scattered people."[40]

Despite official efforts to squelch the spread of Garveyist news and information, Garveyite organizers continued to work throughout sub-Saharan Africa, and the *Negro World* continued to travel up and down the west coast, into the interior, and throughout the vast labor and supply network that connected cities, industrial hubs, farms, and villages throughout central and southern Africa.[41] By 1921, Garvey had begun to backtrack from direct denunciations of the U.S. government, an effort to mollify mounting efforts by American authorities to prosecute him for sedition. But the *Negro World*'s message for Africa—and for the broader colonial world—continued to aggressively publicize, celebrate, and speculate about the very specter of a rising tide of color that European agents feared.

Part of this appeal placed the UNIA at the center of a grand, world-historical narrative of Africa's rebirth. As the standard-bearer for the New Negro movement, the rise of the UNIA was cast in the language of baptism, of spiritual reawakening. "Before Marcus Garvey came upon the scene . . . we Negroes were dead; we were like Lazarus," declared the UNIA's chaplain-general, George Alexander McGuire, in a speech recorded on the first page of the *Negro World*.

> For years we have been satisfied with conditions; we followed the words of the great Booker Washington . . . and did not look beyond the horizon. Our horizons were very narrow indeed; but when there came upon the scene a man whose man has become a name to conjure within Negrodom, we came forth as Lazarus from his grave and now we have cast off that former condition and are brought forth into the full light of humanity—the full light of liberty. We Negroes of Liberty Hall—we Negroes of this cradle of liberty, are all resurrected Negroes.[42]

Such a baptism, argued Garveyites, revealed scripture: "The Garvey Movement is beginning to fulfill the prophecy that Ethiopia shall stretch out her hands unto God [Psalm 68:31] which means that the black men of the world will unite to the one God" and "the white man . . . will leave Africa," declared the Garveyite minister Rev. James M. Webb. This prophetic framing was widely shared by officers, members, and admirers of the organization scattered throughout the world. "The days of Africa's glory must come," declared J. Alfred Walker at the unveiling of the UNIA division in Bluefields, Nicaragua. "Europe has reached the zenith and is now on the decline. . . . Out of the debris of Europe, Africa will rise." A Garveyite from Coffeyville, Kansas, was more succinct: Garveyism embodied nothing less than the "rapid approach of the climax in the human affairs of the universe."[43]

Garvey and his lieutenants did not equivocate on what such a climax implied. "We are coming with a great determination to conquer, not to beg for, not to apologize for, but if needs be to die for the freedom of Africa," Garvey thundered at the opening of the UNIA's International Convention of 1921. "Whether we land in the South or the North or in Central Africa there shall be the battleground for African freedom." From Garvey's perspective, the rise of the Negro, and the rise of colonial peoples more broadly, was a simple matter of arithmetic. "There are more colored people in the world than white people," he observed. "Don't you believe your political scientists that the next world war will be a race war? White man, do you think you can stand up against the combined forces of Japan, China, India, and Africa?" By late 1921, Garvey was trumpeting the success of the UNIA in "carry[ing] its propaganda throughout the world" and spreading "the new spirit of freedom" in Africa.[44] This work was of a piece with the anticolonial rumblings emerging out of Asia, the Middle East, and Latin America—news of which the *Negro World* gleefully publicized with blaring headlines such as "White Race in Peril"; "Bitter Race War to the Death Is Forecast"; "The Tide of Color Goes on Rising."[45] These sentiments were such a pervasive and consistent feature in the *Negro World* that they became part of the common language through which Garveyites in North America, the Caribbean basin, and sub-Saharan Africa came to understand the purpose and the thrust of their movement.[46]

Garveyism and Rumor in South West Africa

The news and ideas broadcast by the *Negro World* were deployed carefully by a group of mission-educated clerks, traders, ministers, and workers who forged a recognizably African Garveyism across the continent. In Nyasaland and the Rhodesias, where political organizing outside of the parameters of the "tribal" governance was forbidden, Garveyites established welfare associations and other front groups that advocated for modest improvements while using the guise of cautious reformism to carry on the work of anticolonial network- and institution-building. In West Africa, intellectuals gleefully embraced the promise of Garvey's transatlantic steamship company, the Black Star Line, and celebrated the UNIA's broader vision of commercial exchange, but they kept a careful distance from Garvey's more direct and inflammatory anticolonial pronouncements.[47] After the crushing failure of the UNIA's colonizationist efforts in Liberia, Garvey himself came to recognize that the work of building Garveyite institutions in Africa must be spearheaded by Africans themselves. "If we have accomplished nothing else but the bringing to the natives of Africa a consciousness of themselves and a desire on their part to free themselves from the thralldom of alien races and nations, we would have justified the existence of this great organization," Garvey argued in 1923. The redemption of Africa "will not mean so much fighting from without as the rising of the people from within with a new consciousness of their power which is gradually being realized." As Garveyite organizer Ernest Wallace explained at a meeting in Basuto-land (Lesotho), African Garveyites were being asked to "cook their own pot."[48]

Even as African Garveyites sought to pursue the steady and strategic work of organization building, the UNIA's prophetic exegesis was not easily contained. The inspirational propaganda of the *Negro World*—news of a great organization rising in America, spreading through Africa, acquiring members by the million, and mobilizing the race in concert with East Asian, South Asian, Middle East, North African, and Latin American anti-imperialists, all in accordance with ancient scripture—had a momentum of its own. Where Garveyism traveled—through the Eastern Cape, to the lower Congo, and into central Africa—rumors of black American liberators, sometimes attached to explosive doctrines of anticolonial self-determination, threatened the postwar efforts by colonial agents of Britain, France, Belgium, and South Africa to strengthen the grasp of the "civilizing mission" on the continent. "The mad dreams and literature of Marcus Garvey . . . were broadcast on the winds," recalled W. D. Cingo in the *Kokstad* (Transkei, South Africa) *Advertiser* in 1927. "Hopes for political and economical emancipation were revived and to-day the word America (i-Melika) is a house-hold word symbolic of nothing else but Bantu National freedom and liberty."[49]

A perfect example of this pattern can be seen in South West Africa, then a protectorate of South Africa, now independent Namibia. UNIA organizing spread north into the protectorate from its central node, in Cape Town, and by early 1921 meetings were being held in the port town of Lüderitz. Led by the spirited president of the Lüderitz division, Fitz Herbert Headly, a West Indian emigrant and chief stevedore employed by Railways and Harbors, the work was then carried into the interior, leading to the establishment of divisions at Wind-hoek and Swakopmund and to activism at Usakos, Karibib, and Okahandja. By early 1922 the UNIA had attracted hundreds of members, including West Indians and Liberians (probably Kru), as well as Herero, Nama, Ovambo, and Hottentot. Members received red identification cards, as well as red, black, and green rosettes, which spread quickly through the protectorate.[50] As one observer remarked, "Garvey suddenly became the man of the day."[51]

As elsewhere in colonized Africa, Headly and other local UNIA leaders focused on bread-and-butter issues. The organization provided medical care and established sickness and death benefits, supported black business owners, set up a local school, and launched a campaign to keep "down the high roll of offenders" and empty the prisons.[52] Headly assured local officials that there was "nothing seditious" about the UNIA's doctrine and that the organization simply endeavored to "bring . . . about the better conditioning [*sic*] of our people as a whole." The UNIA, he explained, "is . . . a humanitarian Charitable, Educational, Social, Friendly, Instructive, and Expansive Society and is founded by [a] person desiring to work for the general uplift of the Negro peoples of the world over."[53]

What Headly omitted from these conversations was the crucial piece of context that so animated African Garveyites. If Headly and other UNIA leaders acknowledged the need for caution, for proceeding in a "Constitutional Manner" in their work, they viewed the goal of this work as nothing less than the freedom of all Africans. The purpose of their organizing, argued Headly, was to arouse the race from its slumber, to declare Africa for the Africans, to establish the "Bond of Unity" among the divided members of the race, and to prepare for "the allotted time" to strike out for liberty. "Our Brothers across the seas are awaiting on you all," he explained to a Herero headman in 1922. "Now is your time to make a bid for Freedom and Liberty before it is too late." Success for the movement had been laid by the spread of Garveyism "to the four parts of Mother Africa." There was no need to fear, because "the same forces that have freed over races and nations must also play their part with the Negroid races." To "prepare to gather up the spoils," Africans must unite, organize, and set to work.[54]

Authorities in South West Africa closely watched the growth of the UNIA in the protectorate, but they did not view it as much of a threat.[55] This began to change toward the end of February 1922, when A. J. Waters, Crown prosecutor for the protectorate, expressed misgivings about "the effect of UNIA propaganda on 'backward' natives in this country."[56] Indeed, if Garveyites carefully couched their message of racial unity and liberation within the cautious framework of lawful organization building, it is easy to understand how this subtlety might be lost on those less embedded in movement strategy sessions. In March, authorities confiscated a letter written in Nama, signed "on behalf of Gawais [Garvey]," that trumpeted the arrival of "our own government" in Africa and the aid of "all black nations of the whole world." The next month, following a meeting held by Garveyites with Herero living at Omaruru, near Windhoek, authorities found writing emblazoned across three flat rocks in tar paint, presumably written by one of the meeting organizers: "This country is not your country, it belongs to . . . Michael [the deceased chief of Omaruru] and the Americans."[57]

By September and October 1922, white observers had begun to fear that a spirit of insurrection was building among the Herero that recalled the mood prior to the Herero Rebellion of 1904 against their former colonial rulers, the Germans. Herero women and men, wearing red, black, and green rosettes, began refusing vaccinations and opposing sheep inspection and stock branding. Herero Christians streamed out of the missions and stopped attending mission schools, awaiting the erection of a church that worshiped "the God of the blacks."[58] Rumors swirled that the "Americans" were on the way, "bringing rifles for the natives." As the head constable at Omaruru reported in November, "The dream of the Hereros is . . . that the Americans will come from North South East and West over the great [hills] and take Windhoek and from there [move] onwards. . . . The faith in this American power that is coming to help the natives is stated to be very strong."[59] In a series of hastily called meetings, UNIA organizer John Mungunda tried to explain, to little effect, that American Garveyites were not on the way. "If I told you that American negroes [sic] were coming to release you, I think you would be satisfied, but it would be a lie," he told the crowd. "I know nothing about America. The society has been formed through American ideas, but Americans only explained it but will not do the work—we must do that."[60] In November, with Hereros, according to one report, "openly threaten[ing] rebellion," and with whites arming themselves response, Headly pleaded with people to keep their heads and to recognize the "peaceable" intentions of the organization, but feared that "our day is near at hand."[61]

Rebellion never erupted. By April 1923, popular support for the Garvey movement had waned. Rumors that Marcus Garvey would arrive in Walvis Bay with a war fleet reignited enthusiasm in early 1924, but expectations were dashed when the fleet did not arrive at the appointed hour. As normalcy returned to the protectorate, Headly continued to doggedly organize for the UNIA. His last dispatch to the *Negro World* came in September 1927—a report of a UNIA meeting in Lüderitz.[62] Missionaries at the Herero Parish, meanwhile, were left grumbling about the renascence of Herero ritual practices, a continued coldness to the European church, and the disconcerting rise of "heathendom."[63]

Conclusion: Freedom Dreams

In his influential book, *Freedom Dreams*, Robin D. G. Kelley sets out to "recover ideas" from the black radical imagination—from dreams of Africa and reparations to solidarities with communists and global peoples of color to articulations of black feminism and surrealism—that might inspire us to dream about what freedom might look like today. The conceit of the text is direct and powerful: In the face of overwhelming pressures and opposition, black activists and intellectuals have forged enduring and magnificent discourses that imagine better worlds; we are wise to understand and celebrate this legacy.[64]

There is unquestionably much to learn from this type of social imagining. But the lessons of the Garvey movement suggest that our exploration of the black radical imagination must not end with soaring visions, lessons for future generations, and dreams.[65] These things give us comfort and inspiration after the fact, but they do not explain very much about who was attracted to a particular message, at a particular time, and why that was the case. They do not measure the extent to which politics—the engagement of peoples of African descent in evolving contests of power—was enacted in meaningful ways. Casting our perception of intellectual production more broadly and diffusely—as a changing set of ideas born from the intersection of imagination, exchange, innovation, and opportunity—welcomes more people into the circle of production than the remarkable women and men whom Kelley chronicles. It insists that we hold ideas to a standard beyond abstraction, that we ask what work they do, what solidarities they inspire, what popular visions they enact, what centers of power they challenge.

During the interwar years, Garveyism emerged as a dynamic and successful tool of politics making because it enacted a freedom dream that spoke powerfully to the experiences, hopes, and frustrations of millions of peoples of African descent. Like pan-African visions before and since, it revealed not a fixed vision but "vocabularies of agency"—a space for the creative, uneven, and sometimes defiant renegotiation of the status quo. Garveyism's legacy rests less in the idea than in the process—in the innovations and deviations and rumors and prophecies and promises and experiments by which it took its form. Or, rather, Garveyism's legacy rests on one big idea—Africa for the Africans!—and on the millions of people who made that idea soar.

Notes

1. Quarterly Report, Mweru-Luapula Province, Kawambwa District, June 10, 1931, Sec 2/434, Vol. 1, National Archives of Zambia, Lusaka [hereafter NAZ].

2. For Kunga, see Ranger, *African Voice*, 200–201. Reports of rumors of black American liberators are widely dispersed across the colonial record. See Memo to Taggart, SNA, May 26, 1924, ZA 1/10, NAZ; Report by D. M. Kennedy, July 30, 1931, Sec 2/434, Vol. 1, NAZ; Testimony of Mubakasa, KSM 3/1/1, NAZ; Extract from Patrol Report, Ndola,

September 24, 1925, ZA 1/10, NAZ; J. B. Thomson to Provincial Commissioner, June 6, 1931, and J. O. Talbot Phibbs, Report on Evidence of Watch Tower, Fort Jameson, June 9, 1932, both in Sec 2/434, Vol. 1, NAZ. See also Cross, "Social History and Millennial Movements," 175.

3. Ewing, *Age of* Garvey, 176–85. This argument has also been made by Shepperson, "Nyasaland and the Millennium," 153–54; Fields, *Revival and Rebellion*, 11–12; R. A. Hill, "Introduction," in *Marcus Garvey and Universal Negro Improvement Association Papers* [hereafter *MGP*], 10:lvi–lvii.

4. For the spread and global contours of the Garvey movement, see Martin, *Race First*; and Ewing, *Age of Garvey*.

5. For this type of organizing in Southern Rhodesia, see West, "The Seeds Are Sown." For Northern Rhodesia, see Ewing, *Age of Garvey*, 186–211.

6. For Caribbean labor unions, see Ewing, "Caribbean Labour Politics." For Cuba, see Guridy, *Forging Diaspora*, 61–106; McLeod, "'Sin dejar de ser cubanos'"; and Sullivan, "'Forging Ahead.'" For Garveyism in West Africa, see Langley, *Pan-Africanism and Nationalism*, 58–91; and Hughes, "Africa and the Garvey Movement." For South Africa and the ANC, see Vinson, *Americans Are Coming*, 63–101; and R. A. Hill and Pirio, "'Africa for the Africans.'"

7. See, for example, Blain, "'We Want to Set the World on Fire.'"

8. R. A. Hill, "Introduction," *MGP*, 10:liii–lix; Vinson, *Americans Are Coming*, 103.

9. Dorman, *Chosen People*, 149; Roll, "Garveyism"; L. Putnam, *Radical Moves*, 49–81.

10. For the views of African Garveyites, see, for example, Sam K. K. Mwase, "Memorandum on Education, Watch Tower and Market," Sec 2/436, Vol. 1, NAZ; and Police Inspector's Report, April 20, 1933, Sec 2/434, Vol. 1, NAZ. For Garvey, see Grant, *Negro with a Hat*, 64.

11. Fields, *Revival and Rebellion*, 12.

12. L. Putnam, *Radical Moves*, 232.

13. The title of this section echoes Robert W. Bagnell's (in)famous takedown of Garvey, "The Madness of Marcus Garvey."

14. W.E.B. Du Bois, interview by Charles Mowbray White, August 22, 1920, and Chandler Owen and A. Philip Randolph, interview by Charles Mowbray White, August 20, 1920, *MGP*, 2:620, 609.

15. Du Bois, "A Lunatic or a Traitor?"

16. Padmore, *Life and Struggles*, 125.

17. Jabavu, "Native Unrest in South Africa," 250.

18. Cronon, *Black Moses*, 203; Stein, *World of Marcus Garvey*, 6; D. L. Lewis, *W.E.B. Du Bois: The Fight for Equality*, 70–75; Gilroy, *Against Race*, 232.

19. Hahn, *Political Worlds*, 119, 159–60.

20. Tuck, *We Ain't What We Ought to Be*, 163.

21. Adi, *Pan-Africanism and Communism*, 17–18. Other examples of this tendency include Gilmore, *Defying Dixie*; and Minkah Makalani's otherwise excellent *In the Cause of Freedom*.

22. For a trenchant critique of scholars' tendency to view the black radical intellectual tradition as derivative of, and bound by, Western intellectual traditions, see Bogues, *Black Heretics, Black Prophets*.

23. The phrase "freedom dreams" is drawn from Robin D. G. Kelley's influential book, *Freedom Dreams*.

24. "Power is exercised rather than possessed; it is not the 'privilege,' acquired or preserved, of the dominant class, but the overall effect of its strategic positions—an effect that is manifested and sometimes extended by the position of those who are dominated." Foucault, *Discipline and Punish,* 26.

25. For the Frazier-Herskovits debate, see Holloway, *Confronting the Veil*, 127–34. For Woodson, see Savage, *Your Spirits Walk beside Us*, 11–14.

26. Trouillot, *Global Transformations*, 1–2, 14–21.

27. V. Das, "Subaltern as Perspective"; Comaroff and Comaroff, "Millennial Capitalism"; Comaroff and Comaroff, "Alien-Nation"; Styers, *Making Magic*; Palmié, *Wizards and Scientists.*

28. See Comaroff and Comaroff, "Millennial Capitalism"; Styers, *Making Magic*, 26; and Palmié, *Wizards and Scientists*, 19.

29. Guha, *Elementary Aspects of Peasant Insurgency*, 225. See also J. C. Scott, *Weapons of the Weak*.

30. Gilroy, *Black Atlantic*. As Brent Hayes Edwards points out, the concept of diaspora was introduced to global black studies by George Shepperson roughly five decades ago. See Edwards, "Uses of Diaspora"; and Shepperson, "African Abroad."

31. Campt, "Crowded Space of Diaspora," 97; Matory, *Black Atlantic Religion*, 273; Lonsdale, "Moral Economy of Mau Mau," 267; Fikes, "Diasporic Governmentality," 56–58. See also Makalani, "Introduction"; and J. N. Brown, *Dropping Anchor, Setting Sail*.

32. Derby, "Beyond Fugitive Speech," 131. See also Parés and Sansi, *Sorcery in the Black Atlantic*.

33. Barber, "Methodology and Vampires," 313.

34. See L. White, *Speaking with Vampires*, 6.

35. Barthes, "The Death of the Author," 147.

36. Michael O. West and William G. Martin, "Contours of the Black International: From Toussaint to Tupac," in West, Martin, and Wilkins, *From Toussaint to Tupac*, 10–11.

37. Hahn, "'Extravagant Expectations,'" 125; Glaude, *Exodus!* 20.

38. Hubert H. Harrison, "The White War and the Colored World," *The Voice*, August 14, 1917, in Perry, *Hubert Harrison Reader*, 203.

39. Captain J. E. Philipps, "Africa for Africans and Pan-Islam," 1917, National Archives of England, London, WO/106/259.

40. R. Lewis, *Marcus Garvey*, 81; Lieutenant Governor of Côte d'Ivoire to Martial-Henri Merlin, December 4, 1921, *MGP*, 9:251–56; Hughes, "Africa and the Garvey Movement," 116; Norden, *Fresh Tracks*, 64.

41. Ewing, *Age of Garvey*, 91–93.

42. Report from Liberty Hall, *Negro World*, April 2, 1921, 1.

43. Rev. James M. Webb, "The Garvey Movement Is Biblical," *Negro World*, December 17, 1921, 10; "Unveiling of Charter in Bluefields, Nicaragua," *Negro World*, March 19, 1921, 5; letter from A. W. Fitz, Coffeyville, Kansas, *Negro World*, June 4, 1921, 2.

44. "Opening Convention Speech by Marcus Garvey," August 1, 1921, *MGP*, 9:129–32; Speech by Marcus Garvey at Liberty Hall, *Negro World*, October 29, 1921, 2.

45. See *Negro World*, April 9, 1921, 10; *Negro World*, July 18, 1925, 2; *Negro World*, July 4,

1925, 7. Other examples of this rhetoric can be found in the following issues of the *Negro World*: "White Correspondent Writes of the 'Black Shadow over Africa,'" August 1, 1925, 2; "Battle Cry 'Africa for the Africans' Disturbs Wilhelm: Ex-Kaiser Rants over Threat to White Supremacy as Seen in New Self-Reliance of African Race," March 19, 1927, 2; "New Crisis in Africa and Asia Seen as Climaxing Native Unrest," March 24, 1928, 2; and "Worried over Progress of Colored Races in Their Struggle for Complete Emancipation, He [Ex-Kaiser Wilhelm] Points to Africa, China and India and Says a Gigantic Battle is Brewing," April 28, 1928, 2.

46. For examples of this rhetoric in South Africa, see Ewing, *Age of Garvey*, 166–68.

47. "Right Oh!" to John E. Bruce, November 1, 1920, and Agbebi to Bruce, May 15, 1920, in group B, box 2, items 188 and 258, John E. Bruce Papers, Schomburg Center for Research in Black Culture, New York Public Library; "Letter from Sierra Leone by 'Dorn,'" *Negro World*, March 26, 1921, 4; Langley, *Pan-Africanism and Nationalism*, 91–92.

48. Speech at Liberty Hall, *Negro World*, March 17, 1923, 1; Report of a Speech by Ernest Wallace, December 23, 1925, *MGP*, 10:351–52.

49. W. D. Cingo in the *Kokstad Advertiser*, September 30, 1927, *MGP*, 10:407. For a summary of the spread of the "myth of the American liberator" in sub-Saharan Africa, see R. A. Hill, "Introduction," *MGP*, 10:liii–lix.

50. C. Lewis Warner to Secretary for South West Africa, Lüderitz, March 20, 1922, *MGP*, 9:386–87; Pirio, "The Role of Garveyism," 261; Report by P.K.K. Atlogbe of UNIA Meeting, Lüderitz, ca. September 10, 1921, R. S. Cope to J. F. Herbst, December 21, 1921, Acting Magistrate, Swakopmund, to Secretary for South West Africa, May 18, 1922, and South West Africa Police Report on UNIA Activities, November 10, 1922, all in *MGP*, 9:204, 279, 425, 673–74.

51. Vedder, "The Herero," 163. By 1922 the Lüderitz division reported 871 dues-paying members. The popularity of Garveyism was equally impressive in Windhoek, where the division also boasted more than eight hundred members. Here's Headly describing his first organizing trip to the interior town: "On my arrival I was met by a vast host of our race. . . . But the real surprise was yet in store for us, for on emerging from those precincts of the station we were met by squadrons of mounted men who escorted us to the location and halted by the superintendent of locations' office, where I was met by a seething mass of humanity to hear the first gospel of Garveyism in Windhoek." *MGP*, 9:xlvii; see also Fitz Herbert Headly, "Conditions of Life among Our Race in the Protectorate," *Negro World*, February 25, 1922, 11.

52. Letter from Fitzherbert [*sic*] Headly, President, Lüderitz Division, S.W. Protectorate, Africa, *Negro World*, October 8, 1921, 11; Pirio, "The Role of Garveyism," 261.

53. Headly to A. C. Warner, Resident Magistrate, Lüderitz, January 27, 1922, and Headly to Gyshert Reitz Hofmeyr, February 2, 1922, *MGP*, 9:321, 348.

54. Headly to Mr. Barnabas, Herero Headman, January 25, 1922, *MGP*, 9:320; Fitz H. Headley [*sic*], "Hon. M. G. Has Made Africans Think Black," *Negro World*, February 11, 1925, 2.

55. "No direct action has been taken [on the UNIA] although the activities of the agents are being cl[osely] watched," reported the Crown prosecutor, A. J. Waters. "No trouble is anticipated as it is unlikely that the Society can acquire any considerable moral or financial stability." Waters to W. Scotland, SW Africa, January 30, 1922, *MGP*, 9:330.

56. A. J. Waters to Magistrate, Lüderitz, February 23, 1922, *MGP*, 9:352.

57. Confiscated letter by Salmon Diedrik (translated from Nama), Statement by Rev. August Kuhlmann, Rhenish Mission Society, Omaruru, April 20, 1922, and Statement by Kuhlmann to SW Africa Police, Omaruru, October 11, 1922, *MGP*, 9:377, 398–99, 614–15.

58. A. G. Drake, CID, SWA, to Commanding Officer, Windhoek, September 9, 1922, *MGP*, 9:591–92; Quarterly Report of Herero Parish, SW Africa, November 2, 1922, *MGP*, 10:724–25.

59. Police Reports, South West Africa, October 26, 1922, and Report by Head Constable Callaghan, Omaruru, October 18, 1922, *MGP*, 9:666, 628.

60. Report of Native Corporal Jacob, South West Africa, n.d., *MGP*, 9:671.

61. Quarterly Report of Herero Parish, SW Africa, November 2, 1922, *MGP*, 10:724; Intercepted Letter from Fitz Herbert Headly to Joseph Hailand, November 14, 1922, *MGP*, 9:684.

62. "Meetings of Luderitz and Belize Branches," *Negro World*, September 10, 1927, 6.

63. Report of Native Corporal Jacob, *MGP*, 9:671. South West African authorities carefully monitored and cataloged rumors swirling about the arrival of black Americans. Several of these reports are reprinted in *MGP*; see 9:614–16, 666, and 10:8–9, 594, 720–26, 732.

64. Kelley, *Freedom Dreams*, xii.

65. This is not to suggest that Kelley himself *does* stop here. For his groundbreaking scholarship applying the work of South Asian subaltern studies to African American history, see Kelley, *Race Rebels*; and Kelley, "'We Are Not What We Seem.'"

9

"The Age of Unrest, the Age of Dissatisfaction"

Marcus Garvey and the Rise of Australian Aboriginal Political Protest, 1920–1929

JOHN MAYNARD

Writing in the aftermath of the Great War, Marcus Garvey declared: "Never before in the history of the world has the spirit of unrest swept over as it has during the past two years." It was, he said, "the age of unrest, the age of dissatisfaction."[1] This surge of unrest was a global phenomenon with oppressed groups around the world including India, Egypt, Ireland, Russia, and Africa clamoring for self-determination and the right to take charge of their own destiny. In Australia the time witnessed the rise of a vibrant pan-Aboriginal political movement intent on demanding Aboriginal rights to land, protecting their children from government removal policy, defending an Indigenous cultural identity, demanding citizenship rights and self-determination in their own country, and requiring that Aboriginal people be placed in charge of Aboriginal affairs. Aboriginal political resistance in the twentieth century emerged, in part, in response to the white, colonial, paternalistic civilizing mission particular to the Australian context. But it also developed in concert with international black influences. This essay will examine the Aboriginal political movement at this critical point of world history, including the transoceanic political influence of Garveyism on its political directives. The existence of Aboriginal links and connections with Garvey and the UNIA takes the Aboriginal political movement offshore and helps break the confinement of the long-entrenched inward, insular, and nationalistic Australian history gazing of the past. Two prominent Aboriginal leaders of the time, Fred Maynard and Tom Lacey, became Garveyites and viewed Garveyism as an answer to Aboriginal issues in Australia.

In this article I consider why they found Garvey's message so relevant. I will conclude with an overview of contemporary Aboriginal Australia and renewed discussions of Marcus Garvey and his legacy.

Background

The history of human occupation of the Australian continent dates back some sixty-five thousand years, and it is now recognized that Aboriginal Australia carries the oldest living memory known to humankind. Aboriginal people remain adamant that their ancestors came directly out of the Dreamtime, from the time before time began, to create the world and everything in it.

Aboriginal longevity on the continent was based upon an egalitarian hunter-gatherer mode of existence. Everything was shared within the group, and great importance was placed upon caring for the environment. Aboriginal cosmology privileged bestowing the world to future generations as it was in the beginning. A tight totemic kinship structure religiously ensured that resources were not depleted beyond what was necessary for life and sustenance.

The sixty-five thousand years' time frame of their successful existence was one that passed through ice ages, rising sea levels, catastrophic droughts, fires, floods, and famines. But the arrival of the British in 1788 was a seismic collision that witnessed destruction of an unparalleled magnitude through invasion, occupation, dispossession, cultural destruction, massacres, segregation, and assimilation. It has been estimated that only four decades after the British established themselves at Port Jackson (Sydney) the Aboriginal population was decimated by somewhere between 60 to 90 percent.[2] This destruction was waged through violence and by the introduction of new diseases. By the turn into the twentieth century the Aboriginal population was estimated at a mere sixty-six thousand people in total.[3]

By the mid- to late nineteenth century the remnants of the Aboriginal population in the Southeast colonies, against all odds, had begun to reestablish ties to their traditional land. These people had petitioned governments for small plots of land, forty to fifty acres, and had combined a mixture of European farming with Aboriginal hunting and gathering techniques with great success. The turn into the twentieth century saw a backflip by state governments, who began to succumb to white farming pressures and strip back these successful Aboriginal farms with no recompense. Aboriginal people were thrown off this land destitute. At the same time, government authorities began to tear very young Aboriginal children away from their families to be institutionalized. The young girls were to be trained as domestic servants for white households and the boys groomed as laborers. There was to be little or no educational opportunities for these children.[4] At the same point in time, the world was engulfed in the Great War. It is now recognized that a thousand Aboriginal men fought for their country in World War I. Like the experiences of Native American and African American soldiers, there was a building resentment that Aboriginal soldiers were not afforded the same rights, privileges, and recognition as non-Indigenous soldiers on their return. The assaults upon Aboriginal land, the taking away of Aboriginal children from their families, and embittered returned Aboriginal soldiers from the Western Front were the catalyst for the rise of Aboriginal political revolt.[5]

More than ninety years ago, my grandfather Fred Maynard established the Australian Aboriginal Progressive Association (AAPA) in Sydney. The AAPA today is recognized as the first united all-Aboriginal political organization to form in Australia. This rising momentum of Aboriginal political discontent was tied to a growing national pan-Aboriginal identity. In 1928, Ben Roundtree, a returned World War I Aboriginal soldier and secretary of the AAPA, wrote a letter to the Commonwealth Government Royal Commission in Canberra on the Constitution. Roundtree forcefully endorsed and supported a national Aboriginal agenda and policy:

> We heartily endorse the views of the commission now sitting at Canberra and pledge ourselves to stand solid behind the commission for the emancipation of the whole of our conditions and people throughout Australia. . . . [O]ur unswerving loyalty is with you in the fight for the federalizing of the whole of Aboriginal affairs and the abolition of state control.[6]

The aftermath of the Great War had witnessed the collapse and disintegration of great empires and severely shaken the foundations of colonialism. As Adam Ewing has observed, there was a "global wave of conservative readjustment" to these challenges, and this had a direct impact on black politics during the 1920s.[7] This was very much the case in Australia as well, with authorities taking a very dim view of the unexpected rise of a very well organized and committed Aboriginal political movement.

AAPA members in Australia were greatly inspired and influenced by Marcus Garvey and his ideology of self-determination and cultural pride.[8] The AAPA logo and motto, "One God, One Aim, One Destiny," was self-evidently adopted from the UNIA, as was the slogan "Australia for Australians." In his poem "Africa for the Africans," Garvey cried:

Europe cries to Europeans, ho!
Asiatics claim Asia, so
Australia for Australians.
And Africa for the Africans.

From an Aboriginal perspective, in adopting the slogan "Australia for Australians" there could be no mistake of who was recognized as Australian, and it represented an Aboriginal "assertion of nationhood."[9]

Oppressed groups around the globe interacted, communicated, and established long-standing connections and affiliations with each other. These networks offered support, encouragement, and, importantly, a sense of communal strength and unity. Aboriginal people had seen the importance of international connection and alliances for more than a century. Aboriginal activists, cricketers, footballers, boxers, circus performers, jockeys, soldiers, and maritime workers either traveled widely or had contact with members of the international black diaspora and subsequently broadened their own perspectives and outlook. This global movement demonstrates the level of mobility and political exchange among oppressed activists. Such global networks between Indigenous and other oppressed groups across the globe challenge distorted national historical understandings that have sought to constrain Indigenous peoples as static within tightly controlled national borders. As Jane Carey and Jane Lydon observed, while "Europeans have been considered 'cosmopolitan,' the mobility of Indigenous people has either been overlooked or understood only as a consequence of the oppressive expansion of European empires."[10] The history of the AAPA and its international connections and influences demonstrates that Indigenous people saw the importance of breaking free from imagined national and state boundaries. Aboriginal people were "cosmopolitan" in their own thinking and actions. They were active agents in taking advantage of opportunities and engaging with international contacts of influence and inspiration. Garveyism was a vehicle that inspired oppressed peoples to challenge the imposed constraints of imperialism. A global sense of unity was comforting and delivered a framework of political ideology that could be reworked to fit the Aboriginal Australian experience.

Like North America and the movement of black people to New York and Harlem, a similar migration to the urban space was witnessed in Australia.[11] The first two decades of the twentieth century saw Aboriginal people fleeing tightening governmental control and heading to Sydney for greater working opportunities and greater freedom. They were refugees in their own country, but the city space offered a heady mix of urbanization and radicalization.

The Coloured Progressive Association

As early as 1902, an organization called the Coloured Progressive Association (CPA) was established in Australia. The organization was composed mainly of members from the "Black Commonwealth," which included non-white people living in Australia as well as visiting West Indian, Indian, African, Maori, and Islander merchant sailors. Additionally, some visiting African Americans and some Aboriginal dockworkers were a part of this group. The CPA was apparently formed in response to the establishment of the "White Australia Policy" and a very inhospitable Australian environment. In 1901 the newly federated Commonwealth of Australia had passed an Immigration Restriction Act targeting people of non-European origin, which became known as the "White Australia Policy." This racist act was initiated as a barrier to Asian and black immigrants having an opportunity to make Australia home. The famed African American newspaper *The Crisis* was scathing of this blatantly racist policy: "There is Australia, a great empty continent containing five million people where it could easily support one hundred million. It is being held for white settlers who do not come, while coloured people are being kept out. Let Australia open its doors to its natural coloured settlers."[12] Criticism of and objections to this policy would fall on deaf ears as the "White Australia Policy" would remain intact until the mid-1960s.

In 1902, members of the CPA sent correspondence to the British House of Commons beseeching them to repeal the policy. In that correspondence the CPA outlined their purpose:

> Coloured races residing in the Commonwealth of Australia are sadly in need of the powerful assistance that a society or union, established for their mutual self-help and protection, will be able to afford them. We are now endeavouring to start such a society. United we shall be able to obtain legal redress whenever our liberties and privileges are threatened and the mere fact that such a society is in existence will of itself prove a mighty barrier against oppression or injustice of any kind. It is believed that every coloured person will gladly join our society as soon as they become acquainted with our aims and objects—United we shall be strong to help and protect.[13]

They later wrote to Secretary of the Colonies Joseph Chamberlain, protesting the newly introduced policy: "The administration of the Bill is vile, and also the general effects are undoubtedly cruel. Aliens of all kinds can enter the Commonwealth, whether they can read or write, as long as they are not black."[14]

The formation of an organization such as the CPA was very important in helping to define the spaces in which Aboriginal people moved and the identifications and alliances they formed with other oppressed groups. These connections were forged between displaced people, engendering the mobility, not just of black populations, but, importantly, of black transnational politics. The CPA may well have disappeared from historical memory except for the visit of African American boxing sensation Jack Johnson to Australia in 1907 and 1908. The CPA held a farewell function in Sydney to honor Johnson in 1907. Jack Johnson was not just a great boxer but also a highly politicized, charismatic, and inspiring figure. Future Aboriginal political leader Fred Maynard was present at that farewell function.

Garvey and the UNIA Down Under

Marcus Garvey's impact upon Aboriginal Australia witnessed a radical shift and awakening awareness of Aboriginal Australians of their national and global political challenges. As will be discussed, the intersection of the publishing and maritime industries enabled a powerful network of communication and support between Aboriginal activists and their counterparts across the globe.

The establishment of a Sydney chapter of the Universal Negro Improvement Association (UNIA) in 1920 was linked back to the earlier CPA, as the secretary of the UNIA Sydney branch was one Robert Usher, a West Indian who had been an office bearer of the CPA during its known years of operation between 1902 and 1912. In reports covered in the *Negro World*, Usher could not contain his enthusiasm on the impact of Marcus Garvey and the UNIA in Australia and that the message was "resounding throughout the length and breadth of this small continent."[15] He later revealed that the black population of Australia was suffering low self-esteem and confidence "but there are some of us who are doing our best to not only keep ourselves out of the mire, but to pull our brothers out as well."[16] Aboriginal activists, including Fred Maynard and Tom Lacey, were members of the Sydney UNIA branch.

Marcus Garvey had recognized, and directed his energies toward, the notion that all black people were "part of a transnational 'nation,' a global race with a common destiny."[17] The ideology of "Garveyism depended on activities that could restore both self-respect and a sense of community—essentially the development of a united black culture."[18] As Lawrence Levine argues, the sudden rise of Garvey and Garveyism was only possible "because blacks retained a healthy consciousness of identity and community. What Garvey did was to provide a political channel and a global perspective for that consciousness."[19] At the head of this network was a global maritime culture and history that connected black and oppressed groups across the global waterfront. The world's wharves, including Australia, proved to be pivotal in the establishment of a highly effective worldwide network of information—it was via the maritime industry that Garvey could send out agents (generally merchant seamen) to spread the message. Connection between sailors and wharf laborers at ports facilitated the weaving of this sophisticated communication system across the sea-lanes. These black seamen carried news and reading material between western Europe and the United States and the Caribbean—in fact, to all corners of the globe.[20] Garvey's newspaper, the *Negro World,* played a significant part in this process. It established a global circulation and, as elsewhere, was eagerly sought after in Australia.[21]

There are several accounts of international black newspapers being sought and made available on Australian docks. These included *The Crisis, Brownies Book, Crusader, Journal of Negro History, Negro World,* and *Emancipator.*[22] Tom Lacey, a member of the Sydney UNIA branch and later treasurer of the AAPA, wrote to Amy Jacques Garvey in 1924: "I would be very grateful to you if you could advise me how to get some of your American papers, the *Negro World* and other papers, so that I could distribute them among our people as it might help to enlighten them a bit."[23] Australian archival sources also indicate the fear on the part of authorities of the spread of what was termed "seditious literature" influencing Aboriginal people.[24] Indeed, the Aboriginal activists saw the papers serving a dual purpose: first, as a means of transmitting their grievances to the black world, and second, as providing firsthand knowledge of what was happening elsewhere. Lacey's letter to the central UNIA branch, which was published in the *Negro World,* pledged the support of ten thousand Aboriginal people in New South Wales and sixty thousand Aboriginal people nationally to Marcus Garvey and his movement. Stating that the Sydney UNIA branch had "not had the time to organize in the other four states yet," Lacey declared his intent to push the message across the country.[25] Evidently, he saw Garveyism as the galvanizing tool and ideology that could forge a united national Aboriginal political movement and agenda. Lacey pointed out that he had been a UNIA member for four years and had recently been elected as the Sydney branch organizer. He explained that Aboriginal people in Australia were held under control by government authorities and departments, with many of the people confined on tightly controlled Aboriginal reserves:

> I hope before long you will be able to send us a delegate down here to Australia and it would mean a great help to us. . . . We have a bit of trouble to see some of our people, as the missionaries have got the most of them, and we have great difficulty in reaching them. The authorities won't allow us to see them unless we can give them (the Aboriginal Board) a clear explanation of what we want them for.[26]

Robert Usher had long-term connections with both Maynard and Lacey dating back to the earlier CPA and the Sydney branch of the UNIA. Usher was aware that Garvey was intending to undertake a world tour in 1923 and expressed the hope that Garvey would include a visit to Sydney on his itinerary. Garvey himself publically acknowledged the Sydney branch:

> The moment I landed in New York I received a cable from Sydney, Australia, where we have a division, who manifested their loyalty 100 per cent, after hearing and reading in the Sydney papers of my arrest here a few weeks ago.[27]

While there is no surviving evidence of why the Sydney UNIA branch suddenly ceased operations in 1924, we can surmise that the Aboriginal activists had recognized the importance of forming their own organization and agenda. Nevertheless, the AAPA would remain greatly influenced by Garveyism, including a platform that promoted self-determination and focused on economic, social, and political reform.

Fred Maynard and Tom Lacey: Aboriginal Garveyites

I will focus here on examining the backgrounds of Fred Maynard and Tom Lacey to ascertain why these men may have connected with Garveyism. Garvey, of course, was likened to a modern-day Moses sent to lead his people to the Promised Land. In similar biblical and religious overtones, both Aboriginal leaders were described as the "moving spirits" of the Aboriginal movement.[28] Tom Lacey was born at Ulladullah on the south coast of New South Wales, within the tribal boundaries of the Yuin Aboriginal people. He was noted as being a "first class cricketer."[29] Lacey received a glowing endorsement: "From end to end of N.S.W. the name of Lacey is known and admired. He is a keen debater and will be hailed as a modern Moses."[30] He was described as an impressive speaker and asserted that if given the opportunity, Aboriginal people could gain the same position "as the coloured people of the United States of America, who have their own colleges and universities."[31] Lacey passed away in the early 1930s, and there is little archival record left other than the references to him during the AAPA's four years of political activity.

Fred Maynard was a Worimi Aboriginal man of the Port Stephens region of New South Wales, situated about two hundred kilometers north of Sydney. The complex and highly politically attuned makeup of the adult Fred Maynard was the result of many varied and impacting events, experiences, and people. The horrific experiences suffered by members of his own family—and his own abandonment and maltreatment as a young boy—then subsequent wide travels and observations of the personal suffering and experiences of many other Aboriginal people in differing locations had a profound impact on Maynard. From a very early age he sought to overcome his own disadvantage and chart his own course through life. His early life experiences were undoubtedly a major component of the underlying forces that drove him in the future. From his own harsh personal experiences and his observations of how Aboriginal people were treated he sought to oppose government policy toward Aboriginal people and try every way possible to instill hope in his people.

Marcus Garvey provided a role model and hero for the Aboriginal leaders to aspire to. Garvey received widespread coverage in the Australian media during the early 1920s, and they were aware of his inspirational activities. His political demands for an independent economic base of operation were of interest to Aboriginal activists who were fighting a losing battle to retain their independent farming ventures during this time period. There are many striking similarities between Fred Maynard and Marcus Garvey. Both were recognized as outstanding and inspiring public speakers. Garvey was a charismatic and powerful demonstrative speaker who captivated audiences wherever he spoke. Even "Du Bois conceded that Garvey's 'singular eloquence' made him 'an extraordinary leader of men.'"[32] Maynard was similarly lauded—"as a public speaker he has few equals in the Commonwealth"[33]—and was described as "an orator of outstanding ability . . . [who] in the not far distant future will loom large in the politics of this country."[34] Maynard addressed a large open-air gathering of Aboriginal people at Greenhills near Kempsey in late 1925: "The interest of the people as they listened to the impassioned appeal of the coloured preacher was remarkable."[35] Maynard and Garvey had both acquired a dictionary as young men and studied it religiously to enhance their knowledge of the English language. Both men were great admirers of Ralph Waldo Emerson and his concept of self-reliance and quoted from him frequently. Maynard's years on the wharf and close connection with visiting black sailors and the availability of black newspapers and manifestos including Garveyism clearly influenced his ideology greatly. Self-educated on a wide variety of topics, and a voracious reader who continued to educate himself,[36] Maynard was aware of international—particularly black—issues, and his association with African American influences and his links to the Garvey movement may have influenced the New South Wales Aborigines Protection Board's attempt to discredit and defame Maynard's Aboriginal background and character. In correspondence from the board to Premier Jack Lang, the inference made was quite explicit: he could not possibly be Aboriginal and his representations "should not be allowed to unduly occupy the Premier's time. Mr Maynard is a full blooded black (either American or South African) whose voluble manner and illogical views are more likely to disturb the Australian Aborigines than achieve for them improvement of conditions."[37]

The Australian Aboriginal Progressive Association

The Australian Aboriginal Progressive Association, which formed in Sydney in 1924, would eventually hold four conferences in Sydney, Kempsey, Grafton, and Lismore. They attracted widespread support from Indigenous communities, establishing thirteen branches and four sub-branches with a membership that exceeded six hundred. Considering that the entire Aboriginal population of New South Wales at that time on government figures was less than seven thousand, and with the greater majority of Aboriginal people confined on restrictive reserves with denied mobility, this was a staggering achievement. They opened their own offices in Crown Street Sydney with the phone connected. News of the AAPA spread rapidly through an established and active Indigenous community network. The formation of the organization filled Aboriginal people with hope and inspiration with the knowledge that some of their own were now speaking out against the oppressive policies that confronted Aboriginal people and communities. One old man "wrote from a far back settlement, asking that someone should come and tell them about the 'Freedom Club.'"[38]

In April 1925, Fred Maynard, in his inaugural address as president of the AAPA, outlined the hopes and dreams of Australian Aboriginal people:

> Brothers and sisters, we have much business to transact so let's get right down to it. We aim at the spiritual, political, industrial and social. We want to work out our own destiny. Our people have not had the courage to stand together in the past, but now we are united, and are determined to work for the preservation for all of those interests, which are near, and dear to us.[39]

His speech marked the opening of the first Aboriginal civil rights convention ever staged in Australia, at St. David's Church and Hall in Surrey Hills. The AAPA was instantly front-page news with headlines trumpeting "On Aborigines Aspirations—First Australians to Help Themselves—Self Determination." More than two hundred Aboriginal people were in attendance, and many had traveled great distances and "heartily supported the objectives of the association."[40] The newspaper coverage highlighted the large, enthusiastic cross section of the Aboriginal community present:

> The old and young were there. The well-dressed matronly woman and the shingled girl of 19. The old man of 60 and the young man of athletic build. All are fighting for the preservation of the rights of Aborigines for self-determination.[41]

The Aboriginal activists were articulate, eloquent, and self-educated statesmen and women far removed from the wider misconceptions of the time period that portrayed Aboriginal people as belonging to the Stone Age, unable to be educated and a dying race. The second conference, in Kempsey, attracted over seven hundred Aboriginal delegates. Fred Maynard closed the conference with the following powerful resolution that was dispatched to all levels of Australian government.

> As it is the proud boast of Australia that every person born beneath the Southern Cross is born free, irrespective of origin, race, colour, creed, religion or any other impediment. We the representatives of the original people, in conference assembled, demand that we shall be accorded the same full right of privileges of citizenship as are enjoyed by all other sections of the community.[42]

The opposition to the AAPA, particularly through police threat, intimidation, and constant surveillance, was responsible for the its being driven underground and disappearing from public view in 1928. The AAPA in Australia, like the UNIA in the United States, rapidly lost momentum during the 1930s. In Garvey's case this was due to the interference of the FBI and subsequent jailing in 1923 on trumped-up mail fraud charges and his eventual deportation from the United States in 1927. The demise of the AAPA can be linked to the onset of the Great Depression and the difficulties Aboriginal men had in maintaining work. But the main cause of the demise of the AAPA was the activities of the police force. David Huggonson has speculated on the level of intimidation that "officers of the Board may have made in relation to taking Maynard's children into state care if he continued his agitation."[43] A revealing 1927 newspaper interview with Maynard indicates the level of intimidation he was subjected to at the time. Maynard stated that "he had been warned on many occasions that the doors of Long Bay [Gaol] were opening for him. He would cheerfully go to gaol for the remainder of his life, he declared, if, by so doing, he could make the people of Australia realise the truly frightful administration of the Aborigines Act."[44] The 1931 Australian Communist Party publication on the *Rights of Aborigines* revealed that the AAPA was destroyed through a coalition of opposition formed between the government's Aborigines Protection Board, the missionaries, and the police.[45]

The Return of Marcus Garvey into Australian Aboriginal Political Consciousness

It is amazing that the history of the Australian Aboriginal Progressive Association for a long period lay forgotten and erased from Australian history and memory. This includes the memory of international black influences, including Garveyism, upon the rise of early Aboriginal political activism. We understand that the resurgence of Aboriginal activism during the 1960s and 1970s drew heavily upon international black inspiration, including Malcolm X, Martin Luther King Jr., and Black Power, but there was little or no recognition of Marcus Garvey's influence five decades before. It has only been because of my own work across the past two decades that the links between early Aboriginal activists and Garveyism have been uncovered. But there has been a recent resurgence of interest—both positive and negative—of Garvey within Aboriginal Australia. High-profile Aboriginal political activist Gary Foley remains a deep devotee of Garveyism and of the continued relevance of the "father of black nationalism." Foley encourages young Aboriginal people to examine, analyze, and incorporate Garveyism and the political ideology of the AAPA into their current thinking.[46] Griffith University Indigenous academic Marcus Waters was equally effusive: "Garvey spent a lifetime healing a people who were victims of oppression, mental and physical slavery. He understood their minds and thinking had to be reformed. Black Nationalism was born to inspire and empower a people who had lost everything."[47]

The Marcus Garvey revival into Australian Aboriginal political memory has not been without some negative and largely uninformed backlash directed at Garvey and Garveyism. Two very prominent Aboriginal leaders and media- and government-supported spokespeople, Marcia Langton and Noel Pearson, have targeted Garvey and Garveyism as a part of their own rhetoric detailing what they perceive to be the current ills of Aboriginal Australia. Pearson has been adamant that for Indigenous people the "extreme position is that of *separatism*. In the United States, black nationalists such as Marcus Garvey actively pursued separatist agendas."[48] Pearson does not articulate Garvey's directive within the context of the time period; nor does he observe that Garveyism was constantly evolving and changing. Langton derides any contemporary Aboriginal demands for self-determination and links those demands to Garvey:

> It is Australia's version of the Marcus Garvey movement of the 1950s Jamaica that dreamt of repatriation of African descendants to Africa and involved proto-Rastafarians in rituals such as waiting on the wharf for their saviour, Emperor Haile Selassie of Ethiopia, to arrive on a ship and rescue them.[49]

Clearly, Langton is unaware that Garvey was long gone by the 1950s and that Haile Selassie did visit Jamaica with much fanfare in 1966. Garvey and Garveyism remain largely misunderstood. It is interesting that Garvey has resurfaced today in Australia simultaneously as a point of inspiration and negativity. I leave the final word on the misinformation, misinterpretations, and just missing understanding of Garvey to the Pulitzer Prize–winning author Steve Hahn:

> There is a deep history of the UNIA about which we know very little, though this seems emblematic of a larger and more curious elision: that is to say, how little we know, at any point in its history, about what is

acknowledged to be the greatest mass movement of people of African descent in the twentieth century. . . . Garveyism won massive support in the 1920s, and its intellectual and political legacies have been profound. It left its mark on every major black social and political movement of the twentieth century (here and abroad).[50]

Although the ripples the AAPA made on the political landscape in Australia may be judged by some as minor, the long-term repercussions on Aboriginal political thinking were far-reaching, and Marcus Garvey's influence played a major role in developing Aboriginal political strategies. The story of the AAPA adds another small piece to the jigsaw of Garvey and his impact around the world.

Conclusion

We are left today to recognize and remember the early Aboriginal freedom fighters who were prepared to bravely step forward to challenge the tight government control over Aboriginal lives in the early decades of the twentieth century. Men like Tom Lacey and Fred Maynard were products of their lived experiences and observations of Aboriginal suffering. It was the connection of these men with African American visitors, literature, and manifestos and the inspiration of Marcus Garvey that left an indelible imprint on their political thinking and strategies. The organization they formed, the Australian Aboriginal Progressive Association, remains as the first united all-Aboriginal political organization to form in Australia, and its platform, directives, motivations, and strategies clearly reveal the influence of Garveyism. Garvey is only now regaining a place in Aboriginal political history, and the contemporary setting remains a complex point of inspiration, contestation, and in some cases derision.

Notes

1. Editorial by Marcus Garvey, November 1, 1920, in R. A. Hill, *Marcus Garvey and Universal Negro Improvement Association Papers* [hereafter *MGP*], 1:lxix.
2. Butlin, *Our Original Aggression*, 175.
3. Bourke, Bourke, and Edwards, *Aboriginal Australia*, 45.
4. Parbury, *Survival*, 80.
5. Maynard, *Fight for Liberty and Freedom*, 39.

6. Letter from Australian Aboriginal (Protection) [*sic*] Progressive Association, published in *The Daylight*, March 31, 1928. It is held at the National Archives of Australia (Canberra), CRS A659/1, 1943/1/1451.

7. Ewing, *Age of Garvey*, 108.

8. Maynard, *Fight for Liberty and Freedom*, 29.

9. Goodall, *Invasion to Embassy*, 152.

10. Carey and Lydon, *Indigenous Networks*, 1.

11. Maynard, "Fred Maynard and Marcus Garvey."

12. *The Crisis* 23, no. 3 (January 1922): 103.

13. Coloured Progressive Association to Dadabhai Naoroji, House of Commons, Finsbury, Central London, November 11, 1902, Dadabhai Naoroji Papers, National Archives of India, Delhi, courtesy of Dinyar Patel, Harvard University.

14. Ibid.

15. *Negro World,* May 5, 1923.

16. Ibid.

17. Marable, *Life of Reinvention*, 18.

18. Ibid.

19. Levine, *Unpredictable Past*, 116.

20. Bandele, *Black Star*, 20.

21. T. Martin, *Race First*, 93.

22. A. Goldsmith to Carter G. Woodson, September 6, 1920, Carter G. Woodson Files 1912–1950, reel 1, series 2, Correspondence, Library of Congress, Washington, DC.

23. *Negro World,* August 2, 1924.

24. For a sense of the concern of Australian authorities, see the documents collected in the National Archives of Australia, Canberra: A467, SF7/26.

25. *Negro World,* August 2, 1924.

26. Ibid.

27. *MGP*, 4:570.

28. *The Northern Star,* August 3, 1927.

29. *Daily Examiner,* December 29, 1926.

30. *The Voice of the North*, October 10, 1927.

31. *The Voice of the North,* January 11, 1926.

32. Levine, *Unpredictable Past*, 121.

33. *The Voice of the North,* October 12, 1925, 18.

34. *The Voice of the North,* January 11, 1925.

35. *Macleay Chronicle*, October 7, 1925, 8.

36. Maynard-Kondek, "Charles Frederick Maynard," 175.

37. E. B. Harkness, Under Secretary to the Premiers Department, New South Wales State Government, Sydney, November 9, 1927, NSW Premiers Department Correspondence Files 9/11/1927, A27/915, New South Wales State Archives, Sydney.

38. *Macleay Chronicle,* August 19, 1925.

39. *Daily Guardian*, April 24, 1924.

40. Ibid.

41. *Daily Guardian*, May 7, 1925.

42. *Macleay Chronicle,* October 7, 1925.

43. Huggonson, "Aborigines and the Aftermath."

44. *Newcastle Sun*, December 7, 1927.

45. *The Workers Weekly*, September 24, 1931.

46. Gary Foley, "The Answer Is a Better Knowledge of History," *Tracker Magazine,* July 15, 2011.

47. Marcus Waters, "Marcus Waters Reflects on Black Nationalism," *The Stringer Independent News,* June 19, 2014.

48. Pearson, *A Rightful Place,* 31.

49. Langton, *Quiet Revolution*, 139.

50. Hahn, *Political Worlds,* 119–20.

10

"No Race Question"

Garveyism and Trinidad's Labor Movement in the Age of Black Internationalism, 1919–1925

JOSÉ ANDRÉS FERNÁNDEZ MONTES DE OCA

In July 1921 the Guianese journalist William Howard Bishop left Port-of-Spain, Trinidad, for London. Bishop was the general secretary of the Trinidad Workingmen's Association (TWA) and the editor of the organization's newspaper, the *Labour Leader*.[1] Colonial officials in Trinidad described him as an agitator, "very strong on the colour question and a loyal supporter of the principles of Marcus Garvey."[2] But Bishop was traveling to London for a different purpose: to represent the TWA at the Labour Party Conference. After spending some time with members of the Labour Party and analyzing the conditions of the working class in London, Bishop wrote a letter home to the members of the TWA, expressing his desire to see the foundation of a labor federation in the West Indies and in British Guiana, improvements for the working class in the West Indies, and the establishment of a representative government in Trinidad—all necessary conditions for "industrial emancipation." Bishop called on his fellow workers to stay organized and pointed to the need for both labor reform and "the introduction into the colony of a popular form of government."[3] Bishop's trip to London marked the beginning of the TWA's period of influence in Trinidad's labor and constitutional politics.

Bishop's multi-pronged connections to international labor, his demands for colonial reform in the British Empire, and his association with Garvey's race-conscious movement raise interesting questions about the interconnectedness of transnational race and class struggles. In the past, authors have emphasized the importance of Marcus Garvey's ideas and organization, the Universal Negro

Improvement Association (UNIA), in the development of the labor movement in Trinidad after 1919.[4] In so doing, they have often overlooked a more complex reality on the ground, among members of the island's working class. To be sure, Garveyite propaganda played a consequential role in the development of Trinidad labor politics. As Tony Martin observes, the leadership of the UNIA and the TWA overlapped, no more so than in the figure of Bishop himself. Articles written by Bishop were reprinted in the official organ of the UNIA, the *Negro World*; in turn, news about Garvey and the UNIA was published in the *Labour Leader*.[5] But as Jerome Teelucksingh has argued, if Garveyite ideas such as universal fraternity among Africans, racial pride and self-esteem, and a sense of nationhood were pertinent to Trinidad's working-class politics, the challenge for the TWA leadership was to reconcile two distinct ideologies, one African diaspora–based, the other grounded in socialism. For Teelucksingh, the broader context of black internationalist and transnational struggles formed a crucial context for the evolving relationship between Garveyism and labor politics in Trinidad.[6]

In this essay, I examine how the TWA combined Garveyism and labor politics, and how it navigated the potential contradictions between class-based and race-based organizing more broadly. I do not study the TWA and the UNIA as grassroots organizations per se. Instead, I focus on the ideas of class and race expressed by working-class leaders at meetings, in police reports, and in newspapers. Scholars have yet to delineate with contemporary primary sources the extent to which Garveyism influenced TWA leadership and the labor movement amid the economic strain, heightened racial tensions, and social distress of post–World War I Trinidad.[7] Nor have scholars attempted to understand local ideas of class and race in relation to the broader range of global black internationalist strands present on the island in those years.

This careful exploration is important if we are to move beyond the identification of black internationalist connections to an exploration of the specific nature of those connections. *Black internationalism* is a term scholars use to describe mutually aware social, cultural, and political struggles for freedom and equality among African-descended people globally. Indeed, black internationalists saw themselves as part of a global community, rooted in the African diaspora experience and in the crafting of transnational solidarities. The concept of black internationalism has allowed authors to fruitfully explore these connections and expressions of solidarity between black struggles across borders and in the face of racial constraints. But in uncovering the existence of these connections, scholars run the risk of obscuring important differences and debates. After all, socialists, communists, and black nationalist followers of Marcus Garvey conceived black internationalism in notably different ways.[8]

My goal is to add to the existing literature on Garveyism and race consciousness in Trinidad a perspective that situates the TWA's ideas on race and class as a local dialogue interacting with global discussions among black radicals about labor organizing, socialism, communism, black nationalism, and pan-Africanism. I reconstruct the multiple connections between the small island of Trinidad in the 1920s and the networks of black internationalists that emerged and extended messages of solidarity from Harlem to London, and from West Africa to the circum-Caribbean.

Authors such as Teelucksingh and Kelvin Singh argue that it was after 1925 that the TWA shifted from a pan-Africanist orientation to a socialist one.[9] My research demonstrates that Trinidad's labor leaders had juxtaposed black internationalist strands—Garveyism among them—with left-wing ideas of class, laborism, and socialism since 1919, and in some sense even before that. All these ideas, sometimes at odds and at other times reconciled, formed part of an ongoing dialogue during early 1920s that shaped the TWA's political discourse on class and race. During the early twentieth century, race consciousness emerged here as elsewhere as a transnational phenomenon connecting ordinary people and articulating ideas of race, class, and citizenship.[10] As a result, in Trinidad the working class demanded democracy and equality, while foregrounding racial subordination as a product of capitalist exploitation. Leaders of the working class incorporated and reconfigured black internationalists' ideas on racial uplift, intellectual improvement, and unity into their political rhetoric.

This project reconstructs the struggle of the Trinidadian working class in the 1920s to define what race consciousness and Garveyism meant to the working class itself. Colonial officials saw the different forms of black internationalism as "Bolshevism," "political agitation," and "seditious," essentially hostile to the government. Their concern generated archival sources that allow us to reconstruct a different picture. The police reports of TWA meetings, Trinidad UNIA meetings, and other activities "among Coloured labour," in addition to the *Labour Leader* publications, offer insight into labor leaders' ideas on class and race. The TWA refused to become a race-based union but nevertheless insisted on talking about race; labor leaders argued repeatedly that racial subordination hindered British principles of equality and accentuated global exploitation. The present research gives insight into Trinidad's political thought in the 1920s as an important moment when local ideas of great importance in the coming decades took shape.

My narrative begins with the 1919 strikes, which illuminate the intersection of Trinidad's local claims with international struggles and ideas. I reconstruct the multiple connections between the small island of Trinidad and the networks of black internationalists that emerged and extended messages of solidarity across the Atlantic. Parallel to the development of the strikes, black internationalists from various denominations visited Trinidad, offering lectures that analyzed race consciousness and labor solidarities; in turn, TWA activists such as Howard Bishop and Arthur Cipriani created inter-class and inter-race connections within Trinidad and with Great Britain. The workers were receptive to international struggles broadcast by these activists and their newspapers, adopting and reconfiguring ideas to promote their complaints and sponsor unity and justice. The program of the TWA was based on class struggle and colonial reform, in clear differentiation to Garvey's race-first doctrine. I argue that in this period the TWA and the UNIA established themselves as different organizations with different goals and principles. The TWA took black internationalist language and embedded it into its own propaganda and political culture.

Black Internationalists in Trinidad's Meeting Halls: Race, Labor Unity, and International Solidarity

The 1919 strikes in Trinidad emerged out of the tumult of the Great War. Inflationary conditions, unmatched by an increase in wage levels, complicated the economic situation of the working class, especially among African descendants and East Indians. The growing number of applications granted for pauper and poverty certificates displayed the widespread distress in the island. The colonial ruling class, aware of stagnant wages and the difficulties working-class families faced to meet minimal requirements in food, clothing, and shelter, did not make any attempt to improve wages.[11] In the context of high unemployment and underemployment, between February and November 1919 civil servants, stevedores, mechanics, porters, and railway workers petitioned for a salary increase. During those months the TWA expanded its membership and attempted to recruit the stevedores and negotiate on their behalf. When the shipping companies refused to settle, the stevedores chose to strike the first week of December 1919.[12]

Throughout 1919, and especially in instances of social distress, colonial authorities saw the spreading strikes as dangerous anti-white uprisings. In July the acting governor in Trinidad, William M. Gordon, wrote to the secretary of state in the Colonial Office that "a very strong feeling of racial antipathy" had spread across the colony. The governor also argued that the "racial antipathy" was fueling local demands for "the establishment of a system of representative government of the Colony by the black race." Gordon and a group of wealthy whites in the colony shared the opinion that the return of dissatisfied soldiers from the British West Indian Regiment, the arrival of a group of men involved in the Cardiff riots in June, and the circulation of newspapers such as the local *Argos* and Marcus Garvey's *Negro World,* ignited the uprisings in Port-of-Spain.[13] From their perspective, the social distress in 1919 was a matter of racial animosity that endangered the colonial government; it appeared to them as nothing but an expression of rage from the black population, rather than a rational response to working-class living conditions.

In response, colonial officials targeted TWA members and others involved in the stevedores' strike. A half dozen people, some of them members of the TWA and others who were active Garveyites, were deported from Trinidad.[14] In April 1920 Trinidad and other West Indian governments passed a Seditious Publications Ordinance, which banned the importation of literature that could stimulate "racial hatred" or contained Bolshevik propaganda. The measure was especially issued against the *Negro World* and other African American newspapers such as *The Crusader, The Emancipator, The Promoter,* and *Crisis.*[15]

Scholars have read such accusations "against the grain" to argue that Marcus Garvey's message of self-reliance, unity, respect, and other ideas on race consciousness had indeed motivated lower classes of African descendants in Trinidad to riot.[16] But not everyone shared the fears of colonial elites. The Constabulary Commission, gathered to clarify the happenings during the 1919 strikes, dismissed the fears of colonial officials and white elites in the island, judging accusations of a *Negro World*–inspired plot to murder white people and overthrow the government "absolutely inconceivable."[17] Rather than being motivated by incoming ideas of race pride or hatred, concluded the commission, the 1919 strikes were motivated by specific local grievances. Neither the enforcement of the Seditious Publications Ordinance nor the surveillance of black activists addressed local aspirations for just working conditions, equality, and political representation in Trinidad. David Headley, president of the TWA, supported the view of the commission, observing that despite the suggestions raised by the wealthiest whites in the colony that the outbreak was due to merely racial stimulus that excited the masses, it was clear that the masses' "self-insurgency" was a movement carried forward by the "spirit of every wage-earner," regardless of color, class, creed, and nationality.[18]

The visions expressed by colonial officials, the white elite, the Constabulary Commission's report, and Headley need not be viewed as contradictory, but rather understood as complementary pieces that illustrate the complexities of local and transnational connections. During 1919, burgeoning ideas of race consciousness, unity, and pride carried by black activists met with local social and political grievances expressed by workers during the strikes and by labor leaders in the meeting halls. The events in 1919 show the articulation of working-class grievances and local and transnational labor initiatives in dialogue with strands of race-conscious internationalism. Workers were attentive to transnational ideas of race and class, and they adopted those ideas to promote their complaints and to articulate their own conceptions of unity and justice.

This dynamic can be seen in the September 1919 visit to Trinidad by the Venezuelan-born journalist and black activist Felix Eugene Michael Hercules.[19] At Port-of-Spain, speaking before a large audience of urban black residents, Hercules delivered a wide-ranging message of unity and race-conscious internationalism that joined conditions in Trinidad to a wide range of global concerns: Africans' living conditions in South Africa; the rights of people of African descent in the southern United States; and the importance of cooperation and the "betterment" of the race "by union and economic principles."[20]

In his introduction of Hercules, the chairman of the meeting, Charles Henry Pierre, a lawyer of mixed Afro-Indian heritage, gave local shape to Hercules's remarks by focusing the audience's attention on local claims for constitutional reform and political participation. Like Hercules, he viewed these demands in a global context, observing that constitutional reform and political participation would have wide-ranging benefits for Africans and peoples of African descent alike.[21]

Another traveler, Demerara-born Rev. A. Theophilus Peters, member of the Congregational Church of Rhode Island, arrived at Port-of-Spain in October 1919. In Trinidad, he was introduced to officials of the TWA who invited him to address several speeches on the "New Negro" at the meeting of the association. The police inspector, Sergeant Sylvester, attended one of the meetings at the Western Boy's School. According to Sylvester, Peters "exhorted the people to join the Association by which he said they would surely benefit by being better treated and get better wages."[22] The *Trinidad Guardian* reported that the meeting was held under the chairmanship of the TWA president Headley. In his opening remarks to the crowded hall, Headley "stated that for them to get all they wanted [the working class] had to marshal their forces . . . in accordance with law and order." Headley also declared that their intention was to expand the association throughout the island and that "when they were thoroughly organized they could affiliate themselves with the Union in Demerara and the 15 other West Indian colonies."[23] As with the Hercules meeting in September, the Peters meeting demonstrated the articulation of two strands: on one hand, Trinidadian claims for constitutional reform and the advocacy for local and regional labor connections; on the other hand, connections with race-based international struggles.

After the 1919 strikes, black spokespersons, journalists, and activists, regardless of their ideological program and origin, were seen as equally dangerous for the colonial authorities, targeted, and followed closely. In December 1919 colonial officials followed the steps of Sierra Leone–born John Eldred Taylor. In 1919 Taylor immigrated to England, where he collaborated with Dusé Mohamed Ali, who, with Taylor's help, launched the *African Times and Orient Review* in July 1912.[24] After the outbreak of the Great War, Taylor met Hercules, with whom he launched the Society of Peoples of African Origin and the *African Telegraph*. In December 1919, the secretary of state informed the governor of Trinidad that Taylor had left for the West Indies. The governor was urged to pay close attention if he attempted to land in the colony.[25]

Taylor never arrived in Trinidad, but his partner did. Hercules came back to Trinidad in December and addressed more meetings right after the stevedores' strike. In Port-of-Spain he interacted with members of the TWA and was introduced at a meeting by Headley. According to a report by the police inspector, Hercules told the workers, "the Capitalist wants your labour and you must show him you are entitled to good wages in return, by going on strike until you get it." Hercules also counseled the workers to "do things in a constitutional manner and you will have our support on the other side of the waters."[26] Once again, his speech brought forth the importance of unity and cooperation. It also stressed the working-class struggle against capitalist exploitation, improvement through constitutional means, and international labor support, ideas that would become the main discourse in which the TWA would base its program.

Hercules was part of an international network of activists whom colonial and U.S. authorities viewed as engaging in race-mongering, regardless of their expressed ideological positions.[27] In a December 1919 letter to Colonel G. H. May, inspector general of the constabulary in Trinidad, the American consul reported that the black agitators' purpose was to "bring about cooperation between the disturbing elements both in our country and in your Colonies."[28]

Instead, the black internationalists who visited Trinidad in 1919 carried ideas that creatively merged an awareness of race-conscious international struggles with an analysis of the dynamics between labor and capital. Regardless of their preferred solution—political reform or revolution, race-based or class-based alliances—they understood themselves to be operating within the constraints of a worldwide system of racial subordination. In the 1920s the TWA would elaborate a program based on labor struggles that incorporated concerns about race and international struggles. It would become—as it had not been previously—the organization that led this activism, leveraging its collective strength among the workers of Trinidad.

The TWA's Political Rhetoric of Class and Race in the Early 1920s

In an article published in 1924 in the *Labour Leader,* William Howard Bishop told his readers that since 1919 he had been under the eye of Trinidadian authorities.[29] He also reported that a squad of detectives under charge of Police Inspector Costelloe came to his house in 1920 with a warrant and searched for seditious literature such as the *Negro World,* the *Messenger,* and the *Crusader.*[30] Indeed, Bishop was under close surveillance. Colonial officials knew that Bishop had moved from Demerara, where he had worked as a teacher, to Trinidad in 1903. They knew that during the 1910s he had become a member of the TWA. According to the colonial reports, Bishop was a very active member of the association during the labor disturbances in December 1919, "very strong on the colour question and a loyal supporter of the principles of Marcus Garvey."[31]

This claim, consistent with authorities' insistence that Garvey's influence was driving working-class unrest, misrepresents the broader complexities that carried the relationship between the TWA and the UNIA, between Garvey's race-first doctrine and the "doctrine of Labour."[32] The TWA leaders' political discourse during the 1920s expressed the tension between the ideas of race and class. The TWA elaborated a program based on labor politics, colonial reform, and socialism.[33] This program developed in close dialogue, yet not in collaboration, with Garveyism and other strands of black internationalism. TWA members identified principles of racial uplift, race consciousness, and self-determination as tools against capitalist subordination, yet they were very specific that their organization was not a race-based one. Meanwhile, Garvey's UNIA in Trinidad conversely assured colonial officials that the organization was not related to any labor union. The TWA and the UNIA maintained a clear differentiation, establishing very visible boundaries. For example, in January 1921, H.D.A. Thompson, president of Trinidad's UNIA, expressed to colonial authorities that the organization did not "uphold strikers" or have any sympathy for "agitators" who attempted to break ordinances, in reference to the 1919 strikes.[34] For their part, in their meetings and pamphlets the TWA members avoided discourses based on race-first rhetoric and focused their discussion on labor dignity, capitalist exploitation, and colonial reform.

Two figures perfectly exemplify the close, yet clearly separate, relationship between the TWA and Trinidad's UNIA: Howard Bishop and Aaron Fitz Brathwaite. Bishop, general-secretary of the TWA, maintained a friendly relation with Garveyite circles. Brathwaite was an important and active member of both the TWA and the UNIA. Their activism represents both the intermittent dialogue between both organizations and their clearly stated boundaries.

As a central figure in Trinidad's labor politics, Bishop maintained a constant dialogue with different friendly societies, mutual-aid societies, and social clubs. In 1922 he gave a speech on the need for black unity at a UNIA Port-of-Spain meeting. Indeed, Bishop was close to the UNIA and kept its members, and the public in general, informed about the UNIA's overall development in the United States and elsewhere. In 1926 the *Negro World* acknowledged Bishop's work on behalf of the organization in Trinidad, congratulating him for his splendid work in keeping UNIA members and friends informed in a country where the *Negro World* was banned. "The *Negro World*," the paper wrote, "extends to this enterprising and race loving young man its best wishes for success in his splendid vocation."[35]

Although colonial authorities defined him as a "loyal supporter of the principles of Marcus Garvey," Bishop was in the main an advocate for labor politics rather than Garveyism. Even as Bishop published news about Garvey and his ideas in the *Labour Leader,* he maintained a distance between himself, his paper, and the aims of Garveyism and the UNIA. In fact, Bishop was very clear about what he viewed as the UNIA's limitations. In a 1923 article he stressed the historical importance of Garvey and Garveyism in the awakening of African-descended people and hailed Garvey as a new Moses who was leading his people out of mental bondage and into a new stage of racial pride and improvement. But Bishop also maintained that the time had come for Garvey to "give place to an Aaron who will lead the dusky skinned children of God and sons of men onward, upward, into regions of life triumphant."[36] He believed that Garvey's time as the great leader was over and that it was up to others to lead the charge forward.

Bishop is better described as a black internationalist than as a Garveyite. He was indeed "very strong on the colour question," as were his fellow associates in the TWA. They identified with principles of racial uplift, race consciousness, and self-determination as tools against capitalist subordination. Far from basing its claims on the New York–based UNIA program, the TWA pursued better conditions for the working class and colonial political reform through peaceful and democratic means. The TWA sought to achieve social change through trade union activism, education, and worker solidarity rather than through an organization that was exclusively designed for the "Negro race," and that advocated the doctrines of racial purity and self-reliance.[37]

Just as the TWA maintained a distance from the UNIA, Garveyites sought to distinguish their activities from the work of labor activists.[38] This was made clear from the moment the UNIA sought permission to organize in Trinidad. In January 1921, H.D.A. Thompson appealed "as a British Subject" to Governor John Robert Chancellor for the establishment of the UNIA on the island. In his petition, Thompson noted that "hundreds of people" in Trinidad were afraid of becoming members of the UNIA because of the Sedition Bill; he assured officials that the UNIA did not support strikers or have any sympathy for agitators who attempted to break ordinances.[39] Similarly, in March 1923, when UNIA high commissioner Richard Hilton Tobitt was denied entry into Trinidad, the Antiguan-born Tobitt described himself as a loyal British subject, held in respect by the government of Bermuda, where he worked as the principal of St. George High School. Tobitt denied rumors that connected him with the "Labour Union" and solemnly swore that he held no union memberships. Instead, he declared himself a member of the UNIA and argued that the organization has been misrepresented by its enemies as well as by its ignorant members.[40]

The UNIA's distancing of itself from any form of labor activism seems paradoxical given the example of Aaron Fitz Brathwaite. During the stevedores' strike in 1919, Brathwaite was a central figure in the negotiation between workers and the shipping companies. He had been a member of the TWA since the 1910s and was also an important member of Trinidad's UNIA structure during the 1920s.[41] But a closer look reveals the ways that Brathwaite and the TWA worked to establish a very clear boundary between their work and Garvey's race-first rhetoric. When questioned by colonial authorities about the UNIA in 1921, Brathwaite explicitly de-emphasized the organization's focus on race consciousness, noting instead its efforts toward education, industrialism, and the development of social, moral, and spiritual skills among the black population, and under the laws of the colony.[42] During the early 1920s, with the police maintaining close surveillance of TWA meetings, references made by members of the association to the "race question" were consistently limited to calls for race unity, accompanied by calls for alliances with fellow workers of other races. TWA leaders constantly declaimed against hatred based on skin color.[43]

The organization's aim, indeed, was to develop an interracial labor movement in the colony. Around May 1921, TWA president Headley published a booklet on the labor conditions in Trinidad from 1919 to 1921. Howard Bishop described the booklet as "the bible" of the working class.[44] In the booklet, Headley argued that capital must recognize the new era under way, an era of needed trust between capital and wage earners, of conciliation and compromise. He called for Trinidad's industrial system to "be strengthened and stabilized in a manner befitting the age of democracy that has just dawned upon the world." If the authorities resisted, workers would come together "to show the Capitalists and the Powers . . . that Labour will keep on clamoring until he gets a fair share of this world's goods which he is entitled."[45]

The TWA consistently organized its program around the principles of workers' self-organization for equality, justice, and democracy. For example, on August 19, 1921, Headley addressed a meeting by pointing out the need for unity among the people regardless of their skin color.[46] During these meetings the TWA handed out flyers calling on workers to join the association:

Labour Revival

Are You a
Wage Earner?

Do you wish **Better Conditions** for yourself and family?

———

Do you wish an

8-Hour Working Day? ...

We promise to surprise and astonish you with facts!

No Race Question   But a constitutional demand for the rights of the working classes.[47]

The fact that the TWA leadership felt the need to declare explicitly "No Race Question" suggests both that the "race question" was a general concern and that they expected some of their potential audience to associate TWA meetings with it. The TWA, however, sought to channel the popular awareness of racialized injustice into a broader analysis of international capitalist subordination. The declaration "No Race Question" articulated an explicit contrast with the Garveyite premise of race unity as a guiding idea, as opposed to class unionism. The flyer centered on issues such as wages and work hours and clearly defined its struggles as a class issue rather than a racial one. It also defined the struggle as "a constitutional demand for the rights of the working classes"; that is, the flyer located the solution within political reforms that would grant a greater voice to colonial subjects within the empire.

The message of class unity—and the disavowal of the "race question"—was part of the TWA's effort to create alliances both locally and internationally. By the mid-1920s, TWA leaders Howard Bishop and the European-descended Arthur Cipriani were making overtures to Trinidad's East Indian community, which remained divided from the African-descended community despite their common class interests.[48] The TWA also maintained important connections with other West Indian labor movements, especially in Barbados and British Guiana. For example, Herbert Critchlow, secretary of the British Guiana Labour Union, visited Trinidad in July 1924 to meet with members of the TWA; meanwhile, the *Labour Leader* published on the activities, dialogues, and friendly relations between the organizations.[49] In February 1924, Cipriani visited Barbados to lecture at the Olympic Theatre in Bridgetown. In his address he emphasized the difference between communism and the "doctrine of Labour." For Cipriani, "The doctrine of Labour" was to take control of the government by legal constitutional means, whereas communism was to take over the government by any means and at any cost. Cipriani observed that communism and socialism were doctrines opposed to each other. Furthermore, he argued that all those who had spoken against socialism, the "doctrine of Labour," "were not only seditious or disloyal but actually treasonable to His Majesty"—a reference to the first-ever Labour prime minister in 1924. Cipriani urged the formation of a workingmen's association in Barbados, and before he left the island such an organization had been started.[50]

In their meetings, messages, and alliances, the TWA members portrayed themselves as part of a global struggle between capital and labor. They saw this as a struggle that would not necessarily end in the destruction of capital but rather in a reconciliation and negotiation that would bring fair conditions, proper distribution of wealth, and ultimately the actual practice of democracy. For them, their role in that struggle was to obtain representative government in the colony, opening the possibility for the working class to have access to positions of power that would enable them to legislate based on the principles of equality and democracy. In their rhetoric, the TWA's leaders were clear to define themselves as a class-based group that sought to incorporate other people into their organization.

Given that the colonial authorities saw black internationalism and Garveyism as being aimed toward hate and rebellion, it is perhaps not surprising that the TWA leaders tried to establish clear boundaries between themselves and the UNIA. In their meetings the TWA leaders rejected race-based discourses and advocated labor unity. In turn, Trinidad's UNIA denied any relations with labor unionism. However, these were boundaries that at times could be crossed in the interest of conciliating shared ideas and goals. During the 1920s the *Labour Leader* consistently dedicated entire sections to analyzing Garveyism, published news about Marcus Garvey's actions, and republished his letters and manifestos. In contrast, the newspaper did not dedicate much attention to the activities of the local UNIA. The following section addresses how the TWA incorporated Garveyism and other forms of black internationalism into its rhetoric.

Garveyism and Black Internationalism in the *Labour Leader*

During the 1920s, articles in the *Labour Leader* worked to define the importance and meanings of race consciousness and, separately but certainly relatedly, Garveyism. Although the Trinidadian UNIA expanded across the island to thirty-two branches by 1927, the newspaper did not pay much attention to its activities.[51] However, it did publish regularly on Marcus Garvey, his organization, and his thoughts. Over the course of the 1920s the *Labour Leader* aligned its editorial vision with black internationalist publications; among them, Garveyism became a source of inspiration in relation to working-class struggles and political rhetoric. News items about Garvey and the UNIA in the *Labour Leader* were mainly taken from U.S., British, or Guianese newspapers. The stories covered a range of topics, from developments in Garvey's life to the UNIA's international demands and struggles.[52]

Scholars who have studied Trinidad's labor movement have argued that

Garveyism was the most important influence among the TWA leadership. I counter that while Garveyism had a prominent presence in the *Labour Leader*'s pages, so did other forms of black internationalism. For the TWA leaders, racial subordination was a product of capitalist exploitation, and the opposite of British principles of liberty and equality. The *Labour Leader* reported consistently about struggles for self-determination and racial justice, and maintained a constant interest in African events. It also expressed a constant interest in the "Negro Progress," not only locally but internationally as well.[53]

In addition, in its publications the newspaper reasoned that race equality was a British principle that should be enforced throughout the colony. For instance, in a December 1922 article the paper reported that a "small but serious attempt to introduce [a] colour bar in respect of restaurants has been made by the management of a parlour." The editors argued that this attempt was against the spirit of equality under the British Crown. With impressive consistency, the editors used this occasion to reiterate their standing argument that officials' denunciations of labor leaders for supposed race-mongering were misplaced. The article recalled the strikes during 1919 when "certain section of the local press told Trinidad . . . that there were agitators in this colony bent upon setting one race against another. That statement and many another equally ridiculous formed the fundament upon which certain clauses of the Seditious Publication Bill were drafted." The unfounded race fear spread by "certain section of the local press" and the fact that a restaurant in Port-of-Spain refused to serve African descendants were both, the editors argued, "utterly out of all consonance with the principles of British Administration for alliance to come into our community."[54] The article stands as a perfect example of the *Labour Leader*'s (and the TWA's) position on race consciousness. Race subordination, seen as a product of capitalist exploitation, contradicted British principles of liberty and equality. Struggles for race equality were struggles for democracy, which, in the case of the West Indies, any British subject was entitled to undertake.

In its concern for race equality and international struggles, the *Labour Leader* maintained a constant attention to African events and African-descended people's accomplishments in general. The paper expressed constant interest for racial justice, putting on display many different manifestations of black internationalism. Those articles covered a wide range of publications, from speeches delivered in U.S. universities about the "Negro" condition to visits of African or African-descended leaders to the Americas. For example, in September 1922 the *Labour Leader* announced the possibility of a visit from King Nama Amoah II of the Gold Coast of Africa. King Nama Amoah II had visited the United States and addressed an Afro-American assembly. The *Labour Leader* reported that the king was connected to the African Progress Union of England, an organization that once facilitated one of Cipriani's tours to England.[55]

Movements for African repatriation and colonization led by African descendants in the Americas were routinely part of the international news published in the *Labour Leader*. In 1922 the paper published an advertisement for the African Colonial Enterprise, founded by Dr. J. Albert Thorne, a Barbados native who sought to repatriate and settle African descendants in Nyasaland (present-day Malawi), along the Zambezi River. Thorne's main objectives were the "repatriation of the exiles" and the "civilization of the natives."[56] News on the African Colonial Enterprise, Garvey's colonization projects, and various African American writings regarding Africans in Africa—expressing a mix of exoticism, civilizationist denigration, condescension, and solidarity—exemplify the *Labour Leader*'s interest in various views of race and African heritage. Local mutual-aid societies and literary and debating societies shared these interests, and the *Labour Leader* covered their Africa-linked initiatives as well.[57] For example, the Tunapuna Debating Society hosted in January 1923 a lecture given by Rev. Farquhar, curate of St. Saviour's Church at St. Joseph, who talked on the "manners and general custom of the cultured and uncultured natives of West Africa." According to Farquhar, the habits of West Africans were foreign to West Indian life, full of superstition and witchcraft. These uncivilized conditions, he argued, put them at a disadvantage against Europeans, who took advantage of their ignorance and superstition.[58] This analysis was not questioned by the *Labour Leader*'s editors in their write-up of the event. The report was consistent with other reports in the newspaper. It indicated an interest in fostering friendly—albeit deeply condescending—bonds with Africans and African descendants across the globe.

The *Labour Leader* presented a diverse array of understandings of race, which paralleled the paper's eclectic approach to labor unionism. Race consciousness—including East Indian consciousness—became part of the newspaper's political rhetoric. In a report on an address by Maharah Singh of the Indian Civil Service before the East Indian section of the Trinidadian community, the paper praised the reception as a "striking lesson in race consciousness, and unity which the Negro element of this population would do well to learn."[59] By presenting readers with a broad view of racial solidarity, the paper revealed the overlap between race-based endeavors and the TWA's political views on capitalist exploitation and shared struggles for justice and rights. By merging race consciousness and labor unionism in this way, the paper reflected a locally specific discourse on class and race in Trinidad's post–Great War period.

For most of the 1920s, the *Labour Leader* reported consistently but sparingly about the activities of the Trinidadian UNIA. The paper noted upcoming local UNIA meetings and briefly summarized their activities.[60] An exception was the paper's account of the funeral service for UNIA member Aurora Walker in Port-of-Spain. Walker was a beloved member of the African Black Cross Nurses. Around four hundred people attended her funeral, including officials from Trinidad's UNIA. The procession during the cortege was composed of Walker's family, followed by the UNIA flag carried by members of the Vanguards, then uniformed members of the Black Cross Nurses, officers of the Port-of-Spain division, and members of the Israelites Friendly Society.[61] The *Labour Leader* also reported on special conventions held by the local UNIA in Port-of-Spain in 1925 and in Couva in 1926, but only provided sparing detail.[62]

From the news items published in the *Labour Leader*, Trinidad's UNIA emerges as an important space for socialization, racial fraternity, and community networking. It never appears as an organization that pursued political and labor reform. In that sense, the boundaries and areas of interactions between the TWA and the UNIA were clear enough. The *Labour Leader* served as a channel where the working classes could express their worries, announce their enterprises, and manifest their opinions. Therefore, the newspaper was opened as well to the Trinidad UNIA's needs.

Considering that the UNIA expanded rapidly across the island during the 1920s and that the different internal structures of the association functioned, the information about the Trinidad UNIA's activities maintained a rather low profile in the *Labour Leader*. Indeed, from the information in the newspaper it is difficult to assess the importance and level of UNIA's grassroots organization in Trinidad. The news regarding its activities in all cases—except special occasions—was similar to the accounts regarding other friendly societies' meetings and their cultural activities. The *Labour Leader*'s pages suggest that, in general, the TWA's leadership maintained friendly and constant relations with many other friendly societies.

In contrast to the low profile given to the Trinidad UNIA in the *Labour Leader*, the paper did publish many news items about Garvey, his organization, and especially about his thoughts. In almost every issue from 1923 onward, the *Labour Leader* reprinted Garvey's ideas, including his emphasis on strong leadership, the need for political and economic independence, unity, and justice. In general, the paper reprinted articles that emphasized Garvey's historical importance in the awakening of the black masses. For example, terms similar to those used by Howard Bishop in 1923, the newspaper reprinted a *Detroit Independent*'s item in 1924. The article argued:

> Those who are broad enough to appreciate Mr. Garvey, and are intelligent of knowing this one point though we fail to agree with all his will be forced to admit that he has laid down a great counter movement of propaganda favorable to the mass of coloured people. . . . The colored people can never hope to attain any lofty place in world affair until they realize the importance of letting their neighbors know their worth. To this end, if no other, Mr. Garvey is laying a foundation that will bear a bumper harvest.[63]

The leaders of Trinidad's working class placed their struggles and demands for constitutional reform as a local manifestation of global changes for democracy, justice, and racial equality. The constant acknowledgment of Garveyism as an uplifting force, as a movement "favorable to the mass of coloured people," evidenced the TWA's intention to present their struggles as part of transnational shared visions for freedom and equality. Garvey's writings were broadly published by the *Labour Leader* during the early 1920s, in striking contrast to the TWA's wariness about issuing its own race-based statements. However, these writings shared values that the TWA leaders also addressed in their meetings, such as unity, collective action, justice, and struggle against exploitation. In his writings, Garvey emphasized that "God created man as master of his own destiny."[64] Thus a "spirit of brotherly love" and equality among African descendants was necessary to gain respect and improve their living conditions.[65] In the articles published in the *Labour Leader*, Garvey called on the people to "get organized" because disunion brings exploitation, robbery, and killing. "Get organized," Garvey said, "and you will compel the world to respect you."[66] The TWA aimed to get across a message to its members that empowered the working class, the mass, to gather them under its red flag, as the only political alternative to end injustice and exploitation in the colony.

Garveyite and TWA views, as presented in the *Labour Leader*, thus appear not as contrary or contradictory but rather as parallel and complementary visions of international struggle. In a 1924 article published in the *Labour Leader*, Garvey argued that African descendants should emancipate themselves and create a nation of their own, to have a country and a government. Garvey's vision was of a redeemed Africa. Alongside the reprinted column of Garvey's words that, by 1924, had come to be a routine feature of the weekly paper, the newspaper usually also printed columns that discussed the relevance of labor unity and brotherhood in contrast to race difference and conflict.[67] This placement of Garveyism matched TWA leaders' ideas of labor unity. Instead of presenting Garveyism and race consciousness as a matter exclusively of the "Negro race," these discussions on the meaning of unity, political independence, and justice resonated as important claims raised by the labor movement in favor of alliances and friendship.

The dialogue between Garveyism and the TWA—along with the marking of explicit differences between them—continued throughout the 1920s, even as the *Labour Leader* continued to serve as a window onto multiple strands of black internationalism. For example, in 1929 the paper published an interview of Arthur Cipriani conducted by Amy Jacques Garvey, Marcus Garvey's second wife. Asked about the impact of UNIA propaganda in Trinidad, Cipriani answered that the UNIA propaganda would not go far, because the organization "gets no support from the educated negroes in Trinidad." He asserted that the average workingman was willing to support the broader movement for race consciousness, and indeed any movement for the "advancement" of his race, but that Garvey's back-to-Africa ideas were not in the best interest of West Indians.[68] This stance of generalized support for any movement for the advance of the "Negro Race" exemplifies the TWA's approach to racial issues.

Rather than a redeemed Africa, the TWA aimed for the redemption of the exploited working class, for a redeemed brotherhood of races, and a redeemed self-government in the island. Labor leaders such as Howard Bishop and Arthur Cipriani constantly referenced the importance of representative government. In the *Labour Leader*, Garveyite ideas of black government, black nationalism, brotherhood, and redeemed Africa coexisted with socialist ideas, labor politics, and news of TWA advances in the island and connections with other working-class movements in the West Indies. As the *Labour Leader* published this somewhat contradictory mix of internationalist visions, the TWA advocated in their meetings interracial alliance of the oppressed, coming together in an organized brotherhood to gain representation in the colonial government.

Conclusions

Trinidad's meeting halls fostered multiple connections. These networks brought together black internationalists with Trinidad's labor leaders and their ideas of labor and political reform. The TWA's leaders established a well-defined political discourse based on class unionism and struggle against capitalist exploitation, rather than Garveyite race-first doctrine. However, these visible boundaries between the TWA and the UNIA could be crossed to conciliate ideas and goals. This was especially significant to craft a political discourse that demanded democracy and equality while addressing racial subordination as a product of capitalist exploitation. The TWA's leadership and the writers of the *Labour Leader* gathered a mix of ideas from a variety of sources: from the calypsos, from visiting black internationalists, from New Negro struggles in Unites States, from the spread and articulation of global Garveyism. These strands formed part of an ongoing dialogue that contributed to shaping the TWA's discourse on class and race. They forged a political discourse that would influence Trinidadian intellectuals in the decades that followed.

Scholars have argued that the emergence of black internationalisms during the interwar period was shaped by the mass migration of West Indian population during the early twentieth century, the intensification of international racism, the experience of the Great War, and the spread of radical global movements such as anarchism, socialism, and communism.[69] I hope that my contribution helps us trace the genealogy of another instance of black internationalism, one whose origins are not in the cosmopolitan streets of Harlem or London but in the docks and TWA meeting halls in Port-of-Spain, where labor politics and race consciousness were synthesized with other visions to craft a unique discourse that brought together an analysis of race, class, and colonial politics in dialogue with an evaluation of global capitalism, international racism, and transnational struggles.

Notes

1. The Trinidad Workingmen's Association, the foremost working-class organization on the island, was founded in 1897 in Port of Spain and by the 1910s had already established links with the British Labour Party. Its core membership was urban skilled African-descended workers. After 1919, as a product of the waterfront workers' strike, the association increased its membership. The *Labour Leader* began publishing in August 1922 and ceased existence in January 1932. See Samaroo and Girvan, "Trinidad Workingmen's Association."

2. Minute Paper from Inspector-General of Constabulary, December 30, 1921, box dated 1921, file no. 13/1921, Colonial Secretary Records [hereafter CSR], National Archive of Trinidad and Tobago [hereafter NATT].

3. Bishop's letter was titled "Open Oversea Letter to the West Indies and to British Guiana." This letter and other documents produced by the TWA can be found in Minute Paper from Inspector-General of Constabulary, January 8, 1921, box dated 1921, file no. 321/1921, CSR, NATT.

4. For an analysis on Garveyism and class formation in the British Caribbean see Bolland, *Politics of Labour*, 155–211. Tony Martin views the TWA as a Garveyite organization, and one of its most thoroughly organized strongholds during the 1920s. See Tony Martin, "Marcus Garvey and Trinidad, 1912–1947," in R. Lewis and Warner-Lewis, *Garvey*, 47–77.

5. T. Martin, "Marcus Garvey and Trinidad," 67.

6. Teelucksingh, *Caribbean Liberators*.

7. For tensions during the postwar era, see Brereton, *History of Modern Trinidad*, 157–76. For working-class politics in Trinidad during this period see K. Singh, *Race and Class Struggles*; Basdeo, *Labour Organization*; and Reddock, *Women, Labour and Politics*, 47–181.

8. Lara Putnam challenges scholars to do a better job of "historicizing connection" in *Radical Moves*, 232. For some other examples of the burgeoning literature on black internationalism, see West, Martin, and Wilkins, *From Toussaint to Tupac*; and Makalani, *In the Cause of Freedom*.

9. K. Singh, *Race and Class Struggles*; Teelucksingh, *Caribbean Liberators*.

10. L. Putnam, *Radical Moves*; Baldwin and Makalani, *Escape from New York*.

11. According to the Colonial Office, prices rose 145 percent during the war. See K. Singh, *Race and Class Struggles*, 15.

12. For more on the strike see Teelucksingh, *Labour and the Decolonization Struggle*, 33–37; and Reddock, *Women, Labour and Politics*, 148–50.

13. Chancellor's Papers, Oxford, box 4/6, folders 1–21, and The National Archives of the U.K., Public Records Office, CO 295/522/7611, in R. A. Hill, *Marcus Garvey and Universal Negro Improvement Association Papers* [hereafter MGP], 11:299–307.

14. The deportees were Rev. Edward Seiler Salmon (TWA), Brutus Ironman, Bruce McConney (TWA), John Sydney de Bourg (TWA), and Charles Duncan O'Neill. Many of them maintained their race and/or working-class activism in different places after deportation. Salmon moved to United States in the 1920s, where he joined the African Orthodox Church. De Bourg became part of the UNIA hierarchy in New York and was elected Leader of the Negroes of the Western Provinces of the West Indies and South and Central America; later on he broke with Garvey. De Bourg, McConney, and Brathwaite, who remained in Trinidad after the strikes, are among those who signed the Declaration of Rights of the Negro Peoples of the World, proclaimed at Garvey's First International Convention in 1920. O'Neill became a socialist leader of the newly formed Barbados Workingmen's Association during the 1920s and 1930s. See Teelucksingh, *Caribbean Liberators*, 19–20; T. Martin, *Pan-African Connection*, 69–70; and Browne, *Race, Class, Politics*.

15. T. Martin, "Marcus Garvey and Trinidad," 54–55.

16. For reports, letters, and accounts on black internationalist and race consciousness in the Caribbean from 1910 to 1920, see *MGP*, volume 11.

17. The commission failed to find evidence that the TWA leadership organized the stevedores' strike. Rather, it became apparent that the unrest during the first three days of December lacked leadership. In addition, the commission noted the connection between the strike and general dissatisfaction among the working classes. Even more important, the commission observed manifestations of interracial sympathy. *Commission of Enquiry into Conduct of Constabulary during Strike 1919,* cabinet B4, box 32, Commission of Enquiry Collection [hereafter CEC], NATT; Minutes of Evidence, vol. 2, 1919–1920, 1164, cabinet B4, box 23, CEC, NATT.

18. Headley, *Labour and Life,* 13.

19. Hercules was co-founder, with John Eldred Taylor, of the London-based Society of Peoples of African Origin (SPAO) and editor of its journal, the *African Telegraph.* The goal of the SPAO was to promote the interest of blacks internationally and to bring their claims to the attention of the British public. Hercules's visit to Trinidad in 1919 was part of his larger West Indian tour. Elkins, "Hercules"; *MGP,* 11:53–54 n. 1, 280 n. 4.

20. Minute Paper from Colonial Secretary to Inspector General, December 15, 1919, box dated 1919, file no. 19/1919, CSR, NATT.

21. *Argos,* September 13, 1919, quoted in Singh, *Race and Class Struggles,* 21.

22. Ibid.

23. *Trinidad Guardian,* October 31, 1919.

24. Marcus Garvey briefly worked for the *African Times and Orient Review* during his stay in London in 1913–14. See R. A. Hill, "Comradeship."

25. *MGP,* 11:53–54 n. 1, 280 n. 4; Elkins, "Hercules"; Secretary of State to Governor of Trinidad, December 13, 1919, box dated 1919, file no. 30/1919, CSR, NATT.

26. Minute Paper from Colonial Secretary, December 15, 1919, box dated 1919, file no. 19/1919, CSR, NATT.

27. *MGP,* 11:79–80.

28. Minute Paper from Governor of Jamaica, August 30, 1919, box dated 1919, file no. 19/1919, CSR, NATT.

29. Bishop became the TWA's general secretary in 1920. In this position he focused on fostering unity between middle-class liberals and the working class during the 1920s. In 1921 he traveled to London and conferred with Colonial Under-Secretary E.F.L. Wood and members of the Labour Party. These contacts raised questions about Trinidadian living conditions in Parliament, members of whom pressed for a commission to visit the West Indies to consider recommendations on constitutional reform. See Reddock, *Women, Labour and Politics,* 124.

30. *Labour Leader,* May 3, 1924. The *Messenger* was published in New York by black American socialists A. Philip Randolph and Chandler Owen. The *Crusader* was the official organ of the New York–based African Blood Brotherhood and was edited by Cyril Briggs.

31. Minute Paper from Inspector-General of Constabulary, December 30, 1921, box dated 1921, file no. 13/1921, CSR, NATT.

32. "Doctrine of Labour" was an expression used by A. A. Cipriani in 1924 to refer to both Labor and Socialism. *Labour Leader,* March 8, 1924.

33. For most of the early 1920s the TWA refers explicitly to politics of labor. By 1924 the *Labour Leader* started showing an explicit interest on socialism. See, for example, *Labour Leader,* June 18 and July 25, 1924.

34. Minute Paper from H.D.A. Thompson, January 5, 1921, box dated 1921, file no. 368/1921, CSR, NATT.

35. *Labour Leader,* September 4, 1926.

36. *Labour Leader,* October 13, 1923.

37. Teelucksingh, *Labour and the Decolonization Struggle,* 20, 47; Teelucksingh, *Caribbean Liberators,* 11.

38. Garvey had shared a platform with socialists such as A. Philip Randolph and W. A. Domingo following the war, but during the 1920s he had sought to distance his organization from socialist and communist politics. In a speech in New York in August 1922, Garvey mentioned that socialism was "another form of white control that the white man [was] going to fasten around the neck of the Negro people of the world." *MGP,* 4:850.

39. Colonial authorities granted permission for the establishment of the UNIA in Trinidad sometime around early 1921. By mid-1921 the Carapichaima division hosted a convention, and for the 1922 convention in New York, in addition to the Trinidadians living in New York, Fitz Aaron Braithwaite was sent as a Trinidad representative. According to Tony Martin, by the early 1920s Trinidad was the most thoroughly organized UNIA stronghold after Cuba. At the 1922 convention de Bourg reported that there were thirty-three branches in the island. Rev. Richard H. Tobitt, UNIA high commissioner, gave the number as 32 in 1923, the year he tried to visit Trinidad. A UNIA headquarters compilation of 1927 named 30 divisions. Minute Paper from H.D.A. Thompson, January 5, 1921, box dated 1921, file no. 368/1921, CSR, NATT. For more information on Trinidad UNIA branches, and the names of several officers in 1927, see T. Martin, "Marcus Garvey and Trinidad," 59–61, 71–72.

40. *Labour Leader,* November 18, 1922, and Minute Paper from Detective Inspector, May 17, 1921, both in box dated 1921, file no. 5/1921, Colonial Secretary Office, CSR, NATT. Rev. Tobitt was the UNIA high commissioner to British Guiana, head of a territory that included French and Dutch Guiana, South America, Bermuda, the Leeward Islands, and Barbados. The legislative council denied his entrance and labeled him "undesirable" in 1923, even though the UNIA had existed legally in Trinidad (as the result of Thompson's successful petition) for the last two years.

41. For example, in 1922 Brathwaite traveled to New York to participate in the UNIA's convention. See T. Martin, *Pan-African Connection,* 77.

42. Minute Paper from Inspector-General of Constabulary, January 8, 1921, box dated 1921, file no. 368/1921, CSR, NATT.

43. Minute Paper from Inspector-General of Constabulary, January 8, 1921, box dated 1921, file no. 321/1921, CSR, NATT.

44. Ibid.

45. Headley, *Labour and Life,* 4; Minute Paper from Inspector-General of Constabulary, January 8, 1921, box dated 1921, file no. 321/1921, CSR, NATT.

46. Minute Paper from Inspector-General of Constabulary, January 8, 1921, box dated 1921, file no. 321/1921, CSR, NATT.

47. Ibid.

48. K. Singh, *Race and Class Struggles,* 49–59, 79, 124–37.

49. *Labour Leader,* July 16, 1924.

50. *Labour Leader,* March 8, 1924.

51. For a list of the branches in Trinidad see T. Martin, "Marcus Garvey and Trinidad," 60.

52. For examples see *Labour Leader,* October 15, October 21, October 28, November 11, 1922.

53. *Labour Leader,* June 30, 1923.

54. *Labour Leader,* December 16, 1922.

55. *Labour Leader,* November 21, 1921.

56. *Labour Leader,* September 23, 1922.

57. For more on the importance of friendly societies in Trinidad since the late nineteenth century, see Cummings, *Barrack-Yard Dwellers,* 64–67.

58. *Labour Leader,* January 20, 1923.

59. *Labour Leader,* October 17, 1925.

60. From roughly 1923 to 1928 the branches that organized most of the meetings were the Port-of-Spain central division, Lily of the Nile, Couva, and Penal. In general, during the meetings the members sang hymns, read Marcus Garvey's or commissioners' letters, prayed, and enjoyed lectures and cultural activities.

61. *Labour Leader,* September 23, 1922. Among their many activities, the UNIA branches in Trinidad also served as friendly societies, paying death and other benefits to its members. See T. Martin, "Marcus Garvey and Trinidad," 60.

62. *Labour Leader,* August 15, 1925, May 8, 1926, June 14, 1926.

63. *Labour Leader,* May 3, 1924.

64. *Labour Leader,* July 9, 1924.

65. *Labour Leader,* July 16, 1924.

66. *Labour Leader,* June 28, 1924.

67. *Labour Leader,* July 25, 1924.

68. *Labour Leader,* June 29, 1929.

69. L. Putnam, *Radical Moves,* 234.

11

Decolonization, Desegregation, and Black Power

Garveyism in Another Era

MICHAEL O. WEST

Structurally, Garveyism was a by-product of the great global black disillusionment that followed World War I. World War II, or more precisely the post–World War II dispensation, opened up new possibilities to address black disillusionment. In the wake of the second global imperialist war of the twentieth century, black people the world over renewed their campaigns against colonialism and apartheid, as the system of institutionalized white supremacy was now called in South Africa. In short, the struggle for decolonization and desegregation had sharpened.

The result was that, between the late 1950s and the early 1960s, decolonization descended on the greater part of Africa.[1] True, the triumph of African decolonization was far from complete. In southern Africa (South Africa; South West Africa, later Namibia; and Rhodesia, later Zimbabwe), the forces of white supremacy obstinately, and brutally, remained in control.[2] With corresponding (and sometimes coordinated) barbarity, Portugal also continued to resist the advancing forces of African nationalism in its colonies of Mozambique, Angola, Guinea-Bissau, and the Cape Verde islands.[3] Nevertheless, most of Africa had formally thrown off the shackles of colonialism by the early 1960s. Concurrently, decolonization came to the larger British-ruled territories in the greater Caribbean, beginning with Jamaica and Trinidad and Tobago.[4]

Decolonization and desegregation were part of the same historical process, just as colonialism and segregation were twinned.[5] In the era of decolonization, black people in the United States launched a frontal attack on apartheid, or Jim

Crow, to use the American moniker.[6] By the mid-1960s, Jim Crow, like colonialism in the greater part of Africa and in the major British Caribbean possessions, had been legally abolished.

These were historic achievements. Decolonization in Africa and the Caribbean and desegregation in the United States removed decades-long barriers to black participation in the political process, from voting to holding public office. With national independence and civil rights also came the elimination, in law if not always in fact, of racist restrictions in public facilities, ranging from hotels and restaurants to toilets and phone booths.

Yet political and social rights, even when they were respected—in many cases, in and out of Africa, authoritarian regimes abrogated or curtailed political rights—did not extend to the economic and cultural realms. Decolonization and desegregation failed to structurally transform the economic systems and cultural norms put in place by colonialism and global apartheid, systems and norms that continued to marginalize and degrade the masses of black people, even while incorporating a privileged minority of blacks.[7] Decolonization and desegregation thus remained incomplete and unfulfilled projects.

Into the void entered Black Power. As universal in its reach and aspirations as Garveyism, Black Power came to demand the completion and fulfillment of the visions and promises of decolonization and desegregation. In those cases where decolonization and desegregation had not yet been achieved, as in the southern African white-settler colonies, the task facing Black Power was not just obtaining economic and cultural empowerment but also winning political and social rights.

Garveyism and Decolonization; or Kwame Nkrumah and the Political Kingdom

No individual of African descent better personified the worldwide fight for decolonization than Kwame Nkrumah, who, in 1957, led Ghana to independence. Ghana was the first territory in sub-Saharan Africa to become a sovereign nation-state (Sudan did so in 1956), and its decolonization was, up to that point, the grandest pan-African event of the post–World War II era. Nkrumah eventually would be turned out of office, overthrown in a classic neocolonial military coup in 1966, the inaugural year of Black Power. On being removed from power, Nkrumah went into exile in Guinea, from where he adopted a variety of new political personas, including as a Black Power militant. Kwame Nkrumah, lately president of Ghana, had made a transition from state power to Black Power, one of the few persons, if not the only one, to have done so.

Not coincidentally, perhaps, Nkrumah held Garvey in high regard.[8] The one, like the other, was possessed of a large imagination. "Hail! United States of Africa—free! / Hail! Motherhood most bright, divinely fair! / State in perfect sisterhood united / Born of truth; mighty thou shalt ever be."[9] So did Garvey the bard summarize his vision of African unity, portraying the continent as a despoiled queen mother finally reunited with her long-lost offspring, a concept at odds with previous generations of pan-Africanists, who had conceived of Africa as the fatherland rather than the motherland.[10]

For all his versatility, Nkrumah is not known to have tried his hand at verse, but Garvey's poem could well serve as a theme song for his public life. As leader of Ghana, Nkrumah was both loved and loathed throughout the continent (and beyond) for his unstinting promotion of African unity—a united states of Africa—an idea which may or may not have had origins in Garveyism but one which, until Nkrumah came along, was best identified with the Universal Negro Improvement Association (UNIA). With a single-mindedness to match Garvey's, the less-than-happily-married Nkrumah reportedly confided to an extramural lover (Garvey was more chaste): "African unity is my first and only love!"[11] *Africa Must Unite,* bellowed the title of one of Nkrumah's most famous books,[12] providing the inspiration for the similarly titled reggae tune, "Africa, Unite, Unite." In this song, the Rastafarian songsters effectively fused the visions of Garvey and Nkrumah.

Ghana's independence doubled as a grand pan-African event, with Nkrumah as the star attraction and the most lionized African political figure of the era, celebrated in prose and poetry. Sometimes the poetry was set to music. Such was the case with the song "They Got It," composed by the Jamaican proto-reggae artist Laurel Aitken.[13] Crooned Aitken: "Ghana is a place we all must love with a blessing that come [*sic*] from above. . . . / And give praise to her prime minister, who is the great Dr. Nkrumah." Among those on hand to praise Nkrumah and witness Ghana's midnight birth was a young Martin Luther King Jr., then just making his way into the politics of protest. On returning to the United States, King preached a Sunday-morning sermon in which, notably, he offered Nkrumah as a modern-day biblical Moses.[14] King himself would later assume the Mosaic Mantle, a topic on which Nkrumah had also discoursed.[15]

Raised a Catholic, Nkrumah converted to Protestantism, making the opposite religious journey as Garvey. As a student in the United States between

1935 and 1945, majoring in theology, among other subjects, Nkrumah became a licensed preacher (although not an ordained minister) in the Presbyterian Church. He graduated at the top of this theology class and, true to his training at historically black Lincoln University in Pennsylvania, took the text of his valedictory address from Psalm 68:31: "Princes shall come out of Egypt; Ethiopia shall soon stretch out her hands unto God."[16] Both his theological training and his preaching stint would serve Nkrumah well when, after World War II, he returned home to the Gold Coast, as colonial Ghana was called, and launched his career as an anticolonial agitator.

Nkrumah's principal weapon against the British colonialists was Gandhian-inflected militant nonviolence, a tactic King also later adopted. Fleet of tongue, like Garvey (and King), Nkrumah freely deployed biblical scripture on the hustings. One scripture, especially, formed the basis of his most famous axiom, namely, Jesus's injunction to "seek ye first the kingdom of God, and his righteousness; and all these things shall be added unto you" (Matthew 6:33). Nkrumah was not the first freedom fighter in the global black emancipatory tradition to single out this particular scripture. As far back as the early eighteenth century, enslaved Africans in colonial Virginia had appealed to that very passage, which resurfaced more than a hundred years later as a decisive theological bedrock of another Virginian, the enslaved revolutionary Nat Turner.[17] Unlike Turner and others, however, Nkrumah did not so much quote Jesus as riff on him. (Black Power protesters at Howard University would demand that the school be renamed Nat Turner University or Garvey University, and that the exiled Nkrumah be hired as its president!) As an anticolonial stump speaker, Nkrumah never tired of advising his audiences: "Seek ye first the political kingdom, and all other things shall be added unto it." Thus was Jesus's "kingdom of God" transformed into the "political kingdom" of African nationalism, that is, decolonization.

Garvey played a role in Nkrumah's conversion to the doctrine of the political kingdom. A voracious consumer of political literature during his student days, Nkrumah read widely in European thought, from nationalism to Marxism. "But I think of all the literature that I studied," he reported, "the book that did more than any other to fire my enthusiasm was *Philosophy and Opinions of Marcus Garvey* published in 1923."[18] As he wrote his autobiography, in which the above lines appeared, Nkrumah is said to have had on his wall a picture of Garvey, and another of Harriet Tubman,[19] perhaps the most beloved female icon in the Black Power movement in the United States.

Nkrumah would soon electrify latter-day Garveyism, meaning UNIA-derived thought and action in the post–World War II era. Shortly after Ghana's independence, his government launched a shipping fleet and, significantly, named it the Black Star Line, after the ill-fated UNIA maritime venture. (Nkrumah also named Ghana's soccer team the Black Stars.) "Why do you call it the Black Star Line?" inquired St. Clair Drake, the outstanding African American scholar and pan-Africanist who was then teaching in Ghana. "That's obvious," Nkrumah responded. "We're vindicating Mr. Garvey." Drake, himself a scion of Garveyism (his father, a preacher and immigrant to the United States from Barbados, was a staunch UNIA supporter), quoted Nkrumah further: "And then with the sense of humor which he and [George] Padmore and these guys had about serious things he said, 'Well Garvey's ship never got over here, but ours will get back over there.'"[20] Some of those "over there," on the west bank of the Atlantic, responded with alacrity. A number of these individuals, still in possession of original Black Star Line paper stocks—now only of sentimental value—wanted to pick up from where the UNIA left off.

Latter-day Garveyites found an outlet for their views in a new publication, *African Opinion: A Journal of Independent Thoughts and Expression*. Inaugurated in 1949 and based in New York City, *African Opinion* continued to publish with some interruption until 1976, practically to the end of the Black Power era. International in scope, *African Opinion* was, quite simply, the preeminent journal of latter-day Garveyism. Few Garvey scholars seem aware of this publication, but it will surely repay their perusal, as well as that of students of decolonization, desegregation, Rastafari, and Black Power, among other movements.

African Opinion reminded some of the UNIA organ, the *Negro World*.[21] One reader hoped *African Opinion* would "continue the program of 'The Negro World,' keep before the Africans and men and women of African blood and descent a central program for racial uplift and advancement."[22] But there was a difference: the *Negro World* was a newspaper; *African Opinion* was a magazine. The model for *African Opinion* appears to have been *International African Opinion*, which published for about a year before folding. Launched in 1938 under the leadership of George Padmore and C.L.R. James, the London-based *International African Opinion* grew out of the solidarity work occasioned by the Ethiopian crisis of 1935, when fascist Italy invaded Ethiopia.[23] From the outset, *African Opinion* lustily embraced Nkrumah as a modern embodiment of Garvey.

Latter-day Garveyites took to the pages of *African Opinion* to discuss any number of issues, including Ghana's Black Star Line. "I am suggesting that the

Black Star Line should be owned, controlled and run completely by Ghana and those of us Garveyites who now hold stocks in it," offered A. Gomez of Havana, Cuba, a land whose latter-day Garveyites were well represented in the "letters to the editor" pages of *African Opinion*. "Arrangements should be made to allow us, original stockholders, to purchase those shares. This is fitting because of our interest in Ghana and the continent at large," Gomez insisted.[24] This was critique, Nkrumah having raised the hopes of the Garveyites, only to turn around and disappoint them. "A shocking turn," protested an article in *African Opinion*, describing the revelation that an Israeli company was managing the Black Star Line and owned 40 percent of its stock. Ghana, the magazine countered, should be allied with the Arab bloc in the struggle against Zionism and seek investment for its shipping company from Africans of the diaspora.[25]

The All-African People's Conference, the Fall of Nkrumah, and the Garveyite Rebuttal

Numbers of Africans of the diaspora were in attendance at the All-African People's Conference (AAPC), an event promoted by and covered in *African Opinion*. Held in Accra, Ghana, in December 1958, the AAPC was the great gift of Nkrumah's Ghana to the struggle for decolonization in Africa, just over a year after Ghana's independence. The AAPC brought together representatives of practically every nationalist and revolutionary movement in Africa, with the objective of planning a final assault on colonialism and white supremacy throughout the continent. Various future icons made their pan-African political debut at the AAPC, among them Frantz Fanon (representing the Algerian armed resistance), Amilcar Cabral (Guinea-Bissau), and Patrice Lumumba (Congo).

It stood to reason that George Padmore, that most iconic of pan-African organizers, would have had a directing hand in this, the greatest gathering (up to that point) of freedom fighters in the history of modern Africa. Indeed, Padmore wanted to call the AAPC the Sixth Pan-African Congress, but Nkrumah vetoed that suggestion.[26] With Nkrumah as his chief aide, Padmore had organized the Fifth Pan-African Congress, held in 1945 in Manchester, England.[27] By the time of the AAPC, however, the roles had been reversed: Padmore was now an aide to Nkrumah, serving as his unofficial minister of pan-African affairs. As it happened, the AAPC would double as a farewell to Padmore, who died less than a year after the event.

Garvey was recognized at the AAPC. In his opening address to the conference, Nkrumah denounced white-settler colonialism in Africa, evoking as he did so that most famous of Garveyite sayings. "We say that Africa belongs to the Africans!" announced Nkrumah,[28] ever so slightly tweaking the Garveyite refrain, "Africa for the Africans," a mantra not original to the UNIA but inherited from previous generations of pan-Africanists. Nkrumah referenced Garvey more directly in his closing address to the AAPC. Calling attention to the longer tradition of pan-African struggles, as he had done in his opening address, Nkrumah said: "A name that springs to mind immediately in this connection is Marcus Garvey. Long before many of us were even conscious of our own degradation, Marcus Garvey fought for African national and racial equality."[29]

The AAPC was one of two conferences that became part of the inspirational prehistory of Black Power. The other was the Bandung Conference, named after the Indonesian city in which it was held in 1955. Nkrumah had been invited to Bandung, but he found it impolitic to attend. The British colonialists, who, along with their American paymasters, opposed the conference, threatened to delay Ghana's independence if Nkrumah went to Bandung.[30] In some ways, the AAPC may be seen as Nkrumah's answer, on an African continental level, to the Bandung Conference, which marked the advent of the Asian-African bloc, or the Third World, in global politics.

One immediate outcome of the AAPC was the formation of a political connection between Nkrumah and Patrice Lumumba. It is universally agreed that the AAPC was an epochal event in Lumumba's political consciousness.[31] Among those joining this consensus was the Garvey scholar John Henrik Clarke. "A high point in Patrice Lumumba's political development came in 1958, when he was permitted to attend the All African Peoples' Conference in Accra, Ghana," Clarke noted.[32] Lumumba was never the same after Accra, which marked the beginning of his evolution into a militant African nationalist implacably opposed to colonialism and its successor, neocolonialism. It was this Lumumba who became Congo's first prime minister when the country obtained independence from Belgium in 1960. Within months he was dead, the first high-profile victim of neocolonialism in postcolonial Africa. "They've lynched our savior, Lumumba, in the old fashion Southern style," declared a leaflet handed out by protesters in Harlem, New York, where latter-day Garveyites were conspicuous among those denouncing the murder of the Congolese leader.[33] From St. Louis, Missouri, Annie B. Lee, a Garveyite since the 1920s and author of multiple letters to the editor of *African Opinion*, added her voice. "We are all shocked over the death of Patricia [*sic*] Lumumba, Premier of the Congo, even the little children," Lee wrote.[34]

No one was more shocked by Lumumba's murder than Nkrumah.[35] Just as the AAPC radicalized Lumumba, so also Lumumba's murder radicalized Nkrumah, who began to reorient Ghana's foreign policy from West to East, even as he became increasingly authoritarian at home. As part of the effort to avenge Lumumba's murder, Nkrumah declared ideological war on neocolonialism, if not actual war on the neocolonial assassins. The literary aftereffect of this campaign was *Neo-Colonialism: The Last Stage of Imperialism*, a book with a distinctly Leninist title and one destined to become a Black Power favorite.[36]

The senior official in charge of American foreign policy toward Africa did not care for Nkrumah's book and gave it a rather nasty review, orally, to Ghana's ambassador to the United States.[37] The handwriting was on the wall. Nkrumah sealed his fate when he announced plans to visit North Vietnam on a peace mission, part of his attempt (unwelcomed by the United States) to negotiate an end to the American war against Vietnam. He was on his way to North Vietnam when the Ghanaian military, acting in concert with the United States and other Western powers, staged a coup against him.[38] That Nkrumah, who would die in exile six years later, had left Ghana for what turned out to be the last time on February 21, 1966, the first anniversary of Malcolm X's assassination, would only reinforce the mystical signs-and-wonders strain in pan-Africanism, a category in which Garveyites were well represented.

Nkrumah, like Lumumba, had fallen victim to neocolonialism. Unlike Lumumba, however, Nkrumah escaped with his life. He would live to fight another day, including as a Black Power partisan. Actually, Nkrumah was always much more adept at contesting power than he was at wielding it. The authoritarianism, the cult of personality, the indifference in the face corruption, in part it seems as a way to control subordinates, had become nauseating in Nkrumah's final years in office.[39] There is a very real sense in which the Ghanaian military officers who ousted him, truckling instruments of neocolonialism that they were, did him a favor.[40] History, at least a certain strain of pan-Africanist history, may not be so gracious as to absolve them, but unwittingly they may well have saved Nkrumah from historical ignominy.

Just as they had done on Lumumba's murder, Garveyites rallied around the ousted Nkrumah. "They were and are still jealous of our Pharaohs," asserted a writer identifying herself only as "Mrs. M. T. E., U.S.A.," possibly because of the heretical nature of her views. In the Exodus story, from which came the trope of the Mosaic Mantle, Egypt's pharaonic ruler is cast as the oppressor. Yet here was Mrs. M. T. E., offering Garvey and Nkrumah as modern-day pharaohs, an idea anathema to a long line of biblically inclined pan-Africanists, including many Garveyites. "We must now put our minds on Garvey, Nkrumah or any of our other great leaders and break the spell," advised the contrarian Mrs. M. T. E.[41]

One of the more loquacious defenders of the ousted Nkrumah was S. B. Gardner, a leader of the UNIA rump in Kingston, Jamaica. The "spirit of Marcus Garvey has been resurrected" in Nkrumah, Gardner announced. "This same God sent Nkrumah to put his image alongside that of Garvey on the minds of African people, not only in Ghana and Africa but in all parts of the world where black people are found," he went on. Gardner concluded with a slogan that would be picked up by other contributors to *African Opinion*, the magazine in which he was writing: "Long Live Nkrumah!"[42]

Gardner was dogged, if not always factually correct, in his defense of Nkrumah, and in turning Nkrumah into a fulfillment of Garvey's alleged prophecy. According to Gardner, when Garvey for the last time was "leaving Jamaica for England, sleeping black men said: 'Garvey, you are finished with the African question.'" Far from being finished with Africa, however, Garvey's whole purpose for migrating was to lay the foundation for realizing his vision of a free and united Africa. "I am going to England where I can find someone to send the message to Mother Africa. We want a United States of Africa," Garvey is said to have told Jamaica's "sleeping black men." In England, Gardner fancifully continued, Garvey "found Dr. Kwame Nkrumah who carried the gospel of the fatherhood of God and the brotherhood of man. And out of this, I can see come the 'Organization of African Unity' of which all Africans are proud to have."[43]

It was all a figment of Gardner's imagination, for there was no such rendezvous between Garvey and Nkrumah. "It was unfortunate that I was never able to meet Garvey," Nkrumah mused in his autobiography, "as he had been deported from the country [the United States] before I arrived" there.[44] It was doubly unfortunate that they never met, since Garvey and Nkrumah were on British soil concurrently, if only for a couple of weeks. Nkrumah even visited London, where Garvey then lived, to obtain a visa to enter the United States, but their paths never crossed. By the time Nkrumah returned to England a decade later, just after the end of World War II, Garvey was dead. Yet while transparently fictitious, Gardner's tale about Garvey meeting Nkrumah in England and handing him, Mosaic-like, the mantle of leadership of the African liberation struggle is a testament to the hope and expectation many Garveyites invested in Nkrumah.

Pan-Africanism Reprised: Black Power, Nkrumah, and Garvey

Just as it would have a catalytic role in resurrecting Garvey's legacy, so too Black Power assisted mightily in Nkrumah's political rebirth. No sooner had the Ghana coup happened than writers of diverse political stripes began to hold forth on Nkrumah's "rise and fall."[45] Nkrumah had indeed fallen, stripped of the state power he had wielded for nearly a decade with Garvey-like cocksuredness. (The cock, or rooster, was the symbol of Nkrumah's Convention People's Party.) What the political obituarists failed to notice was that Nkrumah immediately rose again, this time in the firmament of Black Power, which, in Nkrumah's own words, had "descended on the world like a thunder-cloud flashing its lightning" in 1966, the very year of the Ghana coup.[46]

The half of Nkrumah's Black Power story has not yet been told, but it is a remarkable tale of the triumph of the pan-African spirit over political adversity. Playing the role of elder statesman that he was, at least in relation to his mostly youthful interlocutors, the exiled Nkrumah held court for numerous visiting Black Power notables and delegations from various parts of the world at his seaside villa in Conakry, Guinea. Nkrumah's Black Power correspondence was even more prodigious.[47] A keen student of the movement, he kept abreast of the Black Power literature, while contributing to that literature himself.[48]

In addition to being a Black Power subject, Nkrumah was an object of the movement. As an object of Black Power, Nkrumah was often paired with three of his contemporaries whose lives and labors, political and intellectual, were also lauded and held up as worthy of emulation, namely, Patrice Lumumba, Frantz Fanon, and Malcolm X, all three of whom were now dead. Together, these men—Nkrumah, Lumumba, Fanon, and Malcolm—formed a patriarchal foursome that was celebrated in the prose, poetry, and iconography of Black Power.

Then there was Garvey, who also emerged as a key Black Power icon. Poetry, always among the most democratic forms of literary expression in political movements, was a favorite Black Power genre. All the key Black Power heroes, dead and alive, became subjects of the poetry produced by movement militants. Garvey, however, had the distinction of being apparently one of the few heroes of Black Power whose poetry was quoted by a Black Power fellow bard. The poem in question was Garvey's "The Black Women,"[49] and the Black Power fellow bard was Obi Egbuna, the Nigerian-born British Black Power figure and noted Nkrumah disciple.[50] Black Power paralleled Garveyism both in its celebration of black womanhood, especially black feminine beauty, and in its insistence on keeping the actual black woman under subjection, endeavors that did not go unchallenged in either movement.[51] It was thus entirely appropriate that Egbuna, a prominent Black Power celebrator of black feminine beauty, should have sought inspiration from Garvey. "As I looked at you, I felt as if a voice were whispering Garvey's words inside me," Egbuna confided to a black female paramour. Egbuna then quoted directly from Garvey's poetical paean: "Black queen of beauty, thou hast given color to the world! / Among other women thou are royal and the fairest! / Like the brightest jewels in the regal diadem."[52]

As a Garvey-admiring, Nkrumah-idolizing jewel in the global Black Power leadership, Egbuna was rivaled only by Stokely Carmichael. A foundational figure in the emergence of Black Power, much admired by Egbuna, among others, Carmichael was also the movement's most loose-footed emissary, traveling the world with the Black Power message from his base in the United States. Carmichael had Garveyite roots, too. *African Opinion*, which gave him lavish coverage, was not wide of the mark when it summed up Carmichael's biography thus: "Born in Trinidad, West Indies, grew from childhood in the United States, young Stokely became involved in the tide of African nationalism generated by Marcus Garvey."[53] Carmichael himself remembered that the "Harlem stepladder speakers had a profound effect on me." And, he added, "many of them were remnants or offshoots of the Garvey movement."[54] It seemed also that Carmichael came by his penchant for patriarchal heroes honestly. Garvey, he allowed, was his father's "great hero."[55]

In turn, Nkrumah became Carmichael's great hero. "I have been waiting for and seeking for a black man outside of our generation who knows what is going on," a youthful Carmichael confessed, after several years in the Black Power trenches. "I have found one—Dr. Nkrumah. He knows precisely what the struggle is," Carmichael revealed.[56] Having located the path "from Black Power back to Pan-Africanism," as he testified at the point of discovery, Carmichael never wavered in his embrace of Nkrumah and Nkrumaism.[57] Carmichael eventually abandoned the United States and moved to Guinea, the better to learn at Nkrumah's feet. On arrival in Guinea, Carmichael also assigned himself the task of doing whatever it took, including engaging in armed combat, to help make real the most quixotic aspiration of his teacher—that is, "restore Nkrumah to the leadership of Ghana."[58] Carmichael, like others, failed that assignment. He failed to add as well that, like emigrants at all times and in all places, he was not just attracted to something and that, in moving to Guinea, he was also fleeing from something. In particular, Carmichael was escaping the wrath of his increasing legion of detractors in the Black Power movement in the United States, to say nothing of the repressive and murderous policies and practices of the American state. Unofficially, at any rate, Carmichael's Garveyite-like relocation—Garvey himself never set foot on the soil of continental Africa—was accompanied by a nomenclatorial makeover. Stokely Carmichael became Kwame Ture, in honor of Nkrumah and Nkrumah's host in exile, Guinean president Sékou Touré.

The Nkrumah that Carmichael, Egbuna, and other Black Power advocates embraced was a man who had become a definer of what he now called "the armed phase of the African Revolution."[59] With no personal experience in armed struggle, on being removed from power Nkrumah took to the "revolutionary path," at least discursively.[60] Rather imperiously, he even wrote a manual on guerrilla warfare, a text that became part of the global Black Power syllabus.[61] Additionally, other works by Nkrumah, including the above-mentioned *Africa Must Unite* and *Neo-Colonialism*, along with his Black Power essays, were widely read in Black Power circles globally. *African Opinion*, the organ of latter-day Garveyism, was among the publications that recommended Nkrumah's writings to its readers throughout the Black Power era.

Amy Jacques Garvey, the Garvey Renaissance, and Black Power

In 1970, John Henrik Clarke noted that "we are now in the midst of a Marcus Garvey Renaissance."[62] Clarke made his observation in the introduction to a new edition of *Garvey and Garveyism*, a book originally published, or rather self-published, in 1963 and written by Amy Jacques Garvey.[63] The Marcus Garvey renaissance about which Clarke spoke coincided with the rise of Black Power. Very likely, the renewed interest in Garvey and Garveyism would not have happened, or at least would not have happened at the time it did and in the way it did, but for the rise of Black Power. Far from being coincidental, the Garvey renaissance was inextricably linked to the Black Power phenomenon.

Her husband's second wife, Jacques Garvey had labored long and hard in the discursive vineyard of Garveyism. She would also contribute greatly to the Garveyite revival in the era of Black Power. Indeed, Jacques Garvey may be said to have launched the field, establishing herself as the veritable matriarch of Garvey studies. Exactly four decades before *Garvey and Garveyism* appeared in 1963, she had edited *Philosophy and Opinions of Marcus Garvey*, the first collection of her husband's writings.[64] Jacques Garvey would even contribute to Garvey studies posthumously, after her death in 1973.[65]

In life, Jacques Garvey's experiences as author, editor, and activist prepared her well for the coming of Black Power. Long since back in Jamaica, after stints in the United States and Britain with her late husband, she was a key figure in delivering the message of Garveyism to exponents of Black Power. Promptly on Black Power's emergence as an identifiable political force, Jacques Garvey took to elucidating its historical "source and course," which she unhesitatingly identified as Marcus Garvey. She also quoted Malcolm X copiously and called attention to his family background, noting that both of his parents were Garveyites.[66] Jacques Garvey's discourse on Black Power further cited Martin Luther King Jr., a critic of Black Power, although a thoughtful one.[67] On a visit to Jamaica just months after Malcolm's death, King had lauded Marcus Garvey as "the first man on a mass scale and level to give millions of Negroes a sense of dignity and destiny, and make the Negro feel he was somebody."[68]

More than a mere deliverer of Garveyism to Black Power, Jacques Garvey became a Black Power personality in her own right, with connections far and wide in the movement. Writing in 1968, that glorious year of revolutionary insurgency worldwide,[69] with Black Power front and center, Jacques Garvey was in her element. Notably, her article appeared in a London-based magazine that Nkrumah had founded while he was still president of Ghana, and which he continued to support after being removed from power. "NUCLEAR POWER is misused to decimate people and destroy countries," averred Jacques Garvey, who had visited Nkrumah's Ghana, which strongly opposed French military nuclear tests in the Sahara.[70] Whereas nuclear energy was being generated by powerful nations (most of them white, although China had acquired the bomb by then) toward destructive ends, "BLACK POWER is generated to protect people from injustices and wrongs," Jacques Garvey offered. Black Power, she went on, was impervious to the ideological radioactivity of white supremacists, who "cannot tap its source, although they can destroy some of its exponents." Black Power was indestructible because "it is in every black man, woman and child's heart to get his Human Rights, and to keep them." As always, Jacques Garvey traced the "source" of Black Power back to Marcus Garvey. "It is the SPIRIT OF GARVEYISM, it is an IDEAL, A GOAL, A WORKING PHILOSOPHY," she concluded her assessment of Black Power. "IT IS ETERNAL in the breasts of peoples of African descent everywhere."[71]

Black Power in Jamaica: Garveyism, Rastafari, and Walter Rodney

Jacques Garvey's essays, focused as they were on Marcus Garvey as a source of Black Power, were inattentive to Rastafari. In Jamaica, however, Rastafari was a key base of support for Black Power, even if the most visible representatives of the movement came from other sectors of society, especially the university-educated, radical intelligentsia, a category in which Rastafarians were (then) sparsely represented.[72] Nevertheless, by the era of Black Power, Rastafari had become "a force that black intellectuals could not ignore," as Monique Bedasse has noted.[73] It was, perhaps, also appropriate that sustained engagement between black intellectuals and Rastafarians should have begun in Jamaica, the birthplace of Rastafari. Nor should the Rastafari prominence in Jamaican Black Power have been surprising. With its emphasis on black economic empowerment and its affirmation of African-centered black cultural worth, Black Power in many respects was an ideology tailor-made for Rastafari. That signature Black Power mantra—"black is beautiful"—had long been a Rastafari axiom.

Black Power, however, was a double-edged sword. Great debating society that it was, with numerous schools of thought contending and as many ideological flowers blooming, Black Power advocates often agreed on little beyond the basic goals, a multifariousness that was at once the great strength and weakness of the movement. So it was with economic empowerment, where the debate featured models ranging from socialist to capitalist, from cooperative to individualistic.[74] In this medley, the traditional Rastafari emphasis on artisanship, craftsmanship, and Garveyite-aligned "social entrepreneurship," as Caroline Shenaz Hossein has called it, found recognition.[75] In the realm of African-centered cultural affirmation, long a point of consensus with many (although not all) Garveyites, Rastafari also was in lockstep with Black Power. And just as Rastafari emerged, in part, on the wings of Garveyism, so too Rastafari spread alongside Black Power, even to places not known to have been directly touched by Garveyism, such as the indigenous communities of New Zealand.[76]

Walter Rodney was familiar with Rastafari, along with Garveyism and Black Power. He was also instrumental in bringing all three—Rastafari, Garveyism, and Black Power—into dialogue and, more importantly, political coordination on Jamaican soil. This was one of the more unique fusions between the old and the new, which, everywhere in the world, was a hallmark of Black Power. For the neocolonial Jamaican government, however, the amalgamation of Garveyism, Rastafari, and Black Power was a dangerous, even seditious, political arrangement. For his part in effecting this arrangement, the Guyanese-born Rodney, whose job as a university lecturer had brought him to Jamaica (he went to the same university as an undergraduate), would be singled out for special punishment. He was unceremoniously expelled from Jamaica, an action reminiscent of Garvey's deportation from the United States.[77] The saving grace was that Rodney was spared the full-court treatment accorded Garvey. Although persecuted in the Jamaican press, Rodney was not prosecuted in the country's courts; while jeered, he was never jailed. In Jamaica, as elsewhere in the Caribbean—and the world—expulsion and exclusion (denial of visas) were among the weapons wielded by governments in the war on Black Power, an undertaking in state repression that was as far-flung and as deeply coordinated as the movement itself.[78]

Discursively, the outstanding outcome of Rodney's expulsion from Jamaica was the publication of his collected Black Power essays and speeches, *The Groundings with My Brothers.*[79] The collection was appropriately, if androcentrically, titled: the bulk of Rodney's "groundings," Rastafari language for debating, was conducted with male Rastafarians. *Groundings* belonged to a familiar literary genre: the Black Power primer. History, philosophy, protest, policy, autobiography, and organizing manual rolled into one, as a category the Black Power primer had something in common with the slave narrative of old. As central to Black Power as the slave narrative was to abolitionism, the Black Power primer was as ubiquitous as the Black Power movement itself, produced worldwide.[80]

Rodney's *Groundings* was the best-known primer to come out of the Caribbean, and it stood out for the extent of its engagements with Garvey. With few exceptions, Black Power primers everywhere acknowledged and celebrated Garvey, but few cited and quoted him as extensively as *Groundings* did. The reason is not far to seek: location. Rodney's primer was based largely on "groundings" with Jamaican Rastafarian and Garveyite interlocutors, who were often the same people.

Seemingly echoing Amy Jacques Garvey, Rodney placed Marcus Garvey at the foundation of Black Power. Garvey, he announced, "was one of the first advocates of Black Power, and is still today the greatest spokesman ever to have been produced by the movement of black consciousness." Rodney also noted the universality of Garvey's interests. "He spoke," Rodney said, "to all Africans on the earth, whether they lived in Africa, South America, the West Indies or North America, and he made blacks aware of their strength when united."[81] There were similarities in the worldwide reaction to both Garveyism and Black Power, Rodney went on: "Whenever an oppressed black man shouts for equality he is called a racist." Predictably, the racist epithet was also hurled at Rodney, whose accusers ranged from black, Black Power–hating Jamaican officials to white, Black Power–hating U.S. diplomats stationed in Jamaica. "This was said of Marcus Garvey in his day," Rodney summed up. "Imagine that!"[82]

When all is said and done, that is what Garveyism was about—imagination. At the moment of imagining the UNIA, Garvey, on his own telling, patriarchally posed a series of questions: "'Where is the black man's Government?' 'Where is his King and his kingdom?' 'Where is his President, his country, and his ambassador, his army, his navy, his men of big affairs?'" He searched in vain before concluding, with characteristic self-possession: "I could not find them, and then I declared, 'I will help to make them.'"[83] Garvey and, more especially, the vast movement that would be named in his honor did not succeed in making manifest the dream herein summarized—that is, the decolonization and unification of continental Africa, with the option of repatriation for Africans of the diaspora. Rather, the great historic achievement of Garveyism was this: it powerfully nurtured and transmitted the vision of global black liberation that it inherited, and refined, from previous generations of struggles and strugglers.

Black Power became a key inheritor of the Garveyite mantle, more consciously in some places than in others. The movements for decolonization and desegregation, which, however indirectly and inconsistently, owed an inspirational debt to Garveyism, and sometimes also an ideological and organizational one, had failed to make good on the socioeconomic promises of the struggle against colonialism and apartheid/Jim Crow. Or, to use language made famous by Kwame Nkrumah—"seek ye first the political kingdom, and all other things shall be added unto it"—the political kingdom (decolonization and desegregation) had been won, but the addition (socioeconomic improvement) had not been made, at least not in the form and amount expected. Then there was the cultural alienation, that is, the continued devalorization of blackness in all its forms, attendant on decolonization and desegregation. Black Power emerged to address these deficits.

Pointedly, Black Power demanded a "second emancipation."[84] This was at once an indictment of the failures of decolonization and desegregation and an appropriation of the legacy of abolitionism, meaning the first emancipation. Here, as elsewhere, Garveyism, which had also laid claim to the antislavery legacy, offered Black Power a model. Black Power adherents admitted as much. One poet spoke for them, placing Garvey in a familiar lineup of male figures: "statues of saints and heroes/Malcolm! Garvey! / Into fading mottled statues of saints and heroes / Nat Turner, Denmark Vesey."[85] Not for nothing was the UNIA formed (in 1914) on the first day of August, dubbed Emancipation Day, in commemoration of the official end of slavery in the British Empire, which was followed by four more years of semi-slavery, euphemistically called "apprenticeship." The celebration of Emancipation Day was hardly limited to the British Caribbean colonies, with free African Americans in the United States heartily partaking in the period leading up to the U.S. Civil War.[86]

Intellectually, the nexus of Garveyism and Black Power would have far-reaching, and long-lasting, effects. Black Power revived interest in Garvey as a thinker and an activist, and in Garveyism as an idea and a movement. Garvey's writings formed part of the Black Power syllabus, while Black Power primers generally acknowledged Garvey and Garveyism as important forerunners. Garvey also appeared in another Black Power literary genre: collected sayings of the movement's icons and heroes, a project modeled on a runaway best-seller in that era, albeit one that enjoyed the benefit of state subsidy and sponsorship, namely, Chairman Mao's *Little Red Book*.[87] The interest thus sparked was a key factor, arguably the decisive factor, in the ensuing "renaissance" in Garvey studies. More than four decades later, the renaissance continues unabated. This very collection, *Global Garveyism*, is part of the legacy of the rebirth in Garvey studies emanating from the era of Black Power and powerfully shaped by scholars, and scholarly networks, deeply influenced by the Black Power phenomenon.

Notes

1. Hargreaves, *Decolonization in Africa*; Cooper, *Decolonization and African Society*.
2. Saul, *Flawed Freedom*.
3. Macqueen, *Decolonization of Portuguese Africa*.
4. Mawby, *Ordering Independence*.
5. See, for example, Fredrickson, *White Supremacy*; Cell, *Highest Stage of White Supremacy*; Fredrickson, *Black Liberation*.
6. On the use of the apartheid concept in the study of U.S. racism, see Massey and Denton, *American Apartheid*; Grady-Willis, *Challenging U.S. Apartheid*; Washington, *Medical Apartheid*.
7. Mamdani, *Citizen and Subject*.

8. Duffield, "Marcus Garvey and Kwame Nkrumah"; M. W. Williams, "Marcus Garvey and Kwame Nkrumah."

9. T. Martin, *Poetical Works of Marcus Garvey*, 23.

10. See, for example, Edward Wilmot Blyden, "The Call of Providence to the Descendants of Africa in America," in Moses, *Classical Black Nationalism*, 190–95; Henry McNeal Turner, "The American Negro and His Fatherland," ibid., 221; and W.E.B. Du Bois, "The Conservation of Races," ibid., 236. Ghana's independence anthem of 1957 also spoke of the "fatherland." Three years later, and with Nkrumah now in the authoritarian phase of his rule, a new version of the anthem dropped the fatherland reference in favor of personal celebration of the leader: "Hail our Nation's Founder for whom we pray."

11. Marais, *Kwame Nkrumah*, 86.

12. Nkrumah, *Africa Must Unite*.

13. Coester, "Ghana Is the Name We Wish to Proclaim," 1–4.

14. Martin Luther King Jr., "The Birth of a New Nation," in Carson and Shepard, *A Call to Conscience*, 17–41.

15. Nkrumah, *Ghana*, 184.

16. Ibid., 32.

17. Sensbach, "Freedom from Heaven," 498; Greenberg, *Confessions of Nat Turner*, 45–46.

18. Nkrumah, *Ghana*, 45.

19. "Black Power: Dilemmas and Contradictions, 1945–1966," folder 29, box 22, Papers of St. Clair Drake, Schomburg Center for Research in Black Culture, New York Public Library.

20. Shepperson and Drake, "Fifth Pan-African Conference," 64.

21. The *Negro World* ceased publishing in 1933; its namesake, the *New Negro World*, came into existence in 1940. See Blain, "'We Want to Set the World on Fire.'"

22. Letter to the editor, *African Opinion* 1, nos. 5–8 (April–May 1950): 20.

23. Quest, "George Padmore." While united in their opposition to the Italian conquest of Ethiopia, Padmore and James differed in approach to the U.S. invasion and occupation of Haiti. Padmore vociferously and consistently attacked U.S. imperialism in Haiti, whereas James, author of the best-known book on the Haitian Revolution in any language, had surprisingly little to say about occupied Haiti. By contrast, the Italian conquest of Ethiopia had a significant impact on the writing of James's Haitian revolutionary book, *The Black Jacobins*. See Dalleo, *American Imperialism's Undead*, 25–43, 149–72; and Høgsbjerg, "C.L.R. James and Italy's Conquest of Ethiopia."

24. Letter to the editor, *African Opinion* 5, nos. 5–6 (January–February 1960): 10.

25. "'Black Star Line' in Quicksand," *African Opinion* 4, nos. 5–6 (February–March 1958): 8–9.

26. Drake to Padmore, May 22, 1958, folder 23, box 8, Drake Papers, Schomburg Center; W. S. Thompson, *Ghana's Foreign Policy*, 58.

27. There is some tension between the accounts of the Fifth Pan-African Congress written by Padmore and Nkrumah. See Padmore, *Pan-Africanism or Communism?* 52–55.

28. For Nkrumah's opening address, see http://www.columbia.edu/itc/history/mann/w3005/nkrumba.html.

29. Quoted in Jacques Garvey, *Garvey and Garveyism*, 319.

30. Tarling, "'Ah-Ah'"; Ampiah, *Political and Moral Imperatives*, 127–36; Vitalis, "Midnight Ride."

31. Musambachime, "Changing Political Personality." For Lumumba's speech at the AAPC, see Van Lierde, *Lumumba Speaks*, 55–58.

32. Clarke was reviewing the English translation of Lumumba's autobiography, *Congo My Country*. See *Freedomways* 3, no. 1 (1963): 119–20 (quotation on 120).

33. Robert I. Teague, "Negroes Say Conditions in U.S. Explain Nationalists Militancy," *New York Times*, March 2, 1961, 1 and 17.

34. Letter to the editor, *African Opinion* 6, nos. 1–2 (January–February 1964): 4. There was a delay in publishing the letter, caused by interruption in bringing out the magazine.

35. Nkrumah, *Challenge of the Congo*.

36. Nkrumah, *Neo-Colonialism*. The Leninist inspiration came from Lenin, *Imperialism*.

37. Rahman, *Regime Change of Kwame Nkrumah*, 196–97.

38. Meyer, *Dr. Nkrumah's Last Journey*.

39. Owusu, *Uses and Abuses of Political Power*; Fuller, *Building the Ghanaian Nation-State*.

40. For personal accounts by two of the coup leaders, see Afrifa, *Ghana Coup*; Ocran, *Politics of the Sword*.

41. Letter to the editor, *African Opinion* 8, nos. 3–4 (August–September 1967): 4.

42. Letter to the editor, *African Opinion* 8, nos. 1–2 (May–June 1967): 4.

43. Letter to the editor, *African Opinion* 9, nos. 3–4 (October–November 1969): 3. Nkrumah indeed had a directing hand in the formation in 1963 of the Organization of African Unity (now the African Union), although it fell well short of his ideas about African unity. Later, as an exile, he wrote off the Organization of African Unity, calling it "as dead as a doornail." See Milne, *Kwame Nkrumah*, 360.

44. Nkrumah, *Ghana*, 45.

45. See, for example, Bretton, *Rise and Fall of Kwame Nkrumah*; Van Lare, *Rise and Fall of Kwame Nkrumah*; and C.L.R. James, "The Rise of Fall of Nkrumah."

46. Kwame Nkrumah, "The Spectre of Black Power," in Nkrumah, *Revolutionary Path*, 421–28 (quotation on 423).

47. Milne, *Kwame Nkrumah*.

48. Nkrumah, "The Spectre of Black Power"; Nkrumah, "The Struggle Continues: Message to the Black People of Britain," in Nkrumah, *Revolutionary Path*, 429–31; Nkrumah, *Axioms of Kwame Nkrumah*.

49. T. Martin, *Poetical Works of Marcus Garvey*, 44–45.

50. On Egbuna's role in British Black Power, see Egbuna, *Destroy This Temple*; Angelo, "Black Panthers in London"; and Bunce and Field, "Obi B. Egbuna, C.L.R. James."

51. Taylor, *Veiled Garvey*; T. Martin, *Amy Ashwood Garvey*; Ford, *Liberated Threads*; Farmer, *Remaking Black Power*.

52. Egbuna, *Diary of a Homeless Prodigal*, 87.

53. *African Opinion* 9, nos. 7–8 (July–August 1970): 3.

54. Carmichael, *Ready for Revolution*, 100.

55. Ibid., 227.

56. Carmichael, "Pan-Africanism—Land and Power," 41. On Carmichael's relation with Nkrumah more broadly, see P. E. Joseph, *Stokely*.

57. Carmichael, *Stokely Speaks*, 221–27. The term given to Nkrumah's ideas is spelled "Nkrumaism," without an "h," not "Nkrumahism," as many have it. For a summary of Nkrumah's thinking, see Biney, *Political and Social Thought*.

58. Carmichael, *Ready for Revolution*, 690.

59. Nkrumah, *Handbook of Revolutionary Warfare*.

60. Nkrumah, *Revolutionary Path*.

61. Nkrumah, *Handbook of Revolutionary Warfare*. Other guerrilla manuals, written by the likes Mao Tse-tung and Che Guevara, both experienced revolutionary warriors, also formed part of the Black Power syllabus, becoming required reading for movement militants. See Mao, *On Guerrilla Warfare*.

62. John Henrik Clarke, "Introduction," in Jacques Garvey, *Garvey and Garveyism*, vii.

63. On Jacques Garvey's travails in getting her book published, see Taylor, *Veiled Garvey*, 223–24, 231–32.

64. Jacques Garvey, *Philosophy and Opinions*.

65. Jacques Garvey appeared as follows on the cover and title page of *Marcus Garvey and the Vision of Africa*, John Henrik Clarke's 1974 edited collection: "With the assistance of Amy Jacques Garvey." There are indications that Jacques Garvey believed she had done more than merely "assist" Clarke and deserved the title of coeditor. See Taylor, *Veiled Garvey*, 231. On Jacques Garvey's posthumous contribution to Garvey scholarship, see also Garvey, Essien-Udom, and Jacques Garvey, *More Philosophy and Opinions of Marcus Garvey*.

66. A. Jacques Garvey, "The Source and Course of Black Power in America: The Dynamic Leadership of Garvey," *Kingston Star*, October 4, 1966; A. Jacques Garvey, "The Source and Course of Black Power in America: When Negroes Got Sense of Destiny," *Kingston Star*, October 6, 1966.

67. Martin Luther King Jr., "Black Power," in Carson, *Autobiography of Martin Luther King*, 314–32.

68. Jacques Garvey, "The Source and Course of Black Power in America."

69. Kurlansky, *1968*.

70. Allman, "Nuclear Imperialism." In a related vein, see Intondi, *African Americans against the Bomb*.

71. Amy Jacques Garvey, "Marcus Mosiah Garvey," *Africa and the World*, May 1968, 25–26 (quotations on 26).

72. Rupert Lewis, "Jamaican Black Power in the 1960s," in Quinn, *Black Power in the Caribbean*, 53–75.

73. Bedasse, *Jah Kingdom*, 169.

74. See, for example, L. W. Hill and Rabig, *Business of Black Power*.

75. Hossein, "Case Study."

76. Shilliam, *Black Pacific*.

77. On Rodney's ordeal in Jamaica, see R. Lewis, *Walter Rodney's Intellectual and Political Thought*, 85–123; and West, "Walter Rodney and Black Power."

78. On the surveillance and repression of Garveyism, see Elkins, "'Unrest among the Negroes'"; and Kornweibel, *"Seeing Red."* On the tracking of Black Power in the Caribbean

by U.S. intelligence, which coordinated closely with the region's intelligence services, see Central Intelligence Agency, "Black Radicalism in the Caribbean—Another Look," June 12, 1970, p. 13, Approved for Release 2008/10/28: CIA-RDP85T00875R001100090030-4, U.S. National Archives, College Park, MD; and West, "Walter Rodney and Black Power." On the repression of Black Power in the United States, see Churchill and Vander Wall, *The COINTELPRO Papers;* and O'Reilly, *Racial Matters.*

79. Rodney, *Groundings with My Brothers.*

80. Some of the more prominent book-length, single-authored examples include Cleaver, *Soul on Ice;* H. R. Brown, *Die Nigger Die;* Seale, *Seize the Time;* Egbuna, *Destroy This Temple;* and Stubbs, *I Write What I Like.* Other Black Power primers only came out in the post–Black Power era; these include Hyde, *X Communication;* and Kamarakafego, *Me One!*

81. Rodney, *Groundings with My Brothers,* 20–21.

82. Ibid., 24. On U.S. diplomats and Rodney, see West, "Walter Rodney and Black Power."

83. Marcus Garvey, "A Journey of Self-Discovery," in Clarke, *Marcus Garvey,* 71–76 (quotation on 73).

84. For instance, the first really international Black Power conclave, the Congress of Black Writers, held in 1968 in Montreal, Canada, was subtitled "Towards the Second Emancipation."

85. Albert E. Haynes Jr., "ECLIPSE," in Baraka and Neal, *Black Fire,* 406–9 (quotation on 408). For a deeper study of the connections between the antislavery tradition and Black Power in the United States, see Woodard, *Nation within a Nation.*

86. Kerr-Ritchie, *Rites of August First;* Kachun, *Festivals of Freedom.*

87. For an example of Garvey in the collected sayings of Black Power icons and heroes, see Maglangbayan, *The Black Handbook.* On the worldwide impact of the *Little Red Book,* see Cook, *Mao's Little Red Book.*

Bibliography

Adeleke, Tunde. *UnAfrican Americans: Nineteenth-Century Black Nationalists and the Civilizing Mission*. Lexington: University Press of Kentucky, 1998.

Adi, Hakim. *Pan-Africanism and Communism: The Communist International, Africa and the Diaspora, 1919–1939*. Trenton, NJ: Africa World Press, 2013.

Adi, Hakim, and Marika Sherwood, eds. *Pan-African History: Political Figures from Africa and the Diaspora since 1787*. New York, 2003.

Adler, Karen S. "'Always Leading Our Men in Service and Sacrifice': Amy Jacques Garvey, Feminist Black Nationalist." *Gender and Society* 6, no. 3 (1992): 346–75.

Afrifa, Colonel A. A. *The Ghana Coup: 24th February 1966*. London: Frank Cass & Co., 1967.

Ahlman, Jeffrey S. "The Algerian Question in Nkrumah's Ghana, 1958–1960: Debating 'Violence' and 'Nonviolence' in African Decolonization." *Africa Today* 57, no. 2 (2010): 67–84.

Ali, Drew. *The Holy Koran of the Moorish Holy Temple of Science*. Riverdale, IL: Califa Media, 2014.

Allman, Jean. "The Disappearing of Hannah Kudjoe: Nationalism, Feminism, and the Tyrannies of History." *Journal of Women's History* 21, no. 3 (2009): 13–35.

———. "Nuclear Imperialism and the Pan-African Struggle for Peace and Freedom: Ghana, 1959–1962." *Souls* 10, no. 2 (2008): 83–102.

Altink, Henrice. *Destined for a Life of Service: Defining African-Jamaican Womanhood, 1865–1938*. Manchester: Manchester University Press, 2011.

Ampiah, Kweku. *The Political and Moral Imperatives of the Bandung Conference of 1955: The Reactions of the US, UK, and Japan*. Folkstone, UK: Global Oriental, 2007.

Anderson, Benedict R. *Imagined Communities: Reflections on the Origin and Spread of Nationalism*. 1983. London: Verso, 1991.

Anderson, Carol. *Eyes off the Prize: The United Nations and the African American Struggle for Human Rights, 1944–1955*. New York: Cambridge University Press, 2003.

Anderson, Karen Tucker. "Last Hired, First Fired: Black Women Workers during World War II." *Journal of American History* 69, no. 1 (1982): 82–97.

Angelo, Anne-Marie. "The Black Panthers in London, 1967–1972: A Diasporic Struggle Navigates the Black Atlantic." *Radical History Review* 103 (2009): 17–35.

Arroyo, Jossianna. *Writing Secrecy in Caribbean Freemasonry*. New York: Palgrave Macmillan, 2013.

Asante, S.K.B. *Pan-African Protest: West Africa and the Italo-Ethiopian Crisis, 1934–1941*. London: Longman, 1977.

Ashdown, Peter. *Garveyism in Belize*. Benque Viejo del Carmen, Belize: Published for SPEAR by Cubola Productions, 1990.

———. "Marcus Garvey, the UNIA and the Black Cause in British Honduras." *Journal of Caribbean History* 15 (1981): 41–55.

Austin, David. *Fear of a Black Nation: Race, Sex, and Security in Sixties Montreal*. Toronto: Between the Lines, 2013.

Babson, Steve. *Working Detroit: The Making of a Union Town*. Detroit: Wayne State University Press, 1996.

Bagnell, Robert W. "The Madness of Marcus Garvey." *The Messenger*, March 1923, 638–48.

Bair, Barbara. "'Ethiopia Shall Stretch Forth Her Hands Unto God': Laura Kofey and the Gendered Vision of Redemption in the Garvey Movement." In *A Mighty Baptism: Race, Gender, and the Creation of American Protestantism*, ed. Susan Juster and Lisa MacFarlane, 38–61. Ithaca: Cornell University Press, 1996.

———. "Garveyism and Contested Political Terrain in 1920s Virginia." In *Afro-Virginian History and Culture*, ed. John Saillaint, 227–49. New York: Garland, 1999.

———. "Pan-Africanism as Process: Adelaide Casey Hayford, Garveyism, and the Cultural Roots of Nationalism." In *Imagining Home: Class, Culture, and Nationalism in the African Diaspora*, ed. Sidney J. Lemelle and Robin D. G. Kelley, 121–44. London: Verso, 1994.

———. "Remapping the Black/White Body: Sexuality, Nationalism, and Biracial Antimiscegenation Activism in 1920s Virginia." In *Sex, Love, Race: Crossing Boundaries in North American History*, ed. Martha Hodes, 399–420. New York: New York University Press, 1999.

———. "Renegotiating Liberty: Garveyism, Women, and Grassroots Organizing in Virginia." In *Women of the American South: A Multicultural Reader*, ed. Christie Anne Farnham, 220–40. New York: New York University Press, 1997.

———. "True Women, Real Men: Gender, Ideology, and Social Roles in the Garvey Movement." In *Gender Domains: Rethinking Public and Private in Women's History*, ed. Dorothy O. Helly and Susan M. Reverby, 154–66. Ithaca: Cornell University Press, 1992.

Baker, Houston A., Jr. *Modernism and the Harlem Renaissance*. Chicago: University of Chicago Press, 1987.

Baldwin, Davarian L. *Chicago's New Negroes: Modernity, the Great Migration, and Black Urban Life*. Chapel Hill: University of North Carolina Press, 2007.

Baldwin, Davarian L., and Minkah Makalani, eds. *Escape from New York: The New Negro Renaissance Beyond Harlem*. Minneapolis: University of Minnesota Press, 2013.

Bandele, Ramla. *Black Star: African American Activism in the International Political Economy*. Urbana: University of Illinois Press, 2008.

Baraka, Amiri, and Larry Neal, eds. *Black Fire: An Anthology of Afro-American Writing*. 1968. Baltimore: Black Classic Press, 2007.

Barber, Karin. "Methodology and Vampires." *Journal of Southern African Studies* 29, no. 1 (2003): 312–14.

Barthes, Roland. "The Death of the Author." In *Image-Music-Text*, trans. Stephen Heath, 142–48. New York: Hill and Wang, 1977.

Basdeo, Sahadeo. *Labour Organization and and Labour Reform in Trinidad, 1919–1939*. Trinidad and Tobago: Lexicon Trinidad, 2003.

Bashford, Alison, and Philippa Levine, eds. *The Oxford Handbook of the History of Eugenics*. Oxford: Oxford University Press, 2010.

Bates, Beth. *The Making of Black Detroit in the Age of Henry Ford*. Chapel Hill: University of North Carolina Press, 2012.

Batiste, Stephanie. *Darkening Mirrors: Imperial Representation in Depression-Era African American Performance*. Durham: Duke University Press, 2011.

Bedasse, Monique A. *Jah Kingdom: Rastafarians, Tanzania, and Pan-Africanism in the Age of Decolonization*. Chapel Hill: University of North Carolina Press, 2017.

Bedford, William van Lare. *The Rise and Fall of Kwame Nkrumah and Its Impact on the Rest of Africa*. Accra-Tema: State Publishing Corporation, 1967.

Beinart, William, and Colin Bundy. *Hidden Struggles in Rural South Africa: Politics and Popular Movements in the Transkei and Eastern Cape, 1890–1930*. Johannesburg: Ravan Press, 1987.

Berger, Iris. "African Women's Movements in the Twentieth Century: A Hidden History." *African Studies Review* 57, no. 3 (2014): 1–19.

Biney, Ama. *The Political and Social Thought of Kwame Nkrumah*. New York: Palgrave Macmillan, 2011.

Birmingham, David. *The Decolonization of Africa*. 2nd ed. Athens: Ohio University Press, 1996.

Blain, Keisha N. "'Confraternity among All Darker Races': Mittie Maude Lena Gorder and the Practice of Black (Inter)nationalism in Chicago, 1932–1942." *Palimpsest: A Journal on Women, Gender, and the Black International* 5, no. 2 (2006): 151–81.

———. *Set the World on Fire: Black Nationalist Women and the Global Struggle for Freedom*. Philadelphia: University of Pennsylvania Press, 2018.

———. "'We Want to Set the World on Fire': Black Nationalist Women and Diasporic Politics in the *New Negro World*, 1940–1944." *Journal of Social History* 49, no. 1 (2015): 194–212.

Blain, Keisha N., Asia Leeds, and Ula Taylor. "Women, Gender Politics, and Pan-Africanism." *Women, Gender, and Families of Color* 4, no. 2 (2016): 139–45.

Blyden, Edward Wilmot. *Christianity, Islam and the Negro Race*. London: W. B. Whittingham, 1887.

Bogues, Anthony. *Black Heretics, Black Prophets: Radical Political Intellectuals*. New York: Routledge, 2003.

Bolland, O. Nigel. *The Politics of Labour in the British Caribbean: The Social Origins of Authoritarianism and Democracy in the Labour Movement*. Kingston, Jamaica: Ian Randle, 2001.

Bourbonnais, Nicole. *Birth Control in the Decolonizing Caribbean: Reproductive Politics and Practice on Four Islands, 1930–1970*. New York: Cambridge University Press, 2016.

Bourgois, Philippe I. *Ethnicity at Work: Divided Labor on a Central African Banana Plantation*. Baltimore: Johns Hopkins University Press, 1989.

Bourke, Colin, Eleanor Bourke, and Bill Edwards. *Aboriginal Australia*. Brisbane: University of Queensland Press, 2004.

Bowen, Merle L. "The Struggle for Black Land Rights in Brazil." *Africa and Black Diaspora: An International Journal* 3, no. 2 (2010): 147–68.

Bracey, John H., Jr., August Meier, and Elliott Rudwick, eds. *Black Nationalism in America*. Indianapolis: Bobbs-Merrill, 1970.

Bradford, Helen. *A Taste of Freedom: The ICU in Rural South Africa, 1924–1930*. New Haven: Yale University Press, 1987.

Brandt, Nat. *Harlem at Work: The Black Experience in WWII*. Syracuse: Syracuse University Press, 1996.

Brereton, Bridget. *A History of Modern Trinidad, 1783–1962*. Kingston, Jamaica: Heinemann, 1981.

Bretton, Harry L. *The Rise and Fall of Kwame Nkrumah: A Study of Personal Rule in Africa*. New York: Praeger, 1967.

Brinkley, Douglas, and David R. Facey-Crowther, eds. *The Atlantic Charter*. New York: St. Martin's Prss, 1994.

Brooks, Joanna, and John Saillant, eds. *"Face Zion Forward": First Writers of the Black Atlantic, 1785–1798*. Boston: Northeastern University Press, 2002.

Brown, H. Rap. *Die Nigger Die!* New York: Dial Press, 1969.

Brown, Jacqueline Nassy. *Dropping Anchor, Setting Sail: Geographies of Race in Black Liverpool*. Princeton, NJ: Princeton University Press, 2005.

Browne, David. *Race, Class, Politics and the Struggle for Empowerment in Barbados, 1914–1937*. Kingston, Jamaica: Ian Randle, 2012.

Buckley, Gail Lumet. *American Patriots: The Story of Blacks in the Military from the Revolution to Desert Storm*. New York: Random House, 2001.

Buck-Morss, Susan. *Hegel, Haiti, and Universal History*. Pittsburgh: University of Pittsburgh Press, 2009.

Bunce, R. E. R., and Paul Field. "Obi B. Egbuna, C.L.R. James and the Birth of Black Power in Britain: Black Radicalism in Britain, 1967–1972." *Twentieth Century British History* 22, no. 3 (2010): 391–414.

Burkett, Randall K. *Black Redemption: Churchmen Speak for the Garvey Movement*. Philadelphia: Temple University Press, 1978.

———. *Garveyism as a Religious Movement: The Institutionalization of a Black Civil Religion*. Metuchen, NJ: Scarecrow Press, 1978.

Burnett, Carla. "'Are We Slaves or Free Men?' Labor, Race, Garveyism, and the 1920 Panama Canal Strike." Ph.D diss., University of Illinois at Chicago, 2004.

———. "'Unity Is Strength': Labor, Race, Garveyism, and the 1920 Panama Canal Strike." *Global South* 6, no. 2 (2013): 39–64.

Bush, Barbara. *Imperialism, Race, and Resistance: Africa and Britain, 1919–1945*. New York: Routledge, 1999.

Bush, Rod. *We Are Not What We Seem: Black Nationalism and Class Struggle in the American Century*. New York: New York University Press, 1998.

Butlin, Noel. *Our Original Aggression: Aboriginal Populations of Southeastern Australia, 1788–1850*. Sydney: Allen & Unwin, 1983.

Bynum, Cornelius. *A. Philip Randolph and the Struggle for Civil Rights*. Urbana: University of Illinois Press, 2010.

Byrd, Brandon R. "'To Start Something to Help These People': African American Women and the Occupation of Haiti, 1915–1934." *Journal of Haitian Studies* 21, no. 2 (2015): 154–80.

Byrd, James P. *Sacred Scripture, Sacred War: The Bible and the American Revolution*. Oxford: Oxford University Press, 2013.

Cabrita, Joel. *Text and Authority in the South African Nazaretha Church*. Cambridge: Cambridge University Press, 2014.

Callahan, Allen Dwight. *The Talking Book: African Americans and the Bible*. New Haven: Yale University Press, 2006.

Campbell, Horace. *Rasta and Resistance: From Marcus Garvey to Walter Rodney*. Trenton, NJ: Africa World Press, 1987.

Campbell, James. *Middle Passages: African American Journeys to Africa, 1787–2005*. New York: Penguin Press, 2006.

———. *Songs of Zion: The African Methodist Episcopal Church in the United States and South Africa*. New York: Oxford University Press, 1995.

Campt, Tina. "The Crowded Space of Diaspora: Intercultural Address and the Tensions of Diasporic Relation." *Radical History Review* 83 (Spring 2002): 94–111.

Carew, Jan. *Ghost in Our Blood: With Malcolm X in Africa, England, and the Caribbean*. Chicago: Lawrence Hill Books, 1994.

Carey, Jane, and Jane Lydon, eds. *Indigenous Networks: Mobility, Connections and Exchange*. London: Routledge, 2014.

Carmichael, Stokely. "Pan-Africanism—Land and Power." *Black Scholar* 1, no. 1 (1969): 36–43.

———. *Ready for Revolution: The Life and Struggles of Stokely Carmichael [Kwame Ture]*. With Ekwueme Michael Thelwell. New York: Scribner, 2003.

———. *Stokely Speaks: From Black Power to Pan-Africanism*. 1971. Chicago: Chicago Review Press, 2007.

Carson, Clayborne, ed. *The Autobiography of Martin Luther King, Jr.* New York: Grand Central Publishing, 1999.

Carson, Clayborne, and Chris Shepard, eds. *A Call to Conscience: The Landmark Speeches of Dr. Martin Luther King, Jr.* New York: Grand Central Publishing, 2001.

Carton, Benedict. *Blood from Your Children: The Colonial Origins of Generational Conflict in South Africa*. Charlottesville: University of Virginia Press, 2000.

Castillo Bueno, María de los Reyes, and Daisy Rubiera Castillo. *Reyita: The Life of a Black Cuban Woman in the Twentieth Century*. Durham: Duke University Press, 2000.

Catron, John W. *Embracing Protestantism: Black Identities in the Atlantic World*. Gainesville: University Press of Florida, 2016.

Cell, John. *The Highest Stage of White Supremacy: The Origins of Segregation in South Africa and the American South*. Cambridge: Cambridge University Press, 1982.

Césaire, Aimé. *Discourse on Colonialism*. Trans. Joan Pinkham. 1955. New York: Monthly Review Press, 2000.

————. *Notebook of a Return to the Native Land*. Trans. Clayton Eshleman and Annette Smith. Middletown, CT: Wesleyan University Press, 2011.

Chailloux Laffita, Graciela, and Robert Whitney. "British Subjects y Pichones en Cuba." In *De dónde son los cubanos*, ed. Graciela Chailloux Laffita, 53–115. La Habana: Editorial de Ciencias Sociales, 2007.

Chapman, Erin D. *Prove It On Me: New Negroes, Sex, and Popular Culture in the 1920s*. New York: Oxford University Press, 2012.

Charlton, Audrey. "'Cat Born in Oven Is Not Bread': Jamaican and Barbadian Immigrants in Cuba between 1900–1959." PhD diss., Columbia University, 2005.

Chéry, Tshepo Masango. "Kingdoms of the Earth: Coloured Identity, African-Initiated Churches, and the Politics of Black Nationalism in South Africa, 1892 to 1948." PhD diss., University of Pennsylvania, 2012.

Chomsky, Aviva. *West Indian Workers and the United Fruit Company in Costa Rica, 1870–1940*. Baton Rouge: Louisiana State University Press, 1996.

Christensen, Jeanne. *Rastafari Reasoning and the Rasta Woman: Gender Constructions in the Shaping of Rastafari Livity*. Latham: Lexington Books, 2014.

Christian, Mark. "Marcus Garvey and the Universal Negro Improvement Association (UNIA): With Special Reference to the 'Lost' Parade in Columbus, Ohio, September 25, 1923." *Western Journal of Black Studies* 28 (2004): 424–34.

Churchill, Ward, and Jim Vander Wall. *The COINTELPRO Papers: Documents from the FBI's Secret Wars against Domestic Dissent*. Boston: South End Press, 1990.

Clarke, John Henrik, ed. *Marcus Garvey and the Vision of Africa*. New York: Random House, 1974.

Clavin, Matthew J. *Toussaint Louverture and the American Civil War: The Promise and Peril of a Second Haitian Revolution*. Philadelphia: University of Pennsylvania Press, 2010.

Cleaver, Eldridge. *Soul on Ice*. New York: A Delta Book, 1968.

Clegg, Claude, III. *An Original Man: The Life and Times of Elijah Muhammad*. New York: St. Martin's Press, 1997.

————. *The Price of Liberty: African Americans and the Making of Liberia*. Chapel Hill: University of North Carolina Press, 2003.

Coester, Markus. "'Ghana Is the Name We Wish to Proclaim': Two Popular Caribbean Voices and the Independence of Ghana." *Ntama: Journal of African Music and Popular Culture*, April 26, 2004.

Colby, Jason M. *The Business of Empire: United Fruit, Race, and U.S. Expansion in Central America*. Ithaca, NY: Cornell University Press, 2011.

Comaroff, Jean, and John L. Comaroff. "Alien-Nation: Zombies, Immigrants, and Millennial Capitalism." *South Atlantic Quarterly* 101, no. 4 (2002): 779–805.

————. "Millennial Capitalism: First Thoughts on a Second Coming." *Public Culture* 12, no. 2 (2000): 291–343.

Conniff, Michael L. *Black Labor on a White Canal: Panama, 1904–1981*. Pittsburgh: University of Pittsburgh Press, 1985.

Cook, Alexander C., ed. *Mao's Little Red Book: A Global History*. Cambridge: Cambridge University Press, 2014.

Cooper, Frederick. *Decolonization and African Society: The Labor Question in French and British Africa*. Cambridge: Cambridge University Press, 1996.

Corbould, Clare. "At the Feet of Dessalines: Performing Haiti's Revolution during the New Negro Renaissance." In *Beyond Blackface: African Americans and the Creation of American Popular Culture, 1890–1930*, ed. W. Fitzhugh Brundage, 259–88. Chapel Hill: University of North Carolina Press, 2011.

Corinealdi, Kaysha. "Envisioning Multiple Citizenships: West Indian Panamanians and Creating Community in the Canal Zone Neocolony." *Global South* 6, no. 2 (2013): 87–106.

Crais, Clifton. *The Politics of Evil: Magic, State Power, and the Political Imagination*. Cambridge: Cambridge University Press, 2002.

Craton, Michal. *Testing the Chains: Resistance to Slavery in the British West Indies*. Ithaca: Cornell University Press, 2009.

Cronon, E. David. *Black Moses: The Story of Marcus Garvey and the Universal Negro Improvement Association*. Madison: University of Wisconsin Press, 1955.

———. "Review of *Garvey and Garveyism* by A. Jacques Garvey." *Caribbean Studies* 5, no. 2 (1965): 74–75.

Cross, Sholto. "Social History and Millennial Movements: The Watch Tower in South Central Africa." *Social Compass* 24, no. 1 (1977): 83–95.

Crump, William L. *The Story of Kappa Alpha Psi: A History of the Beginnings and Development of a College Greek Letter Organization, 1911–1991*. 4th ed. Philadelphia: Kappa Alpha Phi Fraternity, 1991.

Cruse, Harold. *The Crisis of the Negro Intellectual*. New York: Morrow, 1967.

Cugoano, Ottobah. *Thoughts and Sentiments on the Evil and Wicked Traffic of the Slavery and the Commerce of the Human Species*. London, 1787.

Cummings, James Damian. *Barrack-Yard Dwellers*. Kingston, Jamaica: University of the West Indies, 2004.

Curran, Andrew S. *The Anatomy of Blackness: Science and Slavery in the Age of Enlightenment*. Baltimore: Johns Hopkins University Press, 2011.

Curthoys, Ann. "The Lying Name of 'Government': Empire, Mobility and Political Rights." In *Indigenous Networks: Mobility, Connections and Exchange*, ed. Jane Carey and Jane Lydon, 75–94. London: Routledge, 2014.

Curtis, Edward E., IV, and Danielle Brune Sigler, eds. *The New Black Gods: Arthur Huff Fauset and the Study of African American Religions*. Bloomington: Indiana University Press, 2009.

Curwood, Anastasia. *Stormy Weather: Middle-Class African American Marriages between the Two World Wars*. Chapel Hill: University of North Carolina Press, 2010.

Dalleo, Raphael. *American Imperialism's Undead: The Occupation of Haiti and the Rise of Caribbean Anticolonialism*. Charlottesville: University of Virginia Press, 2016.

Dalrymple, Daniel A. "In the Shadow of Garvey: Garveyites in New York City and the British Caribbean, 1925–1950." PhD diss., Michigan State University, 2008.

———. "'Reclaiming the Fallen': The Universal Negro Improvement Association Central Division, New York 1935–1942." *Journal of Black Studies* 45, no. 1 (2014): 19–36.

Das, Santanu, ed. *Race, Empire and First World War Writing*. Cambridge: Cambridge University Press, 2011.

Das, Veena. "Subaltern as Perspective." In *Subaltern Studies: Writings on South Asian History and Society, Vol. VI*, ed. Ranajit Guha, 310–24. Delhi: Oxford University Press, 1989.

Davidson, Apollon, et al., eds. *South Africa and the Communist International: A Documentary History*. 2 vols. London: Frank Cass, 2003.

Davis, Angela Y. *Freedom Is a Constant Struggle: Ferguson, Palestine, and the Foundations of a Movement*. Chicago: Haymarket Books, 2016.

Dawson, Michael C. *Black Visions: The Roots of Contemporary African-American Political Ideologies*. Chicago: University of Chicago Press, 2001.

DeCaro, Louis A., Jr. *Malcolm and the Cross: The Nation of Islam, Malcolm X, and Christianity*. New York: New York University Press, 1998.

Delany, Martin R. *The Condition, Elevation, Emigration, and Destiny of the Colored People of the United States and Official Report of the Niger Valley Exploration Party*. Amherst, NY: Humanity Books, 2004.

Derby, Lauren. "Beyond Fugitive Speech: Rumor and Affect in Caribbean History." *Small Axe* 18, no. 2 (2014): 123–40.

Désulmé, Mythra. "Garvey and Haiti." *International Journal of African Renaissance Studies* 3, no. 2 (2008): 102–14.

De Witte, Ludo. *The Assassination of Lumumba*. Trans. Ann Wright and Renée Fenby. London: Verso, 2001.

Dillard, Angela D. *Faith in the City: Preaching Radical Social Change in Detroit*. Ann Arbor: University of Michigan Press, 2007.

Dillon, Elizabeth Maddock, and Michael J. Drexler, eds. *The Haitian Revolution and the Early United States: Histories, Textualities, Geographies*. Philadelphia: University of Pennsylvania Press, 2016.

Dolinar, Brian, ed. *The Negro in Illinois: The WPA Papers*. Urbana: University of Illinois Press, 2013.

Donkoh, Wilhelmina J. "Nkrumah and His 'Chicks': An Examination of Women and the Organizational Strategies of the CPP." In *Africa's Many Divides and Africa's Future: Pursuing Nkrumah's Vision of Pan-Africanism in an Era of Globalization*, ed. Charles Quist-Adade and Vincent Dodoo, 99–121. Newcastle upon Tyne: Cambridge Scholars Publishing, 2015.

Dorman, Jacob S. *Chosen People: The Rise of American Black Israelite Religions*. Oxford: Oxford University Press, 2013.

Dossett, Kate. *Bridging Race Divides: Black Nationalism, Feminism, and Integration in the United States, 1896–1935*. Gainesville: University Press of Florida, 2008.

Drake, St. Clair. *The Redemption of Africa and Black Religion*. Chicago: Third World Press, 1970.

Drake, St. Clair, and Horace Cayton. *Black Metropolis: A Study of Negro Life in a Northern City*. Rev. ed. Chicago: University of Chicago Press, 1993.

Dubey, Madhu. *Black Women Novelists and the Nationalist Aesthetic*. Bloomington: Indiana University Press, 1994.

Dubois, Laurent. *Avengers of the New World: The Story of the Haitian Revolution*. Cambridge: Harvard University Press, 2004.

———. "Dessalines Toro d'Haiti." *William and Mary Quarterly* 69, no. 3 (2012): 541–48.

Du Bois, W.E.B. *Black Reconstruction*. New York: Harcourt, Brace, 1935.

———. "Close Ranks." *The Crisis* 16, no. 3 (July 1918): 111.

———. "A Lunatic or a Traitor?" *The Crisis* 28, no. 1 (1924): 8–9.

———. *The Souls of Black Folk*. 1903. New York: Dover, 1994.

Duffield, Ian. "Marcus Garvey and Kwame Nkrumah." *History Today* 31, no. 3 (1981): 24–30.

Duncan, Mae Najiyyah. *A Survey of Cincinnati's Black Press and Its Editors, 1844–2010*. Bloomington, IN: Xlibris, 2011.

Duncan, Natanya. "The Efficient Womanhood of the Universal Negro Improvement Association, 1919–1930." PhD diss., University of Florida, 2009.

———. "'If Our Men Hesitate Then the Women of the Race Must Come Forward': Henrietta Vinton Davis and the UNIA in New York." *New York History* 95, no. 4 (2014): 558–83.

———. "Princess Laura Kofey and the Reverse Atlantic Experience." In *The American South and the Atlantic World*, ed. Brian Ward, Martyn Bone, and William A. Link, 218–37. Gainesville: University Press of Florida, 2013.

Dunn, D. Elwood. *Liberia and the United States during the Cold War: Limits of Reciprocity*. New York: Palgrave, 2009.

Dunn, D. Elwood, Amos J. Beyan, and Carl Patrick Burrowes. *Historical Dictionary of Liberia*. 2nd ed. Lanham, MD: Scarecrow Press, 2001.

Dunn, James Alexander. *Dangerous Neighbors: The Making of the Haitian Revolution in Early America*. Philadelphia: University of Pennsylvania Press, 2016.

Earley, Charity Adams. *One Woman's Army: A Black Officer Remembers the WAC*. College Station: Texas A&M University Press, 1989.

Edgar, Robert. "Garveyism in Africa: Dr. Wellington and the American Movement in the Transkei." *Ufahamu: A Journal of African Studies* 6, no. 3 (1976): 31–57.

———. "New Religious Movements." In *Missions and Empire*, ed. Norman Etherington, 216–37. Oxford: Oxford University Press, 2005.

Edgar, Robert, and Hilary Sapire. *African Apocalypse: The Story of Nontetha Nkwenkwe, a Twentieth-Century South African Prophet*. Athens: Ohio University Press, 2000.

Edwards, Brent Hayes. "The Uses of Diaspora." *Social Text* 66 (Spring 2011): 45–73.

Egbuna, Obi. *Destroy this Temple: The Voice of Black Power in Britain*. New York: William Morrow, 1971.

———. *Diary of a Homeless Prodigal*. Enugu, Nigeria: Fourth Dimension, 1978.

Elkins, W. F. "Black Power in the British West Indies: The Trinidad Longshoremen's Strike of 1919." *Science and Society* 31, no. 1 (Winter 1969): 71–75.

———. "Hercules and the Society of Peoples of African Origin." *Caribbean Studies* 11, no. 4 (1972): 47–59.

———. "Suppression of the *Negro World* in the British West Indies." *Science and Society* 35, no. 3 (Fall 1971): 344–47.

———. "'Unrest among the Negroes': A British Document of 1919." *Science and Society* 32, no. 1 (1968): 66–79.

Equiano, Olaudah. *The Interesting Narrative and Other Writings*. New York: Penguin Classics, 2003.

Erlank, Natasha. "The Current State of South African Scholarship in the Social Sciences." *African Studies* 67, no. 1 (2008): 121–36.

Erskine, Noel Leo. *From Garvey to Marley: Rastafari Theology*. Gainesville: University Press of Florida, 2005.

Essien-Udom, E. U. *Black Nationalism: A Search for an Identity in America*. Chicago: University of Chicago Press, 1962.

Evans, Ivan. *Bureaucracy and Race: Native Administration in South Africa*. Berkeley: University of California Press, 1997.

Ewing, Adam. *The Age of Garvey: How a Jamaican Activist Created a Mass Movement and Changed Global Black Politics*. Princeton, NJ: Princeton University Press, 2014.

———. "Caribbean Labour Politics in the Age of Garvey, 1918–1938." *Race and Class* 55, no. 1 (2013): 23–45.

———. "The Challenge of Garveyism Studies." *Modern American History* 1, no. 3 (2018), forthcoming.

Eze, Emmanuel Chukwudi, ed. *Race and the Enlightenment: A Reader*. Cambridge, MA: Blackwell, 1997.

Farmer, Ashley D. *Remaking Black Power: How Black Women Transformed an Era*. Chapel Hill: University of North Carolina Press, 2017.

Farwell, Byron. *The Great War in Africa, 1914–1918*. New York: Norton, 1986.

Fernández Robaina, Tomás. "Marcus Garvey in Cuba: Urrutia, Cubans, and Black Nationalism." In *Between Race and Empire: African Americans and Cubans before the Cuban Revolution*, ed. Lisa Brock and Digna Castañeda Fuertes, 120–28. Philadelphia: Temple University Press, 1998.

Ferrer, Ada. *Freedom's Mirror: Cuba and Haiti in the Age of Revolution*. New York: Cambridge University Press, 2014.

Fields, Karen. *Revival and Rebellion in Colonial Central Africa*. Princeton, NJ: Princeton University Press, 1985.

Figueroa, Victor. *Prophetic Visions of the Past: Pan-Caribbean Representations of the Haitian Revolution*. Columbus: Ohio State University Press, 2015.

Fikes, Kesha. "Diasporic Governmentality: On the Gendered Limits of Migrant Wage-Labour in Portugal." *Feminist Review* 90 (2008): 48–67.

Fiorenza, Elisabeth Schüssler, ed. *Searching the Scriptures: A Feminist Introduction*. London: SCM Press, 1994.

Fischer, Sibylle. *Modernity Disavowed: Haiti and the Cultures of Slavery in the Age of Revolution*. Durham: Duke University Press, 2004.

Fitzgerald, Michael W. "'We Have Found a Moses': Theodore Bilbo, Black Nationalism, and the Greater Liberia Bill of 1939." *Journal of Southern History* 63, no. 2 (1997): 293–320.

Ford, Tanisha. *Liberated Threads: Black Women, Style, and the Global Politics of Soul*. Chapel Hill: University of North Carolina Press, 2015.

Ford-Smith, Honor. "Unruly Virtues of the Spectacular: Performing Engendered Nationalisms in the UNIA in Jamaica." *Interventions: International Journal of Postcolonial Studies* 6, no. 1 (2004): 18–44.

Foucault, Michel. *Discipline and Punish: The Birth of the Prison*. Trans. Alan Sheridan. New York: Vintage Books, 1995.

———. *The History of Sexuality: Volume 1: An Introduction.* New York: Vintage Books, 1990.

Fredrickson, George. *Black Liberation: A Comparative Study of Black Ideologies in the United States and South Africa.* New York: Oxford University Press, 1995.

———. *White Supremacy: A Comparative Study in American and South African History.* New York: Oxford University Press, 1981.

Frey, Sylvia R. *Water from the Rock: Black Resistance in a Revolutionary Age.* Princeton, NJ: Princeton University Press, 1991.

Fuller, Harcourt. *Building the Ghanaian Nation-State: Kwame Nkrumah's Symbolic Nationalism.* New York: Palgrave Macmillan, 2014.

Garnes, Walterio Lord. "Marcus Garvey and the UNIA in the Memory of West Indian Residents in Cuba." *76 King Street. The Journal of Liberty Hall: The Legacy of Marcus Garvey* 1 (2009): 130–44.

Garraway, Doris L., ed. *The Tree of Liberty: Cultural Legacies of the Haitian Revolution in the Atlantic World.* Charlottesville: University of Virginia Press, 2008.

Garvey, Marcus, E. U. Essien-Udom, and Amy Jacques Garvey. *More Philosophy and Opinions of Marcus Garvey.* Totowa, NJ: Cass, 1977.

Gasa, Nomboniso. *Women in South African History: Basus'iimbokodo, Bawel'imilambo/ They Remove Boulders and Cross Rivers.* Pretoria: HSRC Press, 2008.

Geggus, David Patrick. *Haitian Revolutionary Studies.* Bloomington: Indiana University Press, 2002.

———, ed. *The Impact of the Haitian Revolution in the Atlantic World.* Columbia: University of South Carolina Press, 2001.

Geggus, David Patrick, and Norman Fiering, eds. *The World of the Haitian Revolution.* Bloomington: Indiana University Press, 2009.

Geiss, Imanuel. *The Pan-African Movement: A History of Pan-Africanism in America, Europe and Africa.* Trans. Ann Keep. New York: Africana Publishing Co., 1974.

Gellman, Erik S. *Death Blow to Jim Crow: The National Negro Congress and the Rise of Militant Civil Rights.* Chapel Hill: University of North Carolina Press, 2014.

Gilmore, Glenda Elizabeth. *Defying Dixie: The Radical Roots of Civil Rights, 1919–1950.* New York: Norton, 2008.

Gilroy, Paul. *Against Race: Imagining Political Culture beyond the Color Line.* Cambridge: Harvard University Press, 2000.

———. *The Black Atlantic: Modernity and Double Consciousness.* Cambridge: Harvard University Press, 1993.

Giovannetti, Jorge L. "Black British Subjects in Cuba: Race, Ethnicity, Nation, and Identity in the Migratory Experience, 1898–1938." PhD diss., University of North London, 2001.

———. "The Elusive Organization of Identity: Race, Religion, and Empire among Caribbean Migrants in Cuba." *Small Axe* 19 (2006): 1–27.

Girard, Philippe. "Black Talleyrand: Toussaint Louverture's Diplomacy, 1798–1802." *William and Mary Quarterly* 66, no. 1 (2009): 87–124.

———. "Jean-Jacques Dessalines and the Atlantic System: A Reappraisal." *William and Mary Quarterly* 69, no. 3 (2012): 649–82.

———. "Rebelles with a Cause: Women in the Haitian War of Independence, 1802–04." *Gender and History* 21, no. 1 (2009): 60–85.

Glaude, Eddie S. *Exodus! Religion, Race, and Nation in Early Nineteenth-Century Black America.* Chicago: University of Chicago Press, 2000.

Glick, Jeremy Matthew. *The Black Radical Tragic: Performances, Aesthetics, and the Unfinished Haitian Revolution.* New York: New York University Press, 2016.

Gomez, Michael A. *Black Crescent: The Experience and Legacy of American Muslims in the Americas.* Cambridge: Cambridge University Press, 2005.

———, ed. *Diasporic Africa: A Reader.* New York: New York University Press, 2006.

———. *Exchanging Our Country Marks: The Transformation of African Identities in the Colonial and Antebellum South.* Chapel Hill: University of North Carolina Press, 1998.

Goodall, Heather. *Invasion to Embassy: Land in Aboriginal Politics in New South Wales, 1770–1972* Sydney: Allen & Unwin, 1997.

Gore, Dayo F. *Radicalism at the Crossroads: African American Women Activists in the Cold War.* New York: New York University Press, 2011.

Grady-Willis, Winston A. *Challenging U.S. Apartheid: Atlanta and Black Struggles for Human Rights, 1960–1977.* Durham: Duke University Press, 2006.

Grant, Colin. *Negro with a Hat: The Rise and Fall of Marcus Garvey.* Oxford: Oxford University Press, 2008.

Greenberg, Kenneth S., ed. *The Confessions of Nat Turner and Related Documents.* Boston: Bedford Books of St. Martin's Press, 1996.

———, ed. *Nat Turner: A Slave Rebellion in History and Memory.* Oxford: Oxford University Press, 2003.

Greene, Julie. *The Canal Builders: Making America's Empire at the Panama Canal.* New York: Penguin Press, 2009.

Gregg, Veronica Marie, ed. *Caribbean Women: An Anthology of Non-Fiction Writing, 1890–1980.* Notre Dame: University of Notre Dame Press, 2005.

Grimes, Ronald. *Beginnings in Ritual Studies.* Scotts Valley, CA: CreateSpace Independent Publishing Platform, 2010.

Grossman, James. *Land of Hope: Chicago, Black Southerners, and the Great Migration.* Chicago: University of Chicago Press, 1989.

Guevara, Ernesto Che. *Guerrilla Warfare.* New York: Monthly Review Press, 1961.

Guha, Ranajit. *Elementary Aspects of Peasant Insurgency in Colonial India.* Delhi: Oxford University Press, 1983.

Guridy, Frank A. "'Enemies of the White Race': The Machadista State and the UNIA in Cuba." *Caribbean Studies* 31, no. 1 (January–June 2003): 107–37.

———. *Forging Diaspora: Afro-Cubans and African Americans in a World of Empire and Jim Crow.* Chapel Hill: University of North Carolina Press, 2010.

———. "Making New Negroes in Cuba: Garveyism as a Transcultural Movement." In *Escape from New York: The New Negro Renaissance beyond Harlem,* ed. Davarian L. Baldwin and Minkah Makalani, 183–203. Minneapolis: University of Minnesota Press, 2013.

Hahn, Steven. "'Extravagant Expectations' of Freedom: Rumor, Political Struggle, and the Christmas Insurrection Scare of 1865 in the American South." *Past and Present* 157 (1997): 122–58.

————. *A Nation under Our Feet: Black Political Struggles in the Rural South from Slavery to the Great Migration*. Cambridge: Harvard University Press, 2003.

————. *The Political Worlds of Slavery and Freedom*. Cambridge: Harvard University Press, 2009.

Hargreaves, John D. *Decolonization in Africa*. London: Longman, 1988.

Harold, Claudrena N. "Reconfiguring the Roots and Routes of New Negro Activism: The Garvey Movement in New Orleans." In *Escape from New York: The New Negro Renaissance beyond Harlem*, ed. Davarian L. Baldwin and Minkah Makalani, 205–24. Minneapolis: University of Minnesota Press, 2013.

————. *The Rise and Fall of the Garvey Movement in the Urban South, 1918–1942*. New York: Routledge, 2007.

Harpelle, Ronald. "Cross Currents in the Western Caribbean: Marcus Garvey and the UNIA in Central America." *Caribbean Studies* 31, no. 1 (January–June 2003): 35–73.

————. *The West Indians of Costa Rica: Race, Class, and the Integration of an Ethnic Minority*. Montreal: McGill-Queen's University Press, 2001.

Harris, Joseph E. *African-American Reactions to War in Ethiopia, 1936–1941*. Baton Rouge: Louisiana State University Press, 1994.

Harrison, Hubert H. *When Africa Awakes*. 1920. Baltimore: Black Classic Press, 1997.

Hart, Richard. *Towards Decolonisation: Political, Labour and Economic Developments in Jamaica, 1938–1945*. Kingston, Jamaica: Canoe Press, 1999.

Hassim, Shireen. *Women's Organizations and Democracy in South Africa: Contesting Authority*. Madison: University of Wisconsin Press, 2006.

Haynes, Rosetta R. *Radical Spiritual Motherhood: Autobiography and Empowerment in Nineteenth-Century African American Women*. Baton Rouge: Louisiana State University Press, 2011.

Headley, David. *Labour and Life*. Trinidad: Trinidad Workingmen's Association, 1921.

Healy-Clancy, Meghan. "The Family Politics of the Federation of South African Women: A History of Public Motherhood in Women's Antiracist Activism." *Signs: A Journal of Women in Culture and Society* 42, no. 4 (2017): 843–66.

————. "To Control Their Own Destiny: The Politics of Home and the Feminization of Schooling in Colonial Natal." *Journal of Southern African Studies* 37, no. 2 (2011): 247–64.

————. "Women and the Problem of Family in African Nationalist History and Historiography." *South African Historical Journal* 64, no. 3 (2012): 450–71.

————. *A World of Their Own: A History of South African Women's Education*. Charlottesville: University of Virginia Press, 2014.

Healy-Clancy, Meghan, and Jason Hickel, eds. *Ekhaya: The Politics of Home in Kwa-Zulu Natal*. Pietermaritzburg: University of KwaZulu-Natal Press, 2014.

Hedlin, Ethel Wolfskill. "Earnest Cox and Colonization: A White Racist's Response to Black Repatriation, 1923–1966." PhD diss., Duke University Press, 1974.

Hill, Laura Warren, and Julia Rabig, eds. *The Business of Black Power: Community Development, Capitalism, and Corporate Responsibility in Postwar America*. Rochester: University of Rochester Press, 2012.

Hill, Robert A., ed. *The Black Man: A Monthly Magazine of Negro Thought and Opinion*. Millwood, NY: Kraus-Thomson Organization Limited, 1975.

———. "Black Zionism: Marcus Garvey and the Jewish Question." In *African Americans and Jews in the Twentieth Century: Studies in Convergence and Conflict*, ed. V. P. Franklin, 105–22. Columbia: University of Missouri Press, 1998.

———. "Boundaries of Belonging: Essay on Comparative Caribbean Garveyism." *Caribbean Studies* 31, no. 1 (January–June 2003): 10–33.

———. "The Case of Marcus Garvey." In *Mail Fraud Charges against Marcus Garvey: Hearing before the Subcommittee on Criminal Justice of the Committee of the Judiciary, House of Representatives, July 28, 1987*. Washington, DC: U.S. Government Printing Office, Serial No. 69, 1988.

———. "'Comradeship of the More Advanced Races': Marcus Garvey and the Brotherhood Movement in Britain, 1913–1914." *Small Axe* 17, no. 1 (2013): 50–70.

———. *Dread History: Leonard P. Howell and Millenarian Visions in the Early Rastafarian Religion*. Kingston, Jamaica: Miguel Lorne, 2001.

———, ed. *The Marcus Garvey and Universal Negro Improvement Association Papers*. 13 vols. Berkeley: University of California Press, 1983–2016.

Hill, Robert A., and Barbara Bair, eds. *Marcus Garvey: Life and Lessons: A Centenary Companion to the Marcus Garvey and Universal Negro Improvement Association Papers*. Berkeley: University of California Press, 1988.

Hill, Robert A., and Gregory Pirio. "'Africa for the Africans': The Garvey Movement in South Africa, 1920–1940." In *The Politics of Race, Class and Nationalism in Twentieth-Century South Africa*, ed. Shula Marks and Stanley Trapido, 209–53. London: Longman, 1987.

Hine, Darlene Clark, and John McClusky, eds. *The Black Chicago Renaissance*. Urbana: University of Illinois Press, 2012.

Hinks, Peter P., ed. *David Walker's Appeal to the Coloured Citizens of the World*. University Park: Pennsylvania State University Press, 2000.

Hinks, Peter P., and Stephen Kantrowitz, eds. *All Men Free and Brethren: Essay on the History of African American Freemasonry*. Ithaca: Cornell University Press, 2013.

Hodgson, Dorothy, and Judith Byfield, eds. *Global Africa: Into the Twenty-First Century*. Berkeley: University of California Press, 2017.

Høgsbjerg, Christian. "C.L.R. James and Italy's Conquest of Ethiopia." *Socialist History* 28 (2006): 17–36.

Holloway, Jonathan Scott. *Confronting the Veil: Abram Harris Jr., E. Franklin Frazier, and Ralph Bunche, 1919–1941*. Chapel Hill: University of North Carolina Press, 2002.

Holly, James Theodore. *A Vindication of the Capacity of the Negro Race for Self-Government and Civilized Progress*. New Haven: W.H. Stanley, 1857.

Holt, Thomas C. *Children of Fire: A History of African Americans*. New York: Hill and Wang, 2011.

Honey, Maureen, ed. *Bitter Fruit: African American Women in World War II*. Columbia: University of Missouri Press, 1999.

Hooker, James R. *Black Revolutionary: George Padmore's Path from Communism to Pan-Africanism*. New York: Praeger, 1970.

Horne, Gerald. *Confronting Black Jacobins: The United States, the Haitian Revolution, and the Origins of the Dominican Republic*. New York: Monthly Review Press, 2015.

Hossein, Caroline Shenaz. "A Case Study of the Influence of Garveyism among the African Diaspora." *Social and Economic Studies*, 66, nos. 3–4 (2017): 151–75.

Howe, Glenford D. *Race, War and Nationalism: A Social History of West Indians in the First World War*. Kingston, Jamaica: Ian Randle, 2002.

Howell, Leonard Percival [G. G. Maragh, pseud.]. *The Promised Key*. 1935. New York: A&B Publishers Group, 2001.

Huggins, Nathan Irvin. *Harlem Renaissance*. London: Oxford University Press, 1971.

Huggonson, David. "Aborigines and the Aftermath of the Great War." *Australian Aboriginal Studies* 1 (1993): 2–9.

Hughes, Arnold. "Africa and the Garvey Movement in the Interwar Years." In *Garvey: Africa, Europe, and the Americas*, ed. Rupert Lewis and Maureen Warner-Lewis, 111–35. Kingston, Jamaica: Institute of Social and Economic Research, University of the West Indies, 1986.

Hunt, Alfred L. *Haiti's Influence on Antebellum America: Slumbering Volcano in the Caribbean*. Baton Rouge: Louisiana State University Press, 1998.

Hyde, Evan X. *X Communication: Selected Writings*. Belize City: Angelus Press, 1995.

Intondi, Vincent J. *African Americans against the Bomb: Nuclear Weapons, Colonialism, and the Black Freedom Movement*. Stanford: Stanford University Press, 2014.

Issa, Jahi U. "The Universal Negro Improvement Association in Louisiana: Creating a Provisional Government in Exile." PhD diss., Howard University, 2005.

Ivaska, Andrew. *Cultured States: Youth, Gender, and Modern Style in 1960s Dar es Salaam*. Durham: Duke University Press, 2011.

Jabavu, D.D.T. "Native Unrest in South Africa." *International Review of Missions* 19, no. 42 (1922): 249–59.

Jacques Garvey, Amy. *Black Power in America: Marcus Garvey's Impact on Jamaica and Africa*. Kingston, Jamaica: United Printers, 1968.

———. *Garvey and Garveyism*. 1963. New York: Octagon Books, 1978.

———, ed. *Philosophy and Opinions of Marcus Garvey*. Originally published in two volumes in 1923 and 1925. Dover, MA: The Majority Press, 1986.

James, Ariel. *Banes: Imperialismo Y Nación En Una Plantación Azucarera*. La Habana: Editorial de Ciencias Sociales, 1976.

James, C. Boyd. *Garvey, Garveyism, and the Antinomies of Black Redemption*. Trenton, NJ: Africa World Press, 2009.

James, C.L.R. *The Black Jacobins: Toussaint L'Ouverture and the San Domingo Revolution*. 2nd ed., rev. New York: Vintage, 1963.

———. *A History of Pan-African Revolt*. 1938. Chicago: Charles H. Kerr, 1995.

———. *Nkrumah and the Ghana Revolution*. Westport, CT: Lawrence Hill, 1977.

———. "The Rise and Fall of Nkrumah." In *The C.L.R. James Reader,* ed. Anna Grimshaw, 354–61. Oxford: Blackwell, 1993.

James, Joy, and T. Denean Sharpley Whiting, eds. *The Black Feminist Reader*. Malden, MA: Blackwell, 2000.

James, Leslie. *George Padmore and Decolonization from Below: Pan-Africanism, the Cold War, and the End of Empire*. New York: Palgrave Macmillan, 2015.

James, Rawn, Jr. *The Double V: How Wars, Protest, and Harry Truman Desegregated America's Military*. Bloomsbury Publishing, 2013.

James, Winston. "Culture, Labor, and Race in the Shadow of US Capital." In *The Caribbean: A History of the Region and Its Peoples*, ed. Stephan Palmié and Francisco A. Scarano, 445–58. Chicago: University of Chicago Press, 2011.

———. *Holding Aloft the Banner of Ethiopia: Caribbean Radicalism in Early Twentieth-Century America*. London: Verso, 1998.

Jenkins, Robin. "Linking Up the Golden Gate: Garveyism in the San Francisco Bay Area, 1919–1925." *Journal of Black Studies* 39, no. 2 (2008): 266–80.

Jenkinson, Jacqueline. *Black 1919: Riots, Resistance and Racism in Imperial Britain*. Liverpool: Liverpool University Press, 2009.

Jenson, Deborah. "Jean-Jacques Dessalines and the African Character of the Haitian Revolution." *William and Mary Quarterly* 69, no. 3 (2012): 615–38.

Johnson, Morris. *Archbishop Daniel William Alexander and the African Orthodox Church*. San Francisco: International Scholars, 1999.

Jolly, Kenneth S. *"By Our Own Strength": William Sherrill, the UNIA, and the Fight for African American Self-Determination in Detroit*. New York: Peter Lang, 2013.

Jonas, Raymond. *The Battle of Adwa: African Victory in the Age of Empire*. Cambridge: Harvard University Press, 2011.

Joseph, Celucien. "The Rhetoric of Prayer: Dutty Boukman, the Discourse of 'Freedom from Below,' and the Politics of God." *Journal of Race, Ethnicity, and Religion* 2, no. 9 (2011): 1–33.

Joseph, Peniel E. *Stokely: A Life*. New York: Basic Civitas, 2014.

———. *Waiting 'Til the Midnight Hour: A Narrative History of Black Power in America*. New York: Henry Holt, 2006.

Kachun, Mitch. *Festivals of Freedom: Memory and Meaning in African American Emancipation Celebrations, 1808–1915*. Amherst: University of Massachusetts Press, 2003.

Kaisary, Philip. *The Haitian Revolution in the Literary Imagination: Radical Horizons, Conservative Constraints*. Charlottesville: University of Virginia Press, 2014.

Kallaway, Peter, ed. *Apartheid and Education: The Education of Black South Africans*. Johannesburg: Ravan Press, 1984.

Kamarakafego, Pauulu. *Me One! The Autobiography of Dr. Pauulu Kamarakafego*. Bermuda: PK Publishing, 2002.

Kay, Roy. *The Ethiopian Prophecy in Black American Letters*. Gainesville: University Press of Florida, 2011.

Kelley, Robin D. G. "'But a Local Phase of a World Problem': Black History's Global Vision, 1883–1950." *Journal of American History* 86, no. 3 (1999): 1045–77.

———. *Freedom Dreams: The Black Radical Imagination*. Boston: Beacon Press, 2002.

———. *Race Rebels: Culture, Politics, and the Black Working Class*. New York: The Free Press, 1994.

———. "'We Are Not What We Seem': Black Working-Class Opposition in the Jim Crow South." *Journal of American History* 80, no. 1 (1993): 75–112.

Kemp, Amanda D. "'Up from Slavery' and Other Narratives: Black South African Performances of the American Negro (1920–1943)." PhD diss., Northwestern University, 1997.

Kemp, Amanda D., and Robert Trent Vinson. "'Poking Holes in the Sky': Professor James

Thaele, American Negroes, and Modernity in 1920s Segregationist South Africa." *African Studies Review* 43, no. 1 (2000): 141–59.

Kerr-Ritchie, J. R. *Rites of August First: Emancipation Day in the Black Atlantic World.* Baton Rouge: Louisiana State University Press, 2007.

Kertzer, David I. *The Pope and Mussolini: The Secret History of Pius XI and the Rise of Fascism in Europe.* New York: Random House Trade Paperbacks, 2014.

Kidd, Colin. *The Forging of Races: Race and Scripture in the Protestant Atlantic World, 1600–2000.* Cambridge: Cambridge University Press, 2006.

Kitching, G. N. *Class and Economic Change in Kenya: The Making of an African Petite Bourgeoisie, 1905–1970.* New Haven: Yale University Press, 1980.

Knight, Frederick C. *Working the Diaspora: The Impact of African Labor on the Anglo-American World, 1650–1850.* New York: New York University Press, 2010.

Knowles, Asa S., ed. *International Encyclopedia of Higher Education.* San Francisco: Jossey-Bass, 1977.

Kornweibel, Theodore, Jr. *"Seeing Red": Federal Campaigns against Black Militancy, 1919–1925.* Bloomington: Indiana University Press, 1998.

Krugler, David F. *1919, the Year of Racial Violence: How African Americans Fought Back.* New York: Cambridge University Press, 2014.

Kurlansky, Mark. *1968: The Year That Rocked the World.* New York: Ballantine Books, 2004.

Landau, Paul. *Popular Politics in the History of South Africa, 1400 to 1948.* Cambridge: Cambridge University Press, 2010.

Landers, Jane G. *Atlantic Creoles in the Age of Revolution.* Cambridge: Harvard University Press, 2010.

Langley, J. Ayodele. *Pan-Africanism and Nationalism in West Africa, 1900–1945.* London: Oxford University Press, 1973.

Langton, Marcia. *The Quiet Revolution: Indigenous People and the Resources Boom.* Boyer Lectures 2012. Sydney: ABC Books, 2012.

Larebo, Haile M. *The Building of an Empire: Italian Land Policy and Practice in Ethiopia, 1935–1941.* Oxford: Clarendon Press, 1994.

Lauck, Jon K. *The Lost Region: Toward a Revival of Midwestern History.* Iowa City: University of Iowa Press, 2013.

Leeds, Asia. "Representations of Race, Entanglements of Power: Whiteness, Garveyism, and Redemptive Geographies in Costa Rica, 1921–1950." PhD diss., University of California, Berkeley, 2010.

———. "Toward the 'Higher Type of Womanhood': The Gendered Contours of Garveyism and the Making of Redemptive Geographies in Costa Rica, 1922–1941." *Palimpsest: A Journal of Women, Gender, and the Black International* 2, no. 1 (2013): 1–27.

Lemelle, Sidney J., and Robin D. G. Kelley, eds. *Imagining Home: Class, Culture, and Nationalism in the African Diaspora.* New York: Verso, 1994.

Lenin, Vladimir Il'ich. *Imperialism: The Highest Stage of Capitalism.* 1917. Moscow: Foreign Language Pub. House, 1951.

Lentz-Smith, Adriane. *Freedom Struggles: African Americans and World War I.* Cambridge: Harvard University Press, 2009.

Levine, Lawrence W. *Black Culture and Black Consciousness: Afro-American Folk Thought from Slavery to Freedom*. New York: Oxford University Press, 1977.

———. "Marcus Garvey and the Politics of Revitalization." In *Black Leaders of the Twentieth Century*, ed. John Hope Franklin and August Meier, 105–38. Urbana: University of Illinois Press, 1982.

———. *The Unpredictable Past: Explorations in American Cultural History*. New York: Oxford University Press, 1993.

Levine, Robert S. *Martin Delany, Frederick Douglass, and the Politics of Representative Identity*. Chapel Hill: University of North Carolina Press, 1997.

Lewis, David Levering, ed. *W.E.B. Du Bois: A Reader*. New York: Henry Holt, 1995.

———. *W.E.B. Du Bois: The Fight for Equality in the American Century, 1919–1963*. New York: Henry Holt, 1995.

———. *When Harlem Was in Vogue*. New York: Penguin Books, 1979.

Lewis, Gordon K. "Review of *Garvey and Garveyism* by A. Jacques Garvey." *Caribbean Quarterly* 10, no. 3 (1964): 50–52.

Lewis, Rupert. "Marcus Garvey and the Early Rastafarians." In *Rastafari: A Universal Philosophy in the Third Millennium*, ed. Werner Zips, 42–58. Kingston, Jamaica: Ian Randle, 2006.

———. *Marcus Garvey: Anti-Colonial Champion*. Trenton, NJ: Africa World Press, 1988.

———. *Walter Rodney's Intellectual and Political Thought*. Detroit: Wayne State University Press, 1998.

Lewis, Rupert, and Patrick Bryan, eds. *Garvey: His Work and Impact*. Kingston, Jamaica: Institute of Social and Economic Research, University of the West Indies, 1988.

Lewis, Rupert, and Maureen Warner-Lewis, eds. *Garvey: Africa, Europe, and the Americas*. Kingston, Jamaica: Institute of Social and Economic Research, University of the West Indies, 1986.

Lincoln, C. Eric. *The Black Muslims of America*. 3rd ed. Grand Rapids, MI: Eerdmans, 1994.

Logan, Rayford Whittingham. *The Diplomatic Relations of the United States with Haiti, 1776–1891*. Chapel Hill: University of North Carolina Press, 1941.

Lonsdale, John. "The Moral Economy of Mau Mau: The Problem." In *Unhappy Valley: Conflict in Kenya and Africa*, ed. Bruce Berman and John Lonsdale, 265–314. London: James Currey, 1992.

Lowney, John. "Haiti and Black Transnationalism: Remapping the Migrant Geography of *Home to Harlem*." *African American Review* 34, no. 3 (2000): 413–29.

Lucander, David. *Winning the War for Democracy: The March on Washington Movement*. Urbana: University of Illinois Press, 2014.

Luther, Martin. *Works of Martin Luther: With Introductions and Notes*. Grand Rapids, MI: Baker Book House, 1982.

Macpherson, Anne. "Colonial Matriarchs: Garveyism, Maternalism, and Belize's Black Cross Nurses, 1920–1952." *Gender and History* 15, no. 3 (November 2003): 507–27.

———. *From Colony to Nation: Women Activists and the Gendering of Politics in Belize, 1912–1982*. Lincoln: University of Nebraska Press, 2007.

Macqueen, Norrie. *The Decolonization of Portuguese Africa: Metropolitan Revolution and the Dissolution of Empire*. London: Longman, 1997.

Magaziner, Daniel R. *The Art of Life in South Africa*. Athens: Ohio University Press, 2016.

———. *The Law and the Prophets: Black Consciousness in South Africa, 1968–1977*. Athens: Ohio University Press, 2010.

Maglangbayan, Shawna, ed. *The Black Handbook*. Chicago: Third World Press, 1975.

Makalani, Minkah. *In the Cause of Freedom: Radical Black Internationalism from Harlem to London, 1917–1939*. Chapel Hill: University of North Carolina Press, 2011.

———. "Introduction: Diaspora and the Localities of Race." *Social Text* 27, no. 1 (2009): 1–9.

Mamdani, Mahmood. *Citizen and Subject: Contemporary Africa and the Legacy of Late Colonialism*. Princeton, NJ: Princeton University Press, 1996.

Manela, Erez. *The Wilsonian Moment: Self-Determination and the International Origins of Anticolonial Nationalism*. Oxford: Oxford University Press, 2007.

Mao Tse-tung. *On Guerrilla Warfare*. 1961. Thousand Oaks, CA: BN Publishing, 2007.

Marable, Manning. *African and Caribbean Politics from Kwame Nkrumah to the Grenada Revolution*. London: Verso, 1987.

———. *A Life of Reinvention: Malcolm X*. New York: Viking, 2011.

Marable, Manning, and Vanessa Agard-Jones, eds. *Transnational Blackness: Navigating the Global Color Line*. New York: Palgrave Macmillan, 2008.

Marais, Genoveva. *Kwame Nkrumah: As I Knew Him*. Chichester: Janay Publishing Company, 1972.

Marano, Carla. "'Rising Strongly and Rapidly': The Universal Negro Improvement Association in Canada, 1919–1940." *Canadian Historical Review* 91, no. 2 (2010): 233–59.

———. "'We All Used to Meet at the Hall': Assessing the Significance of the Universal Negro Improvement Association in Toronto, 1900–1950." *Journal of the Canadian Historical Association* 25, no. 1 (2014): 143–75.

Martin, Elizabeth Anne. *Detroit and the Great Migration, 1916–1929*. Ann Arbor: Bentley Historical Library, University of Michigan, 1993.

Martin, Luther H., Huck Gutman, and Patrick H. Hutton, eds. *Technologies of the Self: A Seminar with Michel Foucault*. Amherst: University of Massachusetts Press, 1988.

Martin, Tony. *Amy Ashwood Garvey: Pan-Africanist, Feminist and Mrs. Marcus Garvey No. 1; Or, A Tale of Two Amies*. Dover, MA: Majority Press, 2007.

———. *Literary Garveyism: Garvey, Black Arts, and the Harlem Renaissance*. Dover, MA: Majority Press, 1983.

———. *Marcus Garvey, Hero: A First Biography*. Dover, MA: Majority Press, 1983.

———. *The Pan-African Connection: From Slavery to Garvey and Beyond*. Dover, MA: Majority Press, 1983.

———, ed. *The Poetical Works of Marcus Garvey*. Dover, MA: Majority Press, 1983.

———. *Race First: The Ideological and Organizational Struggles of Marcus Garvey and the Universal Negro Improvement Association*. Westport, CT: Greenwood Press, 1976.

Massey, Douglas S., and Nancy A. Denton. *American Apartheid: Segregation and the Making of the Underclass*. Cambridge: Cambridge University Press, 1993.

Matory, J. Lorand. *Black Atlantic Religion: Tradition, Transnationalism, and Matriarchy in the Afro-Brazilian Candomblé*. Princeton, NJ: Princeton University Press, 2005.

Matthews, Mark D. "'Our Women and What They Think': Amy Jacques Garvey and the *Negro World*." *Black Scholar* 10, nos. 8–9 (1979): 2–18.

Mawby, Spencer. *Ordering Independence: The End of Empire in the Anglophone Caribbean, 1947–69*. New York: Palgrave Macmillan, 2012.

Maynard, John. *Fight for Liberty and Freedom: The Origins of Australian Aboriginal Activism*. Canberra: Aboriginal Studies Press, 2007.

———. "Fred Maynard and Marcus Garvey: Storming the Urban Space." In *Exploring Urban Identities and Histories*, ed. Christine Hansen and Kathleen Butler, 153–60. Canberra: AIATSIS Research Publications, 2013.

———. "'In the Interests of Our People': The Influence of Garveyism on the Rise of Australian Aboriginal Political Activism." *Aboriginal History* 29 (2005): 1–22.

———. "Marching to a Different Beat: The Influence of the International Black Diaspora on Aboriginal Australia." In *Indigenous Networks: Mobility, Connections and Exchange*, ed. Jane Carey and Jane Lydon, 262–72. New York: Routledge, 2014.

Maynard-Kondek, M. "Charles Frederick Maynard: Vision for Justice for Aborigines." In *Unsung Heroes and Heroines*, ed. Suzy Baldwin. Victoria: Greenhouse Publications, 1988.

Mayor's Interracial Committee. *The Negro in Detroit*. Detroit: Detroit Bureau of Governmental Research, 1926.

Mazrui, Ali. "Nkrumah: The Leninist Czar." *Transition* 26 (1966): 8–17.

McCann, James. *People of the Plow: An Agricultural History of Ethiopia, 1800–1990*. Madison: University of Wisconsin Press, 1995.

McDuffie, Erik S. "Chicago, Garveyism, and the History of the Diasporic Midwest." *African and Black Diaspora: An International Journal* 8, no. 2 (2015): 1–17.

———. "The Diasporic Journeys of Louise Little: Grassroots Garveyism, the Midwest, and Community Feminism." *Women, Gender, and Families of Color* 4, no. 2 (2016): 146–70.

———. "Garveyism in Cleveland, Ohio and the History of the Diasporic Midwest, 1920–1975." *African Identities* 9, no. 2 (2011): 163–82.

———. "'A New Day Has Dawned for the UNIA': Garveyism, the Diasporic Midwest, and West Africa, 1920–1980." *Journal of West African History* 2, no. 1 (2016): 73–113.

———. "Obama, the World, and Africa." *Souls: A Critical Journal of Black Politics, Culture, and Society* 14, nos. 1–2 (2012): 28–37.

———. "'[She] devoted twenty minutes condemning all other forms of government but the Soviet': Black Women Radicals in the Garvey Movement and in the Left during the 1920s." In *Diasporic Africa: A Reader*, ed. Michael Gomez, 219–50. New York: New York University Press, 2006.

———. *Sojourning for Freedom: Black Women, American Communism, and the Making of Black Left Feminism*. Durham: Duke University Press, 2011.

McLeod, Marc C. "Garveyism in Cuba, 1920–1940." *Journal of Caribbean History* 30, nos. 1–2 (1996): 132–68.

———. "'Sin dejar de ser cubanos': Cuban Blacks and the Challenges of Garveyism in Cuba." *Caribbean Studies* 31, no. 1 (January–June 2003): 75–105.

———. "Undesirable Aliens: Race, Ethnicity, and Nationalism in the Comparison of Haitian and British West Indian Immigrant Workers in Cuba, 1912–1939." *Journal of Social History* 31, no. 3 (1998): 599–623.

Mears, W.J.G. "A Study in Native Administration in the Transkeian Territories, 1894–1943." Ph.D diss., UNISA, 1947.

Meier, August, and Elliot Rudwick. *CORE: A Study in the Civil Rights Movement, 1942–1968*. New York: Oxford University Press, 1973.

Meriwether, James. *Proudly We Can Be Africans: Black Americans and Africa, 1935–1961*. Chapel Hill: University of North Carolina Press, 2002.

Meyer, Joe-Fio N. *Dr. Nkrumah's Last Journey: The Sensational Viet-Nam U.S. War*. Accra: Advance Press Limited, 1985.

Milne, June, ed. *Kwame Nkrumah, the Conakry Years: His Life and Letters*. London: PANAF, 1990.

Mitchell, Michele. *Righteous Propagation: African Americans and the Politics of Racial Destiny after Reconstruction*. Chapel Hill: University of North Carolina Press, 2004.

Mjagkij, Nina. *Loyalty in Time of Trial: The African American Experience during World War I*. Lanham, MD: Rowman & Littlefield, 2011.

Moore, Brenda L. *To Serve My Country, To Serve My Race: The Story of the Only African American WACS Stationed Overseas during World War II*. New York: New York University Press, 1996.

Moore, Richard B. *Caribbean Militant in Harlem: Collected Writings, 1920–1974*. Bloomington: Indiana University Press, 1988.

Morris, Courtney Desiree. "Becoming Creole, Becoming Black: Migration, Diasporic Self-Making, and the Many Lives of Madame Maymie Leona Turpeau de Mena." *Women, Gender, and Families of Color* 4, no. 2 (2016): 171–95.

Moses, Wilson Jeremiah. *Afrotopia: The Roots of African American Popular History*. Cambridge: Cambridge University Press, 1998.

——. *Alexander Crummell: A Study of Civilization and Discontent*. New York: Oxford University Press, 1989.

——, ed. *Classical Black Nationalism: From the American Revolution to Marcus Garvey*. New York: New York University Press, 1996.

——, ed. *Destiny and Race, Selected Speeches, 1840–1898: Alexander Crummell*. Amherst: University of Massachusetts Press, 1992.

——. *The Golden Age of Black Nationalism, 1850–1925*. New York: Oxford University Press, 1978.

——. *The Wings of Ethiopia: Studies in African American Life and Letters*. Ames: Iowa State University Press, 1990.

Muniz, Humberto García, and Jorge L. Giovannetti, "Garveyismo y racismo en el Caribe: El caso de la población cocola en la República Dominica." *Caribbean Studies* 31, no. 1 (January–June 2003): 139–211.

Murrell, Nathaniel Samuel. "Tuning Hebrew Psalms to Reggae Rhythms: Rastas' Revolutionary Lamentations for Social Change." *CrossCurrents* 50, no. 4 (2000/2001): 525–40.

Murrell, Nathanial Samuel, William David Spencer, and Adrian Anthony McFarlane, eds. *Chanting Down Babylon: The Rastafari Reader*. Philadelphia: Temple University Press, 1998.

Musambachime, Mwelwa C. "The Changing Political Personality of an African Politician: The Case of Patrice Emery Lumumba, 1956–1961." *Genéve-Afrique* 25, no. 2 (1987): 61–78.

Nesbitt, Nick. *Universal Emancipation: The Haitian Revolution and the Radical Enlightenment*. Charlottesville: University of Virginia Press, 2008.

Newman, Richard C., ed. *Black Power and Black Religion: Essays and Reviews*. West Cornwall, CT: Locust Hill Press, 1987.

Newton, Velma. *The Silver Men: West Indian Labour Migrants to Panama, 1850–1914*. Mona, Kingston, Jamaica: Institute of Social and Economic Research, University of the West Indies, 1984.

Nkrumah, Kwame. *Africa Must Unite*. New York: Praeger, 1963.

———. *Axioms of Kwame Nkrumah: Freedom Fighters' Edition*. New York: International Publishers, 1969.

———. *Challenge of the Congo*. London: Panaf Books, 1967.

———. *Ghana: The Autobiography of Kwame Nkrumah*. New York: Nelson, 1957.

———. *Handbook of Revolutionary Warfare: A Guide to the Armed Phase of the African Revolution*. London: Panaf Books, 1968.

———. *Neo-Colonialism: The Last Stage of Imperialism*. London: Nelson, 1965.

———. *Revolutionary Path*. New York: International Publishers, 1973.

Ngavirue, Zedekiah. "On Wearing the Victor's Uniforms and Replacing Their Churches: Southwest Africa (Namibia) 1920–1950." In *Cargo Cults and Millenarian Movements: Transoceanic Comparisons of New Religious Movements*, ed. G. W. Trompf, 391–424. Berlin: Mouton de Gruyter, 1990.

Norden, Hermann. *Fresh Tracks in the Belgian Congo: From the Uganda Border to the Mouth of the Congo*. London: Witherby, 1924.

Obeng, Samuel, ed. *Selected Speeches of Dr. Kwame Nkrumah: First President of the Republic of Ghana*. Accra: Advance Press Limited, 1963.

Ocran, A. K. *Politics of the Sword: A Personal Memoir on Military Involvement in Ghana and the Problems of Military Government*. London: Rex Collings, 1977.

Ogbar, Jeffrey O. G. *Black Power: Radical Politics and African American Identity*. Baltimore: Johns Hopkins University Press, 2004.

Okonkwo, R. L. "The Garvey Movement in British West Africa." *Journal of African History* 21, no. 1 (1980): 105–17.

Oldfield, J. R., ed. *Civilization and Black Progress: Selected Writings of Alexander Crummell on the South*. Charlottesville: University Press of Virginia, 1995.

Olisanwuche, Esedebe P. *Pan-Africanism: The Idea and Movement, 1776–1991*. Washington, DC: Howard University Press, 1994.

Olusanya, G. O. "Notes on the Lagos Branch of the Universal Negro Improvement Association." *Journal of Business and Social Studies* (Lagos) 1 (1970): 133–43.

O'Neill, Peter D., and David Lloyd, eds. *The Black and Green Atlantic: Cross-Currents of the African and Irish Diasporas*. New York: Palgrave Macmillan, 2009.

Opie, Frederick Douglass. "Garveyism and Labor Organization on the Caribbean Coast of Guatemala, 1920–1921." *Journal of African American History* 94, no. 2 (Spring, 2009): 153–71.

O'Reilly, Kenneth. *Racial Matters: The FBI's Secret File on Black America, 1960–1972*. New York: Free Press, 1991.

Owusu, Maxwell. *Uses and Abuses of Political Power: A Case Study of Continuity and Change in the Politics of Ghana*. Chicago: University of Chicago Press, 1970.

Padmore, George. *The Gold Coast Revolution: The Struggle of an African People from Slavery to Freedom*. London: Dennis Dobson, 1953.

———, ed. *History of the Pan-African Congress: Colonial and Coloured Unity, a Programme of Action*. Manchester: Pan-African Federation, 1945.

———. *The Life and Struggles of Negro Toilers*. 1931. Hollywood, CA: Sun Dance Press, 1971.

———. *Pan-Africanism or Communism? The Coming Struggle for Africa*. London: Dennis Dobson, 1956.

Page, Melvin E., ed. *Africa and the First World War*. London: Macmillan, 1987.

Paice, Edward. *World War I: The African Front*. New York: Pegasus Books, 2010.

Palmié, Stephan. *Wizards and Scientists: Explorations in Afro-Cuban Modernity and Tradition*. Durham: Duke University Press, 2002.

Pamphile, Leon D. "The NAACP and the American Occupation of Haiti, 1915–1934." *Phylon* 67, no. 1 (1986): 91–100.

Parbury, Nigel. *Survival: A History of Aboriginal Life in New South Wales*. Sydney: NSW Department of Aboriginal Affairs, 2005.

Parés, Luis Nicolau, and Roger Sansi, eds. *Sorcery in the Black Atlantic*. Chicago: University of Chicago Press, 2011.

Parker, Jeffrey W. "Sex at a Crossroads: The Gender Politics of Racial Uplift Activism in Panama, 1918–32." *Women, Gender, and Families of Color* 4, no. 2 (2016): 196–211.

Paton, Diana, and Maarit Forde, eds. *Obeah and Other Powers: The Politics of Caribbean Religion and Healing*. Durham: Duke University Press, 2012.

Patterson, Orlando. *Slavery and Social Death: A Comparative Study*. Cambridge: Harvard University Press, 1982.

Pearson, Noel. *A Rightful Place: Race, Recognition, and a More Complete Commonweath*. Melbourne: Black Inc. Books, 2014.

Peiries, J. B. *The Dead Will Arise: Nongqawuse and the Great Xhosa Cattle-Killing Movement of 1856–7*. Johannesburg: Ravan Press, 1989.

Pérez de la Riva, Juan. "Cuba y la migraciòn antillana, 1900–1931." In *La república neocolonial: Anuario de estudios cubanos II*, ed. Juan Pérez de la Riva et al., 3–75. La Habana: Editorial de Ciencias Sociales, 1979.

Pérez Nakao, Yurisay. *Inmigración españoa, jamaicana, y árabe a Banes: Historia, cultura, y tradiciones*. Holguín, Cuba: Ediciones Holguín, 2008.

———. "Inmigracón jamaicana a Banes: Historia, cultura y tradiciones." *Del Caribe* 50 (2007): 68–78.

Perry, Jeffrey B., ed. *A Hubert Harrison Reader*. Middletown, CT: Wesleyan University Press, 2001.

———. *Hubert Harrison: The Voice of Harlem Radicalism, 1883–1918*. New York: Columbia University Press, 2009.

Pettersburgh, Fitz Balintine. *The Royal Parchment Scroll of Black Supremacy*. 1926. Kingston, Jamaica: Miguel Lorne, 2003.

Phillips, Kimberley L. *AlabamaNorth: African-American Migrants, Community, and Working-Class Activism in Cleveland, 1915–45*. Urbana: University of Illinois Press, 1999.

Pirio, Gregory. "The Role of Garveyism in the Making of Namibian Nationalism." In *Namibia 1884–1984: Readings on Namibia's History and Society*, ed. Brian Wood, 259–67. London: Namibia Support Committee, 1988.

Plummer, Brenda Gayle. "The Afro-American Response to the Occupation of Haiti, 1915–1934." *Phylon* 43, no. 2 (1982): 125–43.

———. "Garveyism in Haiti during the US Occupation." *Journal of Haitian Studies* 21, no. 2 (2015): 68–87.

———. *Haiti and the Great Powers, 1902–1915*. Baton Rouge: Louisiana State University Press, 1988.

Polenberg, Richard. *War and Society: The United States, 1941–1945*. Westport, CT: Greenwood Press, 1980.

Polsgrove, Carol. *Ending British Rule in Africa: Writers in a Common Cause*. Manchester: Manchester University Press, 2009.

Polyné, Millery. *From Douglass to Duvalier: U.S. African Americans, Haiti, and Pan Americanism, 1870–1964*. Gainesville: University Press of Florida, 2010.

Post, Ken. *Arise Ye Starvelings: The Jamaican Labour Rebellion of 1938 and Its Aftermath*. The Hague: Martinus Nijoff, 1978.

———. "The Bible as Ideology: Ethiopianism in Jamaica, 1930–38." In *African Perspectives: Papers in the History, Politics and Economics of Africa Presented to Thomas Hodgkin*, ed. Christopher Allen and R.W. Johnson, 185–207. Cambridge: At the University Press, 1970.

Prince, Simon. "'Do What the Afro-Americans Are Doing': Black Power and the Start of the Northern Ireland Troubles." *Journal of Contemporary History* 50, no. 3 (2015): 516–35.

Putnam, Aric. *The Insistent Call: Rhetorical Moments in Black Anticolonialism, 1929–1937*. Amherst: University of Massachusetts Press, 2012.

Putnam, Lara. "Borderlands and Border Crossers: Migrants and Boundaries in the Greater Caribbean, 1840–1940." *Small Axe* 18, no. 1 (2014): 7–21.

———. *The Company They Kept: Migrants and the Politics of Gender in Caribbean Costa Rica, 1870–1960*. Chapel Hill: University of North Carolina Press, 2002.

———. "Eventually Alien: The Multigenerational Saga of British West Indians in Central America and Beyond, 1880–1940." In *Blacks and Blackness in Central America: Between Race and Place*, ed. Lowell Gudmundson and Justin Wolfe, 278–306. Durham: Duke University Press, 2010.

———. "Global Child-Saving, Transatlantic Maternalism, and the Pathologization of Caribbean Childhood, 1930s–1940s." *Atlantic Studies: Global Currents* 11, no. 4 (2014): 491–514.

———. "'Nothing Matters but Color': Transnational Circuits, the Interwar Caribbean, and the Black International." In *From Toussaint to Tupac: The Black International since the Age of Revolution*, ed. Michael O. West, William G. Martin, and Fanon Che Wilkins, 107–29. Chapel Hill: University of North Carolina Press, 2009.

———. *Radical Moves: Caribbean Migrants and the Politics of Race in the Jazz Age*. Chapel Hill: University of North Carolina Press, 2013.

Pybus, Cassandra. *Epic Journeys of Freedom: Runaway Slaves of the American Revolution and Their Global Quest for Liberty*. Boston: Beacon Press, 2006.

Quest, Matthew. "George Padmore and C.L.R. James's International African Opinion." In *George Padmore: Pan-African Revolutionary*, ed. Fitzroy Baptiste and Rupert Lewis, 105–32. Kingston, Jamaica: Ian Randle, 2009.

Quinn, Kate, ed. *Black Power in the Caribbean*. Gainesville: University Press of Florida, 2014.

Rahman, Ahmad A. *The Regime Change of Kwame Nkrumah: Epic Heroism in Africa and the Diaspora*. New York: Palgrave Macmillan, 2007.

Ranger, Terence. *The African Voice in Southern Rhodesia, 1898–1930*. Evanston: Northwestern University Press, 1970.

Ransby, Barbara. *Eslanda: The Large and Unconventional Life of Mrs. Paul Robeson*. New Haven: Yale University Press, 2013.

Redding, Sean. "Legal Minors and Social Children: African Women and Taxation in the Transkei, 1880–1950." *African Studies Review* 36 (1993): 49–74.

———. "'Maybe Freedom Will Come from You': Christian Prophecies and Rumors in the Development of Rural Resistance in South Africa, 1948–1961." *Journal of Religion in Africa* 40, no. 2 (2010): 163–91.

———. *Sorcery and Sovereignty: Taxation, Power, and Rebellion in Rural South Africa*. Athens: Ohio University Press, 2006.

———. "Women as Diviners and Christian Converts in Rural South Africa, c. 1880–1963." *Journal of African History* 57, no. 3 (2016): 367–89.

Reddock, Rhoda. "The First Mrs. Garvey: Pan-Africanism and Feminism in the Early 20th Century British Colonial Caribbean." *Feminist Africa* 19 (1994): 58–77.

———. *Women, Labour and Politics in Trinidad and Tobago: A History*. London: Zed Books, 1994.

Reed, Christopher Robert. *Black Chicago's First Century*. Vol. 1, *1833–1900*. Columbia: University of Missouri Press, 2005.

Renda, Mary A. *Taking Haiti: Military Occupation and the Culture of U.S. Imperialism, 1915–1940*. Chapel Hill: University of North Carolina Press, 2001.

Robeson, Paul. *Here I Stand*. Boston: Beacon Press, 1958.

Robinson, Cedric J. *Black Marxism: The Making of the Black Radical Tradition*. 1983. Chapel Hill: University of North Carolina Press, 2000.

Rodney, Walter. *The Groundings with My Brothers*. London: Bogle-L'Ouverture, 1969.

———. *How Europe Underdeveloped Africa*. Dar es Salaam: Tanzania Publishing House, 1972.

Rodríguez, Pedro Pablo. "Marcus Garvey en Cuba." *Anales del Caribe* 7–8 (1987–88): 279–301.

Rogers, J. A. *World's Great Men of Color*. Vol. 2, edited with an introduction, commentary, and bibliographical notes by John Henrik Clarke. New York: Simon and Schuster, 1947.

Rogers, Robert Athlyi. *The Holy Piby*. 1924. Northampton, UK: White Crane Publishing, 2011.

Rolinson, Mary G. *Grassroots Garveyism: The UNIA in the Rural South, 1920–1927*. Chapel Hill: University of North Carolina Press, 2007.

———. "The Universal Negro Improvement Association in Georgia: Southern Strongholds of Garveyism." In *Georgia in Black and White: Explorations in the Race Rela-*

tions of a Southern State, 1865–1950, ed. John C. Inscoe, 202–24. Athens: University of Georgia Press, 1994.

Roll, Jarod. "Garveyism and the Eschatology of African Redemption in the Rural South, 1920–1936." *Religion and American Culture: A Journal of Interpretation* 20, no. 1 (2010): 27–56.

———. *Spirit of Rebellion: Labor and Religion in the New Cotton South*. Urbana: University of Illinois Press, 2010.

Román, Reinaldo L. "Scandalous Race: Garveyism, the Bomba, and the Discourse of Blackness in 1920s Puerto Rico." *Caribbean Studies* 31, no. 1 (January–June 2003): 213–59.

Rowley, Hazel. *Richard Wright: The Life and Times*. New York: Henry Holt, 2001.

Runcie, John. "The Influence of Marcus Garvey and the Universal Negro Improvement Association in Sierra Leone." *Africana Research Bulletin* 12, no. 3 (1983): 3–42.

Saliba, John A. "The New Ethnography and the Study of Religion." *Journal for the Scientific Study of Religion* 13 (1974): 145–59.

Samaroo, Brinsley, and Cherita Girvan. "The Trinidad Workingmen's Association and the Origin of Popular Protest in a Crown Colony," *Social and Economic Studies* 21, no. 2 (1972): 205–22.

Satter, Beryl. "Marcus Garvey, Father Divine, and the Gender Politics of Race Difference and Race Neutrality." *American Quarterly* 48, no. 1 (1996): 43–76.

Saul, John S. *Flawed Freedom: Rethinking Southern African Liberation*. Toronto: Between the Lines, 2014.

Savage, Barbara Dianne. *Your Spirits Walk beside Us: The Politics of Black Religion*. Cambridge: Harvard University Press, 2008.

Schmidt, Hans. *The United States Occupation of Haiti, 1915–1934*. New Brunswick, NJ: Rutgers University Press, 1971.

Scott, James C. *Weapons of the Weak: Everyday Forms of Peasant Resistance*. New Haven: Yale University Press, 1985.

Scott, William R. *The Sons of Sheba's Race: African-Americans and the Italo-Ethiopian War, 1935–1941*. Bloomington: Indiana University Press, 1993.

Seale, Bobby. *Seize the Time: The Story of the Black Panther Party and Huey P. Newton*. New York: Random House, 1970.

Sellers, Allison Paige. "The 'Black Man's Bible': The *Holy Piby*, Garveyism, and Black Supremacy in the Interwar Years." *Journal of Africana Religions* 3, no. 3 (2015): 325–42.

Semley, Lorelle. *Mother Is Gold, Father Is Glass: Gender and Colonialism in a Yoruba Town*. Bloomington: Indiana University Press, 2011.

———. "Public Motherhood in West Africa as Theory and Practice." *Gender and History* 24, no. 3 (2012): 600–616.

Sensbach, Jon. "Freedom from Heaven: State Violence and Religious Protest in the Early Black Atlantic." *Journal of Africana Religions* 3, no. 4 (2015): 495–503.

Seraile, William. "Henrietta Vinton Davis and the Garvey Movement." *Afro-Americans in New York Life and History* 7, no. 2 (1983): 7–24.

Shannon, Magdaline W. *Jean Price-Mars, the Haitian Elite and the American Occupation, 1919–1935*. New York: St. Martin's Press, 1996.

Shepperson, George. "The African Abroad, or the African Diaspora." In *Emerging*

Themes of African History: Proceedings of the International Congress of African Historians, ed. T. O. Ranger, 152–76. Nairobi: East African Publishing House, 1968.

———. "Ethiopianism and African Nationalism." *Phylon* 14 (1953): 9–18.

———. "Notes on Negro American Influences on the Emergence of African Nationalism." *Journal of African History* 1, no. 2 (1960): 299–312.

———. "Nyasaland and the Millennium." In *Millennial Dreams in Action: Studies in Revolutionary Religious Movements*, ed. Sylvia L. Thrupp, 144–59. New York: Schocken, 1970.

———. "Pan-Africanism and 'Pan-Africanism': Some Historical Notes." *Phylon* 23 (Winter 1962): 346–58.

Shepperson, George, and St. Clair Drake. "The Fifth Pan-African Conference, 1945 and the All African People's Congress, 1958." *Contributions to Black Studies* 8 (1986–87): 35–66.

Sherwood, Marika. *Kwame Nkrumah: The Years Abroad, 1935–1947*. Legon, Ghana: Freedom Publishers, 1996.

Shilliam, Robbie. *The Black Pacific: Anti-Colonial Struggles and Oceanic Connections*. London: Bloomsbury, 2015.

Singh, Kelvin. *Race and Class Struggles in a Colonial State: Trinidad, 1917–1945*. Kingston, Jamaica: University of the West Indies Press, 1994.

Singh, Nikhil Pal. *Black Is a Country: Race and the Unfinished Struggle for Democracy*. Cambridge: Harvard University Press, 2004.

Sirleaf, Ellen Johnson. *This Child Will Be Great: Memoir of a Remarkable Life by Africa's First Woman President*. New York: HarperCollins, 2009.

Slate, Nico, ed. *Black Power beyond Borders: The Global Dimensions of the Black Power Movement*. New York: Palgrave Macmillan, 2012.

Smith, Matthew J. "Capture Land: Jamaica, Haiti, and the United States Occupation." *Journal of Haitian Studies* 21, no. 2 (2015): 181–206.

———. "'To Place Ourselves in History': The Haitian Revolution in British West Indian Thought before *The Black Jacobins*. In *The Black Jacobins Reader*, ed. Charles Forsdick and Christian Høgsbjerg, 178–93. Durham: Duke University Press, 2017.

Smith, Richard. *Jamaican Volunteers in the First World War: Race, Empire and First World War Writing*. Cambridge: Cambridge University Press, 2011.

Smith-Irvin, Jeannette, ed. *Footsoldiers of the Universal Negro Improvement Association (Their Own Words)*. Trenton, NJ: Africa World Press, 1989.

Solomon, Mark. *The Cry Was Unity: Communists and African Americans, 1917–1936*. Jackson: University Press of Mississippi, 1998.

Spady, James G. *Marcus Garvey: Jazz, Reggae, Hip Hop and the African Diaspora*. Philadelphia: Marcus Garvey Foundation, 2011.

Stanley, Eric A., and Nat Smith, eds. *Captive Genders: Trans Embodiment and the Prison Industrial Complex*. Edinburgh: AK Press, 2011.

Stein, Judith. *The World of Marcus Garvey: Race and Class in Modern Society*. Baton Rouge: Louisiana State University Press, 1986.

Stephens, Michelle Ann. *Black Empire: The Masculine Global Imaginary of Caribbean Intellectuals in the United States, 1914–1962*. Durham: Duke University Press, 2005.

Stephens, Ronald J. "Garveyism in Idlewild, 1927–1936." *Journal of Black Studies* 34, no. 4 (2004): 462–88.

———. *Idlewild: The Rise, Decline, and Rebirth of a Unique African American Resort Town.* Ann Arbor: University of Michigan Press, 2013.

———. "The Influence of Marcus Mosiah and Amy Jacques Garvey: On the Rise of Garveyism in Colorado." In *Enduring Legacies: Ethnic Histories and Cultures of Colorado*, ed. Arturo Aldama, 139–58. Boulder: University of Colorado Press, 2010.

———. "Methodological Considerations for Micro Studies of UNIA Divisions: Some Notes Calling on an Ethno-Historical Analysis." *Journal of Black Studies* 39, no. 2 (2008): 281–315.

Stovall, Tyler. "Colour Blind France? Colonial Workers during the First World War." *Race and Class* 35 (1993): 35–55.

Strachan, Hew. *The First World War in Africa.* Oxford: Oxford University Press, 2004.

Strang, G. Bruce. *On the Fiery March: Mussolini Prepares for War.* Westport, CT: Praeger, 2003.

Stubbs, Aelred, ed. *I Write What I Like, Steve Biko: A Selection of His Writings.* London: Bowerdean Press, 1978.

Styers, Randall. *Making Magic: Religion, Magic, and Science in the Modern World.* Oxford: Oxford University Press, 2004.

Suggs, Henry Lewis. "The Response of the African American Press to the United States Occupation of Haiti, 1915–1934." *Journal of Negro History* 7, nos. 1–4 (1988): 33–45.

Sugrue, T. J. *The Origins of the Urban Crisis: Race and Inequality in Postwar Detroit.* Princeton, NJ: Princeton University Press, 1996.

Sullivan, Frances Peace. "'Forging Ahead' in Banes, Cuba: Garveyism in a United Fruit Company Town." *New West Indian Guide* 88 (2014): 231–61.

———. "Radical Solidarities: U.S. Capitalism, Community Building, and Popular Internationalism in Cuba's Eastern Sugar Zone, 1919–1939. Ph.D. diss., New York University.

———. "Review of *The Marcus Garvey and Universal Negro Improvement Association Papers, Vol. XI: The Caribbean Diaspora, 1910–1920.*" *Caribbean Studies* 41, no. 1 (2013): 218–25.

Sundiata, Ibrahim K. *Brothers and Strangers: Black Zion, Black Slavery, 1914–1940.* Durham: Duke University Press, 2003.

Sundquist, Eric J., ed. *The Oxford W.E.B. Du Bois Reader.* New York: Oxford University Press, 1996.

Swan, Quito. "Bermuda Looks to the East: Marcus Garvey, the UNIA, and Bermuda, 1920–1931." *Wadabagei: A Journal of the Caribbean and Its Diasporas* 13, no. 1 (2010): 29–61.

———. *Black Power in Bermuda: The Struggle for Decolonization.* New York: Palgrave Macmillan, 2009.

Sweet, James H. *Recreating Africa: Culture, Kinship, and Religion in the African-Portuguese World, 1441–1770.* Chapel Hill: University of North Carolina Press, 2003.

Tafari, I. Jabulani. *A Rastafari View of Marcus Mosiah Garvey: Patriarch, Prophet, Philosopher.* Chicago: Frontline Books Edition, 1995.

Tarling, Nicholas. "'Ah-Ah': Britain and the Bandung Conference of 1955." *Journal of Southeast Asian Studies* 23, no. 1 (1992): 74–111.

Taylor, Ula Y. "Intellectual Pan-African Feminists: Amy Ashwood-Garvey and Amy Jacques Garvey." *ABAFAZI: The Simmons College Journal of Women of African Descent* 9, no. 1 (1998): 10–18.

———. "'Negro Women Are Great Thinkers as Well as Doers': Amy Jacques-Garvey and Community Feminism in the United States, 1924–1927." *Journal of Women's History* 12, no. 2 (Summer 2000): 104–26.

———. *The Promise of Patriarchy: Women and the Nation of Islam.* Chapel Hill: University of North Carolina Press, 2017.

———. "Street Strollers: Grounding the Theory of Black Women Intellectuals." *Afro-Americans in New York Life and History* 30, no. 2 (2006): 153–71.

———. *The Veiled Garvey: The Life and Times of Amy Jacques Garvey.* Chapel Hill: University of North Carolina Press, 2002.

Teelucksingh, Jerome. *Caribbean Liberators: Bold, Brilliant, and Black Personalities and Organizations.* Palo Alto, CA: Academica Press, 2013.

———. *Labour and the Decolonization Struggle in Trinidad and Tobago.* New York: Palgrave Macmillan, 2015.

Terry-Thompson, A. C. *The History of the African Orthodox Church.* New York: Beacon Press, 1956.

Thomas, Richard W. *Life for Us Is What We Make It: Building Black Community in Detroit, 1915–1945.* Bloomington: Indiana University Press, 1992.

Thompson, Joseph. "From Judah to Jamaica: The Psalms in Rastafari Reggae." *Religion and the Arts* 16, no. 4 (2012): 328–56.

Thompson, W. Scott. *Ghana's Foreign Policy, 1957–1966: Diplomacy, Ideology, and the New State.* Princeton, NJ: Princeton University Press, 1969.

Thornton, John, and Linda Heywood. *Central Africans, Atlantic Creoles, and the Foundation of the Americas.* Cambridge: Cambridge University Press, 2007.

Tindale, Norman. *Aboriginal Tribes of Australia.* Los Angeles: University of California Press, 1974.

Tinson, Christopher M. *Radical Intellect: Liberator Magazine and Black Activism in the 1960s.* Chapel Hill: University of North Carolina Press, 2017.

Tolbert, Emory. "Outpost Garveyism and the UNIA Rank and File." *Journal of Black Studies* 5, no. 3 (1975): 233–53.

———. *The UNIA and Black Los Angeles: Ideology and Community in the American Garvey Movement.* Los Angeles: Center for Afro-American Studies UCLA, 1980.

Trometter, Alyssa L. "Malcolm X and the Aboriginal Black Power Movement in Australia, 1967–1972." *Journal of African American History* 100, no. 2 (2015): 226–49.

Trouillot, Michel-Rolph. *Global Transformations: Anthropology and the Modern World.* New York: Palgrave Macmillan, 2003.

———. *Silencing the Past: Power and the Production of History.* Boston: Beacon Press, 1995.

Tuck, Stephen. *We Ain't What We Ought to Be: The Black Freedom Struggle from Emancipation to Obama.* Cambridge: Harvard University Press, 2010.

Turner, Ann, ed. *On Trial: Black Power in Australia*. South Yarra: Heinemann Educational Australia, 1975.

Turner, Richard Brent. *Islam in the African-American Experience*. Bloomington: Indiana University Press, 1997.

Tuttle, William. *Race Riot: Chicago in the Red Summer of 1919*. Urbana: University of Illinois Press, 1970.

Vahed, Goolam, and Thembisa Waetjen. *Schooling Muslims in Natal: Identity, State, and the Orient Islamic Educational Institute*. Pietermaritzburg: University of Kwa-Zulu Natal Press, 2015.

Van der Spuy, Patricia, and Lindsay Clowes. "'A Living Testimony of the Heights to Which a Woman Can Rise': Sarojini Naidu, Cissie Gool and the Politics of Women's Leadership in South Africa in the 1920s." *South African Historical Journal* 64, no. 2 (2012): 343–63.

Van Lierde, Jean, ed. *Lumumba Speaks: The Speeches and Writings of Patrice Lumumba, 1958–1961*. Trans. Helen R. Lane. Boston: Little, Brown, 1972.

Vassell, Linnette Silvera. "Voluntary Women's Associations in Jamaica: The Jamaica Federation of Women, 1944–1962." M. Phil, Department of History, The University of the West Indies, 1993.

Vedder, H. "The Herero." In *The Native Tribes of South West Africa*, ed. C.H.L. Hahn, H. Vedder, and L. Fourie, 153–208. Cape Town: Cape Times Limited, 1928.

Vincent, Theodore G. *Black Power and the Garvey Movement*. Berkeley, CA: Ramparts Press, 1971.

Vinson, Robert Trent. *The Americans Are Coming! Dreams of African American Liberation in Segregationist South Africa*. Athens: Ohio University Press, 2012.

———. "'Sea Kaffirs': 'American Negroes' and the Gospel of Garveyism in Early Twentieth-Century Cape Town." *Journal of African History* 47, no. 2 (2006): 281–303.

Vitalis, Robert. "The Midnight Ride of Kwame Nkrumah and Other Fables of Bandung (Ban-doong)." *Humanity* 4, no. 2 (2013): 261–88.

Von Eschen, Penny M. *Race against Empire: Black Americans and Anticolonialism, 1937–1957*. Ithaca: Cornell University Press, 1997.

Vought, Kip. "Racial Stirrings in Colored Town: The UNIA in Miami during the 1920s." *Tequesta* 60 (2000): 56–73.

Wacker, Grant. *Heaven Below: Early Pentecostals and American Culture*. Cambridge: Harvard University Press, 2001.

Walker, Cherryl, ed. *Women and Gender in Southern Africa to 1945*. Cape Town: David Philip, 1990.

———. *Women and Resistance in South Africa*. Cape Town: David Philip, 1982.

Washington, Harriet A. *Medical Apartheid: The Dark History of Medical Experimentation on Black Americans from Colonial Times to the Present*. New York: Doubleday, 2006.

Watkins-Owens, Irma. *Blood Relations: Caribbean Immigrants and the Harlem Community, 1900–1930*. Bloomington: Indiana University Press, 1996.

Watson, Sonja Stephenson. *The Politics of Race in Panama: Afro-Hispanic and West Indian Literary Discourses of Contention*. Gainesville: University Press of Florida, 2015.

Weisenfeld, Judith. *New World A-Coming: Black Religion and Racial Identity during the Great Migration*. New York: New York University Press, 2016.

Weiss, Holger. *Framing a Radical African Atlantic: African American Agency, West African Intellectuals, and the International Trade Union Committee of Negro Workers.* Leiden: Brill, 2014.

West, Michael O. "History vs. Historical Memory: Rosie Douglas, Black Power on Campus, and the Canadian Color Conceit, Part 1." *Palimpsest* 6, no. 1 (2017): 84–100.

———. "Kwame Nkrumah and Ali Mazrui: An Analysis of the 1967 *Transition* Debate." *Journal of Pan African Studies* 8, no. 6 (2015): 122–40.

———. *The Rise of an African Middle Class: Colonial Zimbabwe, 1898–1965.* Bloomington: Indiana University Press, 2002.

———. "The Seeds Are Sown: The Impact of Garveyism in Zimbabwe in the Interwar Years." *International Journal of African Historical Studies* 35, nos. 2–3 (2002): 335–62.

———. "Walter Rodney and Black Power: Jamaican Intelligence and US Diplomacy." *African Journal of Criminology and Justice Studies* 1, no. 2 (2005): 1–50.

West, Michael O., William G. Martin, and Fanon Che Wilkins, eds. *From Toussaint to Tupac: The Black International since the Age of Revolution.* Chapel Hill: University of North Carolina Press, 2009.

Whitaker, Robert. *On the Laps of Gods: The Red Summer of 1919 and the Struggle for Justice That Remade a Nation.* New York: Crown, 2008.

White, E. Francis. "African on My Mind: Gender, Counter Discourse and African-American Nationalism." *Journal of Women's History* 2 (1990): 73–97.

White, Luis. *Speaking with Vampires: Rumor and History in Colonial Africa.* Berkeley: University of California Press, 2000.

———. "Vampire Priests of Central Africa: African Debates about Labor and Religion in Colonial Northern Zambia." *Comparative Studies in Society and History* 35, no. 4 (October 1993): 746–72.

Williams, Delores S. *Sisters in the Wilderness: The Challenge of Womanist God-Talk.* Maryknoll, NY: Orbis Books, 1993.

Williams, Michael W. "Marcus Garvey and Kwame Nkrumah: A Case of Ideological Assimilation, Advancement, and Refinement." *Western Journal of Black Studies* 7, no. 2 (1983): 94–102.

Wilson, Sunnie, with John Cohassey. *Toast of the Town: The Life and Times of Sunnie Wilson.* Detroit: Wayne State University Press, 1998.

Wintz, Cary D., ed. *African American Political Thought, 1890–1930: Washington, Du Bois, Garvey, and Randolph.* Armonk, NY: M. E. Sharpe, 1996.

Woodard, Komozi. *A Nation within a Nation: Amiri Baraka (LeRoi Jones) & Black Power Politics.* Chapel Hill: University of North Carolina Press, 1999.

Wright, Marcia. "Maji Maji: Prophecy and Historiography." In *Revealing Prophets: Prophecy in Eastern African History*, ed. David Anderson and Douglas H. Johnson, 124–45. Athens: Ohio University Press, 1995.

Wright, Richard. *Black Power: A Record of Reactions in a Land of Pathos.* New York: Harper, 1954.

Wynn, Neil A. *The African American Experience during World War II.* Lanham, MD: Rowman & Littlefield, 2010.

X, Malcolm. *The Autobiography of Malcolm X.* As told to Alex Haley. 1965. New York: Ballantine Books, 1992.

Yong, Amos, and Estrelda Y. Alexander, eds. *Afro-Pentecostalism: Black Pentecostal and Charismatic Christianity in History and Culture*. New York: New York University Press, 2011.

Zachernuk, Philip S. *Colonial Subjects: An African Intelligentsia and Atlantic Ideas*. Charlottesville: University of Virginia Press, 2000.

Zackodnik, Teresa. "Recirculation and Feminist Black Internationalism in Jessie Fauset's 'The Looking Glass' and Amy Jacques Garvey's 'Our Women and What They Think,'" *Modernism/modernity* 19, no. 3 (2012): 437–59.

Zumoff, J. A. "Black Caribbean Labor Radicalism in Panama, 1914–1921." *Journal of Social History* 47, no. 2 (2013): 429–57.

Contributors

KEISHA N. BLAIN teaches history at the University of Pittsburgh. She is author of *Set the World on Fire: Black Nationalist Women and the Global Struggle for Freedom*. She is also coeditor of *Charleston Syllabus: Readings on Race, Racism, and Racial Violence* and *New Perspectives on the Black Intellectual Tradition*.

NICOLE BOURBONNAIS is assistant professor of international history at the Graduate Institute of International and Development Studies in Geneva, Switzerland, with a focus on gender, sex, and reproduction in the twentieth century. She is author of *Birth Control in the Decolonizing Caribbean: Reproductive Politics and Practice on Four Islands, 1930–1970* as well as several articles exploring the intersections between black activism and women's rights and the rise of the global family planning movement.

ADAM EWING is associate professor of African American studies at Virginia Commonwealth University. He is the author of *The Age of Garvey: How a Jamaican Activist Created a Mass Movement and Changed Global Black Politics* and editor of *The Essential Writings of Robert A. Hill*.

JOSÉ ANDRÉS FERNÁNDEZ MONTES DE OCA is a graduate student in history at the University of Pittsburgh. He has studied race and social organization in Port Limón, Costa Rica, and Trinidad and Tobago during the early twentieth century. His doctoral dissertation research is on the topic of rural development in Jamaica across the years of decolonization and independence.

JOHN MAYNARD is chair of Aboriginal history and director of the Purai Global Indigenous and Diaspora Research Studies Centre at the University of Newcastle. His publications have concentrated on the history of Australian race relations and intersections of Aboriginal political and social history. He is the author of several books, including *Aboriginal Stars of the Turf*, *Fight for Liberty and Freedom*, and *The Aboriginal Soccer Tribe*.

ERIK S. MCDUFFIE is associate professor in the Department of African American Studies, the Center for African Studies, and the Department of History at the University of Illinois–Champaign. He is the author of the award-winning book *Sojourning for Freedom: Black Women, American Communism, and the Making of Black Left Feminism*. He is currently working on a new book, tentatively titled *Garveyism in the Diasporic Midwest: The American Heartland and Global Black Freedom, 1920–1980*.

RONALD J. STEPHENS is professor of African American studies in the School of Interdisciplinary Studies at Purdue University. He is the author of *Idlewild: The Rise, Decline and Rebirth of a Unique African American Resort Town* and of several groundbreaking local studies on the Garvey movement in the United States. He is editor of *Robert Franklin Williams Speaks: A Documentary History*.

FRANCES PEACE SULLIVAN is assistant professor of history at Simmons College, where she teaches about Latin America and the Caribbean. Her scholarship is on transnational social and political movements in the greater Caribbean basin during the early to mid-twentieth century. She is currently working on a book manuscript titled *Cosmopolitan Enclaves: Foreign Capital and Popular Internationalism in Cuba's Eastern Sugar Zone, 1919–1939*.

ROBERT TRENT VINSON, Cummings Associate Professor of History and Africana Studies at William & Mary, is the author of *The Americans Are Coming! The Dream of African American Liberation in Segregationist South Africa* and *Albert Luthuli: Mandela before Mandela*. He is also the coauthor of two books in preparation, *Shaka's Progeny: Zulu Peoples and Cultures in the United States and South Africa, 1800–2000* and *Crossing the Water: African Americans and South Africa, 1890–1965*.

MICHAEL O. WEST is professor of sociology, Africana studies, and history at Binghamton University. He has published broadly in the fields of southern African history, pan-Africanism, African studies, African diaspora studies, and African American studies. His current research centers on the Black Power movement in global perspectives.

Index

Page numbers in *italics* indicate illustrations.

Ethiopian Expectation, 30–33, 39, 46–47, 55n80

Ethiopianism, 174, 186, 189, 215

Ethiopian National Anthem, 73, 75, 79, 85n61

Ethiopian News, 147

Eugenics, 156

Evangelical Revival (Great Awakening), 16–18

Ewing, Adam, 9, 61, 69, 71, 80, 92, 134, 151, 162, 205, 228

Fanon, Frantz, 270, 274

Feminism, 140, 162, 167n131, 220; community feminism, 141, 196

Feminist critiques, 142–43, 177

Feminist movement, 141–42, 146, 158, 161

Fields, Karen, 207

Fifth Pan-African Congress, Manchester, 169, 177–78, 270, 282n27

Fifty-Fourth Massachusetts Regiment, 19

Fikes, Kesha, 212

Firestone Rubber Company, 96, 110n38

Foley, Gary, 237–38

Ford, Henry, 116, 120

Ford-Smith, Honor, 141, 158, 163n32, 169

Foucault, Michel, 210

Frazier, E. Franklin, 210

French Revolution, 24, 35

"From Greenland's Icy Mountains," 73

Gardner, S. B., 273

Garnet, Henry Highland, 17–18

Garvey, Amy Ashwood. *See* Ashwood Garvey, Amy

Garvey, Amy Jacques, 34–35, 169, 232, 259; and Black Power, 276–79; community feminism of, 141; and Fifth Pan-African Congress, 178; as Garvey scholar, 2–6, 9, 111n49, 183; and Harmony Division, 148, 150, 159; pan-Africanism and, 172–73, 177; and *Philosophy and Opinions*, 32; as UNIA leader, 140–41, 144; and white supremacists, 111n43

Garvey, Marcus, 108, 144–45, 178; and African liberation flag, 101; arrest of, 3, 118, 237; and Australia, 226–29, 231, 233–35, 237–39; and Black Power, 50, 99, 274–78; civilizationist views of, 93; collaborations with white supremacists, 110n39; and communism, 27–29, 98; and Craigen, 8,

114–15, 118, 120–25, 129; critics of, 22, 27, 29–30, 35, 208; and Cuba, 59–60, 64–65, 70–71, 73; death of, 10, 107, 171; deportation of, 3, 119, 123, 237, 279–81; emigrationist views of, 96–97; and Ethiopian crisis, 49–50, 58n168; and freemasonry, 17; and gender, 140–42, 155, 158, 171; ideology of, 6–7, 60–61, 65, 69, 80, 89, 115, 171, 231–32; influence of, 15, 36–45, 217–20; influence in Africa of, 101, 103, 105, 182, 215; in London, 262n24; labor politics of, 61–62; later years of, 11; and Louverture, 16, 24–29, 32–33; as mass leader, 7, 205–6, 216–17; as Negro Moses, 33–35, 213, 233, 250; and the New Negro movement, 2, 24, 214; and Nkrumah, 267–69, 271, 273; and pan-Africanism, 15–16, 30–32, 51, 147; poetry of, 23, 26, 33; posthumous influence of, 171–72, 274; and propaganda, 20; and Rastafarianism, 50; scholarly views of, 4–5, 53n30, 183, 206–7, 208–11; and South Africa, 182–83, 194–96; speaking tour of, 139–40; influence in Trinidad, 242–46, 249–51, 254, 256–59; and UNIA, 2–4, 21, 89, 171, 206; and U.S. Midwest, 94, 116–19; views on socialism, 263n38; and the Watchtower movement, 207; and Zionist movement, 175

Garvey Club, 173

Garveyism, 74, 182–83, 194, 204n92, 206–14, 216–17, 219; Africa and, 20, 197; African Blood Brotherhood and, 27; and *African Opinion*, 269–70; and Australia, 226, 229, 233, 238–39; and Black Power, 50–51, 99, 266, 277–81; and British West Indies, 59, 67; and civilizationism, 93; in Cuba, 66, 69; emergence of, 2–3; emigrationism and, 19–20; gender and, 8–9, 93, 140, 171; as global movement, 1, 3, 8–11, 61–62, 71, 114, 133, 194, 197–98; and grassroots, 114, 184, 197; ideology of, 7, 171, 216–17; and Irish independence movement, 21; in Jamaica, 145; in Liberia, 90, 96, 98, 100–104, 108; and Nkrumah, 267–69; pan-Africanism and, 15–18; and popular politics, 206–7, 210–12, 221, 232; and Rastafarianism, 38, 40, 278–79; and revivalism, 30–32, 46; and rumor, 215, 217–19; scholarship on, 2, 4–6, 12, 65, 92, 111n49, 208–9, 276–77; second period

www.ingramcontent.com/pod-product-compliance
Lightning Source LLC
Chambersburg PA
CBHW020823270326
41928CB00006B/418